Daughter of Riches

By the same author

Oriental Hotel
The Emerald Valley
Women and War
The Black Mountains
The Hills and the Valley
Inherit the Skies
Folly's Child

DAUGHTER OF RICHES

Janet Tanner

BCA

LONDON · NEW YORK · SYDNEY · TORONTO

This edition published 1992 by
BCA
by arrangement with Random Century

CN 5856

Phototypeset by Intype, London
Printed in Great Britain by
Mackays of Chatham PLC, Chatham, Kent

War is the child of pride
And pride the daughter of riches
                    Jonathan Swift (1667–1745)

Chapter one
St Helier, Jersey, 1990

The file was at the very bottom of the cupboard, coated with a thin layer of dust and securely tied with pink legal tape, a fat file with a few bits of paper sticking out of it, creased over on the edges and clearly marked in thick black ink as well as with a typed stick-on label.

ATTORNEY GENERAL v. SOPHIA LANGLOIS — November 1972

Dan Deffains pulled it out and sat back on his heels looking at it with interest. He had been hating every moment of the job he had to do. Bad enough that his father, successful advocate and thoroughly decent human being, should have been struck down so unexpectedly in what had still been his prime, worse that it had fallen to Dan to turn out the office around which his father's whole life had revolved. For one thing it was a painful duty — he had thought the world of the old man although they had not always seen eye to eye — and there was so much of the essence of the man still there, so much that had refused to die with him. But besides this the task was also time consuming and tedious. Daniel Deffains Senior had worked from the same office for more than thirty years and it seemed he had never thrown anything away. The strong room was full to bursting, every cupboard and drawer, even the odd corner of floor space, overflowed with masses of old letters and documents that had long since ceased to have any importance. Mostly they were the legacy of long forgotten and, truth to tell, not very interesting cases and everyday law business, and Dan had had little hesitation about consigning them to the shredder.

But not this one. This one was different.

Dan straightened up, dusting down the file with the sleeve of his sweatshirt and sneezing explosively as the resulting cloud tickled his nostrils.

ATTORNEY GENERAL v. SOPHIA LANGLOIS. It had been one of his father's hobby horses, he knew, a case that had never ceased to haunt him even though it had happened almost twenty years ago.

He himself had only been a boy at the time, of course, only eleven years old and far more interested in football, conkers and his beloved bicycle than any murder case, however mysterious, and however glamorous, the leading characters. Later, when he had joined the island police force, against the wishes of his father, who had desperately hoped Dan would follow him into the family law firm, he had wondered about it briefly, remembering his father's preoccupation with Sophia Langlois almost as one remembers a half-forgotten dream — mostly flavour, little substance — and it had not been long before day-to-day policing and current enquiries had driven out all thought of the Langlois case which, even at the time, had been an open-and-shut one. Now, however, it was different. Dan was no longer a policeman. Fate — and a drunken driver — had brought his career to an untimely end two Christmases ago and nowadays Dan earned his living as an investigative reporter. As the label on the file jogged his memory so his interest quickened.

What was it his father had always said? 'She didn't do it. I'm damned sure she didn't. But how could I defend her when she was dead set on proving that she was guilty?'

A corner of Dan's mouth lifted as he saw the glimmerings of an excuse to give himself a break from the tedium of sorting the old files. He got up, a tall athletically built man in denim jeans and a grey sweatshirt, and depressed the button on the intercom that connected with the downstairs office.

'Any chance of a cup of coffee, Carol?'

'Oh I should think so. I'll be right up.'

'Well done.'

He crossed to the window, stretching his legs while he waited for her to arrive. The street below was busy with a constant stream of traffic and he thought that if it was like this now, in April, heaven only knew what it would be like when the season really got under way. That was the trouble with Jersey. The narrow winding lanes had never been meant for thousands of hire cars, all driven by people without the first idea of where they were going.

And they hadn't been meant for drunken drivers either. Not that anywhere on God's earth was meant for them. Swine.

Once upon a time — two years ago — Dan would cheerfully have played executioner to the criminally irresponsible idiot who had spent his Christmas Eve getting steadily legless, then got into his car, ignored, or perhaps not even noticed, a STOP sign at a junction, and driven straight out into the path of Dan's motor cycle. That piece of criminal carelessness had meant the end of Dan's career, for one of his legs had been so badly broken that he was considered no longer fit for active duty.

But Dan's disabling injury had been only part of what the drunken swine had done. There had been worse. Dan's wife of five months, Marianne, had been on the pillion when the accident had happened. Severe as the consequences for Dan had been he knew he had escaped lightly. Marianne had not. She had sustained terrible head injuries and after lying in a coma for almost a month she had died without ever regaining consciousness.

Sweat still rose in a clammy sheen on Dan's skin when he thought about what had happened but he did not want to kill the drunken driver any more; his hatred had burned itself out. Nowadays his bitterness and resentment was reserved for the police force that had thrown him onto the scrapheap just when he had most needed his career to fill the empty days, some semblance of normality to cling to in the midst of his grief and self-recriminations for, in spite of knowing the accident had not been his fault, he had not been able to help blaming himself for what had happened.

In those black days his father had tried once again to talk him into becoming an advocate and joining the law firm of which he was so proud. It wasn't too late, he had insisted. Dan could still train at Caen, as he himself had done, in the old traditional manner. But Dan had refused — rather gracelessly, he now admitted as he mourned his father — though he was still certain he had done the right thing. Sorting these mounds of files had convinced him of that if nothing else. Studied arguments and the finer points of law were not for him. To his less academic

3

mind and impatient nature they held no fascination and certainly no satisfaction. He needed action, excitement or the thrill of the chase to set him alight. He had told his father that at the age of eighteen and nothing really had changed.

'Coffee up.'

Dan turned back from the window as the door swung open and his father's secretary entered bearing an enormous breakfast-sized pottery cup and saucer and a jug of coffee. As the aroma reached him he sniffed appreciatively.

'That smells wonderful,' he said, failing to notice the pleased flush that rose in her cheeks. Members of the opposite sex invariably found Dan attractive and the fact that Carol was an old married woman of thirty-three did not render her immune. Dan was, as she said to her best friend, Sheila, 'all man — not good looking exactly but with the sexiest eyes you ever saw and a smile to turn your spine to water. But,' she usually added, 'to my knowledge he's never so much as looked at another woman since his wife was killed. What a waste!'

Dan turned that famous smile on her now.

'I think I'm making some headway up here at last. How are you doing?'

'All right I suppose. Not that I'm in any hurry. You realise once we get this all cleared up I shall be out of a job?'

His smile died. 'Yes. I'm sorry, Carol, I wish there was something I could do for you but I can't — except of course put in a word for you if I hear of anyone wanting a reliable secretary. Would you be interested if anything of the sort came up?'

Carol grimaced. 'I don't really know. I think it's probably high time I started thinking about staying home and having a family. Bob's been hinting as much for a long while but I couldn't face telling your father I was leaving. I've been here since I was seventeen, you know, and I like to think he depended on me.'

'He did,' Dan said truthfully.

'It's funny, you know, I still can't believe he's dead . . . that I'm not going to see him any more. I keep thinking he's going to come bursting in, looking the way he always did when he'd had a good day in court, and asking me what's new.' She turned away, close to tears suddenly. 'I'm sorry, I don't want to be sentimental. It's just that I was very fond of him.'

4

'I know,' Dan said roughly. 'I miss him too.'

'I'd better get on.' Carol moved to the door with determined briskness. 'Enjoy your coffee.'

Dan lowered himself into his father's big leather chair, his face serious. Funny how it could hit you so suddenly. You'd go on, almost as normal, doing what had to be done, and then all of a sudden you'd realise that the reason you were doing it was because he wouldn't be coming back. Christ, it was hard to believe — a man of his powerful charisma snuffed out just like that in the space of less than an hour. It wasn't even as if he'd been old. Just sixty-five — and with not the slightest intention of retiring.

Dan poured himself a coffee and stirred in two spoonfuls of brown sugar and a portion of cream. Better give this up if he didn't want to go the same way. But not just now. Dan sipped the coffee with relish, pulled the Langlois file towards him and slid off the pink legal tape that bound it.

Let's have a look then, Dad. Let's see what it was that you used to go on about.

Half an hour later the coffee jug was empty and Dan was still reading. Fascinating — especially when one considered that the people involved were so well known in the island. What a stir it must have caused! With a sigh of resignation he closed the dusty manilla covers, then sat thinking about the story that had emerged from the statements, depositions and notes, yellowing now from age.

Sophia Langlois, then aged forty-six years, had been the widow of Bernard Langlois, founder of a leisure agency and a chain of luxury hotels whose very names were synonymous with discreet service and unashamed self-indulgence for the wealthy guests who stayed in them — La Maison Blanche, the Westerley, Les Belles Fleurs, the Belville. Dan knew her by sight though he had never had cause to meet her — a slimly built woman with hair that had turned prematurely to a silvery grey, whose chauffeur-driven Bentley could sometimes be seen slipping through the business and holiday traffic here in St Helier. There was a sereneness about her which made it almost impossible to associate her with scandal of any kind, much less violent death.

5

Yet this was exactly the occurrence which had rocked the island eighteen years ago and the victim had been her son, Louis.

There had been three Langlois sons, Dan had gathered from the file, Louis and Robin, both in their middle to late twenties at the time of Louis's death, and a younger boy, still in his teens. That would be David Langlois, who headed the hotel empire now, Dan realised.

Back in 1972 Bernard, the boys' father, had only recently died — (he must have been even younger than my father, Dan thought; I wonder what caused him to cash in his chips?) and control of the hotel empire had passed to the two older boys. From reading between the lines Dan could see there had been any amount of family friction of one sort or another but presumably no one had foreseen the outcome.

One night in November 1972 Sophia had been to a glittering trade gala in St Helier. She had left early pleading tiredness and her chauffeur had driven her back to the family mansion on the North Coast of the island. Then at about midnight Sophia had made a telephone call to the emergency services. Her very words had been recorded and noted down: 'This is Sophia Langlois at La Grange. I think I need both an ambulance and the police. I have just shot my son.'

Dan leaned back against the soft leather, imagining the furore that telephone call would have unleashed — sirens and flashing blue lights as police cars rushed through the night, their occupants still half-convinced perhaps that this was some kind of sick hoax, telephone calls for a scenes-of-crime officer, a photographer, the centenier of the parish . . . and Sophia's lawyer, his own father. What a night it must have been!

But why, he wondered, frowning, had his father been so insistent Sophia had not done it? Zeal in defence of one's client is all very well, but on paper this was an open and shut case.

Louis Langlois was dead, shot with his own gun. Sophia maintained her guilt from first to last. Clearly the police had believed the story and been only too glad to add it to their 'clear-up rate'. So why had his father gone to his grave convinced of Sophia's innocence?

Dan shook his head, tying the pink tapes around the file and preparing to toss it into the pile for the shredder. Then at the last moment he changed his mind and put it instead on the corner of the desk underneath his car keys and sunglasses.

Perhaps when he had finished here he would have another look at the file, see if there was something he'd missed. He couldn't imagine there would be. If there had been anything, the merest hint of suspicion that someone other than Sophia was responsible, she would never have been prosecuted — not an influential person like her. And at least his father had made sure the charge was not murder but manslaughter. Sophia Langlois had served only just over a year in a mainland gaol and returned to Jersey almost as if nothing had happened. Yet for some reason a question mark had remained in his mind over the whole business.

Now, remembering his father's doubts, expressed on more than one occasion, that Sophia Langlois had been guilty of anything but lack of adherence to the truth, Dan found himself wondering whether it was possible there was indeed more to the story than had ever come out. Had she lied that night when she had rung the police to confess to the killing of her son — and then stuck to the story so stubbornly that she had been prepared to serve a prison sentence rather than retract it? And if so — why?

All the investigative juices that had made Dan a good detective and now helped him make his living uncovering unsuspected frauds and hidden scandals were beginning to run, a heady dose of anticipation and sharp tingling intuition prickling his nerves and senses. What a story it would make if he could uncover some hitherto unsuspected angle to the case that had rocked the island's society almost twenty years ago! What a scoop!

Dan made up his mind that he would certainly study the case and do a few investigations of his own. But exciting though the prospect was, for the moment it was going to have to go on the back burner and wait its turn. He had more pressing, if far less interesting, matters to claim his attention.

Dan sighed, tore his gaze away from the Langlois file and went on with the interminable task of sorting his father's papers.

Chapter two
Sydney, Australia, 1991

Juliet Langlois looked at her mother and father across the kitchen and wondered if she would ever really understand either of them.

Her father, she supposed, was not really such an enigma. His vagueness and his preference for peace-at-all-costs could be said to explain a lot of things. Robin hated arguments, hated conflict of any kind, and was happiest when the world was passing him by. An accountant by profession he loved classical music, good wine and her mother, though not necessarily in that order, and as long as he had them he was quite content with life.

But Molly puzzled Juliet profoundly. How was it possible for anyone to have reached their middle forties and be so ingenuous? How was it possible for anyone to be so ingenuous and yet so secretive? To all intents and purposes Molly conveyed the impression of almost childlike innocence. Her tastes had never matured, she liked frills and ice-cream and easy beat music and hated being left alone. But she was also secretive to the point of paranoia. Certain things always made her clam up and if Juliet tried to pry further she would adopt an attitude of hurt self-righteousness as if to be questioned was a personal insult.

That was the line she was taking now.

'Juliet, can't we just drop the subject? I don't want you to go to Jersey and that is all there is to it.'

Juliet sighed in exasperation, pushing a hand through her mane of light brown hair, shot with golden highlights by exposure to the hot sunshine of a Sydney summer. The summer had gone now but the highlights remained, warm and pleasing to the eye.

'I don't see what all the fuss is about. I was born there, I lived there until I was four years old, my grandma still lives there and so do most of my relatives. I am between jobs. It's an ideal opportunity to go and meet them all. So what objection could there possibly be?'

'It's halfway round the world. You can't go dashing off just like that.'

'Why not, for heaven's sake?'

'You just can't. Besides, Sean wouldn't like it.'

'Sean doesn't own me. He's my boyfriend, not my keeper.'

'I thought the two of you were getting engaged.'

'Don't say it like that, as if it were some sort of life sentence. You know very well we are going to get engaged and probably married next year. But as far as I'm concerned that's all the more reason for me to do this now, before I tie myself down to a home and family. Look, I'm sorry to be so obtuse but I simply don't see what the problem is. If it comes to that, I don't know why neither of you have been back in almost twenty years.'

The silence was sudden and complete. Molly's hazel eyes, just a shade lighter than Juliet's own, took on a dazed expression and it seemed to Juliet that her father, behind his newspaper, had stopped breathing. She laughed a trifle nervously.

'Hey — what have I said?'

'What do you mean? This is all getting extremely silly . . .' Molly fluttered.

'It is, isn't it?' Juliet agreed. 'If you think I can't see that you are hiding something you must think I'm an idiot. For goodness' sake, Mum, tell me what it's all about! What dark secret is there hidden in Jersey that you don't want me to find out about? I'm twenty-three years old and you can't continue to treat me like a child!'

'Some other time, Juliet. I'm due at a meeting of the Museum Society.'

'Oh no, Mum, you can't get out of it so easily.'

'Juliet, please.'

'She's right, Molly.' Robin folded his newspaper and took off his spectacles, rubbing his eyes with his fingers. 'You can't keep it from her for ever.'

'But we agreed . . .'

'When she was a little girl. You thought it would be best.'

'And so did you! You didn't want her to know either!'

'What?' Juliet demanded. 'What didn't you want me to know?'

9

Robin looked at her nervously. Sometimes he found it difficult to believe that this lovely young woman was really his daughter, the baby he had taken for long walks in her push-chair around the mellow-gold-and-green island of Jersey, Channel Islands, the little girl he had taught to swim in their private pool here in Sydney. He remembered her at six, astride her first pony, her legs barely long enough to come even halfway down the pony's plump sides, he remembered her in pink leotard and tights, going to her ballet class at the age of eight. Perhaps that had been the first time he had realised just how pretty she promised to be. But it was impossible, all the same, to reconcile that child – his child — with the young woman she had become. Juliet was not tall by today's standards — five feet six in her rubber-soled flipflops — but she was perfectly proportioned with curves that matched the round prettiness of her face and long shapely legs, tanned to a warm golden brown. If photographs were anything to go by she was very like her grandmother — his mother — had been at her age, except for her eyes. Sophia, his mother, had had eyes of startling amethyst, the most unusual colour he had ever seen in his life.

Robin stood up. There was a weight of sorrow inside him suddenly. *That* was why he'd never told her . . . because he was a coward and some things did not bear thinking about.

'Dad, you can't just leave it there — you have to explain,' Juliet said, planting herself in front of him. He sidestepped her, elegant in his lizard-skin sneakers.

'Your mother will tell you.'

'Oh yes, leave it all to me!' Molly called after him, exasperated, as he went out. 'That's typical of you, isn't it?' There was no reply and she turned to Juliet, a small round woman, fussed and furious now. 'He's always been the same. He just won't . . .'

'I know what he's like. Well, Mum, are you going to tell me what this is all about?'

'You really want to know?'

'For goodness' sake, of course I do! If I hadn't wanted to before I would now. All this secrecy!'

Molly sighed, defeated. All these years they'd kept it from her — for her own good, they'd told themselves, though she had often wondered if that was the real reason and whether they were making a grave mistake. Sometimes over the years she had felt very tired of the lies and half truths and excuses. Robin would not talk about what had happened; Robin never would. It was not his way. But that did not mean they had forgotten, either of them, and sometimes she had wished she had the courage to break the self-imposed silence and remove once and for all the burden of wondering how long it would be before Juliet asked one question too many and refused to be satisfied until she had an answer. Now, it seemed, that moment had come. She looked at her daughter, planted there in front of her as if her flipflops had taken root, looked at the determined expression she had learned to know so well, and knew that this was the time for the truth — or at least, part of it.

'Very well,' she said, fighting the catch in her voice, 'I'll tell you. Your father had a brother . . .'

'Uncle David. Yes.'

'No, not David. David is a lot younger. He was just a boy when it happened. The brother I'm talking about was Louis.'

'*Louis*?'

'Louis was a year or so older than your father. He was . . .' This time there was no hiding the catch. Her voice faltered and she pressed her hand to her mouth for a moment, dangerously close to tears.

'Go on,' Juliet pressed her.

Molly swallowed at the lump in her throat. 'This isn't easy for me, you know.'

'I know. But you've got to try.'

Molly nodded. Sometimes she felt she reacted to Juliet as if the relationship had been turned on its head and Juliet was the parent, stern and kind, and she was the child.

'I am trying, Juliet. You must let me tell you in my own way.' She hesitated. 'There was trouble in the family. Bernard, your grandfather, had died not long before. He was the one who really got the hotel chain going.'

'I thought my great-grandparents, Charles and Lola, did that.'

'They had the first guesthouse, it's true, but it was in a very small way. The vision was all Bernard's and he was quite an autocrat where the business was concerned. During his lifetime neither of the boys were allowed much say in how it was run and in fact he and Louis had quarrelled because he wouldn't give Louis the chance to try out some of his own ideas. Anyway, when he died he left his shares equally between his sons. Louis came back to Jersey and tried to do all the things his father had prevented him from doing and more. The others were trying to stop him and the quarrels began all over again, only this time they got very bad. And then he was shot.'

'Shot?'

'Shot dead at his home, La Grange. And your grandmother confessed to having done it.'

There. It was out. She had said it now. After all the years of silence the words — and the emotions that went with them — should have turned a little rusty but somehow they had not. They seared and shocked just as they always had. Only this time the reaction was reflected in her daughter's face. Beneath her golden tan Juliet turned pale. Whatever she had expected it was not this.

'You mean she *murdered* him?'

'They didn't call it murder. She claimed it was an accident and they believed her — at least the court did.' Molly's eyes were feverishly bright now, but there was a slight furtiveness about her expression. At any other time Juliet might have wondered about it. Not now.

'So that was why you and Daddy left Jersey?' she asked.

'The main reason, yes. You know what your father is like — you can imagine how he hated it all. And we didn't want you growing up with the stigma.'

'But if it was an accident then surely . . .'

Molly snorted, her lips tightening to a cupid's bow of disapproval. All reticence had gone now. The floodgates of the years had opened and the torrent stored up behind them for so long came pouring out.

'A pretty strange accident if you ask me. What was she doing waving a loaded gun about? No, if your grandmother hadn't been such a well-respected lady on first name terms with everybody who was anybody she'd never have got away with it.'

'You mean you think she did murder him?'

'I'm saying I don't believe Louis's death happened the way she said it did, that's all. It was too convenient for too many people. And if I thought that there must have been others who thought the same. Besides . . .' She broke off, her eyes going very far away. For a moment a whole world of emotion played behind them, unnoticed by Juliet, then with an effort, she shut off from it. Once, long ago, in another life it sometimes seemed to her, she had been quite unable to control her feelings or to hide them at all. She knew to her shame that she had often behaved badly and that she had caused a great deal of trouble and heartache to others because of her inability to discipline her emotions. Now, thank God, life had reached a much more even keel and she had trained herself to push the things she did not want to think of to the back of her mind. Even when she was brought face to face with them, as she had been now, at least she could handle herself with a certain amount of self-possession, and recognise the relief that came from knowing that part of the story at any rate was no longer a secret from Juliet. She had even been able to conceal just how much it still hurt to think about Louis − at least she thought she had − and just how frightened she was that the full facts behind his death might still emerge to haunt them all.

But for a moment in spite of all the careful self-control Molly had been unable to stop herself from being carried back in time to that November night, nearly twenty years ago, when Louis had died. For a moment it was as if she were once again standing at the window of her bedroom as she had stood that night, unable to sleep for fear and self-loathing, looking out across the fields and woods, silver in the moonlight, and wondering anxiously where Robin was and why he did not come home. When she could bear it no longer she had telephoned La Grange, hoping to speak to Louis and unburden herself of all the terrors that were driving her mad. But Louis had not been there. Instead Sophia had answered the telephone, a strangely cold Sophia who had cut her off with unusual and inexplicable abruptness. Molly had poured herself a large gin and gone back to the window to wait, praying that the next set of headlights to illuminate the valley would herald Robin's return. But still he did not come. In the end she had taken a sleeping pill and gone to bed. But when the insistent shrilling of the telephone had woken her hours later, he had still not been there. She had stretched out her hand

13

and, finding nothing but cold empty sheet, stumbled out of bed and down the stairs with a head that had seemed to be full of cotton wool and legs that refused to work properly. 'Robin?' she had said stupidly, 'Robin, is that you?' But it was not. It was Viv, Robin's aunt-by-marriage, breaking the news that Louis had been shot and Sophia, Robin's mother, had been arrested . . .

The remembered horror of it choked her now and she felt a moment's blind anger directed at Juliet for bringing it all back.

'So now you see why I don't want you to go to Jersey, Juliet,' she snapped.

'No, not really.' Juliet crossed the kitchen, opened the refrigerator and drew herself a glass of ice-cold water from the reservoir beneath its filter. 'Well — yes, I can see why you don't want me to go, but no, I can't see any reason why I shouldn't.'

'It's the same thing, surely.'

'No. It's not. You don't want me to go because it brings back a lot of bad memories for you and because . . . Well, I suppose you're ashamed. But it's different for me. I don't have any bad memories. I can't really remember anything about Jersey at all, except just sometimes, maybe, when a scent or something will kind of stir me. But even then I can't catch it — I don't know what it is I'm remembering. And as for being ashamed . . . well, it happened so long ago I don't suppose anyone cares any more.'

'You don't know Channel Islanders!'

'I *am* one! So are you. So is Dad. And I want to go and find my roots.'

'Don't, Juliet, please!'

'I'm sorry, Mum, but I think you are being silly.'

'I'm advising you because I am older and wiser than you and I know the sort of trouble you'll stir up.'

'I'm sure you're exaggerating. But in any case you should know that being so mysterious only makes me want to go more.'

Molly turned away abruptly. Suddenly she felt very frightened indeed.

'Very well, Juliet. I suppose I can't stop you. But on your own head be it.'

Robin Langlois walked unseeingly around his garden, hands

14

thrust into the pockets of his casual, knee-length shorts, chin almost resting on his white cotton polo shirt.

It was a large garden — space was not at a premium here in the suburbs of Sydney — and Robin often buried himself in it when he wanted to escape from some show down or even from unwanted visitors. What he did not often do was allow himself to think about the past. They'd left all that behind, he and Molly, when they had come to Australia. It had been a fresh start in every way. No more demanding business meetings — Robin had always hated being on the board of a Hotel and Leisure Group, prestigious as the Langlois Group had been in Jersey — no more pretending to be something he wasn't, and, most important of all, no more Louis.

Not that Louis would have been there if they had stayed in Jersey, of course. Louis was dead. But his ghost would have haunted them, Robin knew. If they had stayed they would never have been rid of him.

God, how I hated him! Robin thought now, amazed, as he always was, at the strength of feeling his brother could arouse in him when he was, where most things were concerned, the most placid of men. But then Louis had always managed to hit him where it hurt. First, as children, there had been the awful soul-destroying suspicion that for some reason his mother preferred Louis. His father hadn't — he could never remember his father being anything but scrupulously fair. But that didn't make up for knowing that Louis was Sophia's favourite. Robin adored his mother and the evidence of her favour for his brother festered in his heart.

Then there was the business. Louis had a quicksilver mind where business was concerned. He also had maverick ideas that had caused dreadful friction, but he had still managed to make Robin feel like a clumsy lumbering idiot. When he and Bernard had fallen out and Louis had gone away Robin had tried very hard to fit into his shoes but clearly he had not succeeded. Bernard's will had returned Louis to his former position of power and it had seemed to Robin that his father must have decided Louis's wild schemes were preferable to what Robin had come to see as his own incompetence.

Lastly, but most importantly, there was Molly. Robin thought

15

he could probably have forgiven Louis everything if it hadn't been for Molly. Even as children when they had all played together he had known that Molly liked Louis best and it had hurt just as much as knowing he was Sophia's favourite. But when they had grown older and Robin had fallen in love with Molly it had hurt a great deal more.

Not that Louis ever did anything but flirt with her in the early days. But Robin had seen the way Molly looked at Louis and came alive when he was there and he had known that he was really only the consolation prize. When they had been married he had wished he could lock her away in a glass case he loved her so much. But at least Louis had been off the scene, travelling the world somewhere after falling out with his father.

Robin had just begun to gain confidence when Louis had returned and to his horror he had discovered that the fact that Molly was now his wife seemed to have given her an added attraction in Louis's eyes. He had watched helplessly, unsure just how far Louis was prepared to go, knowing that to act rashly would be to play into Louis's hands. It was, after all, nothing but a game to Louis, a game of power and one-upmanship. His pleasure came from tormenting his brother with the knowledge that he could take his wife from him any time he chose to do so. He didn't really want her — if he had been in love with her Robin thought maybe he could have found some excuse for him — but no, he wasn't in love with her. Robin thought Louis had never been in love with anyone but himself. All he had wanted was the satisfaction of knowing he had only to whistle and she would come running.

Robin shook his head sadly. Once, long ago, he had thought he knew exactly how Cain had felt when he had killed Abel. Now the hatred and the anger was no more than an ache of sadness and poignant regret.

He wished Juliet hadn't raked it all up but he could see how she felt. Her family were still there in Jersey, her grandmother Sophia, Aunt Catherine, Sophia's sister, Paul and Viv, her brother and sister-in-law and his own younger brother David and David's wife Deborah. David and Deborah had come to Australia to visit once when Juliet was about ten but there had been a certain amount of strain in the air and they had never

16

repeated the visit. And Robin, Molly and Juliet had never returned to Jersey.

She has a whole heritage there that fate has deprived her of, Robin thought. It's only right she should go and find it. And if it makes her think twice about getting engaged to Sean it might not be such a bad thing. I don't think she is one hundred per cent sure and I wouldn't want to see her steam-rollered into something she might regret.

He straightened up, a tall rangey man with a slight stoop as if at one time, at least, he had borne all the cares of the world on his shoulders.

Perhaps he'd better go back inside and see if Molly was all right. Really it was the least he could do.

Sean Richardson idly tangled a hand in Juliet's thick fall of hair, playing with the little kiss curls made by the short ends at the nape of her neck, and though his tone was intentionally light his eyes were shadowed.

'You're not serious about going to England, are you, Julie?'

She jerked her head around to look at him and he knew she had seen right through his pretence at the casual, couldn't-care-less approach.

'Perfectly serious. Why shouldn't I be?'

He swallowed. There was no way he was going to tell her the truth – that he was very afraid that if she went he might lose her. It sounded so feeble and in any case he really wasn't sure why he should feel that way. They had been going out together for three years now, since they'd met at art school where Juliet had been studying interior design and he had been doing 3-D. They'd been on the Student Union together and the relationship had stuck. They'd helped one another with their projects, taken all their holidays together, slept together. Now they were talking about getting engaged and married, two steps that he, as a free-thinking art student, had never dreamed for a moment that he would even consider. But to put a ring on her finger seemed the only way to make certain she stayed with him — if he could get a ring on her finger! Sean wasn't totally confident that he could. All very well for her to talk vaguely about getting engaged on her next birthday, that was some comfortable way off. If she felt

17

as he did why wouldn't she move in with him *now*? He had this apartment, not paradise but not bad either, three good-sized rooms and a little back yard, and he was doing quite well with his career and making the sort of salary that would have seemed like riches to him two short years ago when he had been a student. But there was something elusive about Juliet. A quick-silver quality that made him love her all the more but at the same time unsettled him and made him feel very unsure of himself.

Stay here and let's get married now, he wanted to say, but he was afraid to. Instead he settled for the least controversial reason he could think of for persuading her to stay in Australia.

'What about your new job?'

'I don't start that for another month and I'm sure they'd hold it for me a bit longer if I asked them. I am going to be a very small fish in a very large pool when I go to Darby Grace. They have plenty of extremely talented designers and I dare say it will be ages before they allow me even a sniff of a project of my own.'

'You've been doing your own projects very successfully at the Dream Machine.'

'On a quite different scale, though, and I went straight into that from college, remember. I think I'm due for a bit of a break and Darby Grace as good as said so. I shall come back refreshed and ready to give my all to my career.'

'There will be a little bit left over for me, I hope!'

'Oh Sean, you know there will!'

'I still wish you wouldn't go.'

'For goodness' sake!' She wriggled round to face him. 'Nobody wants me to go it seems. Mum and Dad had a go at me this afternoon about it, though their reason was quite different to yours. It seems we have a rather chequered family history.'

He laughed, tossing his light sand-coloured hair back from his long, angular face.

'I can't believe that. I thought your Jersey family were supposed to be real swells. Unlike my convict forbears.'

'It's true — really! It seems my grandmother murdered her son, my Uncle Louis. That was the reason Mum and Dad came to Australia, to get away from the scandal . . .' She broke off.

18

He was staring at her with a shocked expression. 'Why are you looking at me like that?'

'You are joking, Julie?'

'No, I'm not joking. I know it sounds pretty incredible — I couldn't believe it either at first. Not so much that it happened, although that's pretty spooky, but to think they've kept it a secret from me all these years. Unbelievable!'

'They're having you on.'

'No, they're not. If you'd seen their faces . . . I *thought* it was strange we've never been back, not for a single holiday. I mean, I know it's the other side of the world but in a jet aeroplane it's not that far — a matter of hours on Concorde.'

'And your family, I suppose, could well afford Concorde. No going the cheapest way the bucket shop can provide for them!'

'Don't start that again. I can't bear it when you get all assy and left-wing. OK, they've got money, but it's no big deal.'

'No, it's only a big deal for the poor sods with nothing. All right — I'm sorry — I'll get back to the point. I think this murder business is just a story to stop you going and I don't believe a word of it.' He said it almost fiercely as if that was what he wanted to think and she was surprised to realise she had shocked him.

So much for the revolutionary left-wing artist. So much for the native born Australian who boasted of being descended from deported convicts. Beneath it all Sean really had a very puritanical soul.

'If that's their reasoning I'm afraid they've got it totally wrong,' she said with forced lightness. 'I'm quite determined to go now and see what my family is really like.'

'Let me come too.'

'Sean, don't be silly. You certainly haven't got a month's holiday just now. Look, I'm going. I'm going on my own and that's that.'

She leaned over, kissing him and sliding her arms around his neck. It was the one way she knew of shutting him up, the one infallible way, and as always it worked. He picked her up bodily, slipping an arm beneath her knees and another round her shoulders and carried her to the bed. This was the part she always liked best, the teasing, the little love games, the erotic

19

feel of his body, hard and hot, before he undressed her. Why was it always better when there were clothes between, when the feeling of soaring urgency was motivating her, making her want . . . want . . . it. And why when it happened was it always such a let down? Each time when she experienced the sharp cords of desire she thought, yes, yes, yes. Tonight it will be different. Only it never was. When she felt him naked, when he entered her, always she was aware of wanting to scream at him to wind the film back, quickly, before it was too late, always she found herself sobered by the intimate contact as surely as if someone had dowsed her with a bucket of icy water.

There's something wrong with me, Juliet sometimes thought. I'm not normal. But she was afraid to tell anyone how she felt and especially not Sean. It didn't seem fair when he enjoyed doing it so much.

Tonight, as if the thought that he was about to lose her had imbued Sean with a sense of urgency, it was over quickly and Juliet was left feeling even more beached than usual since the desire the initial contact had aroused had had no time to wear off.

'Cigarette?' Sean was reaching for the packet on the shelf beside the bed.

'No thanks.' She'd given up over a year ago but Sean had never got it into his head. 'It's a revolting habit,' she said now, irritated with him without really knowing why. 'Just look how brown the ceiling is and imagine the colour your lungs will be if you keep it up.'

'So what?'

'Don't you care?'

'Not much. I enjoy smoking. A short life and a merry one, I say.'

'That is a stupid attitude at your age. Anyway, you smell disgusting.'

'Well thanks! I love you too!'

A rush of penitence overcame her. Why was she treating him so badly?

'I'm sorry, Sean, I guess I'm a bit edgy tonight. It was probably more of a shock than I realised, finding out that my grandmother served time for the murder of her own son. And it's not just that either. I have this feeling there's more.'

'More?' Sean pulled on his cigarette and aimed a stream of smoke at the offending brown of the ceiling. 'What do you mean, more?'

'I don't know really.' Juliet spoke slowly as if she was only just piecing together impressions which she had not fully appreciated before.

'I'm just not sure even now that they've told me the full story. They were so . . . secretive, both of them.'

'Twenty years of silence.'

'I suppose so. Perhaps it's just as they said, that they thought there was no need for me to know. Perhaps they were protecting me.'

'Who else would they have been protecting?'

'Themselves.' It came out almost as a reflex and as she realised what she had said she shivered. 'That could be the reason they didn't want me to know and don't want me to go back to Jersey. They're hiding something — not just about my grandmother and Uncle Louis but about themselves.'

'Julie! You're letting your imagination run away with you.'

'Maybe, but Dad couldn't even stay in the room to talk about it, and Mum was . . . very strange.'

'What could they be hiding?'

'I don't know. But Mum could hardly bring herself to say his name. Louis. All my life I've had an Uncle Louis and I didn't know.'

'All your life you *haven't* had an Uncle Louis. He was dead.'

'Not until I was four.'

'And you don't remember him at all?'

She shook her head. 'I don't *think* so. Though strangely enough now I know about him and what happened I almost *can*. It's like it's there on the edges of my mind only I can't quite catch it. A bit like a very blurred old negative of a photograph.'

'Maybe now it will start developing.'

'Especially if I go back to Jersey.' She shivered suddenly. 'Sean – I'm scared.'

He ground out his cigarette and put his arm around her.

'Don't go, then.'

She leaned against him, feeling his shoulder comfortably solid behind her head, and was tempted for a moment to agree. Her life, after all, was here. Her new job with its challenges and the promise of rewards, her friends, her parents, Sean who loved her and wanted to marry her. He'd be good to her, she knew, and she loved him too — didn't she? So why was she leaving it all behind to fly across the world alone to a home she barely remembered and relatives who were total strangers? Well, maybe that was not so unnatural. In the beginning when she'd first got the idea it had seemed simply like a good idea for a short break — a holiday, no more no less. Only now it had taken on a whole new complexion, now suddenly there was something sinister, menacing even, in the thought of delving into the past. What Pandora's box was she about to open? Would she do well to forget the whole thing, commit herself to Sean here and now and settle down to marriage and her new job? Perhaps. But even as she thought it she knew she could not do it. She owed herself this one. Until she went back to Jersey and saw for herself the past would remain with her, a constant enigma she would be unable to forget. And when it haunted her she would probably blame Sean for not having allowed her to do what she wanted to do. Unfair, but human nature all the same.

'I'm sorry, but I have to go, Sean,' she said. 'Now, more than ever, I have to go.'

He nodded, kissed her and reached for another cigarette.

'OK. Well, don't be gone too long, Julie. I'm going to miss you like hell.'

She snuggled into him, relishing the moment.

'And I'll miss you. We'll get engaged as soon as I get back, all right? We won't even wait for my birthday, if that's what you want.'

He smiled but it was a rueful smile. He very much wished he could believe she meant it.

Chapter three
Jersey, Channel Islands, 1991

As the plane began its descent Juliet craned her neck to catch her first glimpse for almost twenty years of the island of Jersey.

How small it was! she thought in astonishment, the compact settlement which she imagined must be St Helier, so different from the endless sprawl of Sydney, the little patches of green edged with roads and lanes like a hotchpotch of material scraps sewn into a patchwork quilt, the whole of which might have been totally lost in the vastness of just one sweep of Australian countryside. All around it was the sea, banded in shades of green and blue, beautiful but less hurtful to the eye than the brilliant azure and silver of Sydney harbour. But at least the sun was shining! When the QANTAS jumbo jet had put down at Heathrow it had left the sun behind above a thick cloud base and the effect of descending into a damp morning had been unexpectedly depressing. All very well for the captain to have warned them: 'It is raining in London and the temperature is 11c, 52f,' after a long hot Australian summer and a flight that had involved stops in Singapore and Bahrain, the cool greyness had been just too much of a culture shock.

Wheels touched tarmac, the engines went into reverse and the little jet slowed and taxied towards the airport buildings. As Juliet unbuckled her lap belt and reached into the locker for her bag a nerve throbbed in her throat. She was here now — no going back. Well . . . she *could* go and claim her luggage and book straight on to a flight back to England, she supposed, and chuckled softly to herself at the thought. What a cop-out that would be! Halfway round the world for nothing and her Jersey family all wondering where she had got to. They had promised to meet her at the airport, were presumably waiting now somewhere beyond the Customs Hall. How would she know them? Would they have a board with her name written on it like the tour companies and hire car firms did? Or *their* name, like the hotel courtesy buses? Since they owned a chain of hotels perhaps that was not as silly as it sounded.

Juliet emerged from the cabin and paused for just a moment, sniffing the air. Fascinating how every part of the world smelled different. Then she went down the flight of steps and started across the tarmac.

As the first passengers began filtering through Customs Deborah Langlois stood up from the low bucket seat where she had been sitting and strolled to a vantage point near the door. As she did so the eyes of practically everyone else waiting in the lounge followed her but Deborah scarcely noticed. People looked at her wherever she went and had done for so long now that she accepted it as a fact of life. As a child her tumble of fair curls and her clear turquoise eyes had made adults treat her a little like a living doll, as a teenager, when her curves had developed, she had learned to use her looks to get what she wanted. Now those days were well and truly behind her. At thirty-six Deborah had wealth, position and power — and it showed. Youthful prettiness had matured into beauty, extreme fashion tastes blossomed to style and flair, and confidence had grown from what had once been almost chronic insecurity. As the wife of the Managing Director of the Langlois Hotel and Leisure Group, Deborah's photograph often graced the society pages of *Harpers and Queen* and the *Lady* or figured in the gossip columns of the *Daily Mail* or the *Express*, the very epitome of sophistication, elegance and glamour.

Occasionally a reporter with a nose for a story would ask an awkward question or two about Deborah's past but for some reason the trail had never led very far. Always Jersey's monied elite had closed ranks. Deborah was the wife of David Langlois now. Did it really matter who she had been or where she had sprung from? As for those who tried to pursue the question with Debbie herself, most of them soon gave up, won over by the sheer power of her charm.

I never knew my father, Debbie would tell them, and my mother died when I was in my teens. She was a vicar's daughter, her family had disowned her because of me, so I never knew

24

them at all. But please — I wouldn't like to cause them any embarrassment. I know it sounds ridiculous in this day and age but older people like them can still be extremely puritanical, and really, for modern tastes, there's no scandal at all. Just a rebellious daughter and a love child.

Her turquoise eyes would meet theirs, clear and seemingly transparent, and they almost always found themselves believing her and what was more actually wanting to protect her. There had been scandals in the Langlois family but they had already been done to death in the gossip columns and none of them had had anything to do with Deborah. It had been her misfortune that she had been caught up in them. What was the point of demolishing the reputation of someone who admitted so readily to shortcomings in her pedigree? Invariably the journalists enjoyed a drink and a cigarette with Deborah and went on their way feeling privileged to have met her and never realising for a moment the wonderful copy they had failed to unearth.

If she had lived on the mainland, Deborah sometimes thought, she would never have got away with it. But this was Jersey, a law unto itself, and the expanse of English Channel dividing it from the mainland made an effective moat. The secrets of Deborah's past remained hidden and these days the reporters did not bother her at all.

She stood now in the airport lounge, a slim elegant woman wearing a jacket and trousers in peach silk suiting, her shoulder length silver blonde hair taken up into a classic chignon, dark glasses dangling from a slender hand on which the nails had been painted to the exact same shade of peach as her suit. The craze for flat heeled pumps had passed Deborah by; at just short of five feet five she had never felt she was tall enough to wear them and still look elegant. As a teenager she had teetered on stilettos, ignoring the platform soles of the early seventies as she was now ignoring the 'flatty', but nowadays the high heels she wore were the very last word in tasteful glamour, they came from Manolo Blahnik and Russell and Bromley, and the soft leather bag swinging from her shoulder was unmistakeably Gucci. Most of Deborah's clothes bore designer labels, Versace and Ungaro, Lagerfeld and Krizia and even her underwear was La Perla — 'You must be crazy, paying so much for a pair of knickers!' Catherine, her husband's aunt, had once said. Catherine took a great delight in the outrageous comments for which she was renowned and Deborah had merely smiled and said nothing. She had no intention of explaining that the secret spring of her confidence lay in the wearing of designer clothes and without them she could sometimes, even now, feel slightly gauche. A little girl dressed up in her mother's best or an actress playing a part, neither was the image Deborah wanted to project. She had worked so hard at being who she was; to let even the smallest weakness show could be disastrous.

The first passengers from the Jersey Airways flight came through customs and Deborah glanced at them critically. When she had offered to come and meet her husband's niece she had had no doubts she would know her; now, suddenly she was not so sure. The photograph Sophia, her mother-in-law, had shown her might bear little or no resemblance to the girl from Australia. Photographs could be very deceptive. Juliet might even — heaven forbid — resemble her mother! A muscle in Deborah's stomach tightened at the thought and she felt again an echo of the dismay which had been her first reaction when Sophia had told her Juliet was coming to Jersey.

Oh no. Not Molly's daughter . . .

She had hidden her feelings, of course. To allow them to show would have been to let Sophia — and more importantly, David — know that for her the past was not dead but only dormant. It was almost twenty years since she had seen Molly but the hatred she felt for her — and the jealousy — remained as strong as ever. Never mind that she was happy and successful now, never mind that she knew she had been very fortunate indeed in the way things had turned out. Once Molly had hurt her so much that the wound could never quite heal; the thought of her could get beneath the skin of elegant sophisticated Deborah Langlois and turn her, like Cinderella at the stroke of midnight, into the girl she had once been — frightened, desperate and madly in love with a man who no longer cared for her. To all intents and purposes Deborah had put it all behind her and she had seldom if ever spared a thought for Molly in years. But the news that her daughter was coming to Jersey had brought it all back as fresh as if it had been yesterday.

26

The tide of memory had disturbed Deborah for a few days. She had even considered taking a holiday in order to avoid Molly's daughter. She had been promising herself a trip to New York for ages; she had only to telephone her friends there and she could hop on a plane and put the Atlantic ocean between her and Juliet. But even as the thought occurred to her she knew she could not do it. To leave Jersey just now, with Juliet arriving, would be far too pointed. Sophia and David would be bound to know what was in her mind and Deborah knew her pride would not allow that. So with characteristic directness she had decided to take the bull by the horns. When the family had discussed who should meet Juliet at the airport Deborah had offered. 'It will be much nicer for her than being met by Perry. A chauffeur might be impressive but also very impersonal,' she had said, and hoped that neither David nor Sophia had seen through her and guessed her real motive — to get that initial meeting over with sooner rather than later and lay the ghost.

Now, however, as she watched and waited, Deborah's throat was dry and she felt a little sick with apprehension.

The trickle of passengers continued — not too many, for it was not yet the time of year when every plane would disgorge a full complement of holidaymakers on to the tarmac. There were one or two businessmen, a young man with a child, several middle-aged couples taking early holidays but no one who could be by the remotest stretch of the imagination Juliet. Perhaps she had missed the plane, Deborah thought. It was possible her flight from Australia had been delayed and she had arrived too late to make the connection, too late even to telephone La Grange and explain what had happened. She moved a trifle restlessly, betraying her nervousness by the way she was suddenly fiddling with the earpiece of her sunglasses.

She isn't coming. All this for nothing. I'll have to go home and tell Sophia she wasn't on the plane . . .

And then suddenly there she was.

The moment she came into view Deborah knew it was her though she did not look too much like her photograph and mercifully she didn't look like Molly either. She was taller, slimmer, fairer. She wore a mini skirt, a cropped jacket in lemon denim and the sort of flatty sandals Deborah would have spurned

27

but which, on her long legs, looked just right. Everything about her was young and vibrant and with that tan she could only have come from Australia or a holiday in a sunspot such as the Bahamas.

Deborah's fingers tightened around her bag. Then her lips curved, hiding the nub of nervousness she was still feeling, and she crossed the airport lounge.

'Hello — you must be Juliet. I'm Deborah.'

The car was a white Mercedes coupé and it suited Deborah perfectly, Juliet decided — they had the same elegant lines and touch of class. But the car also felt as if it wanted to go a great deal faster than the winding lanes permitted. Was that also true of Deborah? She somehow thought it might be, but she liked her anyway. With all that glamour she could have been off-putting but somehow she was not. She had a nice smile and a nice voice, not in the least plummy but light and musical and Juliet, used to laid-back Sydneyside drawl, thought she could have listened to it forever.

'You'll like La Grange,' she was saying now as the Mercedes swung down a steeply sloping and curving lane between banks of hydrangeas, big as small trees. 'It's a beautiful house in a beautiful spot.'

'Dad has told me about it,' Juliet said. 'He says the thing he liked best about it was that there was nothing but woodland and fern-covered cliffs between the house and the sea. When he was a little boy he used to sneak out on summer evenings when he was supposed to be in bed and go down the valley, through the woods and onto the cliff path. Then he'd pretend he was a smuggler or something. He was never caught — he said his mother doesn't know about it to this day.'

Deborah laughed. 'Well well! Robin never struck me as a rebel.'

'He isn't. He's a romantic.' She paused. 'It's funny, when he talks about his home in Jersey he always means La Grange, though he had a house of his own after he married Mum, where I was born and lived when I was a little girl.'

'Green Banks. Yes. That is very nice too. Do you remember it at all?'

28

Juliet shook her head. 'Not really. Snatches, perhaps. But I was only four when we left.'

'Yes of course. Well, we'll go over one day and have a look at it if you like. From the outside, of course. I don't actually know the people who live there now. I think it's changed hands a couple of times in the last twenty years. Perhaps when you see it it will jog your memory.'

'Perhaps it will. Sometimes I think I can remember a big sunny room with a rocking horse. And there are certain smells that kind of tickle my memory — furniture polish is one, lavender is another.'

'I think there was a lavender bush in the kitchen garden. Yes, it was a very nice house. Not in the same class as La Grange, though. David and I are very lucky that Sophia allows us to share it with her.'

Sophia. Hearing her grandmother referred to by her Christian name was a slight shock. 'Mama,' Robin always said, and Molly never called her anything but 'your mother'.

'Have you and Uncle David always lived there?' she asked.

'Yes. It seemed only sensible. It would have been much too large for just one person and in any case I don't think Sophia wanted to be alone. She suggested we should stay.'

'I see.' Again Juliet felt a slight jar of shock. She knew instinctively that Deborah meant that Sophia had not wanted to be alone after what had happened and to hear her refer to it so casually, albeit obliquely, was disconcerting. But then of course to Deborah it would be a fact of life, something she had lived with for so long that it no longer caused so much as a ripple on the surface.

The lane curved steeply and as the Mercedes rounded the bend a vista opened suddenly, a glimpse of blue sea framed by bright fresh greens and yellows. The sight was so unexpected and so beautiful it took Juliet's breath away, then, as quickly, it was gone, lost behind the high hedgerows which were already burgeoning into the new season's life.

'Almost there,' Deborah said.

She turned the Mercedes into a tree-lined drive. Renewed nervousness made Juliet's mouth dry again. And then, through the trees, she saw it — an impressively large Regency style house of Jersey granite. Six casement windows protruded from the great slate roof directly above the six upper storey windows; the tall arched door and five ground floor windows completed the perfect symmetry of the design. A small ornamental fountain played on the lawn that fronted the house and twin box trees stood sentinel. The blend of formality with the wild beauty of the wooded area beyond was stunning; for the second time in almost as few minutes Juliet caught her breath.

So this was La Grange. This was the family home she could scarcely remember. And also the scene of the murder that had changed all their lives including, of course, her own. The enormity of it was more overwhelming than Juliet could ever have imagined it would be and she sat in complete awestruck silence as the strange pot-pourri of half-forgotten, dreamlike familiarity teased her senses.

I might have been only four but part of me does remember. There were raised voices, there were tears. I was very frightened. I knew something terrible was happening but no one would tell me what it was. And then they took me away. . . .

Deborah pulled on the handbrake and switched off the engine. She smiled at Juliet, seemingly unaware of the turmoil of emotions.

'Shall we go in?' she suggested.

From the window of her sitting-room on the first floor Sophia Langlois had seen the Mercedes turn into the drive. She rose swiftly from the chair which she had positioned especially for that purpose and went through the connecting door into her bedroom to tidy her already immaculate hair and collect her jacket. Then she hesitated in the doorway, waiting.

Sophia would never have admitted to anyone that she had been watching eagerly for her granddaughter's arrival; she had hardly admitted it to herself. Always poised, always in complete possession of herself, it was totally out of character that she should be peering out from behind the curtains, taking her eye off the drive only to check the time by the anniversary clock which Bernard had bought for her to celebrate the first year of their marriage. But today was different — and very special. Today Juliet was coming home.

30

A tiny pulse of excitement beat in Sophia's throat beneath the elegant tie neck of her violet silk blouse. Many terrible things had happened in her lifetime; she had had her share of tragedy and trouble, and they had left their mark on her. But she did not brood over them now. It was in the past, all of it, and no longer mattered. But Juliet mattered, Juliet was the future and because of what had happened she had lost Juliet. It was the one aspect of the whole business she still regretted — had ever regretted if it came to that — and there had been plenty of times when she had thought she would never see Juliet again. But now she was here.

Suddenly Sophia could not wait a moment longer. She hurried to the window, not caring whether she was seen or not. The Mercedes had drawn up on the gravel turn around and Deborah was getting out — Deborah who had been so much more than a daughter-in-law to her, Deborah, to whom she was perhaps closer than anyone in the world. What would I have done without her? Sophia often wondered, and blessed the day when she had taken pity on a young and frightened girl. But today even Deborah had faded into insignificance.

At first glance as she came around the rear of the car Sophia could scarcely believe her eyes. She had known, of course, that Juliet was a young woman now. She had photographs which Robin had sent her from Australia to prove it. The snapshots and the portraits which were always tucked inside her birthday and Christmas cards had marked the passage of the years — Juliet on the beach — cooking steaks on the 'barbie' in the garden — dressed for a grand ball in a fairytale gown of emerald green trimmed with black lace — on the arm of a young man with long hair and an easy open smile — drinking a champagne birthday toast. But photographs were oddly unreal. In spite of them it was still a shock to see Juliet as she now was.

Disorientated, Sophia found herself remembering the last time she had seen her granddaughter. She had been wearing a plaid kilt and frilly white blouse, long white knee socks and black patent ankle strap shoes and her hair had been a cap of shining gold. Sophia had gazed at her, imprinting the image on her memory to last her through the years, and now suddenly it was there again like a well-worn photograph superimposed on the

31

image of a tall young woman in a cropped lemon denim jacket and mini skirt.

Oh Juliet how much I have missed! she thought, unexpected tears blurring her vision. If only your mother had not felt the need to take you away . . . if only I had been able to visit just once or twice . . . when it was all over.

But it wouldn't have worked. Neither Robin nor Molly would have wanted to see her. Molly had never forgiven her and Robin. . . . No, it was best she had stayed away.

Now, at last, Juliet was here — here because she wanted to be.

Sophia turned to run downstairs. For the first time in many years she felt as if she were a young girl again.

'I suppose,' Vivienne Carteret said, 'she'll be here by now.'

'What?' Paul, Sophia's brother, looked up from his newspaper, peering over the top of his gold-rimmed half-spectacles at his wife who was pouring herself a pre-dinner gin and tonic. 'Who?'

'Well Juliet of course!' Viv tasted her drink, added a touch more tonic, then crossed the room to her favourite chair, a black leather lounger with enormous comfortable wings. 'Your niece, my dear — or great-niece, to be more accurate. She was due to fly in from Australia today.'

'Oh yes,' Paul said, returning to his newspaper. 'David was saying something about it at the office. She's staying at La Grange, isn't she?'

'Of course she is! Where else would she stay?'

Paul chuckled. He was a big man who had once been handsome; now his complexion gave away the fact that he, like his wife, drank a little more than was good for him and his once firm chin had sagged into heavy jowls. Life had thrown a good measure of traumas and disappointments in Paul's path. Now, in the calmer backwaters of middle-age, he had discovered the pleasures of self-indulgence, and both the earlier struggles and the more recent excesses of easy living as well as some wildly irresponsible patches along the way had left their mark on him.

'So — the little fledgling is back in the family nest,' he

remarked wryly. 'I'll bet Robin and Molly had something to say about that!'

'Probably,' Viv agreed. Privately she had never had a great deal of time for either of them; Robin struck her as an ineffectual wimp and Molly was over-emotional and childish. She had a great deal to answer for, Viv had always thought. If she had faced up to her responsibilities things might have been very different. 'I wonder if Juliet knows now about Louis and your sister?' she said reflectively.

Paul glanced up again, reaching for the whisky tumbler on the small occasional table at his elbow.

'Well of course she knows.'

'She didn't. When David and Deborah went over to visit Molly asked them not to say anything about it. She said she and Robin had decided it was best for Juliet not to be told.'

'But that was when she was a child. She's a grown woman now, for God's sake. They must have told her!'

Viv twisted the tumbler between her hands so that the rings which she wore on almost every finger clicked against the glass.

'I wouldn't bank on it. Molly was one of the most secretive women I ever met as well as being one of the silliest. And you know how she was about Louis. She must have been just about the only person who didn't think Sophia had done the world a service by shooting him.'

'Viv, for God's sake!' Paul exploded. He should be used to his wife by now — after nearly fifty years of marriage there was nothing she could do that could surprise him, yet he still found himself shocked by her outspokenness.

'It's true!' Viv smiled faintly, deep lines biting into her smooth plump face above the scarlet gash of her mouth. 'Louis had so many enemies half the island would have been picked up for questioning about his death if Sophia hadn't confessed. I even wondered at the time if *you* had done it.'

'I beg your pardon!' Paul's already high colour deepened a shade so that it was almost puce. Viv smiled again. She was never happier than when she was causing a sensation, mild or otherwise.

'You had the opportunity. You were out that night I seem to remember and you always were very cagey about where you had been. And you certainly had the motive. We were going through an exceedingly bad patch if I remember rightly — and Louis was making things a hundred times worse. He couldn't have died at a better time for us, now could he? Admit it, Paul!'

Paul set his glass down. Little beads of sweat were standing out on his forehead as memories returned to him, clear as yesterday. Viv was quite right, it had been a terrible time for them and Louis had been his chief tormentor. For one thing Paul had owed him a great deal of money. He had had no one but himself to blame for that, of course — he had a weakness for gambling and Louis had exploited it. Then, just to make matters worse, Bernard had died and when the boys came into their father's shares Louis had tried to squeeze Paul out of the business. He could never have done it in Bernard's lifetime — though it had been Bernard, in truth, who had been responsible for building up the hotel and leisure empire he had never forgotten that he had owed his start to Paul's — and Sophia's — parents, Charles and Lola. Without them there would have been nothing and Bernard had recognised that; whatever Paul's shortcomings he had covered for them. Not Louis. Louis was ruthless and hard as well as clever and sly. He would have disposed of Paul with the same lack of compassion that he might crush a wasp that irritated him — no, not just with lack of compassion but with an obvious pleasure too.

Louis had loved power, he had enjoyed making people squirm. But the cocky little bastard had died at exactly the right moment. The debts had been put to one side and forgotten — Paul had discovered to his relief that Louis had not made any record of them beyond the casual IOUs he had deposited in the office safe and Paul had disposed of them by simply flushing them down the lavatory. Since Louis had not left any dependents this had not troubled his conscience over much. As for Paul's position in the company, he had suddenly realised it was sounder than it had been at any time since Bernard's death. With Louis no longer there to run things, Sophia in prison, Robin emigrating to Australia and David still too young for serious responsibility Paul had found himself in the driving seat. From that moment on he had made the most of his opportunities. Fate, he knew, would never deal him a better hand. By the time David was old

34

enough to take up his heritage and become the figurehead of his father's empire, Paul had established himself as elder statesman. David had never suggested, as Louis had, that his services would no longer be required and if he questioned Paul's decisions he did so with a certain amount of deference and respect. Not that he was weak like Robin either. No, David had managed to steer a course between the extremes of his two elder brothers.

Perhaps, Paul thought, of the three boys David was the most like Bernard — clear-sighted and even-handed, tempering decisiveness with tact, able to implement even unpopular innovations with the minimum of resistance from the staff, and with the knack of eliciting loyalty from each and every one of them because each believed he was an important cog in the organisation who also mattered as a private individual.

Man-management was the secret of David's success, Paul decided; with it he did not need to be a financial genius or even a brilliant businessman, for there were always those who would carry out these tasks for him willingly and well. But it did not occur to Paul that in David's handling of him, Paul, lay perhaps the most skilful piece of man-management of all!

Paul folded his newspaper and put it down on the table beside his glass, then he removed his half-spectacles, folding them and putting them into the soft leather case in his breast pocket. His hand was shaking slightly.

'Do we have to talk about Louis?'

Viv shrugged and ran her fingers through her hair in a gesture that had remained unchanged since the days of her youth. Her hair had been her crowning glory in those days, luxuriant, flaming red, and she had been very proud of it. For a long time after it had begun to fade she had continued to have it dyed to something approximating its original shade, then one day she had caught sight of herself in the mirror and realised that it no longer made her look stunning but old — a harridan, she had thought in disgust. The next day she had asked her hairdresser to do whatever was necessary to achieve a more natural colour and now only a silver rinse brightened the head of hair that had once been the talk of Jersey. But old habits die hard; Viv still tossed her head as she had used to do, still flicked her fingers

35

through her hair as a careless gesture which nevertheless rarely failed to attract attention.

'No, dear, we don't have to talk about Louis if it makes you uncomfortable. But it might be a good idea to brush up on all your pretend responses when his name is mentioned — the ones you perfected twenty years ago.'

'What the hell do you mean?'

'Exactly what I say. Twenty years ago you were very good at hiding just how much you hated Louis. Now I'm afraid you're out of practice. You really have become quite transparent.'

'For God's sake, Viv, I don't understand.'

'Don't you?' Her green eyes, clear as chips of emerald glass, regarded him coolly. 'Then let me spell it out for you. Robin's daughter is in Jersey. We are going to meet and socialise with her — we are going to dinner at La Grange tomorrow night, remember? It is quite on the cards that she is going to want to talk about Louis.'

'Over dinner, with Sophia sitting there? Surely not!'

'Well no, obviously not then. But we are two of the only people who knew exactly what happened. It is my bet that at some point Juliet's curiosity is going to get the better of her. So, my darling . . .', she raised her glass to him, 'I suggest you had better be prepared!'

'Oh Juliet, my dear, you have no idea how good it is to have you here!' Sophia said.

Dinner was over, a pleasant informal meal when Juliet had felt surprisingly at ease in the company of the three relatives who were also virtual strangers. Now David and Deborah had tactfully withdrawn to their own apartments, leaving Sophia and Juliet alone.

'It's lovely to be here. I only wish I'd come a very long time ago,' Juliet agreed, sipping coffee from a tiny gold-rimmed bone china cup and enjoying the comfortable glow that had begun with a glass of celebratory champagne and spread along with her share of a bottle of fine wine from David's well-stocked cellar. 'But being here, in this house, is the strangest feeling . . . I don't *really* remember and yet I do. Do you know what I mean?'

'I do indeed. And one thing I promise. Practically nothing

36

has changed — on the ground floor at any rate. Deborah has redecorated the rooms she and David use, of course. Several times over. But down here even when the paint is freshened or the wallpaper replaced the overall effect remains the same — mainly, I suppose, because rightly or wrongly I cling to the stubborn belief I could not improve upon it.'

'I'm sure you couldn't,' Juliet said.

'Well that, my dear, is praise indeed! After all, you are a professional, aren't you?'

Juliet laughed. Yes, she was a professional now — but it still amused her to hear someone actually say it, and besides she was not at all sure that she had looked at La Grange through professional eyes. The moment she had stepped into the entrance hall with its granite flagstone floor, sculptured plaster ceiling rose and mouldings and sweeping staircase she had been transported back in time. It was not only the sight of the place that had done this but the smell — beeswax polish on the bannisters and the beautiful carved wood table, mingling with the slightly musty, though not unpleasant, smell that emanated from the enormous arrangement of dried flowers that filled and brightened one corner. Standing there Juliet had almost been able to hear the patter of a child's sandals on the flagstone — her own sandals, the smart but functional leather Clarks she had worn when she was little.

From the hall she had been taken to the drawing-room, less familiar because she had spent less time there. But she could appreciate it all the same, and enjoy the luxurious yet restful feel that came from the careful blending of shades of cream and apricot. Her practised eye had taken in the velvet curtains and watered silk wall hangings, the furniture which mixed the elegant with the comfortable — a peach chaise, an intricately carved love-seat, and a sofa and easy chairs so deep and inviting that she wished she could immediately sink into them. One wall was lined with book shelves; rich leather bindings bearing the lettering of rare first editions rubbed shoulders with well-loved childrens' classics — *Alice in Wonderland*, *The Wind in the Willows*, *The Water Babies*. The lamps — table lamps and standards — were shaded in watered silk and all around were the treasures of a lifetime's collecting — graceful art nouveau looking not the least bit out of place alongside Regency silver and Oriental jade. Only the carpet jarred slightly — wall to wall cream, deep, luxurious and immaculate. Somehow Juliet would have expected an enormous and beautiful Aubusson or something similar, gracing a floor of polished woodblocks.

Into the dining-room and here her instinct had proved correct. The floor was indeed woodblocked and carpeted with a sweeping circle of rich red, strong enough to complement the dark oak furniture, a long sideboard displaying a whole array of chafing dishes, chairs beautifully fashioned and upholstered in a red Regency stripe silk and a huge rectangular table laid now with crisp white linen, heavy silver and fine sparkling crystal. Yet impressive as every piece in the room was, it was totally dominated by the portrait which hung over the Victorian mantel.

'Grandfather!' Juliet had exclaimed.

'Yes, that is Bernard, your grandfather, but he never saw his portrait, I'm afraid. I had it painted after his death,' Sophia said, then, seeing Juliet's puzzled expression, she chuckled, a hint of mischief creeping into her poised demeanour. 'He'd never have been able to sit still long enough for anyone to paint him. Bernard was a do-er, and he'd have considered it a terrible waste of time. But I felt it was only fitting, as the founder of the family firm, that he should have his portrait in a place of honour, so I commissioned an artist to paint it from a photograph.'

'Is it a good likeness?' Juliet asked.

'Yes, I think so.'

Juliet took in the strong face, the firm chin, the half-smiling mouth.

'He looks kind.'

'Yes,' Sophia said simply. 'He was.'

Something in her tone caught at a chord deep within Juliet; she lowered her eyes from the portrait to her grandmother. There was a faraway look in her sparkling amethyst eyes and a softness about her mouth.

She really loved him, Juliet thought. Perhaps she still does. My grandfather — Father's father.

There was nothing in him that reminded her of her father, though. If anything Robin was more like his mother with slanting eyes and high cheekbones. 'I have Russian blood,' Robin some-times explained. 'Lola, my grandmother, was White Russian.'

David, on the other hand, was certainly like his father. During the meal Juliet had found her eyes straying more than once between her uncle and the portrait of her grandfather. Looking at David it was easy to see exactly what Bernard must have looked like at his age — even with the added years the similarity was striking — the set of the eyes, the shape of the jawline, the slightly hooked nose. For David himself it must be like a glimpse of his own future. So, David was almost a younger version of his father. But who had Louis been like? But there were no photographs to tell her and curious as she was she knew this was not the right time to ask.

Once more Juliet glanced at her grandmother. What had she expected of a woman who had killed her own son? She honestly did not know. The enigma had plagued her from the moment Molly had told her what had happened. But whatever she had expected, whatever images had half-formed in her imagination, they certainly bore no relation to the reality.

At sixty-six Sophia was still trim, still elegant. Her hair, though heavily streaked with silver now, was a shining cap, her eyes — those incredible amethyst eyes — still sparkled, unmarred by the deep crowsfeet or dark circles one might have expected, though in places the skin looked paper thin as if she had been rather ill at some time. Her taste was impeccable — her silk blouse had obviously been chosen because it was the exact same colour as her eyes, yet it also complemented her Chanel suit of cream wool. Her legs were still good, her calves shapely and ankles trim above a pair of black patent pumps with high slender heels. Yet none of this was necessarily incompatible with the ruthlessness one might have expected. No, it was her smile which gave the lie to that. In all her life Juliet did not think she had seen one sweeter. And now, as Sophia looked at the portrait of her husband, it was there again.

She never killed anyone! Juliet thought, shocking herself with her own vehemence. I don't believe she could ever take a gun and kill anyone — especially not her own son. And what is more if she had done, it would be haunting her now.

A woman who could do something like that and then return

to live in the house where it had all happened would be a very hard woman. Whatever else she might be Juliet would have staked her life on that one fact — Sophia was not hard. She turned her smile now on Juliet and it seemed that not only her mouth turned upwards but her whole face — no wonder she looked so young, Juliet thought. Then she leaned forward, taking Juliet's hand in her own.

'All those years!' she said with a sigh. 'My only grandchild and I've missed all your growing up. At the risk of driving you away for another twenty years I am going to tell you how sad that makes me. But now I hope we are going to make up for it. And I want you to begin by telling me everything — all about yourself.'

Juliet smiled back. 'Well, all right. But first do you think I could have another cup of coffee?'

'Of course you could! I'm sorry — I'm being a terrible hostess.'

'You most certainly are not!'

'My only excuse is that all I can think about is getting to know you.'

'I know,' Juliet said, sipping at her fresh cup of coffee and thinking that her own curiosity would have to wait.

By the time she climbed the stairs to the guest room on the first floor in which she would be staying Juliet was more puzzled than ever by the enigma that was her grandmother.

She had been keen to hear every detail of Juliet's life, drawing out stories that Juliet had never told anyone, never thought anyone would find the least bit interesting — and she had shown a perception and wisdom that had been a little disconcerting, going straight to the heart of matters which Juliet had skated over.

'Did you *like* riding?' she had asked with that particular directness when Juliet had told her about the pony that she had been given for her sixth birthday and Juliet had had to admit that no, actually she didn't. It was not an admission she had made to her parents for a very long time; she had been afraid they would think her dreadfully ungrateful and perhaps a little peculiar, or, worse, a coward. It was only after a really bad fall that she had got up the courage to admit she found it daunting to be expected to control an animal so much bigger than she was, particularly since her legs were too short to allow her to balance properly on the plump pony and she was forever sliding down and toppling off and was then unable to get back on again. Molly had been very sniffy about the whole thing — Juliet thought she probably fancied herself as the mother of a future Australian team show jumper or three-day eventer and she had indeed made Juliet feel something of a failure. Her grandmother, however, seemed to understand, anticipate the reaction, just as she understood when Juliet told her how she loved to play the piano and how she had had to beg to be allowed to learn the violin — 'I don't think I can stand the caterwauling!' Molly had said.

But perhaps most startling of all was the way her grandmother had honed in on her feelings for Sean.

'You have a boyfriend?'

'Yes. I met him at college. He was a year above me so he's really settled in his job now and doing very well. We are probably going to get engaged when I go home and get married next year.' Juliet was sure she had not given away any clue to her doubts but Sophia's voice had been serious.

'You're very young.'

'Not *that* young. I'm twenty-three. Quite a few of the girls I was at school with are married already — mothers, even.'

'Yes. Yes, I suppose so. I was still in my teens when I married your grandfather. Well, as long as you are quite sure you love him. That is the most important thing.' Her startling amethyst eyes, shadowed now, searched Juliet's. 'You *are* sure?'

A nerve jumped in Juliet's throat. Yes, she wanted to say, — more because she did not want to discuss her deepest feelings with anyone at all, especially a grandmother she had only just met than because she believed it — but somehow she could not. She had the strangest feeling that Sophia was looking right into her heart and seeing the doubts that she had tried so hard to ignore.

'Juliet?' Sophia pressed her. 'You do love him?'

Juliet found her voice. 'Of course I do.'

For a moment longer those sharp eyes continued to hold hers, then Sophia nodded.

41

'That's all right then. If you love him that is all that matters.'

But Juliet felt instinctively that she was not completely satisfied and she wondered how long it would be before Sophia returned to the subject.

The guest room had a bathroom en suite. Juliet washed her face, brushed her teeth and slipped between the cool cotton sheets. She was very tired now — it had been a long day and jet-lag (which she always denied) was catching up with her. So many questions! she thought as the room drifted away from her. So many . . .

It was only just as she was on the point of sleep that another thought occurred to her. If Sophia cared so much, felt such a passionate interest in her one and only grandchild, why had she never once come to visit? Australia was half a world away from Jersey, the secrets of the past need never have been mentioned if the family had preferred them not to be. Yet she had not come. Instinctively Juliet sensed a gulf between her parents and Sophia that had not yet been adequately explained and her drowsy mind worried at it. But she was too tired to be able to think clearly. The pieces of the jigsaw were shuffling round and round in her mind, confused and oddly distorted. Then they were slipping further and further away and a few moments later Juliet was asleep.

Chapter four

'Juliet, my dear, how very nice!'

Catherine Carteret was working in the garden of her cottage when the Metro which Deborah had hired for Juliet drew up at the gate and her great-niece slid out from behind the steering wheel.

Catherine straightened up, jamming her wide-brimmed straw hat more firmly down on to her iron grey curls, a small round woman with just enough similarity to Sophia to mark them out as sisters but a good many differences too. Where Sophia had poise Catherine seemed to be in a perpetual tizzy, where Sophia could be silent and mysterious Catherine was, and always had been, a chatterbox. Those who remembered them as children retained a vision of Catherine as bouncy, pretty and always laughing, not as beautiful as Sophia but with more than her fair share of personality, and nowadays she was known for her sense of fun and the wicked pleasure she derived from saying quite outrageous things. Yet surprisingly Catherine had never married. Soon after the war she left Jersey for England, trained as a teacher and spent her entire working life at schools in and around the most deprived areas of London.

The family had long since given up trying to understand what had motivated her; Catherine was a law unto herself. Then, just when they had thought that she had left Jersey for ever she had proved them wrong yet again. When she had reached the age of sixty, a year ago, she had retired from her profession, sold the flat which she had occupied for more than thirty years and returned to the island where she had been born. Sophia had suggested she should move into La Grange to keep her company — fond as she was of Deborah and David she liked the idea of having her sister around, especially since they both now had plenty of time on their hands. But Catherine had declined

43

the offer. She had been on her own too long now to be able to fit in with anyone else, she explained, and she had bought herself a charming cottage in the very heart of the island.

For all her reluctance to live with them, however, Catherine saw a good deal of her family. She was one of the few people who got along with Vivienne and usually had dinner with her and Paul at least once a week, and she was a frequent visitor at La Grange. She was delighted now to see Juliet, whom she had pressed to visit her, and she hurried to the gate to greet her — albeit with a warning.

'You'd better not leave your car there. The road is dreadfully twisty and not very wide. I'll open the gate so you can bring it into the drive. Then we'll go in and have a cup of tea.'

'Sorry — I'm not used to being so cramped for space,' Juliet apologised when she had parked the car behind Catherine's on the tarmacadammed drive.

Catherine led the way into the cottage, throwing her hat down on a comfortably cushioned chair in the kitchen and setting the kettle on the stove. Instantly a smell of burning sugar filled the kitchen.

'Damn,' Catherine said. 'I must have spilled something on that ring again. Oh well, it'll burn off, won't it?'

Juliet smiled. There really was no point of comparison between Catherine and the rest of the family. At La Grange Sophia employed a housekeeper, a daily woman and a gardener, and Viv, though her home was smaller and much less elaborate, had all the paid help she needed to avoid carrying out any onerous domestic chores for herself. All of them lived a lifestyle of unashamed luxury — paid for, presumably, by the success of the hotel and leisure empire.

And fashioned on the same lines, Juliet thought wryly. One of the first things she had done on arriving in Jersey had been to look around each of the four hotels and she had been duly impressed by what she had seen. En suite bathrooms were furnished with monogrammed towels and bathrobes, a heated towel rail and a special line in toiletries. In the bedrooms a television set received satellite programmes as well as the usual channels, there was a stereo radio console and each room had its own well-stocked and refrigerated mini bar. But this was just the beginning of the special care lavished on the guests who were, from the moment they walked through the doors, treated as honoured visitors. Regardless of the hour of day or night porters whisked luggage upstairs in one of the huge mirrored lifts while receptionists took orders for morning papers, laundry and special dietary requirements. Five minutes after arrival a pot of tea was delivered to the room (a trick Bernard had borrowed from the great hotels of the Far East) and when the maid turned down the beds at night she laid a chocolate or a flower on the pillow.

Juliet, used to the much more functional life of well-to-do but not excessively wealthy Australia, was fascinated and amused, as she was when she had visited the smart offices that formed the hub of the Langlois empire. As David had shown her along the corridor, carpeted and hung with framed water colours, to the board room where a buffet lunch had been laid out in her honour she had noticed the deference with which staff treated him and thought that it was easy to imagine the other members of the family commanding exactly the same respect.

Perhaps, she thought, it was because they expected it that they were treated like visiting royalty — even Sophia, who had served time for the killing of her son, would still merit the same approach from the staff, most of whom had probably long since forgotten what had happened anyway. But Catherine was quite different. The staff might like her very much indeed — they almost certainly did — but their approach would reflect her own friendliness. Catherine did not stand on ceremony. She had no time for it at all. It was not that she was embarrassed exactly by the glamour and opulence, rather that it had quite simply passed her by. She did not notice it and certainly did not seek any special treatment and because of this Juliet was totally at ease with her in a way it was not possible to be totally at ease with the others after only a week's acquaintance however much she might like them. They belonged, quite obviously, to the island's aristocracy. Catherine, not to put too fine a point on it, was unashamedly *ordinary*.

'So — what do you think of Jersey?' Catherine asked, setting out large pottery mugs on the scrubbed wood table and dropping a one-cup teabag into each. 'Is it as you expected? Oh — do

45

move my hat and sit down. There's a peg behind the door but I'm afraid I'm very lazy about using it.'

Juliet took the hat and hung it up with some difficulty since a raincoat, a cardigan and a PVC apron bearing the legend *Colman's Mustard* were already in occupation.

'I think Jersey is beautiful,' she said, returning to the cushioned carver, 'though I was pretty staggered at how small it is. One side to the other in a couple of hours or even less! It takes that long to get out of the Sydney suburbs!'

'Perhaps that has something to do with the traffic,' Catherine suggested.

'Well perhaps. But it's size too. Have you ever been to Australia, Aunt Catherine?'

Catherine shook her head. 'No, I haven't. I always meant to but I never did.'

'You should have done. Mum and Dad would have been pleased to see you.'

'Yes.' Catherine turned, the kettle in her hand, and briefly Juliet caught the most uncompromising look on her expressive face. So totally at odds with her usual open and friendly smile was it that Juliet's stomach knotted with sudden shock. Catherine's generous mouth had hardened, her eyes narrowed. The look passed as suddenly as it had appeared but Juliet was left in no doubt as to what it had meant. Either Robin or Molly was far from being Catherine's favourite person. She had never come to Australia because she had not wanted to see either one or both of them.

Not for the first time Juliet found herself wondering just why her parents had emigrated. All her life they had given her vague answers to the question — they liked the idea of the sunshine, Robin had disliked being tied up with the business, they wanted space and freedom. When they had dropped the bombshell story of the family scandal and had added the explanation that they had wanted to give her a fresh start away from the wagging tongues she had accepted it at face value. Now, however, she found herself wondering if perhaps there had been additional reasons. Had there been trouble between her parents and the rest of the family? Might that not explain why there had been so little contact over the years? And had it been a long standing feud or was it all connected, somehow, with Louis's death?

Catherine was pouring boiling water onto the teabags without the slightest hint of apology or even awareness that such relaxed methods were not at all in keeping with the way the other members of the family entertained.

'So,' she asked gaily, 'are *we* as you expected us to be?'

Juliet took a spoon and began squashing the teabag against the side of the mug.

'I didn't really know what to expect. I knew your names and that I got cheques at birthdays and Christmas and that was about all. But there was a great deal I didn't know. A great deal I'd never been told.'

'You mean . . .' There was a wary look in Catherine's eyes.

'It was only when I announced my intention of visiting Jersey that Mum and Dad told me . . . well, about Grandma.'

'You didn't know?' Catherine said, startled.

'No. I had no idea at all.'

'Good heavens! Still, I suppose that shouldn't surprise me really. Your mother always liked her little secrets. Even so . . .'

Juliet extracted the teabag from her mug and put it on the saucer Catherine had placed in the centre of the table for that purpose. Quite suddenly her mind was made up.

'Aunt Catherine . . . what did happen?'

'I thought you said they had told you at long last.'

'Well yes, but only the bare bones really — that Dad had two brothers, not one as I'd always believed, and when Grandpa died Louis, the eldest, tried to run things his way and caused a lot of trouble. Because of this there was a terrible quarrel and Grandma shot Louis, for which she went to prison. But there's a lot I don't understand and to be honest I have the feeling Mum still hasn't told me everything.'

'I see.' Catherine turned to take the lid off a large square tin of assorted cream biscuits. She was all too aware of how transparent she could be and the last thing she wanted now was for Juliet to read her thoughts — that almost certainly Molly would not have told her daughter everything.

If I were her I think *I'd* be inclined to keep quiet about certain aspects and I'm not secretive as she is! Catherine thought wryly.

47

Aloud she said: 'I don't know that I can tell you much more than you already know — I was away from Jersey when it happened. In London. I taught there, you know, for many years.'

Juliet's face fell.

'Almost everyone could tell you more than I could,' Catherine continued. 'Your Uncle Paul and your father were responsible for sorting everything out.'

'I expect Daddy hated that.'

'I expect he did. The bulk of the responsibility fell to Paul, I believe. David was too young to be much involved — he was only nineteen at the time and still at college.'

'You mean he wasn't in Jersey when it happened?'

'Oh yes, he was. He'd had a bad dose of 'flu and came home to recuperate. So you see any of them would be far better placed than me to answer your questions.' She selected a bourbon cream, bit into it and pushed the tin towards Juliet. 'Do have one. They're delicious.'

Juliet shook her head. 'No thanks. I'd better not. I'm going out for dinner with Grandma this evening and she tends to go in for four courses at least.'

'She is probably making up for the time when she had to live on the food provided by one of Her Majesty's institutions,' Catherine said drily.

'It must have been quite dreadful for her,' Juliet said, shocked that Catherine could joke about it.

'I'm sure it was. Luckily for her she got off very lightly. I dare say her previous good character and her standing in the island helped in that respect but her light sentence owed a good deal to Daniel Deffains.'

'Daniel Deffains?'

'Her advocate. He did a first rate job under very difficult circumstances.'

Juliet wrapped her hands around her mug.

'Frankly I find the whole thing almost beyond belief. It seemed incredible when Mum told me about it and now that I've met Grandma . . . well, I just can't believe she could have done something like that.'

Catherine nodded. The evasiveness had gone now; she simply looked sad and a little puzzled.

'I know. We all felt the same way.'

'So if nobody believed she did it why was she found guilty?' Juliet asked. 'It simply doesn't make sense.'

'She was found guilty because she insisted she *was* guilty,' Catherine said gently.

'So what exactly happened?'

'Sophia had been to a gala in St Helier. She got home shortly before midnight — her chauffeur dropped her off at the front door of La Grange. Twenty minutes later the emergency services received a telephone call from Sophia asking for the police and an ambulance. She said she had shot Louis.'

'And they believed her.'

'Well — Louis was dead.'

'But it's not unheard of for people to make false confessions, is it?'

'I don't know, Juliet.'

'But you thought at the time . . .'

'Like you I couldn't believe Sophia could have done something like that, and neither did Daniel Deffains. I'm certain that was the reason he did such a magnificent job on her behalf. If anyone but Dan had been defending her she could very well have ended up with a much longer sentence.' Catherine was a little flushed and breathless but Juliet did not notice.

'But even he couldn't get her off entirely,' she said, still faintly accusing.

'You don't understand, my dear. He was totally hamstrung . . .' Catherine broke off, remembering the impassioned conversation she had had with the advocate when she had come dashing home to Jersey on hearing of her sister's arrest.

'How could you let them charge her, Daniel?' she had demanded furiously. 'It's ludicrous — crazy!'

'Sophia insists she was responsible,' Daniel had said, his eyes behind his gold rimmed spectacles haunted with anxiety. 'She wants to plead guilty and take whatever punishment is meted out to her. All I can do is try to put her case as sympathetically as possible.'

49

'But she didn't do it!'

'She says she did. She is my client, Catherine; it's my duty to go along with her wishes. The whole thing is a trifle unusual, it's true. Generally speaking it is a client's innocence I have to believe in if I am to represent them. But unusual or not the ethics are the same. I have to do my best for her on the basis of believing what she tells me. I can't go running around playing policeman — I don't have the brief to do that.'

'I see. You don't want to help her!' Catherine had flared.

'Of course I want to help her. Good heavens, I've known you both all my life. Nothing would please me more than to go into court and prove her innocent. But she is quite determined I should not do that.'

'She gave him nothing to go on,' Catherine said now to Juliet. 'From first to last she insisted that she and Louis had quarrelled and she had accidentally shot him.'

'But how could that have happened?'

'Oh, Juliet, I don't know. It was all so long ago. All I know is I simply couldn't believe it. Sophia worshipped Louis. Of all the boys he was . . . very special to her. And besides . . .' She broke off, biting her lip.

'Besides what?'

'Sophia was afraid of guns,' Catherine said, choosing her words with care. 'I found it very difficult to believe she had been handling one, let alone that she actually pulled the trigger, accidentally or otherwise.'

'She had a phobia, you mean?'

Catherine hesitated. 'Something like that.'

'So — why didn't you stand up in court and say so?'

'Oh Juliet . . .' Catherine sighed. 'Because she asked me not to.'

'But *why*?'

'Sophia was determined to take the blame for Louis's death.'

'You mean she was protecting someone?'

'I don't know. We went through all kinds of theories at the time. I even remember wondering if she had simply been unhinged by the whole thing and really believed she *had* done it. As I said, she adored Louis. It occurred to me to wonder if he might have been killed by an intruder and she had found him

50

when she came in from the gala and . . . just flipped. But the police wouldn't hear of such a thing. And considering what a very strong, calm and resourceful person Sophia is it does seem very unlikely.'

'Maybe.' Juliet's face had set in a determined line. 'But I'm sure Grandma didn't kill Louis. I've been sure from the moment I met her. It's nothing to do with anything anyone has told me, it's just a gut feeling. And you have it too, don't you?'

'Yes. But I think you should remember that we are talking about something which happened a very long time ago. I know it's new to you and it's understandable you should be interested. But we have lived with it for almost twenty years.'

'What difference does that make?'

'We have accepted it and put it behind us. I don't mind talking to you about it but you might find other members of the family less eager to do so. I think you would be wise to do as we have done and forget it ever happened.'

'How can you say that?' Juliet's eyes were feverishly bright. 'If Grandma didn't kill Louis, if she served a prison sentence for a crime she did not commit, then surely it's only right that we should try to clear her name? To be honest, I can't understand why you did not pursue it at the time.'

'Juliet, I've told you . . .'

'I know. I hear what you say. But you must see how it looks to me. She is my grandmother, remember.'

'And my sister.'

'Yes, but that's not quite the same.' Juliet broke off, not sure how to express the deep-seated need she was beginning to feel which went beyond proving Sophia's innocence for her sake alone — the need to know for herself whether she was the granddaughter of a murderess and what blood any children she might have would carry in their veins. It was not something that had occurred to her immediately, rather it had crept up on her insidiously, beginning with the look she had seen in Sean's eyes when she had told him the story Molly had told her. It really was not very nice to feel that you might be the direct descendant of someone who could do such a dreadful thing and in a way Juliet could understand Sean's shock at learning that she might

51

be; illogical or not it did actually matter more than she would have ever believed possible.

'Juliet,' Catherine said, 'don't drag it all up again. Let it rest.' There was a note of pleading in her voice and she leaned forward and touched her great-niece's arm. 'For your own sake, for your own peace of mind, leave well alone.'

A moment's sharp unease prickled over Juliet's skin.

'Why?' she asked.

Catherine hesitated. Her cheeks were faintly flushed and she could no longer meet Juliet's eyes.

'All families have skeletons in the cupboard, Juliet. There is nothing unusual in that. But sometimes it is best if they stay there. Almost always it's best.'

Again a shiver of discomfort whispered up the back of Juliet's neck. What was her aunt talking about? But perhaps she had probed enough for one afternoon.

'I'm sorry, Aunt Catherine, I'm asking far too many questions,' she said with forced lightness. 'And besides, I think I should be getting back. I'm being taken out to dinner tonight, to one of the hotels. It's just won a special award for its cuisine — chefs' hats, or something.'

'I think you will find they all have, my dear,' Catherine said, laughing. 'I expect you are going to Les Belles Fleurs; that has the most elaborate restaurant. But I know Sophia's special favourite is the smallest and most intimate — La Maison Blanche.'

'The one that began it all. Of course, she lived there as a child.'

'We all did,' Catherine said, reminding Juliet that she was Sophia's sister. 'Nicky and Paul, Sophia and me.'

'Nicky — he was killed in the war, wasn't he?'

'He . . . died.'

'Oh, I thought Dad said . . .'

Catherine smiled sadly. 'Family skeletons again, my dear. I will tell you about that one when you've more time but I warn you, it's a sad story. Now . . .'

'Yes, I really must go. Grandma wouldn't want to take me out to dinner looking like this.'

'I think you look very nice. Turquoise suits you and you have the legs to wear a mini skirt. Would that I could say the same!'

She reached for her straw hat, jammed it on to her irrepressible grey curls and followed Juliet to the door. At the gate Juliet turned to wave and Catherine thought with a stab of surprise how like Sophia as a young girl she looked. The thought reminded her again of Juliet's impassioned defence of her grandmother and with it came the sinking sense of dread that she had experienced when Juliet had intimated that she was going to rake up the past.

Oh dear, she hoped she had persuaded her against that. There were so many things better forgotten. But in many ways Catherine could understand very well how Juliet felt. She, too, had been convinced of her sister's innocence. She, too, had been determined to prove it. Only one thing had stopped her from trying and that had been Sophia herself.

Catherine drew a deep steadying breath, remembering that day when she had visited Sophia in custody as clearly as if it had been only yesterday.

'I don't believe you did this, Sophia,' she had said, 'and somehow I am going to make everyone else see you couldn't have done it.'

Sophia's face had been pale and haunted, her amethyst eyes dark with grief. But the hand she had laid on Catherine's arm had been steady and her voice had been clear and strong.

'*I* killed Louis, Catherine! Try to prove otherwise and I swear I will never forgive you!'

Chapter five

At the secluded table in the Rose Room Restaurant at Les Belles Fleurs the Langlois family party had just finished dessert.

'I think you should speak to the chef, David,' Sophia said, laying down her spoon. 'The texture of my fool was far too bland — more like a mousse. A fool should be slightly coarse. And the colouring he has used to decorate that strawberry gâteau can only be described as garish.'

Juliet glanced at her grandmother in surprise. She had seemed such an easy person to be with; this was the first time Juliet had witnessed the formidable professional perfectionism that came into play where the hotels were concerned. Obviously their enormously high standard had not happened by accident and was only maintained by constant vigilance, but all the same Juliet could not help feeling sorry for the chef, who had provided a five-course haute cuisine meal and supervised a sweet trolley groaning under no less than fifteen different desserts.

'My rhum baba was very good,' she volunteered.

Viv laughed. 'Any of them would taste good to me but I daren't eat them. Not with a spreading waistline like mine! I'm afraid I must just wait for the cheese — and then choose Edam!'

'You would be able to eat more interesting things, Viv, if you didn't drink so much,' Sophia said tartly. 'Do you know how many calories there are in alcohol?'

'Well thank you for that advice, Sophia!' Viv reached for her glass and raised it mockingly at her sister-in-law. 'I'm afraid I intend going right on being a sinner. And I must say it has a great deal more going for it than being a plaster saint!'

The pointedness of the remark caused a moment's total silence around the table. Sophia and Viv had never been close; they were essentially too different to be friends, and the family skeletons Catherine had mentioned jangled uncomfortably between them, never mentioned, perhaps not even thought about very often these days, but there all the same, engendering deep-seated resentments and criticisms. Generally, for the sake of family harmony, their mutual antagonism was buried deep beneath a social veneer. Tonight, however, the gloves were off, and without a doubt Sophia had instigated the spat.

Juliet looked down at her plate, embarrassed by the exchange. Then Deborah cut quickly into the awkward silence.

'Talking of drinks I was sampling some of the Australian wines the other day. It's funny, I'd always thought of Oz in terms of Castlemaine XXXX but I can see now how blinkered I have been. They really are very good aren't they, Juliet?'

'I'm glad they're being discovered,' Juliet agreed, relieved at the change of subject. 'The Hunter Valley isn't that far from Sydney — did you visit it when you were over?'

'No. Australia is so vast and we had so little time — thanks to David's fond belief that the Langlois Leisure Chain would collapse if he was away from it for more than a couple of weeks.'

Two attentive waiters removed the dessert dishes, a third brought the cheeseboard to the table, yet another refilled their wine glasses from the bottle of Chablis that had come to the table in a silver ice bucket.

'Not Australian, I'm afraid,' David said with an apologetic smile. 'But almost as good!'

'It's impossible to beat Chablis in my opinion,' Sophia said, and again Juliet was startled by her grandmother's aggressive tone. It simply was not like her — or not like the person Juliet had been allowed to see, at any rate — and the change was disconcerting.

Once again it was Deborah who stepped swiftly in to change the subject. David had recently acquired the land for a large car park near the Westerley, one of the chain of hotels, and at present it was being landscaped with trees, shrubs and flowers with the intention of making it beautiful as well as functional. Juliet found herself admiring the other woman's social skills as she steered the conversation away from dangerous waters by raising the subject of the most recent Langlois project.

'Our gardens are going to rival the Howard Davis Park by the time we have finished with them,' she said, smiling. 'Visitors are going to book into the Westerley simply for the privilege of parking their cars amongst two hundred rose bushes.'

'The Howard Davis Park is famous for its glorious floral displays, Juliet,' Sophia explained. 'It is also the site of a garden of remembrance for a great many poor men who died here during the war. I hope it's not your intention that our car park should also become a cemetery, Deborah!'

Glancing at her grandmother, Juliet was disturbed to see how tired she suddenly looked. There were dark shadows under her eyes and they were accented by the high colour in her cheeks, which might have been caused by the use of a little more blusher than usual or was perhaps a result of the fact that despite the overhead fans it was rather warm in the restaurant.

Perhaps she had been keeping her grandmother up too late, Juliet thought doubtfully. Almost every evening they had remained downstairs in the lovely peaches and cream drawing-room, chatting about anything and everything long after the others had retired to bed.

'Who is responsible for the landscaping of the garden?' Viv asked, emptying her glass and giving a sideways look at the bottle of Chablis to see if there was anything left in it.

'The best firm in Jersey, naturally,' Deborah smiled.

'Assisted by my wife.' David beamed proudly and not for the first time Juliet thought how nice it was that someone who had been married for fifteen years, as David had been, should still be so transparently in love with his wife. At every opportunity David had his arm around her — in the most unobtrusive way, of course, but he never seemed to miss a chance to steer her to her chair or help her in or out of her car. Besides this, he listened when she talked with a rapt expression and could often be caught looking at her with pride and love. Sharp businessman David might be but clearly where Deborah was concerned David was totally vulnerable.

Like Dad with Mum, Juliet thought, for over the years she had seen Robin behave in much the same way with Molly. Not as often nowadays perhaps but still . . . was it a trait of all the Langlois men? She rather fancied she had heard her parents remark on how Bernard had adored Sophia. So what about Louis? He had never married, of course, but had there been a woman in his life whom he would have cheerfully killed for? If only there were someone she could ask — but she knew instinctively that Louis was a taboo subject. It was as if he had never existed at all, so completely had he been cut out of their lives.

'I didn't know you had a talent for gardens, Deborah,' Viv was saying.

'I haven't, Viv. I don't know the first thing about growing things. I just know what I like.'

'And very nice it is too,' David said loyally. 'Deb has an incredible eye for colour.'

She certainly has, Juliet thought. Tonight Deborah was wearing a purple silk dinner suit teamed with a fuchsia pink camisole. Lipstick and nail varnish of exactly the same pink and eyeshadows and blusher several tones lighter completed the stunning all-over effect so that by comparison Juliet felt almost insignificant in her own favourite dress of delicate sorbet shades. If Deborah had designed the garden with half the flair she showed in dressing herself it would certainly be a glorious sight.

'Well well!' Viv was saying. 'A landscaping artiste and an interior designer both in one family — around one table if it comes to that! Whilst Deborah is designing gardens you could be supervising the decor, Juliet. Though I warn you, with the standards expected of Langlois Hotels, it would be a little like painting the Forth Bridge.'

'The Forth Bridge?'

'Sorry — perhaps in Australia you say Sydney Harbour . . .'

A small choking sound made them turn towards the head of the table. Sophia had half-risen. She was holding onto the edge of the table but even so she was swaying slightly.

'Mother!' David was out of his chair in a flash but Deborah was quicker. She reached Sophia in a split second, slipping an arm around the slim wavering figure to steady her.

'Sophia — darling — aren't you feeling well? Sit down! We'll get you a glass of water . . .'

'I'm sorry . . . I'm feeling a little dizzy.' Sophia's voice was shaky. 'I think perhaps one of my tablets . . .'

'Yes, darling, of course. Only sit down for a moment while I find it.' She eased Sophia back into the chair and rummaged in her bag for a small enamelled pill box. An anxious waiter was hovering.

'Could we have a glass of water please?' David said to him. 'My mother is unwell.'

'Of course.' As he hurried away Debbie extracted a pill and passed it to Sophia, who placed it under her tongue.

'I knew she was going to have one of her turns,' Paul muttered. 'I can always tell. When she gets snappy . . .'

'Paul!' Viv hissed.

'It's true. It's a sure sign.'

'But what is it?' Juliet asked anxiously. 'What's wrong with her?'

'It's her heart. She's had the problem for years. It tends to play up when she's been overdoing things.'

'Oh my goodness! Is it my fault?'

'No,' Sophia's voice was faint but also acid with self-mockery. 'Of course it's not your fault, Juliet. It's just me being silly.'

'You are not being silly, Mother. You can't help something like this.'

'I should be able to! Ruining the evening for everyone.'

'The trouble with you, Sophia, is that you don't like it if you're not in complete control of everything and everybody,' Paul said with heavy-handed humour. 'And you haven't ruined the evening anyway. It's all but over and we've all had a wonderful time.'

The waiter reappeared with a carafe of water and a glass. Deborah held it to Sophia's lips and after a moment her colour began to return.

'Feeling better?' Deborah asked.

Sophia smiled unsteadily. 'Yes, my dear. Thank you. I think it's time for me to go home, though. Will you . . . ?'

'Of course.' Deborah took her arm and helped her to her feet again, then she and David armed her out of the room.

'Well,' Viv said, collecting her bag and Deborah's, 'she did look peaky for the minute didn't she?'

'I knew it!' Paul muttered. 'I could see she wasn't feeling too good.'

'So you keep saying,' Viv snapped. 'If you could see it why the hell didn't you warn us instead of letting us sit here in blissful ignorance?'

'She will be all right won't she?' Juliet asked anxiously.

'I expect so. She's had these heart turns for ages, ever since . . .' Viv broke off but Juliet knew exactly what it was she had been going to say. Her grandmother had been having trouble with her heart ever since Louis had died.

'Is there anything I can do, do you think?' Juliet offered.

'I doubt it. Leave her to David and Deborah. They are used to it,' Paul advised. 'Tell you what, I'll run you back to La Grange in my car and we'll stop off for a nightcap since the evening has been cut short. How does that grab you, Viv?'

'It doesn't. I'd rather get home, thank you. But we can go via La Grange. That will save Juliet having to travel in the ambulance.'

The note of sarcasm was so obvious Juliet winced — even now Viv couldn't stop making unpleasant little digs. Juliet experienced a rush of protective love for the grandmother she had only met again so recently.

'There's plenty of room in Uncle David's car,' she said quickly. 'I can sit in the back with Grandma and make sure she is all right.'

Viv's lip curled. 'Oh, I expect Deborah will be doing that,' she said maliciously.

'Juliet is a nice girl,' Paul said as he reversed his black BMW out of its parking space. 'Her heart is in the right place.'

'Mm, you're right,' Viv agreed, getting out a cigarette and lighting it. 'I have to say I half expected a gold digger but she's certainly not that. She is pleasant and intelligent and I rather sense hidden fire, though don't ask me why. Heaven knows, when you think of her parents it's a miracle she has turned out so well.'

'That's a bit harsh, Viv,' Paul said, completing the manoeuvre and setting the car on the road home.

'Is it? Molly is a child who never grew up and Robin . . .' By leaving the sentence unfinished Viv left no room for doubt as to her feelings about Robin. She drew on her Winston and the car began to fill with a cloud of pungent smoke. 'Still, I suppose they at least achieved what we never did — an offspring,' she added wryly.

59

Paul said nothing and after a moment she continued, her voice dangerously bright.

'It's rather strange when you come to think of it how this family has shrunk. There were four of you, after all. One would have expected a dynasty, the sort of family tree that runs off the edge of the paper. And what happened? Nicky dies, Catherine never marries, you . . . have me. Only Sophia has children — three of them. And sons to boot. Three boys to carry on the name of Langlois, if not the Carteret name. But between them those three boys have only managed to produce one child and she is a girl. Ironic, don't you think?'

'If you say so.'

Though Paul liked to think of himself these days as a driving force in the business dealings of the Langlois empire there was a great deal of acquiescence in his nature. At the office he often blustered in a conscious effort to appear forceful and decisive but in private he all too often opted for the easy way out, especially when his wife was at her most loquacious and waspish. Arguing with Viv was tiresome and seldom got him anywhere — he had never known anyone so determined to have the last word — and he had never been able to summon up any enthusiasm to join in her habit of dissecting the vagaries of fate. Now he switched off as he usually did when she began on one of her discourses, deliberately distancing himself so that her rather shrill voice became as much a part of the background as the hum of the engine and he was free to pursue his own undemanding train of thought.

'I wouldn't mind betting David would like a family,' Viv continued. 'A couple of sons to carry on the business when you are all past it and a pretty little girl to sit on his knee and gaze at him with adoring eyes. But somehow I can't see it happening. I can't imagine Deborah . . .'

She laughed suddenly, a snort of mirth so piercing not even he could ignore it.

'What's funny?' he asked.

'The idea of Deborah in a maternity smock, with that wonderful figure of hers of which she is so damned proud going to pot underneath it. No, the Fall of the House of Carteret is down to one thing — the men marry women who can't, or won't, have children.'

She was angling, Paul knew, trying to needle him into saying something he would later regret. That was the trouble with Viv, too much drink sometimes made her maudlin and she would pick away at the old scabs until she revealed the raw and bleeding wound beneath.

'You can say what you like about Deborah, but she has been more than good to Sophia,' he said amiably, trying to divert her from the path of self-destruction he sensed she was set upon, and to his relief the ploy seemed to succeed.

'One could argue that Sophia has not exactly treated Deborah badly,' Viv said, stubbing out her cigarette and closing the ash-tray with a snap. 'She lives in the lap of luxury at La Grange.'

'Married to David she would live in the lap of luxury any-where. I suppose it's true that she would not be married to David if it weren't for Sophia, but daughters-in-law are not known for being as nice to their acquired parents as Deborah is to Sophia. And before you say she's after something I would again point out she has nothing to gain from sucking up to Sophia. No, I think she is genuinely fond of her. She was there, remember, when Sophia needed her most — when a good many of her so-called friends were only too ready to desert her. And she's been there ever since. Quite honestly, I don't know what Sophia would have done without Deborah.'

Viv smiled. 'At risk of sounding a complete cow I would still like to turn that one on its head and ask what Deborah would have done without Sophia. It's not just a question of money — it's much more than that. Look, just ask yourself, Paul — who *is* Deborah? Where did she come from?'

Paul was silent.

'You see?' Viv spread her hands expressively, then folded them around her ample, black organza-clad bosom. 'That is not a question you care to answer, is it? So Paul — I rest my case!'

'Grandma, are you asleep?'

Juliet pushed open Sophia's bedroom door and peeped in. Lights were still burning, two wall lamps and a table lamp, and they bathed the room in a warm glow.

61

'It's all right, my dear, come in.'

Sophia was in bed but propped up against the pillows — stark white embossed cotton which contrasted sharply with the old-fashioned brass bed. Bernard had liked white cotton, to him its fresh crispness had symbolised everything he had wanted from life far more than any more ostentatious material could have done and Sophia had never tried to persuade him into anything else. Let the boys have what they wanted — Sophia had never forgotten Bernard's disgust when Louis had insisted on changing his bedlinen to black satin — 'Good God, what next!' he had exclaimed. 'Anyone would think this was a bordello!' — but she was happy to go along with his wishes. Only one thing had she changed since his death — there was now a frilled white broderie Anglaise beauduvet on the bed instead of the brown and gold throwover and gold wool blankets that Bernard had favoured.

The bed was enormous and they had shared it to the end — not for them the separate bedrooms of the class to which they had been elevated. After her enforced absence Sophia had found returning to it one of the most comforting aspects of her homecoming. Now she eased herself up a little more and patted the bed beside her.

'Sit down, Juliet.'

Juliet sat, half afraid of creasing the broderie Anglaise.

'How are you feeling?'

'Oh, I'm fine now.'

'I find that hard to believe,' Juliet said. 'In fact there are a lot of things I find hard to believe about you, Grandma.'

The moment she said it she regretted it. She hadn't meant to raise the subject at all unless the moment was right, doing so now, with her grandmother unwell, was unforgiveable. 'I'm sorry,' she said quickly.

'It's all right, my dear.' Sophia patted her hand. 'Don't worry. I expect you are a great deal more sensitive about certain things than I am. I will talk to you about it, I promise — though I'm not sure I can tell you any more than you already know. But not tonight.'

'No, of course not . . . I didn't mean . . .'

'I know.' She patted Juliet's hand again but she was not looking at her granddaughter. Juliet, disconcerted, followed the

62

direction of her gaze and saw a photograph in a silver frame on a small occasional table beside the bed. The man in the photograph was not anyone she knew but instinctively she knew exactly who it was for somehow the expression on her grandmother's face identified him more explicitly than any words could have done.

Louis. It had to be Louis. His hair was obviously fair although the photograph was black and white, his face square with regular features. He looked quite young in the photograph, perhaps nineteen or twenty, yet already there was the smallest hint of something less than flattering about the eyes. Oh, he was handsome, yes, without a doubt — the studio portrait endowed him with almost film star good looks — but Juliet thought with a small sense of shock that she was not sure she would trust him.

She could not expect Sophia to think like that, of course. She was his mother. Even if she had killed him . . .

'Whatever must you think of us all?' Sophia asked.

Juliet, engrossed in the photograph, had not noticed her grandmother's shift of attention. Now she jumped almost guiltily as if she had been caught snooping.

'I don't know what you mean.'

'Our way of life here must be very different to what you are used to.'

'It is different, but I've enjoyed myself very much. I really don't think I am going to want to go home.'

'And I for one shall not want you to. But your parents would be very upset, I expect, if we persuaded you to stay. And you have your fiancé too.'

'Yes,' Juliet said and felt her heart sink. Oh God, she thought, why should it *do* that whenever marriage or engagement was mentioned? She loved Sean didn't she . . . *didn't* she? Yet it came to her now that one of the reasons she had so enjoyed the last days was that she had felt absolutely completely free — free from the gentle loving pressures Sean exerted on her, free to be herself with no commitments to anyone.

No sooner had the thought crossed her mind than the guilt came rushing in. Sean would be missing her, wondering about her, and all she could do was relish her freedom.

'Do you think I could phone him?' she asked.

63

'Of course, my dear. Why ever didn't you ask before?'

Juliet did not answer. Because I didn't want to, she thought, and felt the guilty colour rising in her cheeks.

'Go and phone him now,' Sophia continued. 'It will be the middle of the day in Australia, won't it? And you are not to worry about me any more. When I've had a good night's sleep I shall be perfectly fine, you'll see.'

'I certainly hope so. Goodnight, Grandma.'

'Goodnight, Juliet. God bless.'

Something sharp and sweet twisted deep within. A half-forgotten memory — a little girl being tucked into bed — 'Goodnight, God bless.'

'And you, Grandma,' she said.

The line to Sydney was perfect, so clear, Juliet thought, that if it had not been for that split second's delay between speech and reply it would have been impossible to believe that she was halfway across the world.

'How are you?' she asked Sean. 'How is Australia?'

'Much as you left it. I was beginning to think you had deserted us completely.'

'Of course not! It's just that there has hardly been a moment to turn around!' Liar, she thought. 'This is really the first chance I have had to telephone.'

'You're enjoying your holiday then?'

'Yes, it's fantastic. You should see the hotels, Sean. And Grandma's house! Sheer unadulterated luxury.'

'I can see you are not going to want to come back.'

It was what she had said herself earlier but to hear him voice it made her feel dreadfully guilty again. 'What a silly thing to say!'

'Is it?' A pause. 'What about the family mystery?' he asked, tone deliberately light. 'Have you solved it yet?'

'Not yet. But I'm going to.'

'Oh yes. How?'

'I have one or two ideas. But never mind that. Tell me about you. How is the job going?'

They chatted for a few minutes more then Juliet said: 'I'd better go. I'll ring you again.'

'Promise?'

'Promise. Goodnight, Sean.'

'G'day, lady. Love you.'

'Love you too.'

She replaced the receiver, surprised to realise she suddenly felt a little homesick. You see, you *do* miss Sean, she told herself almost aggressively. Hearing his voice had reminded her of the good things they shared and she found herself thinking how nice it would be to crawl into bed beside him, feel his arms around her, gentling her, his lips on hers, his body, hot and hard, pressing into the soft sensitive cushion between her legs. The very thought aroused the excitement in her that was always there at the start of one of their encounters, making her forget for the moment the let down that inevitably followed.

'Did you get through all right?' Deborah asked, coming out of the drawing-room.

'Yes, thank you.'

'Would you like a nightcap?'

Juliet hesitated but only for a moment.

'Yes, I would. It's been quite a night one way or the other, hasn't it?'

Deborah smiled serenely without replying. Does nothing ever phase her? Juliet wondered. She stood now beside the drinks cabinet, stunningly beautiful in her purple and fuchsia pink, the soft shaded standard lamp catching the highlights in her hair and turning them to silver.

'What would you like? Brandy — scotch — a liqueur?'

'Have you any Cointreau?'

'We should have. With ice?'

'Please.'

'David, would you . . . ?'

'Of course.' David, who had been sitting in one of the deep armchairs, long legs stretched out in front of him, got up and made the drinks.

'Does Grandma have these attacks often?' Juliet asked, perching on the little love seat.

'More often than we would like. She's supposed to have the condition under control but the tablets don't always work as well as they should. Frankly she worries us, doesn't she, darling?'

David handed Juliet her Cointreau.

'Things do seem to be getting worse rather than better. That's why I'm so glad you've come now, Juliet. I think we live in fear that one of these days she is going to suffer a heart attack proper and it would have been so sad if that had happened before she had had the chance to see you again.'

Juliet felt slightly sick.

'That's an awful thought! She seemed much better when I went in to see her just now though. Tired and a bit pale, but very cheerful.'

'She is almost always cheerful,' David said, settling back into his comfortable chair. 'Considering the life she's had I think it's a miracle.'

There was a slight pause; Juliet sipped her drink wondering if she dared raise the subject of Louis. This was after all the best opportunity she had had. David had practically raised it himself.

'There was a photograph in her room. Right by her bed. I wondered if that might have been . . . ?' Her voice tailed away. The atmosphere had suddenly grown cold. Juliet looked uncomfortably from one to the other of them, David rigid in his easy chair, Deborah, her fingers curled too tightly around her glass of brandy.

'I'm sorry . . .' she began but Deborah interrupted her.

'Louis,' she said. 'Yes, that photograph is of Louis.' Her voice was strained, determinedly light, but Juliet knew that for the first time since she had arrived she had seen Deborah in less than complete control of herself.

'I didn't mean to pry,' Juliet said hastily.

'Don't be silly, of course you are not prying. It's natural curiosity. He was your uncle, after all.'

'Exactly. But in many ways it's as if he never existed.'

'Oh he existed all right!' That was David, his tone deeply bitter. 'The fact of the matter is my brother was never anything but trouble. He was a strange one — ruthless, selfish, hard as nails . . .'

'And very charming.'

Juliet saw the look that passed between them, the lift of Deborah's chin in a gesture close to defiance as she said it, the wary expression in David's eyes and again she was aware of the

66

powerful emotions it seemed Louis could still evoke, almost twenty years after his death. For a moment it seemed as if the very room was holding its breath, then David tossed back his drink impatiently.

'We don't really want to talk about Louis do we? What sort of a subject is that?' He stood up, loosening his tie. 'I'm going to bed. I have a busy day tomorrow. Greig wants me to go over the accounts with him and that is trying enough even when I have a clear head. You stay down if you want to.'

'No, I think I'm ready to turn in too. Juliet?'

Juliet nodded her agreement. But she was disappointed that the subject of Louis had been dropped so unceremoniously and though she went up to her room it was a long time before she was able to sleep. Images set off by the evening's events were chasing through her mind. Sean . . . half a world away in Australia, loving her, wanting her back; Grandma . . . looking so shockingly frail suddenly; Viv with her acid tongue; Deborah and David exchanging a look that had totally excluded her whilst appearing almost to challenge one another; even her own parents, defensive and secretive as they had been when she had told them she wanted to visit Jersey. And of course, most of all, Louis . . . Louis, whose life had clearly had such a dramatic effect on everyone who knew him and whose death was still shrouded in mystery.

What was the truth of it all? Juliet wondered. And would she ever learn any more than the little she knew already? Probably not. Whenever his name was mentioned the family closed ranks, it seemed. And she, as the next generation, was firmly excluded.

Juliet was not the only one unable to sleep. In her beautiful bedroom, decorated in soft pinks and peaches, Deborah lay quite still, arms wrapped around herself, eyes wide open in an attempt to make the nightmare fade more quickly.

It was a long time now since she had had it. Once upon a time it had come almost every night, then gradually less and less often until nowadays months would pass by without a recurrence of those haunting scenes from the past.

It shouldn't be like this, Deborah had sometimes thought. A dream or a nightmare should be just that — fantasy — not a reliving of something that had actually happened. And some-times it was. Sometimes the same emotions — the fear, the loneliness, the sheer desperation, came in other guises. Not tonight. Tonight she had been whirled back in time to the girl she had once been, Debbie Swift, seventeen years old, with a cloud of back-combed bleached-blonde hair and a pair of bright pink hot-pants, teetering along on three-and-a-half inch heels. Tonight she had known throughout the dream exactly why she was so sad and so frightened and when she had woken at last and raised a shaking hand to wipe away the tears that were filling her eyes she had half expected to feel eyelashes spiky with waterproof mascara instead of soft and lustrous from the nightly treatment with oil and glycerine. Even as reality began to return the aura of that other Debbie remained, reaching out across the years to envelop her. And though she was awake the cameras rolled again before her eyes, showing her glimpses of the night that haunted her.

She knew what had caused this relapse, of course, and it had nothing to do with Sophia's attack, worrying though that was. No, it was the talk of Louis that had sparked it off.

In the darkness a solitary tear welled up in the corner of Deborah's eye and ran down her cheek. She folded her arms around herself more tightly but she could not stop the trembling and soon her whole body was shaking with huge uncontrollable, racking sobs.

Why should she cry for him? God knew he had been nothing but a bastard. But it made no difference. It never had.

Alone in the night Deborah cried as she had often cried before and each and every sob was an echo of his name.

'Oh Louis . . . Louis . . .'

Chapter six

Juliet was awake again very early — the sign of a busy mind, her mother always said, and certainly this morning it seemed to be the case. She had fallen asleep thinking about Louis and the twenty-year-old mystery surrounding his death, now, as she came through the layers of consciousness, it was still there, teasing at her. She eased herself up on the pillows, propping her hands behind her head and trying to force her mind back to her own hazy recollections of the events that had preceded her parents' departure for Australia.

A vague memory of Louis had taken shape on the edges of her mind, an image indistinct as an over-exposed photograph, but she was unsure how much of this was real memory and how much imagination inspired by the snippets of information she had gleaned about him and the photograph beside her grandmother's bed. The memory, if that was what it was, stirred long forgotten emotions, echoes of alarm and anxiety experienced by a four-year-old child who had sensed a threat to the continuance of her secure world in the raised voices behind closed doors, the whispered conversations that ended the moment she entered a room and the strained faces of those closest to her. But there was nothing, no single shred of concrete memory she could get hold of. Each soft focus picture slipped infuriatingly away from her as she tried to grasp it just as a dream slips away on waking.

Juliet pushed her fingers through her sleep-tangled hair, frustrated by her inability to remember. She wanted to know the truth. She wouldn't ever be able to put the past to the back of her mind and get on with the future until she did. But she could not imagine how she could ever get to the bottom of the mystery. Every one of the family was too adept at sliding away from awkward questions. Only an outsider would be likely to tell her something approximating to the truth, someone without

69

emotional involvement. But she did not know anyone and it was all so long ago.

Quite suddenly Juliet's eyes flew wide open and her fingers ceased their abstracted combing of her hair. The advocate who had defended her grandmother — what had Aunt Catherine called him? Dan Deffains, that was it. If she could find him, talk to him, was there just the slimmest chance that *he* might tell her the truth? He might consider it a breach of professional confidence, of course, and she couldn't expect him to reveal anything that had not been made public at the time, but at least she would have the facts.

'I didn't believe she had done it and neither did Dan Deffains,' Aunt Catherine had said. Perhaps, if she approached him in the right way he might explain just why he had had those doubts. Juliet pushed aside the covers and got out of bed. She was trembling slightly from combined anticipation and nervousness. But her mind was already made up. Somehow she would find Dan Deffains and ask for his help.

Juliet sat on her haunches, the telephone balanced on her jean-clad knees, one ear cocked in case someone came downstairs and asked who she was ringing.

She was safe enough for the moment, she thought — David had left for the office, Deborah was taking her shower, usually quite a lengthy process, and Sophia was still in bed, resting. Later on the doctor would come to take a look at her but for the moment the coast seemed to be clear and Juliet had snatched the opportunity to look up the number in the telephone book of the man who had defended Sophia against the charge of causing Louis's death.

Finding the number had proved easier than she had expected — here in Jersey it was common practice to list Christian names rather than just initials. What had surprised her was the address. It sounded more like a private house than a place of business — but then it could be that the advocate had retired. Twenty years was a long time. . . .

She dialled the number and listened to the bell ringing endlessly at the other end of the line. Perhaps she had been wrong in assuming Dan Deffains had retired. Perhaps he was a partner in a legal practice that was listed under someone else's name. If so she had no chance whatever of finding him.

'Hello. Dan Deffains.'

The man's voice was deep and full with a hint of a Jersey accent and ever so slightly impatient as if he was none too pleased to be disturbed. Juliet swallowed at the lump of nervousness that suddenly constricted her throat.

'You won't know me, Mr Deffains, but I am Juliet Langlois. I believe you represented my grandmother, Sophia Langlois at the time she was tried for causing my Uncle Louis's death. I am over here from Australia and I really would like to talk to you about the case. Would it be possible for us to meet?'

There was a moment's complete silence and Juliet held her breath, half-expecting a refusal.

'You are Sophia's granddaughter you say?' There was a sudden edge in his voice that might almost have been excitement. Later Juliet would remember and puzzle over it but for the moment she was too keyed-up and eager to even realise she had noticed it.

'Yes, that's right. I realise it all happened a very long time ago but . . .'

'All right. I can't make today, I'm afraid. I'm totally tied up. But what about tomorrow?'

She could hardly believe it. Somehow she kept the excitement out of her voice. 'Morning or afternoon?'

'Either. Though morning might suit me best. About ten, say? Or is that too early for you?'

'No, that would be fine. Where?'

'Could you come here? You have the address?'

'Oh yes.' A door opened upstairs. Someone was coming. Juliet panicked. 'Thank you. I'll see you tomorrow.'

She replaced the receiver just in time before Deborah came down the stairs, coolly beautiful in cream slacks and peach silk shirt.

'Goodness, that's better! I feel halfway human again. Sophia is looking much more herself this morning, thank God. Have you been in to see her?'

'Yes. Briefly. But I think I'll pop in again.'

She ran up the stairs, feeling a little guilty about the deception

71

but at the same time elated. Dan Deffains might not be able to tell her anything but at least she would have tried. And it wasn't' just idle curiosity either.

I don't believe Grandma killed Louis, Juliet thought. I just don't believe it. And if she didn't kill him, then someone else did, someone who has gone unpunished all these years — worse, has let Grandma take the blame for their actions. And I want to know who it is.

The house was on the east side of St Helier, three stories high, white-stuccoed with a green tiled roof and green paintwork. Juliet parked her hire car on the opposite side of the road and sat for a moment looking up at it. Then she crossed the street to the short flight of stone steps flanked by pots of begonias that looked on the point of bursting into irrepressible pink and scarlet life. As she was about to ring the bell the door was opened by a woman wearing a bright headscarf and a coat which was flying open to reveal a floral apron.

'Yes?' The eyes in her florid face were small and beady.

'I have an appointment with Dan Deffains.'

'Oh.' The woman hesitated, eyeing Juliet with suspicion. Then she went back into the house, closing the door after her as if she were afraid Juliet might sneak inside if she left it ajar. A few moments later she was back. Her eyes were still bead sharp and unfriendly.

'You can go in, he says.' Then: 'I'm off now!' she called back to Dan Deffains, as if to wash her hands of the visitor.

The door closed after her and Juliet stood in the hall waiting and wrinkling her nose appreciatively at the smell of fresh lavender polish. After a few moments a man came down the stairs — a tall man, athletically built, wearing chinos and an open necked shirt. Not handsome, exactly, but there was something about him which was instantly attractive. Perhaps, she thought, it was his smile — a very nice smile which crinkled the corners of his eyes.

'Miss Langlois? I'm Dan Deffains.' The voice was deep dark brown, like thick warmed treacle. It certainly sounded like the voice at the end of the telephone. But he was far too young to

72

be the man she had come to see — early thirties at the very outside.

'I think there must be some mistake,' Juliet said, disconcerted. 'The Dan Deffains I wanted to talk to was the advocate who defended my grandmother twenty years ago.'

'That was my father. Also Dan Deffains. It is a bit confusing, I know. Look — shall we go in?'

He pushed open the door of what was obviously the sitting-room. Sunlight slanted in brightening the mustard-coloured curtains and rugs and glancing off the freshly polished table, but it could not disguise the stark masculinity of the room. No woman lived here, Juliet felt sure. There were no fresh flowers, no ornaments, none of the little touches a woman gives to a room, and what pieces there were were strictly unfrilly — a set of Hogarth cartoons on the wall, hunting knives over the mantel-piece, a plain brass Tilly lamp on the table. Some silver trophies were displayed in a glass fronted cabinet — although 'displayed' was hardly the right word to use, Juliet thought. The trophies looked as if they had simply been put in the cabinet and for-gotten.

The room suited the man, however. He looked completely at home in it.

'I hope I'm not making too much of a nuisance of myself,' Juliet said. 'It's very good of your father to see me. Is he . . . ?'

She broke off. Dan Deffains was looking guilty, almost like a small boy caught stealing the chocolate biscuits.

'I'm afraid there is a bit of a snag there, Miss Langlois. My father died last year.'

'Oh!' Juliet was startled. 'Why didn't you tell me that on the telephone?'

He paused, countering her startled response with a rueful grin.

'I'm sorry — I should have explained on the telephone, I suppose, that I am not the Dan Deffains you thought I was, but I have to admit to having been fascinated by the case involving your grandmother for a very long time. I was only a boy when my father represented her, of course, but I know she was almost a cause celebre as far as he was concerned and I couldn't resist the opportunity of talking to you about it.'

'I don't know what to say.' Juliet's disappointment was as

evident in her voice as it had been in her face. 'I had been hoping your father would be able to tell me something about what happened. As I said earlier I'm over here from Australia — we emigrated when I was four years old — and I thought perhaps as her lawyer he might be able to fill me in with a few details. Since that is obviously not possible I think we are both probably wasting our time.'

Dan Deffains regarded her thoughtfully. He too was disappointed — when she had telephoned he had thought that perhaps at last luck was turning his way and he might find a breakthrough point in the case that had occupied his thoughts for so long, both personally and professionally. But he was better at hiding his feelings than Juliet and in any case, from his point of view all might not be lost. It wasn't going to be handed to him on a plate as he'd thought it might be — but then, what in life was?

'I'm not sure I agree we'd be wasting our time if we were to have a talk.' He ran a hand through his hair, thick, dark and very short. 'Look — can I get you a coffee? Mrs Ozouf put it on for me ten minutes ago so it should be just about ready.'

Juliet hesitated. She couldn't think what he meant and she wondered briefly if he was making a play for her. But in spite of getting her here under false pretences he did not seem the sort of man to avoid being alone with and besides, although she could not see what he could possibly tell her she felt oddly reluctant to close the door on the one link with the past that she had established outside the family.

As if on cue the smell of freshly brewed coffee wafted in from the kitchen and she made up her mind.

'All right, thank you. Though I still don't really see the point.'

'I'll try to explain in a minute. Sit down — I'll fetch the coffee.'

Juliet perched on the edge of a worn brown wing chair, tucking her legs beneath her and wishing she had worn trousers instead of her mini-skirted linen suit. Back at La Grange it had looked sharp and smart, just the thing for a visit to a frowsty old advocate. Here, in this aggressively masculine room, she was acutely aware of her bare legs and felt oddly vulnerable.

'Here we are then.' Dan came back into the room carrying a coffee jug, two mugs and a bowl of sugar on an enamelled tray. The design had faded somewhat, Juliet noticed as he put it down on a low table. But at close quarters the coffee smelled even better.

'So,' Juliet said as he poured, 'why did you say we might not be wasting our time?'

As he pushed the cup towards her across the low table his glance lingered for a moment on her long tanned legs and his mouth quirked into a half-smile. But he said nothing. Somehow he did not think Miss Juliet Langlois would appreciate wisecracks, however honestly flattering they were intended to be!

'My father was an advocate of the old school, French trained at Caen rather than an English lawyer such as you'll find today. He went into what was his father's practice and he had no partners — he liked to work alone. When he died all his current work was turned over to other firms and it fell to me to clear out his office and dispose of his archives. A pretty boring job it was too for the most part and I consigned the bulk of the stuff to the shredder. But one file I kept because it had always fascinated me, just as I knew it had haunted my father. That was the file relating to your grandmother's case.'

'Really?' Juliet sat forward eagerly, annoyance forgotten. 'And you still have it?'

'Yep.' He got up, crossed to the heavy old chiffonier that stood in a corner and took out a cardboard file tied with pink legal tape. Then he brought it over, tossing it carelessly down onto the table beside the coffee cups. 'There we are. ATTORNEY GENERAL v. SOPHIA LANGLOIS — November 1972.'

A nerve jumped in Juliet's throat. She stared down at the file, almost hypnotised by the wording on the label. ATTORNEY GENERAL v SOPHIA LANGLOIS. Seeing it in black and white was a shock somehow, giving substance to what had previously been almost a fiction, something that might never have happened at all.

'It's all there,' Dan was saying. 'Every last detail. Or, to be more precise, every last detail that the principals chose to tell my father.'

His tone was heavy with meaning. Juliet glanced up, meeting his eyes and reading the implication as a confirmation of the same doubts Catherine had expressed.

'You mean . . . you think it's not necessarily the truth?'

'I know my father always believed Sophia was innocent and it played on his mind. He had been in a cleft stick professionally speaking. On the one hand he was governed by his client's instructions and she never said one word to suggest she was anything but guilty. On the other he went to his grave feeling he had let her down by not insisting on persuading her to fight the charges. To be honest I wonder if the whole business had something to do with his early death — he had a heart attack at the age of sixty-five, and we all know stress plays a part in cases of that sort.'

'I'm sorry . . .'

'Not your fault. Nor your grandmother's, come to that. An advocate should be able to live with his own ethical decisions. I mention it only to show you that I do have a very real and personal interest in the case. But to get back to your question as to whether I believe the statements and so on in the file tell the truth, I have to say that if your grandmother was innocent — as my father was convinced she was — then clearly they do not.'

Juliet could feel her skin prickling. She had been so sure she was right, now hearing Dan Deffains's son more or less confirming her suspicions she experienced an emotion midway between elation and apprehension.

'It all dovetails though?' she asked.

'As far as one would expect. But I don't think the case was ever properly investigated. I don't know how much you know about our legal system here but to be honest it leaves something to be desired. The chief officers of law enforcement are civilians, known as the Constable, the centeniers and the vingteniers. In the old days the terms were strictly literal — a centenier was in charge of a hundred households and a vingtenier twenty. Nowadays of course that is no longer the case and there is a professional police force — the 'paid police', as they are somewhat disparagingly called, but they are still answerable to the Honorary police and believe it or not they have no powers of arrest which are all vested in the elected officers.'

'Paid police. Yes, I've heard of them. But I didn't realise the proper police didn't have any powers of arrest. How odd!'

'To the rest of the world it must seem pretty feudal, but that's

76

the way it is here. Until fairly recent times even the Parishes were all separately administered — if a criminal crossed the boundary he couldn't be followed until the law officers had sorted it out between themselves. Pretty ludicrous, really, especially in an island the size of Jersey, and as you can imagine the system causes friction between the Honorary and the paid police. On occasions it can be detrimental to the course of justice. I believe — and so did my father — that Sophia's was a case in point.'

'Why?' Juliet sat forward, cup clasped between her hands, but the coffee untouched.

'There was a fair old feud going on at the time between John Germaine, the centenier and Ivor Fauval, the detective inspector. Germaine was an old school country gentleman type, proud of his position, jealous of Jersey's history and traditions, typical well-to-do middle class. Fauval, on the other hand, was an ordinary career policeman and he resented everything about Germaine — his money, the breeding that oozed out of every elegant pore, and, most of all, the fact that he, Fauval, was answerable to him. That, I think, was the bitter pill he could not swallow. Here he was, a trained professional policeman, required to do the bidding of a man who, in his opinion, just played at the job.'

Juliet frowned. 'Are you saying this Inspector Fauval pressed charges against my grandmother out of spite?' she asked.

'No — simply that it might have made him less anxious to look for any other explanation. Let's face it, he had an open-and-shut case presented to him with Sophia's confession. You could hardly expect him to throw it out because she happened to be a friend of John Germaine — the "boss", so to speak.'

'It sounds as though you have some sympathy with Inspector Fauval,' Juliet said.

'I have — or at least with his point of view. I used to be a policeman myself and I know how galling it can be. In this case, however, I think resentment blinded Fauval to his duty. He knew the Langlois family — your family — were personal friends of the centenier. He knew the embarrassment the whole thing was causing him. And he was envious too of everything your family had — wealth, position, lovely homes, chauffeur-driven cars. When Sophia confessed he was only too glad to take her confession at face value. He marked it down to his clear-up rate and he never investigated it as thoroughly as he should have.'

'I see.' Juliet's mouth was dry. 'And what do you think he would have discovered if he *had* investigated properly?'

Dan's eyes narrowed. 'I don't know, but I wish I did. I thought *you* might be able to fill in some of the blanks.'

'Me!' She stared at him. 'But I've told you — this is all totally new to me. I didn't even know until a few weeks ago that I had an Uncle Louis, much less that my grandmother had stood trial for killing him. My parents never told me and nobody here seems to want to talk about it either. I can understand that in a way. It must be something they would rather forget. But on the other hand the brick wall that goes up does seem a bit excessive. Especially since I get the feeling . . .'

'Yes?'

'I don't think they believe Grandma was guilty either. So why don't they want to get the whole thing out in the open and prove her innocence? She's a sick woman — she has a weak heart. She could have a serious attack and die at any time — wouldn't you think they'd want to clear her name before it's too late?'

'Is that why you telephoned to talk to my father?' Dan asked directly. Faint colour rose in Juliet's cheeks.

'Well, yes, if I'm honest I think it is. I wasn't certain what I expected him to say. I just thought I'd like to hear what happened from an independent source — someone not directly involved. And yes, I suppose I did fancy the idea of playing at detective. It's not a very nice thing, you know, for any of us. My parents emigrated to escape the scandal. I think I was hoping I might find some evidence to clear Grandma's name. But I suppose that is out of the question now.'

'It might not be. If we worked together . . .' He hesitated, trying to gauge what her reaction might be, then he went on: 'Look — I have my father's file. I also have connections with the State of Jersey Police. I might be able to do a bit of digging in the archives. And you are in close contact with most of the people who were involved. You say that they clam up and refuse to talk about what happened. But if you were to ask the right questions perhaps you could get to the truth.'

Juliet shivered suddenly, remembering what Catherine had said about family skeletons and warning her to leave the past well alone.

'So you do think the reason they are so cagey is more than just sensitivity. You think they are hiding something?'

'I should say that is a certainty. One thing my years of police experience taught me is that practically everybody has something to hide. Whether it's important or not is the crux of the matter.'

Juliet bit her lip. All very well in theory to want to get to the bottom of the mystery. All very noble to talk about clearing her grandmother's name. But it was always possible she was starting something that might roar away out of control, reopening old wounds, letting all the mischiefs escape from the Pandora's box that had been tightly locked for almost twenty years. And besides . . .

'What exactly is your interest in this?' she asked.

Momentarily Dan hesitated. Should he tell her the truth? But old habits die hard. Policemen — and investigative reporters — ask questions, not answer them. This had to be played close to his chest.

'I told you — the case has always fascinated me,' he said smoothly. 'I was brought up on it, remember. And I thought you were keen to get at the truth. Look — think about it. If you decide you want to go on, let me know. As I said, I still have police contacts and I can do a spot of digging. But there's no point unless you are prepared to ask a few questions too. It might be difficult. You might even find out some things you would rather not have known. But that's the price we have to pay for the truth.' He stood up, holding out his hand. 'Look, I'm going to have to ask you to excuse me now. I have an appointment I can't miss. Think about what I've said and let me know what you decide. Then perhaps we can talk some more.'

Juliet nodded. 'I'll do that.'

'Good.' There was a hardness about the way he said it and Juliet thought suddenly that it was very easy to believe that he had once been a policeman. Then he smiled again and the impression of steel-like authority was almost instantly dispelled. 'I'll hope to hear from you then.'

'Probably.' She wasn't going to commit herself but already

she knew in her heart that she had made up her mind. Nervous though she might be of starting down this road she wasn't going to let that stop her. Perhaps the rest of the family could live comfortably with a lie and shelter behind her grandmother's courage, she could not. She wanted to know the truth. Then, and only then, would she be able to decide what to do with it.

As Juliet's car turned the corner of the street Dan Deffains went back into the house. Adrenalin was pumping through his veins, lifting him to a state of heightened awareness he rarely experienced these days. That had been one of the good things about being a policeman, he thought, there had been plenty of moments like this. But there had also been the dead times, the frustrations, the irritations. And finally the uncaring impersonal bureaucracy which had thrown him onto the scrapheap just when he had most needed to feel there was still some meaning to his life.

In nightmares Dan still relived the disbelief he had felt at first when he had been told quite bluntly that he would have to be prepared to do a desk job for the rest of his service — 'light duties' they called it — or be invalided out of the force.

'You do understand we can't have disabled officers on the streets,' the chief had said and Dan had blown a fuse.

You can't do this to me — it's my life! he had wanted to say, but it sounded too trite for words, and instead he had pointed out in very colourful language indeed that he did not consider himself disabled, that he was still more mobile than a great many so-called fit men, and he would run himself into the ground to prove it. The chief had been unmoved. He was sorry for Dan, he understood how grief-stricken he must be at Marianne's death and he was sorry to lose one of his best men but that was neither here nor there. He had a job to do and regulations were regulations. Dan would just have to grin and bear it for the time being anyway.

Dan had been in no mood to grin and bear it. He felt sickened and totally let down by the service to which he had given his life and it had not occurred to him that grief might be causing him to over-react. In a fury he had slammed out of the chief's office and out of the police force.

For a while depression had settled on him like a thick fog. The girl he had loved and married was dead and although he knew it was irrational he could not help blaming himself. Now he was out of a job too. Finished at the age of twenty-seven. Christ, there was no point left in living!

When the depression could take him no lower Dan had begun to bob up like a cork in a barrel of water. And the main reason was that he had got hold of a story.

Dan had always had a way with words. Years of report writing had dulled his gift, yet in black moments he took refuge in scribbling about all kinds of things that captured his imagination and much to his own surprise he had managed to sell one or two of them. So when the drug smuggling story presented itself to him he knew exactly what he was going to do with it.

Drug-smuggling was rare in Jersey but not unknown and it was a contact he had made whilst in the police force that set him on the trail of one of the island's most flamboyant characters, a newcomer with a good deal to hide. The resulting exposé made Dan's name as an investigative journalist — not that he wrote under his own name. Instead he used the nom de plume Harry Porter. This was a prudent move — on an island the size of Jersey it did not pay to advertise the fact that a former police-man, son of a prominent advocate, was interested in knocking down icons and sniffing out frauds, dishonesty and less-than-salubrious dealings. There were those who knew, of course, it would have been impossible to keep his identity totally secret, but at least the pen name afforded him a little privacy.

Finding new material was not always easy, however, and the moment Dan had read through the file on the Langlois case whilst clearing out his father's office he had sensed that here was a really big story. Not only did it have all the ingredients to fascinate and compel — wealth and power, scandal, a family dynasty split apart by the quarrels of its members then welded together again so that the cracks barely showed, but also it had the smell of an unsolved mystery. Dan knew his father had gone to his grave convinced of Sophia's innocence and the question had teased him — if Sophia did not kill Louis then who did? And why had she insisted that she was responsible? Was she shielding someone — and if so why? Or had she simply lost her mind through grief and honestly believed herself responsible?

The case had never been investigated properly, Dan was sure of that. For all the reasons he had outlined to Juliet it had suited Ivor Fauval to accept Sophia's story. If he could get to the bottom of it there was a book in it without a doubt, a big humdinging bestseller, and how he would enjoy writing it, combining his writing talents with the interest in criminology that had been born and bred in him! If there was a tiny nugget of spite buried deep in Dan's motivation then he did not consciously realise it. He only knew that his instincts were telling him someone had slipped up badly over this one; if whoever had slipped also happened to be a member of the force which had treated him so heartlessly then he was certainly not going to lose any sleep over it.

But Dan's initial investigations had all drawn blanks. There was simply not enough in the file to give him a single new lead — his father had after all been defending Sophia from the position of her admitted guilt. The statements concerning the movements of the other members of the family on the night Louis died, for instance, were vague and uncorroborated, mentioned only as they pertained to Sophia herself.

'She told me not to drag up private family business,' Dan remembered his father once saying when talking about the case. 'She told me she hadn't hired me to play Perry Mason.'

And so Sophia's secrets had remained hidden and Dan had had no more brief to dig them out than his father had twenty years earlier. He had thought of talking to old friends at police headquarters, calling in a few favours and trying to get access to old files, but he had hesitated to do this too soon and perhaps waste a golden opportunity because he did not know what he was looking for. After a few abortive early enquiries, Dan decided to bide his time and keep an ear to the ground. Sooner or later, he thought, he would come up against somebody who might be in a position to answer some of the questions and once he got that initial lead then he could begin to ferret out the truth. A year had gone by and he was beginning to think he was going to have to break cover and admit an interest in the case.

And then, like a gift from the gods, had come the phone call from the granddaughter. When she had told him who she was his pulses had begun to race. Here was someone as interested as he was in learning the truth — and she was an insider!

For the first time in his life Dan had blessed the fact that he had been christened after his father. All the petty irritation that had come from feeling his parents had denied him his own identity, all the times when having the same name had caused silly confusion, were forgotten. If his name had not been Daniel the chances were she would never have found him at all.

Dan went back into the lounge. He felt exhilarated, alive. The interview had not been easy but he thought he would be hearing from Juliet Langlois again. Briefly his conscience pricked him and he wondered if he should have told her the truth about his interest in the case and that he believed Sophia had been covering up for someone close to her. But he had been too afraid that if he told her she would walk out and not come back and he would lose a chance of the best story he was ever likely to unearth. Investigative reporting, like police work, could be a dirty business. It was something he had to live with and he wouldn't lose any sleep over it. Briefly his mind returned to the doubts he knew had haunted his father over the years. He had a feeling it would please the old man if after all this time justice could be seen to be done. If he needed any sop for his conscience, that was it.

Dan tested the coffee pot. Warm, but not hot. He considered reheating it, then changed his mind and poured himself a whisky instead. A bit early for it really, but he felt like celebrating. Dan raised his glass and silently toasted the Langlois case.

Chapter seven

That afternoon, when she had eaten a hearty lunch of lamb chops, new potatoes and mint fresh from her garden, Catherine Carteret got into her car and drove over to La Grange to visit her sister Sophia. Catherine liked to have her main meal in the middle of the day. It was a habit she had got into during her years of supervising school dinners and now she maintained that eating in the evening gave her indigestion.

The trouble was that eating in the middle of the day tended to make her sleepy. When she had nothing better to do Catherine liked to indulge in a half-hour's nap, but today she had decided she really should go and see Sophia, and she fought off the drowsiness that was tugging at her eyelids, stifled a yawn and made up her mind to the fact that today there would be no luxurious 'forty winks'.

At La Grange she was surprised and alarmed when Deborah told her that Sophia was still in her room, explaining that she had had 'a bit of a turn' the previous evening and was taking things easily. Catherine passed the time of day with Deborah and Juliet, who were going through an album of old family photographs, and hurried up the stairs to Sophia's room, opening the door without knocking and simply announcing her presence with: 'Sophia! It's me! Are you awake?'

She was answered by a short laugh.

'Of course I'm awake, Catherine. We don't all sleep the afternoons away!'

Sophia was seated in her rose-pink boudoir chair overlooking the drive. To Catherine's relief she looked her normal self, a little pale perhaps, but fully, if casually, dressed in well cut navy blue slacks, a cream shirt and sweater in emerald green and navy.

'Deborah told me you'd been poorly!' Catherine said accusingly.

'Oh I had a giddy fit last night — you know what I'm like,' Sophia said lightly. 'I'm fine now but Dr Clavell thought I should take it easy for the day — you know what a fusspot he is.'

'I do indeed,' Catherine said with feeling. Dr Clavell had insisted on a series of costly and time-consuming tests for her last year when she had happened to complain to him about her indigestion. The results had all failed to show anything wrong with her and Catherine had not been able to decide whether to be relieved or annoyed at all the wasted effort. She would be very careful what she said to Dr Clavell in future, she had decided.

'I've been sitting here enjoying the sunshine and reading,' Sophia continued, putting her book down on the table beside her. 'Well — to what do I owe this visit? Did someone telephone and tell you I was unwell?'

'No. I didn't find out about that until I arrived.'

'What then? It's unlike you to give up your afternoon nap to come calling on me.'

'Sophia — will you stop insinuating I do nothing but sleep! I do lots of things in the afternoons. My gardening, for one thing. And when the weather wasn't fit to get out I did some stencils on the wall in my downstairs loo.'

'Stencils?'

'Yes — you know, very like we used to do as children. Only this one came from Laura Ashley Mail Order. I'm very pleased. It's really brightened up the old emulsion having bunches of cherries all over it. And it was great fun.'

Sophia shook her head in disbelief. 'How old are you, Catherine? Sixty-one. Will you never grow up?'

'Probably not,' Catherine said cheerfully.

'Anyway, you haven't answered my question yet — why have you interrupted all this fascinating activity to visit me?'

Catherine pulled a face. 'If you are supposed to be resting and recuperating I'm not sure I ought to tell you.'

'Why not, for heaven's sake? I feel perfectly fine now.'

'I doubt if Dr Clavell would approve.'

'I thought we had agreed Dr Clavell is a fusspot. Anyway,

you can't stop now. I shall work myself back to being ill again wondering what on earth it can be you are being so mysterious about.'

'I could tell you it's some lovely juicy scandal — the latest marriage break-up or illicit love nest.'

'But you won't because I'd know you were lying.' Sophia's face grew serious. 'My guess is that it's something fairly important.'

'Not important exactly.'

'What then?'

'All right. I'll tell you. I just thought you ought to be warned that Juliet has been asking questions about . . . well, about things we would probably rather forget. It seems Robin and Molly have kept her in the dark all these years and now naturally she is curious. I don't want to upset you, Sophia, I just thought you should know, that's all.'

Sophia nodded. 'I admit I suspected as much. She made a comment last night that led me to believe it's on her mind. And as you say, I don't think we can blame her for that.'

'No. We can't. But I wanted to warn you.'

For a moment the sisters sat in silence. For so many years the subject had been a taboo that it was almost impossible to break it now. Catherine had said what she had come to say. Now the conversation would move onto less dangerous ground.

'Are you going to stay and have some tea?' Sophia asked.

'I might as well, mightn't I? It'll be too late to do any gardening by the time I get back.'

'And too late for your nap.'

They both laughed. For the moment the ghosts had been laid once more.

Sophia sat in her boudoir chair looking out into the gathering dusk. She had enjoyed seeing Catherine — in small doses she was great fun and laughing together never failed to make Sophia feel young again. As promised Catherine had stayed for tea and for that Sophia had disobeyed doctor's orders and gone downstairs so that they could share the shortbread and chocolate brownies with Deborah and Juliet — not that Deborah, ever mindful of her figure, had eaten anything!

But when Catherine had left Sophia had pleaded tiredness

and gone back to her room again. It wasn't entirely true. She was a little tired perhaps, more, she thought, from the day's enforced inactivity than from any threat of a recurrence of her heart problems. But the main reason had been that she wanted to be alone, to think.

So Juliet was asking questions. She had been very afraid she might. It was the flipside of the coin that had begun to spin the moment she had learned Juliet was coming to Jersey — heads, the anticipation of the joy of seeing her again after so many wasted years, tails, the fear that she would want to delve into things that were best forgotten.

It would not have been so bad if Robin and Molly had had the sense to tell her at least something of what had happened right from the beginning — that way she would have grown up accepting it as part of her life. But they hadn't. What a pair of ostriches! Sophia thought crossly. One a dreamer, the other a child, both with enough guilty feelings to want to bury the past and pretend it had never happened. But of course it had and now Juliet was naturally curious.

Sophia sighed, smoothing out a little wrinkle at the bridge of her nose. She didn't want Juliet poking around in the past any more than Robin and Molly had wanted it. She knew all too well how dangerous that sort of thing could be. But how could she stop it? Of course, the family would close ranks and keep their own counsel now just as they had then. But all the same . . .

I couldn't bear to lose her again, Sophia thought. The first time she went out of my life I was too numb, too shell-shocked by all that was happening to appreciate just how much I would miss my only granddaughter on the other side of the world. Now I am older, not old, but older, and people are very precious to me.

But then, hadn't they always been? Wasn't it because she had always put the people she cared for first that her life had been so turbulent, so eventful, so disastrous in some ways? Sophia shook her head. For heaven's sake, why go over it now? What good would it achieve?

She really should put the light on. The dark was closing in now. But Sophia sat transfixed. She did not often think about that terrible night, almost twenty years ago, when Louis had died. Some things are too painful to remember, the mind blocks them out, pretends they never happened. That was how it was with Louis's death a good deal of the time. Not now. Now a key had unlocked the past and that key was Juliet.

Sophia stared out into the darkening garden remembering how it had been that night. First there had been the gala, glittering social occasion that it was, marred by her anxieties about the business and the family, a dread that would not go away and which was heightened because the root cause of the trouble was Louis — her beloved Louis — and she could not go on making excuses for him any more. Then there had been the drive home with the sick feeling inside her growing, frightening her because she had come to look upon this particular emotion as a portent of something bad to come. Once upon a time she had tried to tell herself she was being stupid, imaginative and over-emotional, but bitter experience had proved that when trouble was coming her own sixth sense invariably knew it and reacted with this awful mounting panic. Why was it so strong, she had wondered as the chauffeur-driven car had whisked her home? The trouble, whatever it was, must be very close indeed.

Clear across the years she remembered the first glimpse that night of La Grange through the trees that lined the drive. In spite of the lateness of the hour lights had still been burning at several of the ground floor windows and the sight had told her that Louis must be home. She had not known whether to be glad or sorry. At least he had not flown off to London as he so often did at the weekends to seek the sort of high life Jersey — staid old-fashioned Jersey — could not offer him. But when Louis was at home these days there were inevitably arguments — or worse.

Again Sophia let her mind drift and into the vacuum came snatches of conversation.

Le Grand, the chauffeur, as he stopped the Mercedes at the front steps: 'Will there be anything else, Mrs Langlois?'

And her own voice, quite normal in spite of the turmoil within: 'No thank you, Peter. I'll see myself in. You get along home.'

She had stood for a moment on the steps, mentally gathering

88

the courage to go in, hoping perhaps Louis might already be in bed. She didn't want another argument. Not tonight . . .

'Grandma! Would you like a nightcap?' Sophia almost jumped. So lost in her memories had she been that she had not heard Juliet's tap at the door.

'A nightcap?' To her own ears her voice sounded strained and distant.

'Yes. Cocoa? Ovaltine? Or something stronger?'

'No. No, I don't think so.'

'Are you all right?'

'Yes, I'm fine.'

'Then why are you sitting here in the dark?'

'I like the dark, darling.'

Blessed dark, soft and cloying all around, concealing ugliness and a multitude of sins.

'At least have some Ovaltine. It will help you to sleep.'

'Very well.' Sophia could not be bothered to argue any more. 'If you insist. But please don't put the light on, Juliet. Not yet.'

Juliet went out, pulling the door closed behind her. If only it were so simple, Sophia thought. If only a cup of Ovaltine would take away all the memories that haunt me! But there were some things she could never forget. Some things that would stay with her all her life. And one of them was that terrible night.

The darkness outside the window was full of ghosts now. Sophia closed her eyes, pressing her hands across her face in an effort to shut them out but it was no use. The sight of Louis's body was imprinted on her mind forever, she could see it now just as she had seen it then, sprawled across the drawing-room carpet. Blood caked in his blond hair and made a great scarlet splash on the white cotton of his dress shirt; a darker patch was spreading across the carpet. She shuddered now as she had shuddered then, her fingers tightening around the gun that she held in her hand — Louis's own pistol, brought illegally into the island, kept because of vanity and bravado. She had known no good would come of it. Her infallible intuition had warned her. But now it was too late. Louis was dead.

For a few minutes longer she had stood, staring down at his body, numb and shaking. Then she had crossed to the telephone and dialled 999.

'This is Sophia Langlois at La Grange,' she had said when the operator answered. 'I think I need both an ambulance and the police. I have just shot my son.'

They had questioned her, of course. At least, John Germaine, the centenier, had. The police inspector had seemed only too pleased to accept her story. He had sneered, she remembered — sneered was the only word for it. But quite honestly she had been past caring. Nothing mattered any more except that Louis was dead.

That was one of the reasons she had been so impatient with John Germaine — poor John, dragged out of bed to charge one of his oldest and dearest friends with the murder of her son.

'For God's sake *why*, Sophia?' he had demanded, facing her across the scrubbed wood table in the police station interview room. *'Why?'*

She had stared into space. Oh, the brightness of the bare bulb above the table! No wonder she loved the soft dark now! She wondered if she should tell him that she had always known, right from the beginning, that one day something like this would happen, but she knew he would think she had gone quite mad. She didn't want them to think she was mad. That would destroy the last remnants of her pride and her pride was all she had left.

'Sophia, I am asking you what all this is about,' John Germaine had insisted.

'Oh John,' she said softly. 'Surely you must know?'

He had frowned. He looked bleary — as if he had been fast asleep when he had been wakened by the telephone. His hair was untidy and one corner of his collar was tucked inside his pullover whilst the other stuck out.

'No, Sophia, I don't know,' he had said crossly.

'Then, John, I am certainly not going to tell you.'

He was angry. She had known it then and she knew it now. John had never forgiven her for placing him in such a position. But that had been the least of her worries.

I didn't tell them, she thought. And at least the past was never raked up at my trial. It was possible, of course, that islanders with long memories and suspicious minds had talked amongst themselves and unravelled threads that were best forgotten. But

90

at least it had never been made public. She had spared them that.

And not only the others — herself too. There had been some things she had wanted to forget even then and there were also memories she could not bear to have sullied. Whatever had happened wild horses would not have dragged the story from her. If they had sent her to prison for the rest of her life she would still have refused to speak.

It was the vow she had made to herself then and now, looking into the dark garden, Sophia renewed it.

It would remain her secret that it had all begun with Dieter.

Chapter eight
Jersey, 1938

From the woods at the top of the rise the meadow, its grass almost long enough for its second mowing, swept in an unbroken sea to the ribbon of grey ashphalt lane which wound down the valley below. At the gate two bicycles lay carelessly tossed on top of one another into the hedge; halfway across the field two figures were trekking towards the woods. The boy, tall and athletic, strode out purposefully, his long legs easily ploughing a furrow through the grass. The girl, a little on the plump side, and hampered by a full cotton dirndl skirt and sandals, was struggling to keep up.

'Dieter!' she called breathlessly. 'Dieter — wait for me!'

He turned, looking back at her over his shoulder.

'Come on, slowcoach!'

'I can't! I've got a stitch!' But she was laughing as she said it. It seemed she laughed a lot these days.

'We shall be all day at this rate. You can go faster than that!'

'No! I can't, I tell you!'

'Very well. Since I am a gentleman I will wait for you.'

She struggled on towards him, legs aching, heart pounding partly from exertion and partly because of the way he looked standing there, hands thrust into the pockets of his shorts, hair gleaming bright gold in the sunshine, looking at her with a half-smile on his handsome yet rather serious face.

My boyfriend, she thought, pride so sharp it was an almost physical pain eclipsing the stitch in her side. My very own, very first real boyfriend.

When she was within reach he held out his hand to her, pulling her up the last few feet.

'Dieter, don't! I can't! I just can't, I tell you!'

'But I am helping you.'

'No, you're not. My legs won't work any more. You are just pulling my arm out of its socket.'

'Oh poor *liebling*,' he teased. 'Rest then.'

She stopped, hands on hips, turning to look back the way they had come whilst she caught her breath. Beyond the lane were more meadows, flat and golden-green, beyond them the sea, blue as the bluebells that covered the wooded hillsides in spring, meeting and merging with the sky in a band of etherial haze.

Jersey. Forty-five square miles of lush countryside hemmed by a coastline of intricate bays and promontories, beaches, caves, outcrops and cliffs. Jersey — where the wooded valleys ran right down to the sea and the hydrangeas, big as small trees, rioted blue as well as pink through the long flowering season. Jersey, island of granite and shale, the home she loved so much she sometimes felt like throwing herself down full length to embrace the warm fertile earth. A few weeks earlier she had been studying Shakespeare's *Richard II* at school and had been intoxicated by the words of John O'Gaunt. 'This other Eden, demi-paradise, This fortress built by Nature for herself Against infection and the hand of war,' might have been written about England, but Sophia Carteret had thought it a perfect description of Jersey.

'This precious stone set in the silver sea . . .' she murmured to herself now, lost for a moment in the total glory of love and life and being thirteen years old with the world at her feet.

'Better?' Dieter asked and when she nodded he set off again, heading for the highest point of the field, then throwing himself down full length in the grass, hands behind his head, knees raised.

She looked down at him, her heart twisting again with that bitter-sweet sharpness that she somehow instinctively knew was so fleeting that it had to be grabbed with both hands. No — not grabbed, it was too precious for that, but savoured, and begged to stay, please stay . . .

'Dieter,' she tried to say but she could not speak because somehow she was too happy for words that might break the spell and she sat down beside him, curling her legs up beneath the fullness of her dirndl and feeling the grass tickling her bare skin. After a moment Dieter sat up too, putting his arms around her and pulling her gently towards him. As their lips touched a small

93

shiver ran through her and the sharp sweetness grew and spread in her veins so that every bit of her was awakened to trembling life. Together they fell back into the grass, their bodies touching but not clinging, their lips still seeking one another with the eager fearfulness of chaste youth. As the kisses grew longer and deeper she nestled into him, blissfully unaware of the torrent of lust that was roaring through his strong young body and when, unable to bear the fiery demands of frustrated passion a moment longer, he pushed her away, rolling over onto his back, she was quite hurt.

'Don't you like it, Dieter? Don't you want to kiss me any more?'

'Of course — but that is not all I want,' he said gruffly and her cheeks flamed with sudden hot colour as realisation dawned.

'Oh . . . I see . . .'

She eased herself into the crook of his arm, her head lying against his shoulder but the rest of her body carefully avoiding touching his. The sun was warm on her face and she closed her eyes, listening to the rustlings and chirrupings of crickets in the grass and feeling the desire still prickling in her nerve endings and sending little bolts of awareness up her soft inner thighs. She must not encourage Dieter, she knew. That would be very foolish — and very wrong. But oh, she did so want to cuddle close to him again, feel his arms around her, bury her face into his neck and smell the salty tang of his sun-warmed skin, even have his weight on top of her, crushing the grass and the wild flowers, pressing her down into the hard-baked earth. But that would be asking for trouble and trouble was the very last thing Sophia wanted. It wasn't just that she was very afraid of what Mama and Papa would say if she ever brought disgrace on them, though she suspected there would be hell to pay if Mama knew she was even lying here in the grass kissing Dieter — no, it went far deeper than that. Nicely brought up young ladies simply did not allow boys to *do* things to them, unless they wanted to be known as fast, and in any case Sophia thought she would die of embarrassment if Dieter so much as touched her under her clothing, no matter how tingly and excited she might feel when he kissed her.

As the disturbing stirrings began to subside a little Sophia opened her eyes a fraction, squinting at Dieter and thinking how lucky she was to have a boyfriend like him and how careful she must be not to spoil things. She was the envy of all her friends, she knew, for their boyfriends — if they had them at all — were mostly spotty schoolboys whom they had known all their lives, whilst Dieter was seventeen years old (four years her senior), so good-looking it took your breath away, and with all the added glamour that came from being foreign. He was a waiter at the guest house Sophia's parents kept in St Helier and when he had arrived to take up his post at the beginning of the season Sophia had fallen instantly in love with him.

As a rule of thumb Lola Carteret, Sophia's mother, discouraged friendships between her children and the hired staff and she also harboured a deep suspicion — of which she was slightly ashamed — of the Germans as a race. But she had soon been won over by Dieter's charming manners and his conscientious attitude to his work. Another point in his favour was the fact that his own father was in the hotel business at home in the Black Forest and had insisted Dieter should gain experience from the bottom up in other establishments in other countries, whilst also improving his already admirable fluency in English and French.

'He is certainly a cut above the Italian boy we had last year,' Lola had pronounced. 'I must say I wasn't keen to have a foreigner again, especially a German. That horrid little Adolf Hitler is enough to put anyone off them and after fighting them in the war I didn't like the idea of having one under my roof. But I have to admit I was wrong. Dieter is a very nice boy and if you children want to show him around the island when he is not working, you can.'

The 'children' she had in mind were, of course, Sophia's brothers. Nick at seventeen and Paul, who was fourteen, were much of an age with Dieter. But they were a wild pair who had little time for his serious ways and the restrictive hours he had to work and it was not long before they were leaving him out of their plans. It was then that Sophia had seized her opportunity. School had broken up for the long summer holiday and she had persuaded Paul to lend Dieter his bicycle — 'So that I can show him around the island,' she had explained.

A little doubtful about the wisdom of the proposal Lola had suggested that Catherine, the youngest of the four Carteret children, should go along too, but Sophia had bought her sister off with a supply of her favourite sherbet lemons and a promise that she would take her swimming every morning (when Dieter was working) as long as she would make herself scarce in the afternoons (when he was not). Catherine had kept to her side of the bargain, more or less, and Sophia had explained to Lola that she and Dieter would never cover all the lanes of Jersey if they had to do it at the pace of a rather plump eight-year-old.

Even when she had engineered all this, however, Sophia had not been confident in her ability to interest Dieter. For one thing she was afraid she was not nearly attractive enough, even though her long brown hair had a permanent wave in it from being braided into plaits for school at Mama's insistence and her eyes were a highly unusual shade of violet that was invariably commented upon by visitors to the guest house. But like Catherine she tended towards plumpness (because they so often finished up the left-overs in the guest house kitchen, she expected!) and the roundness of her face swamped her neat features — a small straight nose and pretty mouth. Besides this she found herself painfully shy in Dieter's presence and as they cycled out she was ashamed that she could not think of a single clever or amusing thing to say.

But to her relief Dieter seemed not to notice her silence. He was so genuinely interested in everything around him that she was able to relax, telling him the names of the flowers and the birds and the trees and relating the history of the island and the legends that had been handed down concerning the places they visited. And somehow, almost magically, love had blossomed. One day, stopping to rest on one of the wooden seats that dotted the cliff paths, Sophia had turned unexpectedly to see Dieter looking at her, and that look had been like a reflection of the way she felt — happy for no reason except that he was there, excited, as if she stood on the brink of something unknown, but very wonderful, and strangely tender, all at the same time. Her stomach had contracted and she had looked away quickly, feeling the colour rush to her cheeks, but after a minute Dieter had reached for her hand.

96

'May I?'

Sophia had nodded, unable to speak, and she was afraid to take her hand from his in case he was offended or thought she did not like it, even when her fingers prickled with pins-and-needles from remaining still for too long.

Mama, of course, had no idea that Dieter had progressed from being 'a friend' to being her 'boyfriend'. Sophia knew without being told that if Lola suspected for one instant she would put a stop to the outings. She had very strict views on what was proper and Sophia knew she would consider thirteen to be much too young to have a relationship — she had heard her say as much plenty of times when discussing other girls.

'Going out with boys at her age — it's asking for trouble!' she would say severely, her huge violet eyes, a shade darker than Sophia's, flashing dangerously. 'Sixteen is quite young enough, don't you think, Charles?' And Papa, who never argued because he liked the quiet life and knew only too well how volatile Mama could be if aroused, would nod and agree.

Dieter too seemed to realise that any relationship with his employers' daughter would be frowned upon and Sophia felt that in a strange way he felt responsible for her, although of course it could simply be that he was exactly what he seemed — the perfect gentleman. Whichever, both of them behaved with the utmost discretion, never giving Lola the slightest cause for suspicion. But inside Sophia glowed with the wonderful excitement that came from being in love — and somehow she knew that Dieter did too.

Only one shadow lay over the magic world they shared, and as she lay in the scratchy murmuring grass it crept up again on the edges of Sophia's mind like a cloud drifting over the sun. She reached out for a tall grass, snapping the stem, then running her fingers up the length of it to scatter the seeds burgeoning at the top while the unspoken fear nagged her.

At last she could keep silent no longer. She tossed the denuded grass aside.

'Dieter . . . you don't think . . . ?'

He turned his head, looking along at her lazily.

'What?'

'You don't think . . . there's going to be a war?'

97

She felt him stiffen.

'What are you talking about?'

'A war. Between Germany and France. And perhaps England too.'

'Certainly not.' His tone was cold and she felt uncomfortable suddenly and almost guilty for spoiling the idyllic atmosphere.

'But I heard Mama say . . .' She broke off, realising she would only make things worse if she repeated what Lola, with her scornful attitude towards Hitler and the Nazi party had said. 'Well, if Germany invades Czechoslovakia there's bound to be trouble,' she finished lamely.

'Why?' Dieter demanded. 'It's no one else's business, is it? Besides France wouldn't take on Germany, and neither would England. They know they would never win.'

Sophia was silent. In spite of the warmth of the sun she was cold suddenly. It wasn't just the threat of war. Dieter was probably right when he said they wouldn't fight — after all, hadn't Austria allowed Germany to move in and take them over and even seemed quite pleased about it if the newspapers were to be believed, cheering Adolf Hitler as he drove into Vienna and ringing the church bells? No, it was the change in Dieter that frightened her. If he had leaped up and punched the air in a Nazi salute he could scarcely have made his feelings more obvious.

Desperate to rekindle the happy mood of a few minutes earlier she picked another grass and tickled his ear with it.

'Hey, Dieter, don't be a crosspatch! Smile!'

There was still a small frown tucking between his eyebrows, narrowing those very blue eyes, but after a moment his features relaxed and he made a grab for her wrist, pinning her to the ground.

'Now, Miss Carteret, we shall see who is the victor!' he taunted playfully and as he bent his head to kiss her once more Sophia thought that in all honesty she really did not care very much.

She was in love with Dieter — that was all that mattered.

'I think it is high time Dieter went home to Germany.'

Lola Carteret peeled off her stockings, rolled them neatly

together into a ball and glanced at Charles, her husband, who was already in bed and hunched comfortably into the pillows.

'What? Are you mad?' He shifted himself a little grumpily — he was tired and more than ready to go to sleep. A late night discussion with Lola, who always seemed to come to life in the small hours no matter how long her day had been, was the last thing he wanted. But he could hardly let a statement such as she had just made go unchallenged.

'No, I don't think so,' Lola argued. 'I know what you are going to say, Charles — that the season won't be over for another month or more and we are still booked solidly, but I can't help that. The way things are I am not happy about having the boy here any longer. In fact I very much wish I had gone along with my instincts when he applied for the job and not had him here in the first place.'

She stood up, slithering out of her petticoat and into an ivory silk wrap that had seen better days, and Charles thought irrelevantly what an attractive woman she still was. Although she had borne four children her breasts were still firm and voluptuous and her hair, though etched with silver at the temples, fell thick and luxuriant to her shoulders now that she had released it from the neat elongated bun at the nape of her neck which was her habitual daytime style. In the soft lamplight her face too looked smooth and unlined, the ivory skin taut and unblemished over her beautiful high cheekbones, and Charles thought that in some ways she looked younger now than she had done ten years ago when the children were all small and demanding her attention and they had been struggling to make the guest house pay without any help except for an old woman who came in to wash the dinner dishes. Then there had been hollows in her cheeks and dark smudges of tiredness beneath her violet eyes, and he had worried sometimes that it was all too much for her and he would lose her to consumption or pneumonia or one of the other killer diseases that struck down those who worked such long hours with too little rest.

He need not have worried. Lola was made of sterner stuff and he should have realised that, he thought with a wry smile. What else would one expect of a White Russian, daughter of an army officer who had supported Tsar Nicholas and then fought with

99

General Denikin in a desperate attempt to thwart the Bolsheviks? When he had realised the hopelessness of his cause, Lola's father had smuggled her out of Russia, and it was then that Charles had met her. He was a petty officer on the ship that brought her to England and he had fallen madly in love with the beautiful and spirited Russian girl. Before the ship docked he had asked her to marry him — and to his amazement been accepted. For years he was to wonder in his mild way how he had managed to be so lucky, never grasping the truth that Lola was as much attracted by his steady solid strength as he was by her volatile nature. Secretly afraid she had accepted his proposal only as a way of providing herself with a home and a British passport and terrified that once she knew she was safe she would leave him, he had left the Navy as soon as he could and taken Lola home to Jersey. But how to support her? Charles had joined the Navy straight from school; he knew no other life.

To begin with he had found himself a job in the docks in St Helier, but the hours were long and unaccountably Charles felt ashamed of himself. There was nothing wrong with what he was doing, he told himself, but somehow he failed to be convinced. As a petty officer he had had a standing he now lacked and besides Sophia was too good to be the wife of a dock labourer. With her proud, almost haughty, bearing she was out of place amongst the other wives, and Charles resolved to find something better for her.

Their first son, Nicholas, was a year old, however, before the opportunity presented itself. Charles' grandfather died at the ripe old age of ninety-one and his will left everything to Charles — his cottage, a small leaky rowing boat and more money than Charles, or anyone, had ever guessed he had, all hidden beneath the mattress and in jars scattered around the cottage.

'Knowing Grandpa it all came from smuggling, more than likely,' Charles told Lola, almost too stunned by his good fortune to be able to believe it. 'Well, at least it means we shall have a place of our own to live instead of having to share with my parents.'

Lola's eyes narrowed thoughtfully and he hurried on: 'I know it's not much of a place but at least you'll have your own kitchen . . . and I can make love to you at night without thinking they can hear every sound. And besides, it's not fair on them when the baby cries. At their time of life they don't want that.'

'Is true, but all the same I do not think is what I want,' Lola said carefully.

'Oh sweetheart!' He put his arm around her. 'I know I haven't been able to give you much of a life — certainly not what you were used to in Russia. But at least now I have Grandpa's money I shall be able to buy you a few little extras . . . and Nicky too. You know that rocking horse you always wanted for him? I don't see why he shouldn't have it now.'

'No,' Lola said. Her voice was very firm and her shoulders were rigid beneath his touch.

'No? But why?' he asked, puzzled.

'We must not . . .' she paused to think of the right word, 'we must not fritter this money away. Maybe is the only chance you will ever have to get out of the docks. I think, Charles, that we should use your Grandpa's money to set us up in business.'

'Business!' He laughed, then tried to sound serious as he saw her hurt expression. 'Lola, sweetheart, I don't know anything about business. I'm a sailor, remember?'

'Then you go back to sea and leave it to me!' she flashed. 'I've never been in business either but I am willing to try. Is plenty of things that don't require more than common sense and the determination to succeed.'

'Such as?'

'Jersey is beautiful island. Is the perfect place for people to go on holiday. Oh yes, I know, until a few years ago only the rich go on holiday. But times are changing. Transport is easier — the trains, the boats, even motor cars. Soon more people go on holiday, not just for day trip, and when they do they will come to Jersey. I think it will be good if we are ready for that. We sell Grandpa's cottage and buy a house where we can have visitors. Then we have business. Is good idea, don't you think?'

Charles laughed again, not scornfully this time, but more from sheer delight at Lola.

'A boarding establishment, you mean? I don't see you as a landlady, cooking cabbage and keeping a lock on the bathroom door.'

Her finely arched dark brows drew together.

'Why should I cook only cabbage? I make good food. People will like to come and stay with me. Will be very nice boarding house — you see.'

Charles had thought the idea was just a whim that Lola would soon forget, but he was wrong. A few days later when he came home from work at the docks she greeted him with the news that she had found the very place.

'Is big house by harbour,' she told him. 'Dining room looks out to sea. Is room for visitors and for us.'

Charles was tired; all he wanted was to eat his tea and have a rest before going to bed, but Lola's eyes were shining with excitement and he did not have the heart to disappoint her. He put his jacket on again, and leaving Nicky with his parents, they walked down town towards the harbour.

When he saw the house Charles was quite taken aback. It was large and square, three stories high and built of Jersey granite. The paint was peeling on the shutters that framed the windows and a tile or two was missing from the roof — blown down by the winds that gusted in from the sea, Charles supposed — but it was still a very impressive place.

'I don't know that we could afford anything as grand as this,' he began doubtfully, but Lola interrupted him.

'We can afford. I have done sums.'

'Well, we'll have to see . . .' he hesitated. But Lola caught his arm excitedly, looking at him with those huge eyes of hers, and he knew he was lost. Just why she should be so set on running a boarding establishment and waiting on others when her regal bearing made her look as if they should be waiting on her he could not understand, but then it was because she was an enigma to him that made her so irresistible. He adored her and could refuse her nothing. Just as long as she was happy, then so was he.

La Maison Blanche advertising itself as a 'First Class Guest House' opened the following spring. Lola had wanted to change its name to something with a Russian influence but Charles managed to dissuade her.

'If we call it something foreign it might put people off.'

102

'But *La Maison Blanche* is foreign,' Lola protested. 'To me, is foreign. And to English people.'

'But not to Jersey,' Charles explained patiently. 'If they are coming to Jersey they will be prepared to accept French or even Jersey patois. But not Russian.'

At last Lola conceded the point. She was too happy with her new venture to argue for long, although giving in was not something she was in the habit of doing. Besides, she was really too tired to argue. She was working from morning to night to get the boarding house ready for guests, scrubbing floors, washing curtains, cleaning cupboards and even wielding a paintbrush to brighten up peeling window sills and skirting boards, all with Nicky, who could now crawl like lightning and even walk a few steps when he had a mind to, hanging onto her skirts.

When the first letter booking a holiday arrived she wanted to frame it and hang it on the wall but she knew that would never do. Instead she contented herself with putting it into a neat file and entering the names and dates in the thick diary she had bought especially for the purpose, then panicked madly in case the family were the only visitors that particular week — embarrassing! — or the whole of the summer — disastrous! But to her relief the bookings kept coming in a steady trickle. It was still necessary to hang a notice announcing VACANCIES over the brass knocker on the freshly painted front door, but perhaps that was not such a bad thing, Lola decided — at least it gave her the chance to get used to running a guest house a little more gradually.

That summer was one of the most exciting — and the busiest — that she had ever known. The visitors who came were impressed by the smart appearance of *La Maison Blanche* and the amenities it offered. It wasn't everywhere one could get a bath, for instance, even if it did have to be paid for as an extra (a shilling for hot water, fourpence for cold), a cup of tea or coffee could be had at any time of the day for threepence, and the food served at luncheon and dinner was good and wholesome and also different enough to be exciting. As for the landlady . . . more than one entranced visitor went home to tell friends and relatives about the Russian beauty who had looked after them, adding the romantic embellishment that she might even be one of the daughters of the Tsar, not murdered at Ekaterinburg after all but alive and living in St Helier.

Soon the guest house was thriving and the second season Charles gave up his job in the docks and stayed at home to help Lola. There was so much to do besides the cooking and cleaning, which she managed single-handed. There was the paperwork, which Lola found difficult because although she spoke English fluently the written word still puzzled her. There were numerous odd jobs to keep the big old house in good order and there was the garden to maintain — neat flower beds and lawns at the front and a large vegetable plot at the rear where Charles grew fresh vegetables to put on the table for the guests.

But busy as he was Charles still found time to take Grandpa's old boat out for a sail with Nicky sitting proudly in the well. Though he had repaired it so that it was no longer in danger of sinking it still leaked to a certain extent and more often than not he returned Nicky to his mother with his little rompers soaked with sea water.

'My baby will catch pneumonia!' Lola would cry dramatically, but he never did. 'He must be the hardiest child in the whole of the Channel Islands,' she said, but Charles only laughed and remarked that Nicky was exactly like his mother.

When Nicky was two years old Lola discovered she was pregnant again and the following year Paul was born. Where Nicky had been a good child, Paul was a scamp. Even before he could walk he was into everything, shuffling round on his bottom 'like greased lightning' as Charles's mother described it and doing more mischief in a morning than Nicky had done in a week. In the kitchen he was a menace — the moment Lola's back was turned he was pulling tins and jars out of the cupboards and emptying the contents onto the floor; in the bedrooms he untucked the beds as fast as she made them; in the dining-room he had been known to pull at the corner of a tablecloth bringing knives, forks and glasses tumbling down around his ears.

'Never again!' Lola cried in exasperation. 'Is my last child, Charles, you hear me? Never, never again!'

But a year later, in the summer of 1925, just when the season was at its height, the third little Carteret put in her appearance.

'At least she is a girl. Girl will not be so much trouble,' Lola said.

I wouldn't bank on it, Charles thought, but since he knew Lola was holding him entirely responsible for the fact that she had had to go back on her promise to herself he did not say so.

Against all doctor's orders Lola was back in the kitchen cooking for the visitors less than a fortnight after Sophia, as she had named the new baby, was born, and soon the strain began to tell.

Sophia was indeed quite good, but all babies mean broken nights and coupled with the long working days it was simply too much for Lola. First she became weepy and, because of her volatile nature, almost hysterical at times; then the milk dried up so Sophia had to be put on a bottle, much to the nurse's disgust, and lastly she became so thin and drawn that Charles grew frantic with worry. The trouble was she would take absolutely no notice of him. 'I am fine!' she would shout at him. 'Is nothing wrong with me. There can't be, can there! I have too much to do to be ill!'

Her face grew steadily more gaunt, great hollows accentuating her high cheek bones, and her violet eyes looked huge and dark, but still she continued working at the same pace, like an automaton set to self-destruct.

One night Charles woke and found her missing from bed. Worried, he went downstairs in search of her and found her lying on the floor of the kitchen. At first he thought she was dead, then, because the baby's bottle was lying beside her, he thought for a panicky moment that perhaps Sophia had been in her arms and was now lying suffocated beneath her mother's prone body. But he soon realised neither fear was justified. Sophia was still in her cot — for the first time ever she had slept though the night — and Lola was not dead, nor even collapsed in the way he might have feared. She was asleep, deeply, completely asleep, but when at last he managed to wake her she could give no explanation for what she was doing there on the floor.

'But the baby wasn't crying,' he said, trying to make head or tail of it. 'You could have been in bed.'

'I think I woke up and was expecting *her* to wake,' Lola said in an exasperated tone. 'I thought if I made her bottle it would be ready for her and she wouldn't keep crying while I was doing it.'

'But how did you get on the floor?' he asked and she flared up again, close to tears.

'I don't know — I don't know! I suppose I just felt sleepy and lay down.'

'On the kitchen floor? Lola, something has to be done. You are a danger to yourself and the baby if you don't know what you are doing.'

'How danger?' she asked scornfully and he did not even bother to reply. Arguing with her was useless — at least until he had found a solution.

Two days later he presented Lola with a *fait accompli*. His mother had promised to help with the cooking and he had engaged a girl to come in the mornings to help make the beds and clean up and another to wash up in the evenings.

'We can't afford to pay help,' Lola objected.

'If I go back to work in the docks we can.'

'But you hate the docks.'

'I would hate it more if anything happened to you.'

'Very well then. But I don't want your mother in my kitchen. She does things a different way to me.'

'That's just too bad,' Charles said flatly. 'If I can put up with going back to the docks, you can put up with having my mother in the kitchen. It's only for a little while, anyway, until you are strong again.'

'I suppose I haven't any choice,' Lola complained.

'No, you don't,' he said, kissing her.

Looking back over the years Charles supposed that had been the turning point, though there were to be many more ups and downs before they had finally got the guest house running on an even keel. They had gained another daughter, Catherine, who had been born in 1930 when Sophia was five years old, and lost his mother, who had died after a long and painful illness that the doctor had termed 'a growth' the very same year. There had been a couple of very lean years followed by a mini-boom and as the bookings flooded in they had bought the cottage next door to provide an annexe now that their growing family were

106

taking up so much room. They had arranged entertainment for the guests – coach trips every day to places of interest around the island and whist, bridge and chess games after dinner and at least one musical evening each week. Gradually they had increased the staff so that nowadays they employed two waiters, a chambermaid, a maid-of-all-work to prepare vegetables and do the washing up and a gardener. The guest house coach trips had proved so popular that Charles had had the bright idea of setting up an agency to cater for all the visitors to Jersey not just their own guests. He had taken an office in town and the tourists had come flocking to him to arrange their yachting and sea fishing trips, their rounds of golf and theatre tickets as well as their sightseeing tours.

Now, in the summer of 1938, things were going very well, but although the day when Lola had collapsed from exhaustion seemed a very long time ago, when she spoke of getting rid of one of the waiters in mid-season the memories came rushing back to Charles as clearly as if it had been only yesterday.

'I don't understand,' he said, hoisting himself up on his pillow. 'Why do you want to send Dieter home?'

Lola sat down on the edge of the bed, reaching for a jar of cream and smoothing it liberally on to her face and neck.

'For one thing he is German.'

'But you knew that when we took him on,' Charles objected.

'Just so. As I said, I wish I had listened to my own better judgement. I don't like Germans. I never have. I am Russian, remember. In the war . . .'

'That's a long time ago, sweetheart.'

'Perhaps. But my memory is long also. And besides, I'm not so wrong, am I? The things they are doing now are just as bad . . . worse. It's terrible what they are doing to the Jews. And they will try to be masters of Europe, see if I'm not right. Already they have annexed Austria.'

'The Austrians don't seem to mind . . .'

'They didn't have much choice, did they? They are like you, Charles, they like the quiet life. If Hitler came here and tried to take over Jersey, what would you do? Would you fight? No — not you. You would roll over like a little puppy dog and let him tickle your tummy.'

'I most certainly would not!'

'That is what Austria did,' she went on, ignoring him. 'Now Hitler thinks he can do the same with Czechoslovakia. And after that what will he want? He'll never be satisfied, that man. Bullies never are. That is what my father always said and he was a soldier, remember.' Her voice rose proudly.

Yes, and see what happened to him, Charles wanted to say, but he did not.

'I just don't think Dieter should be here at this time,' she went on, smoothing in the last of the cream and turning to face him. 'For his sake, too. You know if there is big trouble people could turn on him. I wouldn't want that — he's only a boy. And he could be trapped here. Suppose communication was cut? Oh, I know you think I'm being alarmist, but it could happen.'

'Another month or six weeks isn't going to make much difference, surely?' Charles protested mildly. 'This thing has been rumbling on for so long now I can't see anything blowing up right now. He'll be going home anyway at the end of the season. I don't see the point of kicking him out because of something that might never happen just when you have got him trained up in your ways.'

'Oh Charles, sometimes you can be so blind, can't you?' Lola ran a hand through her thick dark hair, tossing it back over her shoulder. 'There is another reason I want him away from here. He is much too friendly with Sophia.'

'Sophia?' Charles eased himself up on one elbow, looking at her in blank amazement. 'But Sophia is just a child!'

'Exactly. She is much too young to be involved with a boy. I wouldn't like to see that happen for several years yet. But she has been spending all her free time with him, Charles. They ride off on their bicycles and they are gone for hours. I don't like it.'

'But surely it's harmless. She's just showing him the island. She wouldn't think of anything else at her age.'

'Oh Charles, Charles, as I say you are blind. Haven't you seen the way she looks at him? The way her eyes light up like a roman candle on firework night when he comes into the room? Oh, she may be a child to us but she has a body which will soon be a woman's. And she has feelings, too, that she does not understand. I know when I look at her. I feel it here,' Lola

108

pressed her hand dramatically to her voluptuous bosom, '*here*, Charles, as I felt it when I was a young girl. I know what is happening to her, all right, though she may not. And I am afraid.'

'Hmm,' Charles murmured thoughtfully. Lola was exaggerating, he thought. He hadn't noticed anything different about Sophia, not even her developing body. To him she was still his little girl. But perhaps it was a little unwise to let her spend so much time with a boy several years older than she was — and a foreigner at that.

'Suppose I have a word with her?' he suggested. 'Tell her we don't want her going off with him alone?'

Lola reached for her tortoiseshell brush, vigorously sweeping at her hair.

'It won't do any good — just make her rebellious. If she is feeling as I think she feels she will manage to see him whatever we say — and perhaps deceive us to do it. No, he has got to go. It's the only way. Taking everything into consideration I'm sure there can be nothing but trouble and heartbreak ahead if we don't nip this thing in the bud. I feel it in my bones, Charles.'

He sighed resignedly. Useless to argue with Lola when her mind was made up — and he was very tired.

'I suppose you want me to tell him to go,' he said wearily.

'I think it might be better, coming from you . . .'

'All right,' he said, 'I'll do it tomorrow. I'll tell him it's for his own good, in case Hitler decides to fight.'

'That's right, you tell him.' Lola smiled. She put down the tortoiseshell brush and slid the silk wrap off her smooth creamy shoulders.

'And now, Charles, I think I shall come to bed. I hope you are feeling very sexy!'

'Oh Lola!' he groaned, but already he could feel a stirring of desire. How could she do this to him after almost twenty years of marriage? But she did — and he hoped she always would.

Briefly he thought again of Sophia, still a child yet so very much like her mother. Lucky the man who would eventually win all that fire and passion. But one thing was for sure. It would not be Dieter.

Lola slipped between the sheets beside him and Charles forgot

109

everything else as she snapped off the light and in one smooth movement was in his arms.

Sophia was sitting in the yard at the back of the guest house shelling peas when Dieter found her. She looked up as he came around the corner, reaching for a full pod from the basket at her feet and smiling a greeting.

'Hello! Have you managed to kick that terrible Mrs Mounter out of the dining-room then? Mama says she will stay there all morning if she's allowed to . . .' She broke off. There was no answering smile on Dieter's face. His jaw was set and his blue eyes looked like chips of glass.

'Your father has just dismissed me.'

'What?' The overfull pod popped between her fingers and peas cannoned out into her lap. 'Papa? If this is some sort of joke, Dieter, I don't think it's very funny.'

'I am not joking. I am to go back to Germany now — this week.'

'But that's ridiculous! Why?' Sophia had begun to tremble and she felt sick inside.

'Because there might be a war, he says. He thinks I should go for my own sake.'

'But . . . you don't want to go, do you?'

'Of course not. I told him — my father will be very angry. He will not believe this is the reason I have been sent home — what sensible person would? He will think I have not done my work properly or that I have disgraced myself and that is why I have been dismissed.'

'Oh surely not . . .'

'Yes, and I think it may be the truth. Perhaps they know that you and I . . .'

'But we haven't done anything!'

'*We* know that, but do they? Anyway, I am a German. Nobody here likes Germans very much just now. I have seen the newspapers. They tell lies about us and stoke up hate. Your father does not want a German here waiting at table in his guest house, I think, and especially he does not want him to be friends with his daughter.'

'But that's ridiculous! I'll see about this!'

Sophia leapt up. Peas spilled from the colander on her lap and ran away on the sun-warmed concrete yard. She flounced into the house where Lola was in the kitchen chopping vegetables for soup.

'Where is Papa?' Sophia demanded.

'He has gone to town. Why do you want him?'

'Dieter says Papa has told him he's being sent home to Germany.'

'That's right,' Lola said calmly.

'But Mama — you can't send him away now! Not in the middle of the season.'

'I am afraid the decision has been made, Sophia.'

'But you can't — you can't! Dieter's father will be very angry with him.'

'Nonsense. The way things are he will quite understand.'

'And you will never be able to manage without him.'

'Then you will have to help wait at table, won't you?'

'No! I won't! I won't!'

'Sophia, please keep your voice down,' Lola ordered, recognising, as she so often did, her own wilfulness and hot temper reflected in her daughter. 'You will disturb the guests and I won't have that. I'm sorry if you are upset. You are fond of Dieter, I know. But you must understand you cannot always have things the way you want them.'

'I never do. Never, never, never!' Sophia yelled.

'Please stop behaving like a child, Sophia,' Lola said in her haughtiest tone. 'Otherwise I shall have to treat you like one and send you to your room. I am sorry but as from the end of this week Dieter will no longer be employed here and that is all there is to be said.'

For a moment two pairs of startling violet eyes glowered at one another then the one pair began to fill with tears. Her fierce pride threatened, Sophia turned and ran from the room. She might be only thirteen years old but it was a very long time since she had allowed anyone — even her mother — to see her cry. And however hurt she was this occasion was going to be no exception.

She could not stop the tears, however, when she watched Dieter walk up the gangway of the ship that was to take him away from Jersey no matter how she tried.

'You will write, won't you?' she had begged, standing on the quay and wondering if she dared to take his hand, here, where everyone could see.

'Of course I will.'

'And you'll come back next summer when all this is over?'

'I will try. I don't know what I will be doing then, of course.'

'Oh Dieter, please . . .'

'I have to go.' He bent and kissed her quickly and she longed to cling to him as she had done in the long dry grass but did not dare. He ruffled her hair, picked up his bag and made for the gangway. She watched him striding away from her and felt as if her world were ending.

Dieter found a place at the rail from where he could wave to her and she felt the pain mounting as she stood there on the quayside with nothing to do but watch and wait. The minutes seemed endless as the crew prepared to sail — she almost wished they would hurry so that it would all be over and she could find a quiet spot to cry and relieve the unbearable ache in her throat. But when that happened Dieter would be gone and she did not think she could bear that either . . .

At last the gangway was hauled up, the sirens sounded and the ship began to move slowly away from the quay. She waved, the tears streaming down her face, and stood watching until the ship was no more than a dot on the horizon. Then she went home.

Chapter nine
Jersey, 1938–1939

All through that winter and the following spring as the world held its breath and prayed for a solution to the mounting crisis, Sophia thought of nothing but Dieter. She missed him dreadfully but even worse than this was the gnawing fear that he had forgotten her. Each day she ran to collect the post, eagerly at first, then with the inescapable dread of being disappointed yet again weighing her down. Oh, why didn't he write? She couldn't believe that something which had been so important to her had meant nothing at all to him. In morbid moments she wondered if something terrible had happened to him, but in her heart she knew it was highly unlikely. Perhaps the political situation in Germany was responsible, then. This was an explanation she could almost believe. Although Neville Chamberlain had come back from Munich waving his umbrella and promising 'Peace in our time' the situation was still tense. But even so she could not help feeling that if Dieter loved her as she loved him somehow he would find a way. Gradually her most precious memories with their wonderful aura of romance, flower-scented grass and sun-warmed skin, became tainted with sadness and Sophia sank into the depths of depression.

Because she had a very secretive streak Sophia kept her feelings to herself and buried herself in her music — the one thing that could make her feel marginally better. Night after night she shut herself in the front room where Lola's baby grand occupied pride of place and poured all her passion and pain into thundering out the great compositions.

'Is very good!' Lola said approvingly to Charles as they listened outside the door. 'I think her music teacher is right. If she continues like this she should try to get into one of the London colleges of music, the Guildhall or the Royal. She could be a great performer, Charles.'

Charles looked doubtful. Where did Lola get these grand ideas? Sophia was very good, it was true, and he supposed concert pianists had to begin somewhere, but all the same . . . 'She doesn't sound very happy to me,' he said. 'I think she is still upset about that boy.'

But Lola, though she thought Charles might well be right, merely shrugged and hardened her heart.

'She will get over it,' was all she said.

That summer the guest house was busier than ever. Everyone, it seemed, wanted to make the most of what might be the last summer of peace. Lola had employed two French boys as waiters but there was so much to do that Sophia had to take her turn waiting at table and even Nicky and Paul were roped in to help when they were not busy with their school work.

Charles's agency, too, was booming, and as it became increasingly difficult to cope single-handed he decided the time had come to take on an assistant.

'I thought you were hoping Nicholas would join you,' Lola said when he told her of his decision. 'He is leaving school in the summer, after all.'

'Yes, but I don't think he cares for the idea too much,' Charles replied. He did not add that Nicky had told him he had other plans for he was fairly sure there would be fireworks when Lola got to hear what they were and he could not stand the thought of a row just now. 'I have already interviewed two or three young men for the post,' he hurried on, 'and I think I have made up my mind which one to take on. He is the same age as Nicky, but he left school two years ago, not staying on as Nicky did. There are some problems with finances in the family, I believe, and they needed his wages. But he seems very suitable to me — honest, hardworking and very keen to make something of himself.'

'I see,' Lola said drily. 'And what is the name of this paragon?'

'I don't suppose you would know him,' Charles replied, 'but his name is Bernard Langlois.'

Bernard Langlois whistled as he rode his bicycle along the St Clements coast road. The news, as read by Alvar Liddell of the

114

BBC, might have been bad that day, reporting as it had that Italy and Germany had signed a so-called 'Pact of Steel', but for him personally things had never looked better. For the morning post had brought the letter he had been hoping for — an offer from Charles Carteret of a position with his company, Carteret Tours.

'Are you sure it's secure?' his mother, Edie, had asked sharply when he had showed her the letter. 'I don't know why you want to chop and change, Bernard. At least you know where you are in the electricity offices.'

Bernard had refrained from saying that he knew *exactly* where he was in the electricity company offices — trapped in a dead-end job that had him filing most of his working day and which offered him the prospects of rising to the giddy heights of a clerk if he stayed there long enough and did nothing to disgrace himself in the meantime. It was, of course, as Edie had said, a steady and respectable job and it gave him a regular, if small, wage packet and the prospect of a pension when he retired. But Bernard knew he was worth more than that. He did not want to spend his life filing pieces of paper and filling in forms — and he certainly did not want to have nothing more to look forward to than a gold watch and a few shillings pension at the age of sixty-five. The very thought choked him. But he had been very afraid there were not too many positions of interest open to him, a boy who had been forced to leave school as soon as he was old enough to help his family keep a roof over their heads.

For as long as he could remember Bernard's life seemed to have been dominated by money — or the lack of it. He was the oldest of three sons and home was a small terraced house in St Clements. His father, too, worked for the electricity company, though not in the offices, and his mother, a faded little woman who seemed to spend her entire life on her knees polishing the yards of linoleum that covered the floors of their home, always described him as 'an electrician'. Bernard knew better. His father was not an electrician but an electrician's mate, and not a very good one either if the strange wiring arrangements he was responsible for at home were anything to go by. As a boy, learning physics, Bernard had wondered about the wisdom of some of his father's handiwork, now, as a young man, he was convinced it was a miracle the whole house had not gone up in flames long ago. But he knew it would be more than his life was worth to say so, and he kept silent — though he did make certain his bedroom window was never jammed and would allow him a hasty exit should the necessity arise.

Although it held their lives in such a stranglehold money was never actually discussed in the Langlois household and Bernard was never quite sure whether his father was really so badly paid or his mother a poor manager. But whichever, it had always been only too clear there was very little cash to spare. As a child Bernard had become used to having his pullover darned at the elbows so often that it became a patchwork of different shades of grey, and dinner towards the end of the week always consisted of faggots (which Bernard enjoyed) or tripe and onions (which he did not). But it was when he had won a scholarship to the Grammar School that he had realised for the first time just how hard up his family was.

'He can't go — we can't afford it,' Edie Langlois had said, her lips fastening tightly around the Woodbine cigarette that seemed to be permanently anchored there.

Bernard had wanted to cry from disappointment. But for once his father had spoken up for him.

'Seems a pity, Edie. After all, we don't have to pay.'

'Oh, is that what you think? Where's his uniform coming from then?'

'Well the boy's got to wear something in any case. He can't go to school in his underpants, can he?'

This had set Bernard's two younger brothers sniggering, but Stan Langlois had continued unabashed: 'If he's got to have a pair of trousers they might as well be the colour the school wears as any other.'

'Oh yes, and what about the blazer *with* a badge on the pocket? And a satchel — and a tie — and football boots and shorts, I shouldn't wonder.'

'It's a good chance for the boy,' Stan persisted. 'A chance for him to make something of himself — do better than I did.'

It was the only time Bernard could ever remember hearing his father refer to his failure to get on in life. Ever afterwards

116

he was made to feel as if by attending the Grammar School he was somehow getting above himself.

How the money was found he was never quite certain but to his delight he was able to take up his place wearing the regulation items his mother had referred to and carrying his lunch, a brand new fountain pen and a box of pencils in a somewhat battered leather satchel which Edie had found at a jumble sale and which he had polished lovingly until the worn bits scarcely noticed at all.

Once at the school Bernard had settled down to make the most of his God-given opportunity. He was not the most brilliant of boys and was under no illusion that he was but he soon discovered that by dint of sheer hard work he could not only keep up with the rest of his classmates but actually beat a good many of them. Whilst they surreptitiously passed notes or flicked little balls of rolled-up paper at one another Bernard sat in the front row listening intently and scribbling away as fast as he could with his new but rather scratchy fountain pen. The other boys called him a 'swot' and a 'creep' but the insults rolled off him without causing him too much distress. At primary school, in his jumper with the darned elbows, he had been called worse — and to no purpose. This was different — the start of a path that would lead him to a better life. And besides, he knew he could redeem himself when it came to games. He was an extremely reliable, if fairly uninspired, full back at football and quite a tidy bowler on the cricket field. Bernard knew, as every schoolboy does, that the boy who can hold his own at sport will be forgiven almost anything by his peers.

Unfortunately for Bernard by the time he reached school leaving age the family finances were creaking under the strain of supporting three growing boys and he was put under pressure to go out into the world and get a job. The prospect of wasting his education had sickened him but he had known he had no choice. And as he had gone about his soul-destroyingly mundane jobs in the offices of the electricity company he had made up his mind. One day he was going to make use of his talents and pull himself out of the rut of grinding poverty that had trapped his parents. One day he would have a nice house and a fast car and maybe even a boat. He would travel the world, for business and

117

for pleasure, he would have good food on his table and fine wines in his cellar. Just how he would acquire this Bernard was not sure but he was determined that when the opportunity presented itself he would grasp it with both hands.

Now, as he cycled home along the St Clements coast road, Bernard was thinking that the job Charles Carteret was offering him could very well be that opportunity.

'Visitors to Jersey will come to expect more and more in the way of entertainment — and it is going to be our business to see they get it, whether it be coach tours, boat trips or theatre tickets,' Charles had told him. 'I want a young man with an eye on the future, someone not afraid of hard work, to help me develop what I believe can become a really profitable enterprise.'

That's me, thought Bernard. A young man with an eye on the future. The stiff breeze coming off the sea burned his cheeks and made the breath catch in his throat but he pushed down hard on the pedals, fired up with excited enthusiasm and a sense of destiny encountered stronger than anything he had experienced in his life before.

Somehow it was as if everything he had done had been in preparation for this moment. And Bernard Langlois was very, very sure that Carteret Tours was going to provide him with the springboard to make all his hopes and ambitions bear fruit.

On the day that he left school Nicholas Carteret put his school cap in the dustbin, making sure it was so soiled with kitchen waste that it could never again be worn, and broke the news to his mother that he intended to join the army.

'So — you are a grown man now,' she said, pausing in her inventory of the flour, sugar and dried fruit that she was stock-piling in her walk-in larder against the shortages that she knew would be inevitable if war broke out. 'Is time you decided what you are going to do, Nicholas.'

'Oh, I have decided,' he said — and told her.

Lola listened, growing paler and paler until there was no more colour in her face than in the bag of flour in her hands.

'Nicholas, no! I forbid it!'

'You can't forbid it, Mama. As you just said, I am a grown

118

man. And besides, I'd have thought you would be pleased. Your father was a soldier, so it's in my blood.'

'My father died because he was a soldier. I don't want the same thing to happen to you. Tell me this is not true, Nicholas. Tell me you will forget this stupid idea.'

'I can't, Mama. Besides, if war comes I shall be called up anyway. They are already asking boys of nineteen to register so they can be sent for when they are twenty. I'd rather go now and join the regular army than wait to be sent for.'

For a moment Lola was silent. She could see the sense of his argument. Perhaps it would be advantageous to be a regular soldier rather than a conscript. But the thought of Nicky going to fight at all was almost more than she could bear.

'Wait a little while, Nicholas,' she begged. 'Just long enough to give your mother time to get used to the idea.'

And perhaps to give yourself time to change your mind, she added silently.

Nicky looked downcast. He hated arguing with his mother.

'Well, I'll leave it for a week or so,' he agreed. 'But then I shall write away for all the information. And I have to tell you that nothing you can do will stop me.'

Something did happen, however, if not to stop Nicky enlisting, at least to take his mind off it for the time being. Her name was Vivienne Moran.

Vivienne Moran had a way of attracting boys as a discarded sandwich attracts seagulls on the beach. They flocked around her wherever she went, falling over themselves for her favours, and Nicky was no exception.

Vivienne was nineteen years old, with flaming red hair, creamy skin and the greenest eyes in Jersey, so green and clear they were almost like bits of emerald glass. But it was not her eyes that boys usually noticed first. Top of her assets as far as they were concerned were her breasts — big and thrusting above a tiny handspan of a waist.

Besides being very pretty, Vivienne was vivacious, vital and fun to be with. As if all this was not enough she had the added glamour of having a father who worked in the city of London during the week and flew home at weekends and a mother who had been on the stage.

Nicky met her on the beach — the wonderful expanse of golden sand that follows the entire curve of the bay from St Helier to St Aubin. He had gone there with his friends to swim but as they walked along the sand looking for a place to leave their towels he saw her and forgot all about swimming.

'Who is *that*?' he exclaimed, though he did not expect an answer. In her white two-piece swimsuit with a sun-visor set at a jaunty angle on her flaming red hair she looked for all the world like a film star or model and must almost certainly be a summer visitor. But to his surprise Jack Pickard, one of his friends, knew her.

'That, Nicky old boy, is the lovely Viv Moran. The girl with the most luscious tits in Jersey — for all the good they'll do you!'

'You mean — she lives here?' Nick asked.

'She does. But it's no good you drooling like that. Her old man's got money and plenty of it. She gets around with a crowd of her own sort. And she'd certainly never look at you.'

'Want to bet?' Nicky said.

Apart from a few harmless flirtations and one relationship which had lasted six weeks Nicky had never bothered much with girls though the lack of interest could not have been said to be mutual. Nicky was taller than average, with a body lithe and well-muscled from hours of swimming and tanned from frequent exposure to the sun and sea. His hair was thick with a natural wave, his eyes were the same startling violet as Sophia's. Nicky Carteret had made plenty of female hearts miss a beat but he was virtually unaware of it — and the lack of awareness was part of his charm. Now, however, intoxicated by this stunning girl, he was suddenly buoyed up on a wave of confidence which all that admiration had unconsciously engendered.

Without even responding to the banter of his friends he walked straight up to her and threw himself down on the beach beside her.

'Hi,' he said, 'I'm Nicky Carteret and my friends just bet me you'd turn me down if I asked you for a date. So how about proving them wrong?'

120

She turned quickly with a haughty flick of that flame red hair, ready to slap him down. Then as his eyes met hers, confident, challenging, her expression changed from annoyance and outrage to interest. For a long moment she returned his look, then her eyes slid brazenly over him and a corner of her voluptuous red mouth turned up.

'Why not? Winning a bet is always fun, isn't it?'

'That's just a part of the fun,' Nicky corrected her, amazed by his own cool. 'The best part might be something quite different.'

'So it might be,' she said and again her eyes were tantalising. 'When are you going to take me out — and where are we going to go?'

Nicky's confidence faltered slightly. This girl would be used to the very best — and he had no money of his own to speak of. He certainly could not afford expensive restaurants or entertainments. Then to his relief she said: 'Wait a minute, I have a much better idea. I'm having a party on Saturday night. Why don't you come?'

Nicky did not know whether to be relieved or dismayed. The invitation eased the financial problem but he was not ecstatic at the idea of venturing alone into unknown social territory without even being sure that he would ever get Vivienne on her own. However under the circumstances he had little choice — he would just have to brazen it out.

By Saturday morning his apprehension had increased. He spent far longer than usual over his toilet, Brylcreemed his thick wavy hair into submission and put on his best suit.

Vivienne lived in a converted farmhouse in St Lawrence, a good four miles from La Maison Blanche. Nicky thought about cycling but decided against it. Vivienne's friends probably had their own cars — a bicycle would look extremely gauche. Better to arrive on foot.

It was a hot summer evening and by the time he reached the farmhouse Nicky had had to remove his jacket. But when Vivienne's mother opened the door to him he saw her look of faint surprise and when she led him through to the extensive garden he realised the reason for it. In a suit he was hopelessly overdressed. All the young people were in shorts or even swim wear as they laughed and romped around a large swimming pool.

121

Vivienne, looking lovelier than ever in an emerald green halter-top and matching shorts, greeted him. 'Oh darling, didn't you realise it was a pool party?'

Suddenly Nicky was angry. He could not possibly go all the way home to change and she knew it. She had succeeded in making a complete fool of him. But he had no intention of giving her the satisfaction of seeing him squirm.

'Never mind, it's our date isn't it?' he said, taking her hand in a grip of iron and putting it through his arm. 'You'd better introduce me to your friends, hadn't you?'

He saw her green eyes flash and expected fireworks. But he went on smiling at her, a hard fixed smile, and holding her hand in his arm so that to all her friends by the swimming pool it appeared that she was greeting him with pleasure and a certain amount of intimacy, and after a moment she threw back her head and laughed.

'You're quite a guy, aren't you, Nicky Carteret? All right, come and meet the others. And who knows, I might be able to persuade my brother to lend you a pair of swimming trunks.'

'Don't do me any favours,' Nicky said coldly.

'Mm.' Her eyes ran teasingly over his broad shoulders and the ripple of muscles that was clearly visible beneath the slightly damp shirt. 'Oh no, I think it's *me* I'd be doing a favour. I'm sure you'd look very good in swimming trunks or even better . . . well, you never know, we might just do some skinny-dipping later on . . .'

The meaning behind her words was obvious, her appreciative look intoxicating. But Nicky was determined not to drop his guard so easily. He wanted Miss Vivienne Moran, yes — but he wanted her in *his* time and at *his* instigation, not hers.

An hour or so later, however, when he thought he had made his point and when some of the others were beginning to complain that it was not really very warm in the pool now that the sun had gone down, he accepted Douglas Moran's offer of the loan of a pair of trunks, executed a perfect swallow dive from the spring board and swam a few lengths. Some of the boys, understandably annoyed that his beautiful effortless crawl put their clumsy splashing to shame, gave him black looks and turned their backs, but more than one of the girls watched with admir-

122

ation in her eyes and a heart that was beating a little faster, and Vivienne's smile turned to one of satisfaction.

Much later, when the garden beyond range of the gaily-coloured lanterns was quite dark, she did not protest when he pulled her into the shadows. All evening she had been longing to discover how it would feel to be kissed by that hard full mouth — and she was not disappointed. Nicky Carteret might not be rich, he might not know what was 'u' and 'non-u', as Nancy Mitford had so neatly put it, but oh! he was deliciously sexy, every inch a *real man!*

Over the next few weeks Nicky saw a good deal of Vivienne. Before long, in spite of his unpromising start, he was accepted into her circle and to his relief he discovered it did not involve spending a lot of money. Mostly the entertainment — and the refreshments — were provided by indulgent parents. But Nicky thought that the best times were had when they were enjoying the pleasures that came free — the beach parties and the 'ghost hunts' when they trekked across the causeway at low tide to Elizabeth Castle or clambered around the rocks beneath the forbidding Hermitage where St Helier, for whom the town had been named, was said to have been murdered by pirates in the sixth century. Nicky learned to speak as they spoke, to adopt their lazy, laid-back attitude to life, to ride a fast motor cycle around the shady curving lanes and to pull a champagne cork without losing half the bottle in a foaming fountain — unless of course that was the intention. But he also learned things that made all the rest pale into insignificance. With Vivienne to egg him on and point him in the right direction, Nicky also learned to make love.

For a girl of barely twenty in the year of 1939 Vivienne was surprisingly knowledgeable. She had begun her education very young when she had discovered a paper-covered handbook on the 'intimate side of marriage' in her mother's dressing-table drawer and she had been fascinated by eroticism and the gentle arts of seduction ever since, never missing an opportunity to add to her store of information. She had spent a good deal of time practising sultry looks and provocative poses (which she copied from her collection of film star pin-ups) and much enjoyed trying

123

them out on the boys she met. She had lost her virginity long ago and somewhat disappointingly to a friend of her brother's, but since then she had discovered the power and enjoyment to be had from promising a great deal and delivering almost nothing.

Nicky, on the other hand, was virtually inexperienced — but he had not the slightest intention of letting Vivienne know it. When she tried to initiate petting he was quick to take over, working partly on instinct and partly by turning her own tactics to his advantage, with the result that Vivienne only wanted him more. For the first time in her life she had met a man she could not control and manipulate — and he fascinated her.

'Shall I tell you something, Nicky?' she said to him one afternoon towards the end of August.

They were lying beside the swimming pool, all alone for once. Viv's father, as usual, was in London for the week, her mother and brother were out and none of 'the crowd' had been invited to join them. Viv was lying on a sunbed, shaded by a brightly coloured umbrella because her fair skin freckled and burned if she was not careful. One hand trailed over the edge in a careless pose. She looked lovelier than ever, Nicky thought, and he wondered if he could make love to her here without anyone seeing.

'Tell me what?' he asked lazily.

'Oh — I can't shout. You'll have to come here.'

'If I do will you make it worth my while?'

'Definitely.'

It was one of the games they played with one another, cat and mouse. Nicky felt the rush of desire making his shorts uncomfortably tight and quickly before she could notice and perhaps use the knowledge to her own advantage he rolled off his own sunbed, grabbed her trailing arm and pulled her down on top of him.

'Nicky!' she protested, but he held her fast, the sun-warmed patio stones hot beneath his bare back, the delicious softness of her body moulding to the hardness of his.

'Now — tell me!'

'No! You're a bully!'

'And you love every moment of it.'

He forced her face down to his, holding the back of her neck with one hand and untying the bow of her halter top with the other. She squirmed with pleasure, parting her legs a little to accommodate him and loving the feel of his downy-haired chest against her now-bared nipples. His hands moved to the waist of her shorts, easing them down over her hips so that she lay there on top of him naked, desire for him driving her wild. How could he *do* this to her, she who had always initiated the action, teased the boys and then held back.

'Nicky . . .' She moved against him and the movement only twisted her desire another notch higher. 'Please . . .' she groaned, trying to loosen the tie waist of his shorts without relinquishing the body contact for even a moment.

'Ah-hah! Not until you tell me!' He was sweating with desire himself, the pressure of her upon his body was almost more than flesh and blood could stand. But with Viv it was vital to keep the upper hand. He eased his fingers between her buttocks and felt her arching towards him, her desire almost at screaming pitch. 'Tell me — tell me!'

'All right,' she sobbed, 'but you don't deserve it.'

'Don't deserve what?'

She nuzzled her face into his neck, her tongue found his ear and curved inside, slowly circling before withdrawing to nibble the lobe and whisper: 'I think I'm in love with you.'

'What?' He was so surprised he held her away for a moment and she sobbed again.

'Horrible beast! You promised . . . you promised to do it to me if I told you. I think I'm in love with you! Isn't that good enough for you?'

Shock turned to joy. She loved him, this goddess who played with the emotions of other men! Suddenly he was not just playing at being in control, he *was* in control. He was king of all he surveyed; he could take what he wanted — and he wanted Viv.

With a swift movement he lifted her bodily so that it was she who was lying on the sunwarmed patio and rolled on top of her, pulling down his shorts as he did so. She was moist and open and he thrust into her again and again. Soon, very soon, it was over. Their bodies trembled and clung, moist and heaving for a few moments more, then Nicky sat up abruptly pulling up his shorts.

'Nicky — don't leave me!' she wheedled.

He looked down at her, lying there naked. 'Hadn't you better put some clothes on? Someone might come.'

'I don't care! Don't leave me, please!'

'I'm still here. I'm not going anywhere.'

'I don't mean just now. I mean . . . if there's a war . . . I don't want you to go away and leave me. But then . . .', silkily, cat-like almost, 'you might not be able to anyway.'

He felt a stirring of alarm. 'What are you talking about?'

'Oh Nicky, don't be so dense! We just went all the way, didn't we? I could be going to have a baby. And if I was Daddy would kill you if you went away and left me.'

The alarm escalated to panic as Nicky felt the tentacles of the age-old trap closing in on him.

'You're not pregnant.'

'I might be.'

Her beautiful body, gleaming in the sun, did not stir him now. He felt nothing but a flash of that same anger that had assailed him on the night it had all begun — the night of her party. She had thought she could manipulate him then and she thought she could manipulate him now. Well, he'd see about that.

'For goodness' sake, Viv, cover yourself up!' He reached for her towel, lying on the sunbed, and tossed it down across her. 'If there's a war I shall have to go. There won't be any choice.'

'There won't be a war.' She was almost in tears. He had never seen her this way before.

He tied his shorts and sat down beside her, relenting a little.

'I'll tell you what, Viv. If I promise to come back to you will you promise to wait for me?'

'Oh Nicky, you know I will!'

'Well you had better.' He kissed her again and as they clung together with less urgency but a great deal more tenderness neither of them had any real notion of the horror that they were dismissing so lightly.

On the evening of September 5th, 1939, Sophia walked down to the harbour. The darkness there was complete — no sprinkling

126

of starry lights now from the buoys that bobbed on the inky water, no comforting blink from the lighthouse — and the only sound was the lap of the waves as the stiff breeze drove them against the pier and the seawall. How different it was to the scene this morning when the harbour had been a hive of activity!

It had begun at first light — crowds of people gathering to queue for a boat — holidaymakers, anxious to return home now that war had actually been declared, French reservists responding to their *ordres d'appel* and young Jerseymen who were volunteering to fight for King and country.

Nicky had been amongst them. He had been one of the first in the queue at the recruiting office and they had wasted no time in posting him to a regiment. The whole family had gone down to the pier to see him off and there they had been joined by Vivienne Moran — 'Nicky's girlfriend!' Catherine whispered excitedly to Sophia.

Though she scarcely knew her, Sophia did not like Vivienne much and she knew that Lola did not approve of her either. She was too sure of herself by half, a bit of a show-off and probably spoiled into the bargain. But Sophia had felt sorry for her this morning standing all alone as she watched the ship sail away. Her chin was held high but Sophia knew she would be wondering when, or even if, she would ever see him again and she could identify all too well with what Viv must be feeling.

I felt that way when Dieter left, Sophia thought, and the emptiness in her yawned and spread as the memory of his departure was refreshed. But at least then she had truly believed he was sad about leaving her too. Now she was no longer certain of anything. Even worse, England and Germany were at war. She and Dieter were on opposing sides. For all she knew he, like Nicky, was joining the armed forces — two one-time friends preparing to fight one another.

Sophia stared out over the dark water. Her face was wet and salty. Sophia was not sure whether the wetness was seaspray or tears.

Chapter ten
Jersey and Dunkirk, 1939–1940

Vivienne swung her legs down from the examination couch in Dr Bodell's consulting room and smoothed her skirt with apparent insouciance.

'Well?'

The doctor turned from the small hand basin, drying his hands on a clean towel, and his stern expression made her heart sink. All very well to have thrown caution to the winds in the heat of passion, all very well to have imagined that getting pregnant was a very daring, very avant-garde thing to do. The reality, in the cold light of day, was quite different. With Nicky away, God alone knew where, it was decidedly scary and for the first time in her life Viv had lain awake night after night worrying just what she had got herself into. It was also embarrassing, since Francis Bodell was a friend of her father's.

'Well, Vivienne, I think you already know what I am going to tell you. You are pregnant — about three months, I should say.'

Twin high spots of colour rose in Viv's creamy cheeks. 'Damn.'

'A little more than "damn", I should say.' The doctor replaced the towel on its rail and turned to face her. 'Have you confided in your parents about this?'

Viv shook her head. 'I wanted to be sure first. No point advertising the fact I've been a naughty girl if there was no need.'

'Hmm. Well I am afraid there *is* need. You're going to have to discuss this with them — and soon. And who is the father? Does he know?'

'No, he doesn't know, and I don't want him to. I don't want anyone to know. Can't you do something for me, Dr Bodell?'

The doctor's eyes narrowed a shade. 'What do you mean by that?'

'Oh for goodness' sake, do I have to spell it out?'

'Vivienne, I have to remind you abortion is illegal,' he said sternly.

'I know that. I also know that it's done — and that I wouldn't be the first to ask you to arrange it for me.'

'Vivienne . . .'

'Diane Frayne,' Viv said meaningfully.

The doctor stiffened slightly and she knew he had understood her. Diane Frayne was a friend — and one of Dr Bodell's patients — who had disappeared conveniently for a few days earlier in the year for what had supposedly been an operation for grumbling appendix. Viv, who had heard whispers in their circle, had preferred the unofficial explanation — Diane had been 'in trouble' and Dr Bodell had got her out of it.

Looking now at his face, gone suddenly blank and expressionless, she knew she had been right.

'Well?' she pressed him.

Dr Bodell sighed.

'Vivienne — as you so rightly say operations that would be in the patient's interest are arranged from time to time. However, I think you need to be aware what you are asking me. This is not just some inconvenient illness. It is the beginning of a human life. You may not see it that way at the moment but I have known young women haunted by guilt to the end of their days because they felt they were responsible for murdering their own child.'

'I'd never feel like that. I'm much too sensible.'

'I'm not sure being sensible has anything to do with it, Vivienne.'

'It has everything to do with it!' she exclaimed passionately. 'The world is at war — anything could happen. My boyfriend is away fighting — he might never come back. And besides . . .' she laughed shortly, 'my father would kill me.'

'He is going to have to be told,' Francis Bodell said. 'You are not yet twenty-one, Vivienne. You haven't reached the age when you can be responsible for yourself.'

'How pathetic! But anyway, I don't suppose Daddy will mind half as much as long as nobody else has to know. He'll back me up over this, you need not worry — and he'll pay the bill.'

'It's likely to be hefty.'

'That won't worry Daddy. He doesn't mind how many cheques he signs as long as that is all he's expected to do.'

Francis Bodell said nothing. Though he was a friend of Adrian Moran he thought the assessment was not an unjust one.

'There is one other thing, Vivienne. Sometimes — just sometimes — there might be complications. It is possible this sort of operation could leave you unable to have any more children.'

Viv slid down from the couch. 'That's all right, Doctor. I guess it's a highly unlikely scenario and in any case it's a risk I'm prepared to take. I want an abortion and I'm quite sure my father will pay for it. So please, don't lecture me any more. Just arrange it — as soon as possible.'

By the time Vivienne Moran was admitted to a private hospital as an appendicitis patient in need of surgery the war had been going on for a little under four months and in many ways it seemed hardly to have begun at all. But the black-out and the host of regulations and the wondering if and when anything was going to happen was beginning to get on people's nerves and planning was almost impossible in this strange atmosphere that was neither war nor peace.

Only the Jersey Tourist Committee remained optimistic. The island would be an ideal resort for wartime holidays, they proclaimed — 'far removed from the theatre of war with eternal sands, sea and sunshine' and just the place for war-weary mainlanders to refresh themselves to carry on with the national war effort.

For this, Lola was grateful. Nicky had completed his period of training now and was somewhere in Belgium. Anything that would keep her busy was welcome — and there was nothing like a full guest house to occupy her mind and send her to bed too exhausted to lie awake worrying about where he was and the danger he might be in.

Paul Carteret had a wireless set. He had seen it in the window of Mollett's shop and by pooling the money he had been given for his birthday and Christmas along with every other penny he had been able to earn or scrounge he had managed to buy it.

Now it had pride of place in his bedroom and he spent many happy hours fiddling with the dial to pick up different stations and broadcasts in various foreign languages.

On the second Friday in May he was at home suffering from a bad cold — and bored to tears. He had no one but himself to blame, he knew, for he had exaggerated his symptoms to get a few days' reprieve from his lessons, and Lola had insisted he stay in his room so as not to spread germs through the guest house. Deprived of his liberty and his friends he had read his *Eagle* and *Dandy* comics and even his beloved wireless was beginning to bore him. But since he had nothing else to do he went on playing about with it and so it was that he was first to hear the news of the new German offensive. He rushed downstairs so fast that he almost tripped over his own feet and across to the main hotel building where Lola was working in her office.

She looked up in surprise as he came tearing in. 'Paul! What on earth is wrong?'

'Mama — the Germans have attacked Holland and Belgium.'

A nerve jumped in Lola's throat. Suddenly she felt very sick.

'Attacked? How do you mean, attacked?'

'Bombed. "Widespread raids", it said on the wireless.'

'I see,' Lola said quietly. In that instant she had reverted to being the daughter of a Russian Army Officer, proud, brave and perhaps blinkered too. 'Well, they can bomb all they like but they have the Allies to reckon with. I don't think they will get very far.'

Paul stared at her. 'But what about Nicky?'

Her eyes narrowed and her fingers tightened convulsively on her pen but her voice was still quite level.

'There is nothing we can do but pray it will be over quickly and Nicky will come home safely,' she said. 'Now, I have work to do, Paul. But why don't you go on listening to your wireless and let me know if there are any more developments.'

Over the next weeks Paul listened to his wireless whenever he could but the news he heard brought nothing but increasing gloom. Against all the odds Hitler's armies were thrusting their way across Europe in a seemingly unstoppable tide. By the

131

middle of May they were occupying The Hague and six days later they had reached the Aisne River and Anviers on the Somme, just sixty miles away from Paris. Then at the end of the month came the worst news yet — King Leopold of the Belgians had surrendered and the British troops, with their backs to the sea, could do nothing but hold the line as long as possible to enable an evacuation to take place.

Paul's wireless was scarcely turned off during those anxious days and it was over the crackling air waves that Charles first heard the appeal for an armada of small boats to ferry the men from the beaches to the deeper water where the troop ships would be waiting.

'I could go,' he said to Lola, and she nodded. She was under no illusions about how dangerous it would be. The Germans would stop at nothing to hammer home their advantage and finish off the Allies whilst they had the chance. And Charles' boat, though in quite a different class to the old rowing boat he had inherited from Grandpa Carteret all those years ago, was a small craft to pit against the notorious currents of the Channel and the heavy surf that would be running off the Normandy beaches. But she was filled with pride, all the same, and she was glad to know that beneath his quiet exterior Charles was still the same brave man she had married.

When he left the whole family went down to the harbour to see him off and were amazed at the ferment of activity. Every little boat that could sail was going, it seemed — fishing smacks and motor boats, pleasure craft and even old Joe le Feuvre, wrinkled as a bit of dried-up seaweed, in his battered old ketch *Flighty Lady*.

'Mama?' Catherine said as the little boats moved, one by one, out into the sparkling water, 'do you think Papa will bring Nicky home?'

Lola's mouth softened. She was wearing a vivid red scarf knotted over her hair in what looked like a gesture of defiance but her eyes were suspiciously bright.

'I doubt it, darling,' she said, putting an arm around Catherine and pulling her firm little body close, 'but God willing, someone else will.'

But there was a darkness inside her, a shadow on her heart that refused to go away.

As the German Me 110 swooped over, Nicholas Carteret threw himself face down on the beach automatically covering his head with his hands as the staccato gunfire began and the sand flew up in a cloudy but strangely neat line just a few feet from him.

He was half-expecting to be hit, half-expecting the sharp penetrating pain followed by agony or oblivion, but somehow he was too tired to be frightened any more. For two days and two nights he and half a dozen others of the remnants of his unit had marched towards the sea, forcing themselves into some sort of discipline though their feet were swollen, bruised and blistered and their stomachs aching from hunger. What had become of the rest of their battalion they did not know. They had become separated from them in the hellish confusion that had broken out when the German army had swept through the gap in the French and British lines cutting off their retreat. Their only course of action, they knew, was to make for the sea. There they would be shipped out to regroup and continue the fight. So they had plodded along the lanes, busy with refugees, feeling almost guilty because they still had homes to go to when they could cross the Channel whilst these poor souls were fleeing from theirs. Nicky's tender heart bled for them; a year's soldiering had done nothing to brutalise his essential compassion though the sights he had seen and the grief and anger he had felt in the last weeks had hardened him in other ways. When he looked at the old folk, trudging along with all the belongings they could carry thrust into handcarts; when he saw children not as old as Catherine digging with their bare hands in the fields in the hope of finding a turnip or swede to eat; when they overtook women pushing prams full of bags and children whilst those who were big enough to walk dragged behind holding onto their mother's skirts; then he hated the Germans so much that he knew if he came face to face with one he could kill without compunction. But for the moment there was no chance of that. The most important thing was getting out of France alive to fight another day.

At times Nicky had been convinced that he and the others

133

would never make the sea and when the first tangy whiffs of salt
and seaweed had reached them on the wind he had been wildly
euphoric. But he had soon realised that though the sea might
be in sight, just over the ridge of dunes, home and safety were
as far away as ever. For the beaches were jam packed with men,
trapped between the approaching enemy and the sea, and the
low-flying fighters of the Luftwaffe were using them for target
practice.

'We'll never get out of here!' Des Collins, Nicky's best pal,
said, and there was a note of panic in his voice. 'We're trapped!'

'We'll get out,' Nicky said. But he was not sure if he believed it
and with each German plane that came sweeping over, machine-
gunning and strafing, he believed it less.

The boats were out there, a whole flotilla of little craft which
could get into the beaches where the big ships could not. But
what chance did they stand with the Luftwaffe controlling the
skies?

Nicky raised his head as the Me 110 went away down the
beach and the splutter of gun fire and flying sand became fainter.

'Christ, that was close!'

Des sat up, spitting out sand. 'Too bloody close! We'd better
find some shelter in the dunes until it's dark. Then we might
stand a chance.'

They crawled from shell-hole to shell-hole until they were
back in the dunes where they found themselves a dent beneath
a few tufts of stringy grass. With their hands they dug deeper,
then they crouched in the rat hole they had made, eating the
remains of their emergency supply of chocolate and singing to
keep their spirits up whilst they waited for dark.

Presently a pattern began to emerge. For about ten minutes
the beach and the water's edge would be under fire, then for an
equal amount of time the German attack would be concentrated
on some buildings just above on the coast road and soon the
little boats were taking advantage of the lulls to come in. But
there were so many men to be taken off – the surf was full of
them, wading and shouting, hoping the water would protect
them, and there was a smell of death in the air.

Suddenly it seemed Des had had enough. His fevered eyes

134

saw boats at the water's edge as a man in the desert may see an oasis.

'Come on!' he shouted, jumping out of the shell-hole and running down the beach.

He never saw the shadow of the Me 110, never heard the drone of its engines. Too late Nicky yelled a warning. The air split with an orange arrow of gunfire. One moment Des was running, the next his arms spread wide and he arched back as if he too intended to take to the skies. For a moment he seemed to hang there motionless, silhouetted against the sky, then he took one pace forward and another, his legs buckling more with each step until he pitched forward on to his knees in the sand.

'Des!' Nicky screamed. 'Bloody hell — Des!'

His insides had turned to water now, the shock of seeing his friend mown down in front of his eyes blasting through the exhaustion and the numbness. He pulled himself out of the rat-hole, running down the beach towards Des, now lying twitching oddly whilst the sand turned scarlet beneath him.

This time it was Nicky who failed to notice the enemy aircraft approaching until it was almost overhead. His head jerked around, his expression one of total surprise. Then the hail of bullets caught him, the sand came rushing up to meet him and in the midst of confusion there was nothing but stillness and a white hot pain spreading and floating him towards oblivion.

Paul, Sophia and Catherine were down at the harbour watching the little boats straggle back when they were joined by Bernard Langlois.

Bernard had been working for Charles for nine months now and he was very concerned to hear that Charles had sailed off to France. For one thing Bernard genuinely liked Charles, for another he was all too painfully aware that if anything happened to his employer he would be out of a job.

Not that there was any guarantee that he would have a job much longer in any case. Now that the war was hotting up Bernard could not see that there would be much call for an entertainments agency for visitors for he was very much afraid that in spite of all the assurances of the Tourist Committee there might not be any visitors. If this happened he was not at all sure

135

what he would do. It was possible he would be conscripted into the army, of course, and even if he wasn't perhaps he ought to volunteer. But as long as he still had a job he was reluctant to do that — he did not want to come back and find someone else installed in the position he had come to think of as his own.

Today, however, it seemed selfish even to think of such things. On the other side of the Channel men were fighting and dying — that had to be the first concern of any decent person.

'Is there any news?' Bernard asked, making his way over to where the Carterets were standing in a tight little huddle.

'Of Papa you mean?' Paul said. 'No, I'm afraid there isn't.'

His tone was cool and unfriendly and he turned away, looking out to sea and shading his eyes against the sunlight dancing on the water. Paul was not exactly a snob but he, too, was worried about his father and his anxiety took the form of disdain for a boy he felt was his social inferior.

'What about your brother?' Bernard persisted. 'Wasn't he in Belgium?'

'Yes, he was, but the chance of a Jersey boat picking him up is pretty remote I should think,' Paul said shortly. 'Shouldn't you be working, Langlois? Isn't that what my father pays you for?'

Bernard coloured but before he could reply Sophia spurred up.

'Paul, how can you be so rude? I'm sorry, Bernard, this is all a bit scary. We saw Joe Renouf come back just now and he said it's terrible over there, with German planes bombing everything that moves.'

Her face was pale with anxiety but Bernard thought how pretty she looked, her hair flying loose from a broad Alice band and her eyes flashing indignation on his behalf.

'Look, Langlois, there's nothing you can do here,' Paul said. 'We'll let you know as soon as we hear anything.'

'Thanks, I would be grateful,' Bernard replied, determined that his tone should sound neither subservient nor insolent. 'And tell your father not to worry if he's too exhausted to come in for a day or two. I'll look after things.'

'I bet you will,' Paul said, watching him walk off along the harbour wall and wondering just why the thought filled him with such anger.

'I'm scared,' Catherine said. 'I don't think Papa is ever coming back.'

It was three days now and still there was no word of him. The girls had gone to the kitchen, where Lola was making pastry, because at least there was a certain amount of comfort in being together and neither of them could bear the thought of another day spent with Paul on the harbour looking out to sea for the boat that never came. But here too the tension was almost too much to bear and Lola was glad that although she had a breakfast chef these days she still did all the cooking for the main meal herself. At least it gave her something to keep her busy and she thought it would be better if Sophia and Catherine had something to do too.

'Catherine — I want those apples peeled and sliced,' she instructed. 'And Sophia, you can chop the herbs to make the stuffing for the lamb. No, don't look like that . . . it is better to keep busy. And besides the guests will expect their dinner on time. It is no concern of theirs that we are worried.'

When dinner had come and gone, however, with still no news, and no sign of Paul returning either, even Lola began to show signs of strain.

'Where is that boy?' she demanded crossly. 'You'd think at least he would come home and let us know what is going on . . .' She broke off as the sound of a door slamming echoed through the house. 'Perhaps that is him now. Paul! Come in here! Where do you think you have been all this time?'

'Now, Lola, don't use that tone. Is it any way to greet your husband?' It wasn't Paul — it was Charles! He stood in the doorway looking for all the world like a parody of his usual self, hair blown by the wind into wild quiffs that his mother had used to call 'cockatoos', clothes crumpled, stiff with sea water and stained with oil. His chin sprouted three days' growth of beard, his shirt tail hung out of his trousers at the back. But he was grinning broadly.

'Charles!' Lola cried, rushing towards him. 'You're home!'

She threw herself at him and they embraced, oblivious of

137

Sophia and Catherine, who had leaped up eagerly, and Paul, who stood behind his father in the doorway, grinning. Then she pulled away, holding him at arms' length.

'Wherever do you think you have been, Charles Carteret? I have been worried out of my mind. And just look at the state of you!'

Charles grinned ruefully. 'Yes, sorry about that. My motor packed up and I had to get a tow home. But the boat that helped me out came from Ramsgate and he took me back to his home port.' His voice was quite calm and apologetic — he might almost have been talking about a Sunday morning outing that had gone wrong. But his casual response was deliberate. He had no intention of telling Lola what hell it had been.

'Did you manage to bring anyone out, or did your motor go *before* you went in?' Lola asked.

'Oh, I managed three or four trips,' he said casually. 'And I brought three lads all the way home with me.' Again he did not mention that one of his passengers had been badly wounded — a boy of about Nick's age with a blood-soaked bandage covering his eyes. The boy's mates had led him through the surf to the boat, keeping him afloat when he lost his footing, and hoisted him in, and Charles was very much afraid that the boy had been blinded.

Lola was nodding, satisfied. 'Good. They are all someone's sons. And so many boats went, didn't they? I am sure one of them will have picked up my Nicholas.'

Her voice was strong and confident and Charles did not disillusion her. 'We will wait,' she went on. 'Soon there will be news of him, you will see.'

It came in the form of a telegram. Corporal Nicholas Carteret was in a naval hospital at Weymouth, having been wounded in action in France.

'You see?' Lola cried jubilantly. 'I told you he would be safe! I told you Nicky would come home!'

But the telegram had contained only the barest facts; it did not elaborate on the wounds Nicky had received and it did not tell the story of how he had been rescued.

Fortunately for Nicky two more members of his original unit

who had marched with him to the sea — had seen him hit by enemy fire as he bent over Des's body and at considerable risk to themselves they dragged him to cover when the German plane went away. They knew he was badly hurt but to leave him on the beach was unthinkable. Under cover of darkness they managed to carry him down the beach, his arms straddled around their necks, his legs dragging behind him in the sand, and into one of the little boats that had managed to come in close to shore. Then as he lay helplessly in the boat they protected him with their own bodies first from the angry attack of German planes, then from the icy sea spray that washed over him as the Channel waves broke over bows never intended to withstand such seas. Nicky had been taken to Weymouth and now he was safe from the guns and the bombs and the angry ocean.

But his injuries were terrible. Luckily — or unluckily, as he was to say in his moments of darkest despair — none of his vital organs were damaged, though he needed a transfusion of four pints of blood by the time he reached the naval hospital. But one of the bullets that had torn into him had lodged in his spine, just above the waist, and it had cut clean through the spinal cord.

What Lola did not know as she tossed the telegram down and swung Catherine round and round in a fit of euphoria, was that Nicky's injuries were such that there was no hope of him ever walking again.

Chapter eleven

Viv was desperately worried. It was almost a month now since Dunkirk and she had heard nothing from Nicky. Surely if something terrible had happened to him she would have heard? So why didn't he write? Was he still in France, his whereabouts kept secret for reasons of security, or was he amongst the 'missing'? Viv thought she would go crazy not knowing. But then the whole of her life seemed to have taken on a nightmare quality these days.

The war that had once seemed so distant now seemed terrifyingly close. From the south-facing cliffs it was easy to see the pall of black smoke hanging over the French coast as the retreating Allies burned their oil dumps; the Jersey Defence Volunteer Force were busy drilling up at Fort Regent and a whole army of British troops had arrived, digging trenches, erecting fences and mounting anti-aircraft guns in the People's Park. The schools were closed to allow the children to help with the potato harvest — with so many young men away fighting the farmers were desperately short-handed. But Vivienne saw it all through a fog of misery that clouded her every waking moment and invaded her dreams.

This is my punishment for what I did, she tortured herself. Perhaps now I will never know what it would be like to have Nicky's child.

How ironic it seemed though that a decision she should have taken so lightly should have affected her so deeply. Dr Bodell had warned her, of course, of the way she might feel but she had not listened. Now there was a hollow sadness that never seemed to leave her and she woke night after night from tormented dreams, her face wet with tears though she scarcely knew why she was crying. Sometimes she thought it was because of Nicky. But at other times she knew it was because she was longing for her dead baby.

Throughout those bright summery but nightmarish weeks Viv watched and waited for news. The tired and anxious circles beneath her eyes darkened and deepened and she lost weight because she felt too sick to be able to eat properly. But even when France finally fell she did not realise fully the seriousness of the situation though like everyone else she was frightened to think that the Germans were just the other side of the narrow strip of water. And it came as a complete shock to her when her mother broke the incredible news that the British intended to pull out their troops.

'What are you talking about?' she yelled at Loretta. 'What do you mean — the Channel Islands are not going to be defended? You've got it wrong. You must have!'

'It's true I'm afraid, darling.' Loretta's voice, which had once graced English provincial repertory stages, was light and musical. 'Isn't it a beastly nuisance? They say because we are so close to France it would be practically impossible and the best thing for everyone is to completely demilitarise.'

Viv stared at her mother in disbelief.

'But if we aren't defended surely the Germans will move in and take us over?'

'I expect so. As you can imagine, I've had Daddy on the telephone already insisting we evacuate immediately. He says he is arranging to rent a manor house in Essex for us and wants me to organise a flight straight away.'

Viv turned cold with horror, her mind flying, as it always did, to Nicky. If they went dashing off to Essex how would she ever get news of him? He wouldn't even know where to find her!

'We're not going, are we?' she asked.

Loretta shrugged. 'Well, I expect so, eventually. But I did tell your father no strutting little German was going to panic me into simply turning on my heel and running. I need a few days at least to decide what to take with me and arrange for everything we are leaving behind to be stored.'

Viv almost wept with relief. Thank heavens for her mother's stubbornness and panache! It offered her a small reprieve at least. But the days slipped by and as the arranged departure

141

date of the last Saturday in June came closer with no word of Nicky desperation began to grip her once more. She had no alternative but to go with her mother. But before she went at least she could swallow her pride and visit Nicky's family to try and find out if there was any news and leave a forwarding address. They were not a very friendly lot and the prospect was a daunting one but Viv shrugged off the slightly nervous feeling they instilled in her. Nothing mattered except contacting Nicky and besides she already knew which of the family she was going to see. It certainly would not be Lola, who did nothing to hide her disapproval and dislike of Viv. But Charles had an office in town and Charles was far more accessible. Besides, Viv had always felt a good deal more confident dealing with men than with women. If anyone could tell her something about Nicky it was Charles.

And so, late on the afternoon of Friday, 28th June, Viv took her open-top tourer and set out for St Helier. As she drove, a little too fast, through the narrow lanes a German plane skimmed overhead leaving a white vapour trail in the clear blue sky but she thought nothing of it. German planes had been cruising over the island for the past few days now — this was probably just another one.

Viv pursed her lips and put her foot down hard on the accelerator, far more concerned with what she would say to Charles Carteret than with any inquisitive German. She could get around him, she thought. Provided he was still here!

She began to tremble suddenly, wondering why it had not occurred to her before that the Carterets themselves might have decided to evacuate. Perhaps it was because they seemed so much part of the island — it was impossible to imagine St Helier without them. But now that she came to think about it what point would there be in their staying? They wouldn't have much of a business left now. Who would be able to take a holiday on an island occupied by the enemy?

Oh, let them still be here! Viv prayed. And let them tell me Nicky is safe! In St Helier she parked the tourer, got out and walked along Conway Street looking for the offices of Carteret Tours.

*

142

The Carterets had not left Jersey though there had been plans at first for the children at least to be evacuated to safety.

They had talked about it on the afternoon that the news had broken that the island was to be demilitarised, a hasty family conference around the scrubbed pine table in the kitchen of the 'annexe'.

'Is ridiculous — ridiculous!' Lola had stormed. 'How can they wash their hands of us in this way? And to think I was glad that Winston Churchill was in charge instead of Chamberlain! He's as bad — worse! What are we supposed to do, I'd like to know?'

Charles poured himself a straight whisky — unusual enough for him to drink anything stronger than home-brewed beer, unheard of at this time of day!

'You could go to England, you and the children,' he said. 'You'd be safe there.'

Sophia's interest had quickened. She had never left Jersey in the whole of her life.

'What about you?' Lola demanded. 'Would you come with us, Charles?'

'Me?' Charles sounded surprised. 'Oh no, someone has to stay and keep an eye on things here. Jersey is my home. I wouldn't go and leave it to the Germans.'

'Then neither shall I,' Lola said stoutly. 'You are right, Charles. We shouldn't run away. I ran once before — I am not going to do it again. But I think the children should go. I would feel much happier if I knew they were safe.'

'I'm not a child,' Paul objected. 'I don't see why I should miss out on all the fun.'

'Fun!' Lola exploded. 'You think it will be fun? Don't talk such nonsense, you stupid boy!'

'But if you and Papa are staying . . .'

'That is quite different. Besides your sisters will need you there to look after them. No, Paul, not another word. I have better things to do than argue with you. I am going down to the pier now to book you all on to a boat. When I get back I shall expect to find you packed and ready to go.'

Paul scowled but said nothing. Though he was now almost sixteen years old and hated it when she treated him like a child he still had a healthy respect for his mother. The fits of rebelliousness he sometimes experienced at the almost dictatorial way she ran all their lives were almost always undermined by an equally strong desire to please her. From childhood he had learned that Lola expected total obedience and when she got it she was warm, generous and loving. But cross her and all hell was let loose. Her quick volatile temper flared and a sharp smack on the legs or a cuff around the ears was almost inevitable. But the physical reprisal, very rare nowadays, was the least of it and always had been. Much worse was the feeling of guilt she was able to generate, the almost unreasonable sense of having somehow let her down. Paul adored Lola, and however angry and resentful he might be initially when she laid down the law or enforced some rule that he considered stupid or unfair, or chastised him for a piece of naughtiness it was never long before he was crumbling inside, longing for her approval and measuring himself against it – or the lack of it.

To all the children Lola seemed like some incarnate version of St Peter on Judgement Day, ushering them through the portals to warmth, brightness and love or metaphorically banishing them to roast in the fires until they saw the error of their ways, and Paul, perhaps, was more affected by the sway that Lola held than any of them. His rebellion was always the most blatant, his remorse the most bitter. It was so difficult to continue to justify himself once the initial bravado had faded and knowing this he also knew that outright confrontation was useless. Lola always won in the end and he ended up feeling not only impotent but also ashamed of himself both for failing and for defying her in the first place. Now, though his whole body throbbed with the injustice of her arbitrary decision, his instinct for self-preservation made him hold his defiance in check until his mother was safely out of the door. Then, without much hope, for experience had also taught him that Charles very rarely overruled Lola in any matter of importance, he turned to his father.

'I shan't go, Papa. She can't make me.'

Charles sighed. 'Oh Paul, don't make things worse than they already are,' he said wearily. 'Don't you think we have enough to worry about without adding the safety of you and your sisters to the list? Your mother is quite right. If the Germans come —

144

and they are pretty sure to — Jersey won't be a very good place to be.'

'But . . .'

'She knows about these things, remember. She was in Russia at the time of the revolution . . .'

'I wish I had been! It must have been jolly exciting!'

'It might seem that way to you now. That's the trouble when you are young. War seems romantic. But I promise you the reality is different. I expect your brother could tell you that now.'

'At least he's had the chance to find out for himself!' Paul said with feeling. 'She didn't stop him from joining the army.'

'Paul, if the island is occupied and you are still here it won't be your mother who stops you joining the army, it will be the Germans. They'll turn the place into an island prison and you will have to do as they tell you, make no mistake about that. We all shall.' He saw the momentary doubt glimmer in Paul's eyes and went on: 'Now if you are in England, when you are old enough you will be free to do as you like. Surely that is much the best option.'

Paul scuffed the toe of his shoe against the leg of the table. He was beginning to see there was something in what his father said. Free to do as he liked — the prospect was an inviting one. No more Lola laying down the law and refusing to be argued with, no more curfews, perhaps no more school. But he did not want to appear to have been talked round too easily.

'I suppose it's not such a bad idea,' he said grudgingly.

'I'm glad you are beginning to see sense. Though for goodness' sake don't tell your mother what I said about you joining the army.'

For perhaps the first time in his life Paul felt a sense of kinship with his father. As a small boy he had hero-worshipped him, of course, hanging on to his coat tails and following him around, but of recent years he had come to regard him almost as an irrelevance. He was scarcely ever at home since he seemed to work all the hours that God sent at his tourist agency and when he was there he faded into insignificance beside the towering personality of Lola. If he had thought about his feelings for his father at all — and he had not, for Paul was not much given to introspection — he might have noted a certain scorn in the easy dismissal, the disdain one male feels for another who allows a woman to have the last word on virtually everything of importance in what should be his domain and everything else besides. Now, however, he looked at his father and felt that he might be looking at a mirror image of himself.

Being adult, he realised, didn't automatically mean ruling the roost. It didn't mean no longer having precisely the same feelings he had now — the need to be loved and approved of, the sense of guilt at causing needless pain, the moments of rebellion. But perhaps it meant knowing how to cope with them. Papa didn't want Mama yelling at him any more than he did. He wasn't afraid of her, of course, but a quiet life was a good deal more pleasant than a tempestuous one.

The realisation that his father might sometimes feel exactly as he did cheered Paul.

'Don't worry — I won't say anything,' he said conspiratorially. Then another thought occurred to him. 'If I went to England I'd be able to go and see Nicky, too, I suppose.'

'You would indeed.'

'Well, I suppose all things considered it might be all right,' he conceded and felt a lift of excitement at the prospect of the coming adventure.

No sooner had Paul come around to the idea of leaving for England, however, than Lola was back again having had a change of heart.

'The whole place has gone mad!' she exploded, setting her bag down on the table with a thud and taking off her hat. 'You never saw so many people — panicking, all of them! There are queues at the bank — everyone wants to draw out their money, it seems — and the queue at the pier, huh! — it is unbelievable! I should have been there all night! So I have decided. Perhaps it would be better if we all stay together.'

'But I want to go to England, Mama!' Catherine wailed. 'I've packed my case all ready!'

'Then you will just have to unpack it again, won't you?'

'I'll go and queue up if you like,' Paul offered.

Lola looked at him sharply. 'You've changed your tune,

haven't you? Well, it's too late, I'm afraid. Goodness knows what mischief the three of you would get up to without your mother and father to keep an eye on you. I suppose that's what you have been talking about while I was out.'

She nodded her head briskly and Paul wondered how it was that Lola seemed to know instinctively what each of them was thinking and planning as if some sixth sense always helped her to keep them in line. It really was too bad, he thought glumly. He'd never escape now. He didn't know how old Nicky had managed it.

Then he remembered the moment's empathy he had experienced with his father and the memory cheered him once more. Perhaps Charles had his ways of getting around Lola. He might yet prove an ally. Paul made up his mind that the next time he wanted something he would talk to his father first and enlist his help. Quite apart from the prospect of getting his own way with less fuss than it took to fail, Paul found that he liked the idea of getting to know the old man.

That first week when the soldiers left was a strange unreal time of waiting, for what no one was exactly sure. The weather was perfect for June, the sun hot in a cloudless sky, and the uncertainty seemed to hang in the still warm air which occasionally reverberated with the throb of a low-flying German plane. The Union Jack still flew on the top of Fort Regent but the artillery had gone from Elizabeth Castle; the Esplanade was still busy as farmers queued for the weighbridge with their horses and carts and lorries loaded with potatoes to ship, but further along the front men were at work dismantling the criss-cross of wires that had been put across St Aubin's Road to prevent the landing of enemy aircraft. All over the island Constables were checking abandoned houses for animals which might have been left behind and removing any perishable foodstuffs, documents which might give offence to the Germans were being removed from the offices at the States, and the islanders who had decided to remain were busy hiding away their most valuable possessions in places of safety.

Charles helped Lola to hide her hoard of sugar, dried fruit and flour in the attic and bury most of their little stock of spirit

147

bottles along with their valuables in the garden, planting rose cuttings to mark the spots.

'But you are not going to bury my engagement ring. If they want that they will have to cut it from my finger!' Lola declared dramatically, and Charles, in a fit of pessimism, hoped fervently that the time would never come when they would need to sell or barter it in exchange for the necessities of life.

The mood, very unlike him, soon lifted, but he was left with the uncontestable knowledge that he would be bankrupt by the time the Germans came, if not before, unless he trimmed his expenses considerably. With no visitors on the island now he had no income to pay the rent on the tour company office and certainly none for the wages of its employees. And on that afternoon of Friday, 28th June, he decided he had better break the news to Bernard Langlois that until the war was over his service would no longer be required.

From the moment France had fallen Bernard had realised that with Jersey in considerable danger the tourist trade was bound to collapse, and with it his job. He was sorry about it but philosophical. The war wouldn't last for ever and when it was over he would pick up where he had left off. In the meantime he thought perhaps he, like so many others, would anticipate his conscription papers and volunteer for the army.

In spite of this he felt considerable loyalty to Charles Carteret and was reluctant to tell him of his decision. But the moment Charles came into the now totally-quiet office looking serious and beginning: 'Bernard, I'm afraid I have to talk to you,' he knew exactly what was coming.

'Don't worry, I quite understand,' he said when Charles explained that there simply was no point in trying to run a service for tourists when there were none. 'I'm thinking of joining up anyway before they send for me. It seems the least I can do . . .' He hesitated, then asked a trifle awkwardly: 'Have you any more news of your son?'

Charles's face darkened.

'Not a great deal, no. He's been moved to a hospital that specialises in spinal injuries — there's some problem in that area from what we can make out. He was in Weymouth at first, as you know, and his mother wanted to go over and see him, but I talked her out of it, told her I didn't think he'd thank her for it and that no doubt he'd soon be home on convalescent leave. But now I'm not sure I did the right thing. She's worried about him but with things as they are there's no question of travelling now, unless it's for evacuation, and I am beginning to think he may be more seriously wounded than they've let on.'

'Oh, I'm sorry . . .' Bernard broke off, unsure what to say, but he was saved by the deafening sound of an aeroplane approaching very low.

'Dashed Germans! They've been backward and forward over the pier all day watching the potatoes being loaded,' Charles said. 'I don't like it.'

Bernard went to the window, peering out, and saw a girl walking down the street, a tall, luscious girl with striking red hair escaping from beneath an emerald green headscarf, her eyes hidden behind dark glasses. Briefly he wondered who she was. And at that precise moment the world fell in.

The two explosions, one after the other, made the whole building shake and Bernard was thrown backwards across the office in a shower of glass, dust and plaster. For a moment he was so shocked that he lay where he had fallen, unable to move or even think, then, without stopping to wonder if he was hurt, he picked himself up, rushing towards the gaping hole where the window had been.

'Wait — there may be more!' Charles warned, but Bernard took no notice. He could think of nothing but the girl. She must have been in the street when the bomb fell and would certainly have been caught in the blast.

He yanked open the door and ran out. There was debris and broken glass everywhere. A few yards away, tossed against a wall like a rag doll, lay the girl. Her scarf had been torn off by the blast — it fluttered in the gutter like a railway guard's flag — and he could see that her white dress was stained with blood. He ran towards her, sick at heart, trembling with shock and the fear of what he might see when he looked into her face, but driven all the same by the need to help another human being.

149

Then to his unutterable relief he saw her move. He reached her, went to lift her, then changed his mind, afraid of hurting her.

'Are you all right?' he said, knowing it was a stupid question yet saying it all the same.

Her eyes were open though they had a dazed look and her eyelashes fluttered as if she was trying to focus. A half-smile twisted her mouth and she stretched out a hand to him.

'Nicky!' she said.

'Why did they do it?' Lola demanded furiously. 'They are barbarians! They know the island is undefended!'

'Maybe they didn't know,' Charles said, wondering whether he should tell Lola that the girl who had been caught in the blast outside his office had been Nicky's girlfriend, Vivienne. He decided against it. What good would it do? It would only upset her more. And he had other things on his mind.

'I'm wondering if it would be a good idea to move out of St Helier,' he said. 'It's a prime target if they decide to drop more bombs. There's always my cousin Dorothy's cottage over at St Peter. It's been empty since they evacuated to England and I'm sure she wouldn't mind.'

'No, I am not leaving my home,' Lola said firmly. 'But I'd like to know what the Germans think they are up to, all the same.'

'As regards that I'm afraid we shall just have to wait and see,' Charles told her.

It was not long before they found out.

'Everyone is to fly a white flag of surrender, otherwise we shall be bombed again,' Charles told Lola.

Understandably the news made her even more furious.

'Fly white flag? Never! Is humiliating!'

'I'm afraid we have no choice,' Charles said mildly. 'I'm not prepared to see our home go up in smoke to save your pride. We'll hang out one of the big white tablecloths from the restaurant.'

And Lola, though sickened by the prospect, could do nothing but concur.

*

150

A few days later Vivienne regained full consciousness. She opened her eyes to see her mother sitting beside her hospital bed and immediately asked the question that had been buzzing round her fevered brain all the time she had been semi-conscious.

'Is Nicky safe?'

Loretta reached for her daughter's hand, squeezing it. Over and over again in her delirium she had called for Nicky and Loretta, who knew more than Vivienne realised, had put two and two together regarding Viv's presence in Conway Street at the time of the bombing.

'Yes, he's safe,' she said softly.

To her alarm two huge tears squeezed out of the corners of Vivienne's eyes and ran down her cheeks.

'I don't believe you.'

'It's true, darling. He was wounded and he is in hospital, that's probably why he hasn't written to you. But he is safe. That nice young man from the Tour Agency told me. He's been here quite a few times to visit you, you know.'

Viv looked puzzled. She didn't know any young man from a Tour Agency — did she? But that was not important. The only thing that mattered was that Nicky was alive.

'Could I talk to him, do you think?' she asked, forming the words with difficulty because her lips were very dry. 'On the telephone?'

'The young man from the agency?' Loretta asked, startled.

'No . . . no . . . Nicky, of course. If he's in hospital they must have a telephone.'

Loretta felt sick inside. She did not want to tell Vivienne in her present condition that whilst she had been drifting in and out of consciousness the Germans had occupied Jersey. The swastika was now flying over the Town Hall — which they had made their military headquarters — and all telephone lines connecting the island with England had been cut.

'We'll see about that when you're better, young lady,' she said, summoning all her dramatic reserves and remembering a part she had once played in repertory of a strict young nurse. 'Just now it is most important for you to rest and regain your strength.'

151

'So that we can go to England, you mean?' Viv murmured and again Loretta declined to tell her the truth — that Viv's injuries had prevented them from flying out of Jersey before the Germans arrived. Now there could be no question of them leaving. Like it or not they were now trapped along with the rest of the islanders for the duration of the war.

Chapter twelve
1940–1942

The Germans came to Jersey and suddenly nothing was the same. They were not unfriendly, if anything they seemed only too anxious to get along with the islanders, and their priorities were buying up everything they could lay hands on in the shops, swimming and sunbathing on the golden beaches and chatting up those local girls who were not above fraternising. But soon the rules and regulations they imposed and the lack of liberty was getting everyone down.

In many ways, Sophia thought, the awful tedium was worse than the stomach-churning terror she had experienced when she had first seen the hordes of German troops marching through the streets. Nothing was fun any more. The pictures showing at the cinema were all German with English sub-titles and dances and concerts had to be over in time to be home by curfew. It wasn't so bad for Catherine and Paul — Catherine still had her tap-dancing classes at the Donald Journeaux School of Dancing, and Paul and his friends seemed to have great fun seeing how many regulations they could break without getting caught (though Lola had threatened him that she would come down harder on him than any German if she found out he had been crawling under the barbed wire to get to the beach or painting V-signs on walls and pavements — it was much too dangerous to be taken so lightly).

In the long evenings the only entertainment was playing cards, ludo or table skittles, or gathering around the piano to sing whilst Sophia played all the old favourites. But even the piano was no longer the joy to her that it had once been. The occupation had put an end to her hopes of gaining a place at a college of music — cut off from the examining boards practice began to seem pointless and Sophia, angry at the injustice of it, had no heart to play at all unless she was pressed into it by Lola.

All in all war was not a lot of fun, Sophia thought. And living in an occupied country was about as miserable as you could get.

Sophia was all alone at home one afternoon in the autumn of 1941 when a German officer came knocking on the door of La Maison Blanche.

When she looked out of the window and saw him there, looking extremely tall and extremely official in his immaculate grey uniform, her heart missed a beat and she wondered if she could hide and pretend there was no one at home. But it seemed a dreadfully cowardly thing to do and besides Sophia was not at all sure that he had not seen her peeping around the curtains. If he had he might force his way in and that would be worse than ever. Nervously she went to the door and threw it open.

'Yes?'

Face to face the German officer looked bigger than ever and inwardly Sophia quailed. But to her surprise he smiled at her pleasantly and clicked his heels.

'Good afternoon, *fraulein*. Is your father at home?' he asked in perfect English.

Sophia shook her head. 'No, he's out, and my mother too. They have gone to see my little sister dancing in a concert.'

'And you have not gone?'

'No. I had too much homework to do.'

'Ah! I hope you are one of the students who are doing well with your German lessons. Some, I understand, do not wish to learn our language. This is a great pity. If we do not speak the languages how are we ever to understand each other? However, that is not the reason I am here. I have come to tell you that I need your house to provide accommodation for some of my men.' He said it all in exactly the same tone, friendly and conversational, so that for a moment Sophia could hardly believe she had heard him correctly. She knew, of course, that the Germans had requisitioned a good many hotels and guest houses; when they had first occupied the island the Carterets had half expected La Maison Blanche to be on the list. But somehow they had escaped. Now Sophia stared at the tall handsome officer in blank horror.

'I shall have to come back when your father is in and speak

154

with him officially but perhaps while I am here you could show me the facilities,' he said and she felt a bubble of hysteria rising. He might have been a visitor asking for a guided tour before booking a holiday!

'No!' she said sharply. 'I'd rather you waited until they are here.'

For the first time she glimpsed the hint of steel beneath the pleasant exterior. Blue eyes flashed coldly and the smile became fixed.

'It would be most convenient if you were to show me around now,' he said authoritatively.

Sophia began to tremble again. She stood aside and he strode past her into the hall, looking around him with a critical eye. 'Hmm, yes, this I like, better than the big hotels, less impersonal. Now, how many rooms do you have? Show me please.'

Sophia showed him, her resentment growing.

'Good, good,' he said when they had finished their tour. 'The guest house is ideal for some of my men, and my fellow officers and I will take over this part — "the annexe" did you say it was called? It will make nice mess rooms for us.'

Quite suddenly Sophia's indignation overcame her fear.

'And where are we supposed to live?' she demanded.

The officer looked surprised. 'Oh, I am quite sure you will find somewhere. You do not, after all, need all this room for five of you. And your furniture you can leave behind. It will suit us very well.' He looked around, noticed the piano and walked over to it, lifting the lid and tinkling lightly on the keys. Sophia was outraged.

'That's my piano!'

'Really? You are musical? That is good. My son is musical too. And one of the other officers is a good pianist. We shall enjoy your piano, *fraulein*. Now I will leave you. My compliments to your father — please to tell him I shall be moving my men in next week. Good day.' He clicked his heels again, still smiling the same pseudo-friendly smile.

When he had gone Sophia burst into tears of fright and fury and sheer helplessness.

'It's the limit!' Lola cried when they returned from the concert and Sophia told them what had happened. 'They can't do this to us! I shall tell them I won't move from my home!'

'It's no good taking that attitude,' Charles soothed her. 'If you ask me it's a good thing you weren't here when the Jerry came or you'd be on the waiting list for prison by now. If they want the house they'll have it and that is all there is to it. We're lucky they've let us stay here this long.'

'And where are we supposed to go?' Lola demanded.

'There's always my cousin's cottage over at St Peter. We'll go there. It's small, but we can manage. We shall have to.'

'And what about our valuables and the bottles that we buried in the garden? And all the vegetables you've worked so hard to bring on?'

'We'll dig them up when it gets dark — Paul can help me. The potatoes are already harvested and we'll pull the carrots and parsnips. There isn't much we can do about the cabbages — we'll take a week's supply and leave the rest, though I must say I begrudge leaving the Germans so much as a single Brussels sprout!'

Paul and Sophia looked at one another. They had both had the same idea. It was surprising how often they thought like twins.

'Shall we?' Paul asked with a mischievous twinkle.

'Yes,' Sophia nodded.

That night after the vegetables had been harvested they crept out, found Charles's watering can in the outhouse and filled it with a bottle of the disinfectant that was used to keep the drains of the guest house sweet. With just the smallest amount of water to make it go further they sprayed all the remaining cabbages and Brussels sprouts.

'I wouldn't like to be a German with them served up for my dinner,' Paul said, chuckling, and Sophia agreed. She very much hoped that the biggest helping would be on the plate of the one who interfered with her piano!

From the moment they moved out to the cottage everything seemed to get a great deal less pleasant.

It wasn't so much that the cottage was too small for them, though it was certainly cramped — 'No room to swing a cat!' as

156

Lola put it — with only two bedrooms and a small loft under the eaves that Paul had for his room when he had made a rope ladder to reach it. It wasn't even that it was so far out of the way at St Peter after being used to living in St Helier. It was simply that the war had been going on longer and the occupation was biting.

Food was in short supply now, not just luxuries but everyday fare too. Sophia began giving music lessons to a farmer's daughter in exchange for half a pint of milk and a half dozen eggs, but Lola's prudent little stockpile of flour, sugar and currants had long since run out and the cakes and puddings she had once made were nothing but a sweet memory. Pea pods and blackberry leaves went into the teapot in place of tea leaves and Paul and Sophia often cycled to the coast, crept under the barbed wire that edged the beaches and filled a jamjar with sea water which could be boiled off to provide salt. And it was not only food that was scarce. Charles, who had always enjoyed a pipe of tobacco, took to smoking dock leaves and rose petals, and when Lola's broom wore out he replaced the bristles with lengths of rope.

As for new clothes, there were none to be had. Here Catherine, who was still growing, came off worst, for even when Charles cut the toes out of her sandals they were soon hurting her again and when her skirts became too short to be decent Lola had to scout around to find something to make her new ones. At first she achieved this by cutting up dresses of her own and when they had all gone she used the faded chintz curtains which had used to hang in the girls' bedroom and which she had dared to bring with her when they were turned out of La Maison Blanche.

When the first crop of wheat was ready for harvest in the fields near the cottage all three Carterets went to the farm to offer their help, working as hard as they could to earn half a sack to take home to Lola. But on the second day Sophia was disgusted to discover Paul snuggled in a corner of the barn with the farmer's daughter — a big brawny girl of his own age.

Sophia had known Paul was developing an interest in girls. She had seen him flirting often enough, trying out the power that had come from growing to be nearly six feet tall and almost as good looking as Nicky. She had even covered up for him a few times when he had sneaked out on his bicycle to meet one or other of them because she knew Lola would not approve. But discovering him with the beefy, red-faced farmer's daughter shocked her sensibilities and somehow marred the golden image of her elder brother.

'How could you, Paul! She's hideous!' she chided the moment they were alone. Paul flashed her a wicked grin.

'You won't be so bad tempered about it if I can get us an extra bit of butter or even some bacon. Can't you just smell it now, sizzling away?'

'That's immoral!' Sophia snapped, but she could no longer really blame Paul. The prospect of a rasher or two of bacon was already making her mouth water.

A day or two later there was news of yet another restriction. All wireless sets were to be handed in to the authorities.

'My wireless set!' Paul exclaimed, as horrified as Sophia had been at the loss of her piano. 'I saved up for ages for that!'

'And how will we know what's going on?' Sophia chimed in. 'We shall really be cut off if we can't listen to the wireless.'

'I don't think we have any option,' Charles told them. 'It's so big, Paul, it would be very difficult to keep it hidden. But perhaps . . .' He broke off, a sly twinkle in his eyes. 'Perhaps we could get someone to make a little crystal set for us. That should be easy enough to hide. It would be a risk, of course — the Germans would deal very harshly with anyone caught breaking such an important regulation. If you can be fined for riding your bicycles two abreast and sent to prison for insulting Hitler, I dread to think what the punishment would be for holding a wireless set illegally. But I think I'm prepared to take that chance.'

'Do you know someone, Charles, who could do this for us?' Lola asked. She was beginning to look gaunt, her violet eyes huge in a face that was fast losing its smooth roundness.

'I think so, yes. Do you remember Jack Ozouf? He was a wireless operator on my ship. I ran into him the other day and we were talking about old times. I think he could make a crystal set — if we could provide him with the bits and bobs he would need.'

'What sort of bits and bobs?'

'Well, something to make a head piece for a start. I should think a telephone receiver would do very well. We could creep out after lights-out, Paul, and get one from the telephone box down the road.'

He looked at Paul and winked. Paul grinned enthusiastically, enjoying the new found bond of solidarity with his father which the occupation seemed somehow to have strengthened. Paul knew that Charles knew about more than one of his escapades, and he also knew that Charles had not told Lola, who would have been horrified at the risks he took when he joined his friends to daub the town with V-signs or played football with a German helmet, and the feeling of conspiracy that came from knowing he had not only escaped German retribution but also Lola's fury was a heady one.

'When can we do it?' he asked.

'The sooner the better, I should think — before someone else gets the same idea,' Charles said drily.

So Paul's precious wireless set was dutifully handed in, Jack Ozouf was contacted, and the first black moonless night Charles and Paul crept down to the telephone box, cut through the flex and brought the handset back. Their hearts were pounding and their palms damp but they were as triumphant as if they had captured Hitler himself.

When the crystal set was made Lola wrapped it in Catherine's shoe bag and hid it beneath a loose floorboard in the bedroom. Every evening it was brought out so that they could listen to the news and then hidden away again. And though their nerves were always on edge for fear of discovery they all felt a sense of profound satisfaction that they were managing to outwit the Germans over this, if nothing else.

At the end of the summer term Sophia left school. With things as they were there seemed little point in staying on and she was lucky enough to find a job right away — as a junior receptionist with one of the dental practices in St Helier.

'Mr Shenton says he will train me as a dental nurse if I like,' she told Lola.

'Ugh!' Catherine said, squirming, and Lola merely looked sad.

'I suppose it will do for the time being. But I still hope when

159

the war is over you will be able to go to music college in England,' she said.

Somehow, when they talked of the end of the war, it was always on the assumption that when it was all over things would go back to being the way they always had been. And they never for one moment considered the possibility that *Germany* might be the victor.

One day in the middle of August Sophia was sent out by the chief receptionist to post some letters. It was a fine warm day when the sun sparkled on the blue water of the harbour and Sophia decided to take the long route back to the surgery.

As she approached the pier she could see there was a great deal of activity. Her curiosity aroused, she went closer in an effort to find out what was going on.

A ship, flying the German flag, was anchored at the end of the pier.

As always the sight of that hated flag was enough to make Sophia boil inside with rage and frustration but when she caught sight of the human cargo streaming off the ship and on to the pier Sophia's eyes widened in disbelief and horror. There were hundreds of them — bearded, unkempt men, women with matted hair and haunted staring eyes, children so thin that their bones jutted out. Their clothes were filthy and dropping off them, some had rags wrapped around their feet, others staggered barefoot. They lurched and clung together, swaying and stumbling because their poor weak legs had forgotten what dry land felt like.

Sophia stared, trembling with outrage, not wanting to see yet quite unable to tear her eyes away. She knew they must be prisoners of war, sent to join those who had already arrived on the island in the spring. But Sophia had not encountered any of those other prisoners. She had heard talk of them, of course, but that was all and she had never, for one single second, imagined they might look like this.

The procession came nearer, passing so close they could have reached out to touch her, and Sophia shrank back, ashamed of the revulsion that accompanied her pity and horror yet quite unable to help herself. One man, gaunt and lice-ridden, carried

160

a child whose face was covered in sores, a bedraggled woman had a baby at her scrawny breast. All of them stared straight ahead, eyes dead and hopeless in their ravaged faces. And with them, crowing, strutting, pitiless, came the Nazi guards, jabbing at the stragglers with their rifles. Sophia wanted to scream at them, ask them how in God's name they could behave in this inhuman fashion. But the words were nothing but bitter bile in her mouth.

When the procession had passed she forced her trembling legs to move, first into a stumble as halting as the prisoners', then, as the use returned to them, to a run. Sophia fled, breath rasping in her lungs, heart full to bursting. She did not stop until she was back at the surgery.

On the following Sunday afternoon Bernard Langlois was working in the parish of St Peter when he happened to run into Charles.

In the two years since the Germans had come to Jersey and Charles had been forced to close up the offices of Carteret Tours Bernard's life had changed completely. It was not a change for the better, he sometimes thought ruefully, but it had been inevitable and since he had never been one to waste energy fretting about those things over which he had no control, he congratulated himself that under the circumstances, he had really done quite well for himself.

The day after Charles had broken the news to him that the agency was to close he had taken a long walk along the beautiful St Clements coast road. He was still in a state of semi-shock as a result of the bombing on the previous afternoon and the fact that he was now out of a job had been made to seem unimportant by his brush with death. He could very easily have been killed, he realised. Had the bomb fallen on the offices instead of in the street the problem of what to do with his future would have been the least of his worries. At worst there would be no future, at best he could be lying in hospital, terribly injured, like the girl in the white dress. Bernard could not get her out of his mind. However much he tried not to think about her the images kept flashing back — her body, limp and broken, in the midst of the debris, the bloodstains on the white dress, the fluttering emerald headscarf. Several times during the night he had woken, his whole body bathed in perspiration, and lain staring into the darkness seeing it all again. But with daylight Bernard's sound common sense had asserted itself — on a conscious level, at any rate. What had happened had happened. Going over and over it would not change a thing. He hadn't been killed or injured but being grateful for the fact wouldn't keep him or his family in food or keep a roof over their heads. Life had to go on, and he had to make plans for it.

Bernard walked and walked, his chin bent to his chest, hands thrust into his pockets. The sky above the bay was clear blue and unbroken by so much as a single white vapour trail and after a while the stiff breeze off the sea began to clear his head and calm his jangling nerves. But the problem remained — what could he do to earn a living in an island occupied by the enemy?

Perhaps, Bernard thought, he should have gone off and joined the forces whilst he had had the chance instead of delaying out of loyalty to Charles. Thinking of what the German plane had done to the girl yesterday he certainly wished he had — he would like to have been able to personally dispose of the man who had dropped the bomb, and killing a few of his countrymen would have been the next best thing. But there was no point now wasting time regretting his inaction, no point going over what he *should* have done. What mattered now was what he was *going* to do.

Almost as soon as he put the question to himself Bernard was aware of the answer, though at first he tried to avoid it because as a solution it did not appeal to him one iota. But after a few minutes of trying to dream up an acceptable alternative and failing miserably his common sense again took over.

There was nothing for it, he would have to go back to the Electricity Company — if they would have him. Whatever his personal feelings it had a good deal to recommend it. No matter who was in charge in Jersey the basic amenities were still needed — water, electricity, gas and lines of communication — and would be however bad things might become. The Electricity Company could be the lifeline that would provide him with the income that was necessary to his family's survival.

One thing Bernard was determined on, however — he was

162

not going to be trapped in the offices again. He had not the slightest intention of remaining with the utility once the war was over and he thought there were a great many skills that would be far more use to him than understanding the company's filing system.

The very next day Bernard had gone to see his old boss and spelled out what he had in mind — omitting to mention his plans for the day when the war would finally be over. To his immense relief he found himself offered a position as an apprentice engineer — subject, of course, to the approval of the German command.

In practical matters Bernard was a quick learner — in many ways he found it came to him more easily than the academic studies he had sweated over in the classroom. There was an order and a method to the skills he was learning which seemed to him satisfyingly sensible. Now, two years later, he was as capable of doing the job as many men who had spent their lives at it and was certainly better qualified than his father — though he had the kindness and tact not to broadcast the fact. And he was grateful that for the duration of the war at least he was in an occupation that not only paid a reasonable wage but also gave him a certain amount of freedom to move about in an island choked by curfews and restrictions.

On the afternoon when he happened to run into Charles, Bernard had been working on a cable fault in St Peter. He was about to pack up his equipment and head back for St Helier when he glanced up and saw his former employer walking on the opposite side of the road.

Bernard was surprised — he had heard the Carterets had been turned out of their home, but he had no idea they were living in St Peter. He called out a greeting and Charles came across the road, beaming, and as taken by surprise by the chance encounter as Bernard was.

'Bernard! Well, well, what are you doing over here?'

Bernard explained, and Charles chuckled.

'I might have known you wouldn't be kicking your heels for long! I hope this doesn't mean I've lost you for good! I intend to get the agency up and running again as soon as this damned war is over and we're back to normal, you know, and I shall need you to help me.'

Bernard said nothing. This was not the time, he thought, to tell Charles that during the last two years he had given a good deal of thought to what he would do when the war was over and that he had made up his mind to try and set up in business on his own account. An electrical contracting business might fit the bill, he had thought, something that would make use of his newly acquired skills and also give him the chance to be his own boss. Whereas in the old days the job in the tourist agency had seemed an excellent starting point he now felt by the time things 'returned to normal' as Charles put it he would be past the stage where he could be satisfied with being a glorified office boy.

'How are your family? Are they all well?' he asked now.

'As well as anyone can be with all the shortages. I've been out collecting nettles, as you can see. Lola does wonderful things with nettles.' Charles indicated a large bag stuffed to the brim with greenery. 'Look, why don't you drop in and say hello since you're over here? They'd be pleased to see you, I know, and you can try a glass of Lola's excellent rose hip cordial.'

'Well that's very kind but I wouldn't like to impose . . .'

'Nonsense! We hardly ever have visitors these days and Lola does miss it!' Charles shook his head sadly. 'Besides, you look as if you could do with a cool drink. It's a hot afternoon to be working.'

Bernard had been looking forward to getting home, taking off his working clothes and having his tea, but Charles seemed so anxious to press his hospitality it seemed churlish to refuse. He was beginning, Bernard thought, to look a good deal older, with deep furrows forming on his face as if the skin was suddenly too large for the frame, and there was a stoop to his shoulders that had not been there in the days when they had worked together.

Bernard completed packing away his gear and locked up his van and the two men walked together along the lane leading to the Carteret cottage.

'Paul won't be there, I'm afraid,' Charles said, turning into a path which led between burgeoning hydrangeas and curved around the side of the small grey stone cottage. 'Quiet Sunday afternoons at home bore him. But I expect we shall find the others in the garden.'

At the rear corner of the cottage the path passed beneath an archway of climbing roses which had shed their petals like white confetti on to the rough paving stones. Beyond it, a border filled with snapdragons, sweet-william and marigolds edged a small neat lawn where two dilapidated deckchairs had been set out. In one of them Lola was reclining, her skirt draped up rather inelegantly between her knees, in the other Catherine curled like a small plump cat. The moment she saw them Lola sat up, straightening her skirts in embarrassment.

'Just look who I ran into!' Charles called to her. 'It's Bernard. I told him we'd be highly offended if he didn't drop in to say hello, and I promised him a glass of your rose hip cordial. There is some left, I hope?'

Lola rose from the deckchair. Her cheeks were faintly pink.

'The cordial is not all that wonderful, I'm afraid,' she said. 'With no sugar it is not easy to make it taste right. But you are welcome to a glass, Bernard.'

'Thank you. That would be lovely.' But Bernard was not really listening to her and his reply was totally automatic. Although he smiled at her politely, in actual fact he was looking past her at Sophia and wondering in near disbelief if this lovely young woman could really be the chubby schoolgirl he had known.

In the two years since he had last seen her Sophia had changed almost beyond recognition. Now she lay on her stomach on the lawn, propped up on her elbows as she split the stem of a daisy and threaded it lazily on to the chain she was making. Her hair, bobbed now to shoulder length, fell becomingly around her face, her legs, bent at the knees, kicked and crossed just above a deliciously curved rear with an almost childlike grace.

Bernard felt almost weak suddenly and there was a kind of throbbing deep inside him that he had never experienced before.

'Sophia — you could get the cordial for me,' Lola said. 'I put it on the marble slab to keep cool.'

Sophia carefully put the daisy chain down on a book she had been reading and got up. Like everyone else on the island she had lost weight; unlike some it suited her. The puppy fat had gone leaving only flattering curves and mysteriously she looked taller. Because she was wearing shorts her legs were still in evidence — long and lissom, tanned a rich nutty brown by the sun.

She glanced at Bernard as she passed and smiled, a small, almost coquettish twinkle as if she had somehow known what he was thinking. Bernard felt the beginnings of a blush and looked hastily away.

'Come and sit down, Bernard,' Lola said, indicating one of the deckchairs.

'It's all right — you have your chair. I can sit on the grass.' Bernard threw himself down on the lawn, surreptitiously watching the kitchen door for Sophia's return.

A few minutes later she was back with the cordial in a jug covered with a little beaded cloth to keep out the flies. Lola did not miss the fact that she had used the opportunity to put on a bit of lipstick — too precious to use all the time now that it could not be replaced — but Bernard just thought how beautiful she looked. In something of a daze he answered Lola's questions about what he was doing now and he was very relieved when she switched her attention away from him and turned to Charles.

'Did you see anything of the prisoners of war whilst you were out?'

'From the distance. They were down working on the railway again.'

'In all this heat! Oh, is terrible — terrible! The Nazis will rot in hell! Did you know, Bernard, Sophia saw some of them arrive? She said they were treated worse than animals, isn't that so, Sophia?'

Sophia nodded. A shadow had fallen over her face. Bernard felt his heart twist again.

'The trouble is we see so much of them over here,' Lola went on. 'The railway they have been set to build is so close by and they march them over from their camp at St Brelade. Some of them are Russians, you know that? My countrymen, used for slave labour! It breaks my heart!'

'Have you heard about the hospital they are building over in St Lawrence?' Charles asked. 'They have the poor sods tunnelling into solid rock so the whole hospital will be completely underground and safe from any air raid attack. I'd like to put a bomb inside and blow the whole thing to smithereens.' He, too, spoke with an anger that was totally out of character and Bernard paused in his contemplation of Sophia to wonder at the effect the occupation was having on people, changing their whole outlook on life and bringing hitherto deeply buried aggressions to the surface.

When he had finished his glass of cordial Bernard rose reluctantly. His mother had always impressed on him that it was most rude to overstay one's welcome and the last thing he wanted to do was make a bad impression on the Carterets. But even as he thanked them for their hospitality and said his goodbyes his mind was busy. Sometime, somehow, he had to get to see Sophia again. But would she want to see him?

He stole another look at her. She, too, had got up and was following him to the gate. For one wild moment he almost asked her there and then, right in front of her parents, if she would go out with him. But of course he did not do it. Bernard had no wish to make a fool of himself. Something so important had to be thought about and planned carefully.

At the gate Sophia suddenly reached up on tiptoe and placed the daisy chain around his neck.

'Something to remind you of the country when you get back to town,' she said mischievously.

Bernard felt the blush begin again, not just in his face this time but all over his body. But as he walked back to where he had left his van her words sounded like music in his ears and the daisy chain had become to him a laurel wreath.

When Sophia left the dental surgery after work the next evening she was surprised to find Bernard waiting for her.

She had, of course, noticed his interest in her in the garden. Each time she had glanced up she had found him staring at her though he looked quickly away the moment their eyes met and the blush that had spread up his neck when she placed the daisy chain around his neck had not escaped her notice either. But it had been a game to her, a new game, testing out a power she had not known she had and when he had left she had felt a little ashamed of herself for flirting so brazenly though she was still exhilarated by the experience.

167

The trouble was, Sophia thought, she found it impossible to think of herself as an attractive young woman. As a child she had been painfully aware that she was too plump to be beautiful and even her relationship with Dieter had done nothing to change her opinion of herself. What they had shared had somehow, she felt, been *in spite of* the way she looked, some sort of sweet chaste friendship with romantic overtones, not about sexual attraction at all. And of course Dieter had left her. She had never heard from him again and she had eventually allowed herself to come to the painful conclusion that he had forgotten her.

Not, of course, that she had forgotten him. Somehow Sophia doubted that she would ever again experience that total fierce love, the fragile bitter-sweet happiness, the tender dreaming, the way her whole body had seemed to sing and soar. There was only one Dieter — perhaps every woman has only one. First love, perfect, all-consuming and blind. It was over, she told herself, she must put it where it belonged, firmly in the past. But it wasn't that easy, for measured against that love all other emotions seemed pale and tawdry, lacking, somehow the magic she had once known.

Sophia's realisation that she had changed from a rather ordinary looking child into a desirable young woman came as a slow awakening. At first she did not even notice the appreciative looks and when she did she could hardly believe it. She tested them out; when a young man was walking towards her in the street she would hold her head high, pretending not to notice him and then glancing up at the last moment to see if he was looking at her. Invariably he was and the knowledge started a little spiral of excitement deep inside her. After a few times her confidence began to grow and she looked at herself critically and through new eyes, trying to see what it was they saw. But still alongside the confidence was a complementary uncertainty, two ends of the spectrum vying with one another, sending her differing messages. None of the boys ever did more than look; they were usually strangers and she never saw them again. And when it came to boys she knew, friends of Paul for instance, she was usually so afraid of being branded a flirt she behaved so coldly they never dared make an approach. In deep introspective

168

moments Sophia was sure this was because boys did not really find her attractive, they just couldn't help looking, and this made her behave more coolly than ever — she did not want them to think she had erroneous ideas about her own looks — that would be humiliating!

Somehow, with Bernard, it had been different. She had flirted, she knew, and she had actually enjoyed it. With his first blush her confidence had soared and somehow after that she had not been able to stop herself. Only afterwards had she been convinced she must have made a complete fool of herself. And it had honestly not occurred to her for one moment that he might seek her out in an effort to see her again.

When she left the surgery and saw him waiting there she could hardly believe her eyes and her first thought was that he wanted her to take a message of some kind to her father.

'Bernard!' she said. She felt clumsy and awkward, no trace now of the coquetry that had given her such heady power in the garden. 'What do you want?'

A dark flush spread up Bernard's neck. Truth to tell he was feeling just as awkward as she was. He could hardly remember his carefully rehearsed words but he had to say something.

'You know the revues they do at the Opera House? Well, there's a new one on now called *Hello Again* and we've helped them stage one of the scenes — the Electricity Company, that is. I wondered if you'd like to go.'

Sophia was so surprised she, too, was lost for words for a moment.

'I thought tickets for the Opera House Revues were like gold dust!' she said.

'They are. But they've given the Electricity Company some complimentary ones and I've managed to grab a couple for us — if you'd like to come, that is . . .'

'Well . . .' Sophia hesitated, a little frightened suddenly by the startling consequence of her afternoon's flirting. Then, as she saw Bernard's quick defensive look she made up her mind.

'Thank you, Bernard,' she said. 'I'd love to.'

*

169

The show was a triumph and Sophia, who had rarely been to the theatre, enjoyed every moment of it. Bernard, looking very smart in a sports jacket and slacks, met her outside, and the apprehension she had been feeling about her first real grown-up 'date' disappeared in a thrill of pride as he ushered her inside, steering her protectively through the crowds thronging to see the new hit entertainment. By the time the curtain went up every seat had been taken, even the chairs which had been set out in the aisles, and more people were standing at the back. Sophia glimpsed a couple of German officers amongst them and felt a twinge of discomfort. But this was soon forgotten as the smell of the greasepaint wafted out, the orchestra tuned up and the show began. Sophia wondered if Bernard would hold her hand but he made no move and after a while, as the music of Ivor Novello's *Lilac Time* stirred her senses and resurrected the exciting sense of power she had experienced in the garden, she took the initiative and slipped her hand into his. They sat very still, Sophia frightened for a moment by her own boldness, Bernard almost afraid to believe his luck, until the big scene to which the Electricity Company had lent their expertise began.

'This is what we did,' Bernard whispered proudly and Sophia watched in breathless admiration as the spectacle unfolded — the stage in complete blackout whilst the costumes of the performers were all outlined with light. When a flowerseller appeared with a basket full of illuminated flowers she could contain herself no longer and let go of Bernard's hand to clap enthusiastically.

'It's wonderful! Bernard — you are so clever!' she cried above the roar of applause and was delighted when he took her hand again.

When at last the show was over and they were filing out Sophia felt she wished it could have gone on forever. But the evening was almost at an end for she knew Paul would be waiting outside to see her home. There was no way Bernard could have taken her back to St Peter himself and then got home to St Clement before curfew and Lola had insisted it was improper for her to walk home in the black-out alone. When she saw Paul's tall figure waiting her heart sank a little but Bernard caught her arm, holding her back for a moment.

170

'Sophia — can I see you again?'

'Yes,' she replied without hesitation.

She wasn't in love with him, but she had enjoyed herself all the same and she was already looking forward to repeating the exercise.

But that night, for the first time in years, she dreamed of Dieter.

Chapter thirteen

'Mama, do you think we'll ever see Nicky again?' Catherine asked.

It was a winter's evening, past curfew, and all the family with the exception of Paul, who had explained he was staying the night with a friend, were gathered around the kitchen table playing 'sevens' and shivering a little as the fire burned low in the grate. Fuel was in short supply now — Paul and Catherine brought home as many sticks as they could find in the woods and fields but often there was nothing but sawdust to burn.

'Well of course we shall see him again! What a thing to say!' Lola drew a card from her hand and laid it on the table.

'But it seems so long since he went away and we never hear from him and . . .'

'We can't hear from him because he is in England and Jersey is quite cut off,' Charles said. 'You know that, Catherine.'

'Yes and it's hateful! Hateful!' Catherine cried.

'It certainly is but we just have to pray that Nicky is well and safe, as we are,' Lola said. Her voice was level but her haunted eyes told their own story — all very well to try to be philosophical but when it was so long since you had heard from your son and the last news had been that he had been wounded, possibly seriously, it was impossible not to worry. 'One of these days it will all be over,' she said, but Catherine, who was cold, tired and thoroughly fed up with herself, only echoed all their innermost thoughts when she wailed:

'Yes, but when?'

'I think we have played enough cards for tonight,' Charles said. 'Let's finish this game and pack up.'

'Oh Papa . . .' Catherine's voice tailed away as a sudden noise made them all start.

'What was that?' Lola asked sharply.

'There's somebody out there . . .' Charles was already on his feet when it came again, the sound of someone blundering into the corrugated tin of the lean-to shed in the darkness.

'Be careful!' Lola warned as Charles hurried to the door and Sophia slipped out of her chair, taking the poker from the fireplace and following her father. Her heart was hammering but she was determined that if someone was trying to steal their meagre reserves of fuel or vegetables they should not get away with it!

Cautiously Charles lifted the latch and opened the door. 'Who's there?' he called. 'What do you think you are doing?' There was a moment's silence in which Sophia could hear the ragged rasp of breath then a figure appeared out of the darkness. She raised the poker ready to hit out but to her surprise Charles caught her arm. 'Sophia, no!' Next moment the figure materialised in the light spilling out from the doorway, a stumbling figure, gaunt and bearded, holding onto the wall for support. Charles took a step towards him just in time; the man's legs seemed unable to support him a moment longer and with Charles's arms around him he half-fell into the kitchen.

'My God!' Lola gasped. 'It is one of the prisoners!'

It seemed now that Jersey was full of prisoners-of-war. There were thousands of them here now — Polish and Czech, Jews from Alsace and Russians, as well as the Spanish who had been the first to arrive. Whereas that day in August Sophia had stared at them because she had never seen anything quite like them before now, they were all too common a sight as they were marched along the roads to the sites where they were forced to work, building fortifications on the coast, constructing the railway that was almost within sight of the Carterets' cottage and tunnelling into the hillside to build bunkers and the underground hospital. In spite of this Sophia had never grown used to the horror of it or immune to their plight and she was filled with impotent anger whenever she saw them and witnessed the inhuman way they were treated. The soldiers who had charge of them were very different to the ones who marched, singing, along the lanes and arranged entertainments in an attempt to win the friendship of the islanders.

But there was so little anyone could do to help them. Some-

173

times when she saw them queued at the field kitchen for their daily rations of watery gruel Sophia would take some crusts of bread out and drop near them, but often, hungry as they were, they were too afraid of their guards to pick them up. All were pitiful but even so there were some who tore even more painfully at Sophia's tender heart — a skeletal lad, not much older than Catherine, with the terrible hacking cough of consumptive tuberculosis, another, who shivered ceaselessly and convulsively. When they disappeared from the daily procession Sophia tried to tell herself they had been relocated but in her heart she knew it was not so — they were dead, buried in mass graves with no respect and no stone to mark the place where they lay, unmourned by anyone but their companions who were themselves too sick and starved to have any emotion to spare.

Occasionally one of the prisoners escaped and sought shelter at a farm or remote house but the penalty for helping them was instant deportation. Sophia had once asked Lola what she would do if a prisoner ever came to them for assistance and Lola had replied tartly that pity was all very well but the safety of one's family must be the first consideration. Now, however, suddenly faced with this very situation, she did not hesitate.

'Quick, Charles, bring him inside and shut the door!'

Sophia shrank back as the man, still supported by her father, almost staggered into her. His clothes were nothing but filthy rags, hunger had made his eyes huge and hollow and above an unkempt beard his cheekbones made angular ridges in the bluish tinted skin.

Charles eased him into a chair and he slumped there, totally exhausted. Then, as he whispered something hoarse and barely intelligible Lola pressed her hands to her mouth.

'My God, he's Russian! The brandy, Charles, for God's sake give him some brandy!'

Many times the Carterets had been tempted to drown their sorrows in the brandy which they had dug up from the garden at La Maison Blanche and transported here hidden in Catherine's dolls' pram. But the bottles had somehow been too precious to tap. They were an insurance against things getting worse — to be opened only in an emergency. But this was an emergency. Charles went to the dresser, taking down the big three-pint china

174

jug which hung on one of the hooks and extracting the bottle. The label had long since gone, but when Charles opened the bottle the smell of the brandy wafted out, strong and almost stomach-turning. He poured some into a glass and put it to the man's lips but he was almost too far gone to drink it — as Charles tipped the glass a small stream of brandy escaped and dribbled down into the thick beard. After a few minutes, however, the spirit began to revive him and he stirred a little, finishing the drink and mumbling in Russian.

Lola dropped to her haunches beside him, talking to him in his native language, though after so many years of speaking nothing but English she found it strangely awkward. Then she got up, bustling to the small walk-in larder.

'I must get him something to eat — he is starving.'

In the crock were the remains of a loaf which had been intended for breakfast; Lola sliced it and spread it with a little of the precious butter Sophia had earned from the piano lessons she had given this week. The prisoner ate it ravenously.

'Haven't we anything else we can give him?' Sophia asked. 'What about Paul's dinner?'

'Oh yes!' Lola had forgotten about that. Tonight they had had a delicious stew of vegetables and a woodpigeon Charles had managed to shoot. There had been very little meat on it but the flavour it had given to the vegetables had been mouth watering and Lola had set aside a portion for Paul, who had eaten, as well as sleeping, at the friend's house.

The prisoner was recovering a little now, and as the immediate danger of him passing out — or even, heaven forbid, dying — right there in the kitchen, receded, Charles was becoming increasingly edgy.

'How long is it since he escaped?' he asked and once again Lola conversed with the man in Russian.

'He says he slipped away from his working party this afternoon,' she said after a few moments.

Charles frowned. 'They must have missed him by now then. Why haven't they been around looking for him? Well, we've done all we can. He'll have to go now.'

'No!' Lola said sharply.

'What do you mean, no?'

175

'We can't turn him out, Charles. It's bitterly cold. And I'm sure they won't come searching for him now at this time of night.'

'How can you be sure of that?'

'Well, I can't, but . . .'

'And what would we do with him?'

'There's the attic. Paul is not here tonight. He could sleep there.'

'Are you mad? He's probably alive with fleas!'

'Well, let him sleep in the shed then. I'll make up a bed with some blankets. Oh please! He is one of my countrymen and he is very sick. Besides, he is not much older than Nicky. Wouldn't you like to think someone was being kind to him if he was in this position? Dear God, he might be for all we know!'

Charles shook his head. His better judgement was telling him that to harbour this prisoner was an extremely foolhardy thing to do but he knew from experience that arguing with Lola when her mind was made up was a waste of breath. Besides, he supposed she was right — they weren't likely to come looking for him at this hour if they had not already done so.

'Let's get this light out — we don't want to advertise the fact that we are still up. We can manage with a candle. Catherine — you get off to bed. Sophia — fetch the old bedding your mother is talking about.'

The fire had died away now and the kitchen was growing rapidly chilly. When Charles opened the back door to take a peek outside the cold air came rushing in and the Russian began to cough.

'We can't put him outside like a dog!' Lola protested. 'Just listen to that cough — it will turn to pneumonia if he's not looked after. Look, why not let him sleep down here on the floor? I'll put another shovelful of sawdust on the fire and at least he will have one night to recover a little before he has to go off fending for himself again.'

Charles sighed. He was beginning to feel very tired himself. Perhaps there was no harm in doing as Lola wanted and anyway there wasn't a lot of satisfaction in looking after your own skin if you knew you had sacrificed someone else to do it. What was more, if the Germans did come prowling they would be less likely to find him in the house than if he was in the shed — all very well to try to pretend he had crawled in there of his own accord, if he was wrapped in their blankets the story wouldn't hold much water!

'Just for tonight, then,' he agreed reluctantly. 'But tomorrow he has to go.'

Sophia was sleeping badly, continually disturbed by bad dreams. For most of the night she tossed and turned thinking of the Russian downstairs and listening to his bouts of racking coughing. But towards dawn she dozed off, sleeping more heavily than she had done all night, and when the loud banging on the door began she woke with a start, trembling all over.

'What is it?' Catherine asked in terror. She was sitting up in bed, clutching the sheets up to her chin.

Sophia shook her head mutely. She knew what it was all right. The Germans had come, searching for the escaped prisoner. But her lips refused to form the words just as her limbs refused to move.

'Wait a minute can't you!' she heard Charles call as the banging came again. 'What is the matter with you? We are all in bed!'

They must be trying to hide the Russian before opening the door, Sophia realised. But where? There was nowhere to conceal even a cat in the cottage — except perhaps Paul's attic. Oh, why had they not allowed him to go there in the first place? What were a few bugs compared to this?

The thought restored the use to her paralysed limbs. Sophia pushed aside the covers and leaped out of bed. Paul's attic door was opened by means of a long pole; she reached for it, inserted it into the handle and turned. Charles was shepherding the Russian up the stairs. As the attic door swung open Sophia hooked down the rope ladder. 'Quick!' she hissed.

The Russian, clumsy in his haste, grabbed the ladder and hauled himself up. When he had pulled the ladder after him Sophia slammed the door and stood the pole back in the corner. It fell with a crash. At the same time Lola was throwing the old blankets onto Catherine's bed.

'Stay there, you two!' she ordered.

The girls did as they were told, sitting white-faced with their dressing gowns hugged around them as they listened to the sounds of the search below. Then to their horror there were heavy footsteps on the stairs and a German, one of the Feldgendarmerie, came into the room.

Catherine sobbed with fear as he dragged the blankets off the beds but Sophia, though shaking inwardly, managed to glare haughtily at him so that a faint colour rose in his cheeks. Sophia thought he would surely notice that those disreputable old bed-clothes did not belong on their faded, but well-laundered beds, but he did not appear to. Perhaps it was going to be all right . . .

And then the prisoner began to cough.

She froze, numb with horror, at the first muffled explosion and the helpless paroxysm which followed. The German's eyes, cold and blue, turned towards the trap door. 'What is there?' he barked.

Lola was chalky white, her eyes dark with fear.

'Is nothing. Is my son's bedroom.'

'And your son — he has very bad cough, yes?'

'Yes.'

'I don't think so! Show me your son, huh?'

Charles and Lola exchanged glances. They were trapped and they knew it. But neither was willing to allow the enemy to see them grovel.

'Bastard! See for yourself! I show you nothing!' Lola cried defiantly, whilst Charles shouted: 'It's nothing to do with her. Nothing to do with any of them but me. *I* am responsible! *Me* — do you hear?'

The German crossed to the window, threw it open and called to his colleagues. Although he spoke in German his meaning was clear enough. 'In here! I think I have found him!' Then he drew his revolver and turned to Charles. 'Open that door now — or I will shoot.'

'Open it yourself!'

Charles was facing the German defiantly and Sophia instinctively reached for Catherine, trying to protect her with her arms. Then she screamed with shock as the attic door was opened from the inside and the Russian, with a strength born of desperation, launched himself out. He landed full on the German, knocking

178

him to the ground. The revolver cracked, the bullet embedding itself harmlessly in the ceiling, and as the two men rolled over and over together the two girls clung to each other in terror. Then three pairs of boots were thundering up the stairs and the German soldier's colleagues burst into the room. In a matter of moments it was all over. The Russian was overpowered and dragged to his feet; whilst two of the Germans held him with his arms behind his back the first one pounded his fist into the Russian's face again and again until his head rolled drunkenly on his neck, blood pouring from his nose and mouth.

'Take him!' the German ordered, then turned to Charles and Lola. 'And you two — get your coats. You are under arrest!'

For a moment Lola glared haughtily at him, her violet eyes cold with hatred. Then she tossed one glossy braid of hair back over her shoulder, lifted her chin and spat scornfully into the German's face. Instantly his hand shot out, slapping her so hard Sophia heard the click of bone and Lola almost fell. Then he drew a handkerchief from his pocket and wiped away the globule of spit.

'Bitch!' he said in English. 'You will pay for that. And since your temper is so hot I think you do not need your coat. Come!'

He pushed Lola out of the room and down the stairs. Sophia and Catherine huddled at the window watching as Charles and Lola were dragged down the path to the waiting transport. Catherine had begun to sob softly, her breath coming in small staccato hiccoughs, and as Charles and Lola were bundled into the transport her body went rigid for a moment, then she began to scream.

'Mama! Mama! Oh no — no!'

Sophia stood, wild-eyed, poised like a bird ready for flight. A pulse was hammering in her throat, adrenalin coursing through her veins so that her whole body throbbed with it. She had to do something — she couldn't just stand here and watch them take her parents!

The door of the transport slammed, the engine roared.

'Mama!' Catherine screamed again and Sophia's arms tightened around her, turning the small stricken tear-wet face into her chest.

'It's all right,' she heard herself say. 'It will be all right.'

179

But already she knew in her heart it would not be all right. And screamed inwardly as Catherine had screamed at the injustice of it and the terrible impotence she felt knowing there was nothing, nothing she could do to save her beloved parents from the fate that awaited them.

As Sophia had feared Charles and Lola were brought before the court, tried and sentenced to deportation. In spite of all their efforts none of the Carteret children were allowed to see them.

The days passed, muddled and unreal. It was, Sophia thought, a little like living in a limbo world, for their emotions were still muffled by shock and an inability to appreciate yet that this terrible thing had really happened. Each morning Sophia woke half-expecting to hear Lola's strident voice filling the little cottage or Charles' tuneless whistle drifting up the stairs to tell her it had all been a terrible dream. Then, as the silence stretched on, cold and empty, the realisation would come to her that it had not been a dream, and with it the sick ache deep inside her would grow and spread, creeping up her throat to form a choking lump. Quickly, before she could be engulfed by it, she would push aside the covers and go downstairs to make breakfast, forcing herself to pass her parents' room without so much as a glance inside, though she could picture all too well its unnatural tidyness — the bed, which she had made after they had been dragged from it so unceremoniously on the morning of their arrest, unslept in, Lola's cosmetic jars neatly stacked along the dressing table with every lid in place, Charles's pipe lying in the ashtray and his old jacket with the patched sleeves hanging behind the door.

It would stay like that until their return, she promised herself, the furniture dusted and polished, everything in its place. And if sometimes the fear crept up on her that they would never return she pushed it quickly aside. She must believe they would come back one day when the war was over — she must. It was the only way to hang on to her sanity. She couldn't allow herself to go to pieces — she had to be strong for the others.

Both Catherine and Paul had taken what had happened very badly. Those first days Catherine could do nothing but cry — Sophia had even heard her sobbing in her sleep — and she could hardly bear to let Sophia out of her sight. Sophia could understand the terrible insecurity and grief that drove her; in many ways Catherine was still very much a child, having always been fussed over and loved as the youngest of the family, but Catherine's constant presence and her tears imposed an even greater strain on her own self-control. As for Paul, Sophia soon found she could not expect the moral support from him which she might have hoped for. He went out a good deal, disappearing for hours on end and often not returning until long after curfew so that Sophia was terrified he too would be caught and questioned by the occupying forces and many a night she stood at the window, peeping between the curtains into the pitch black night, her nerves in tatters as she prayed anxiously for his return. But when he was in the house he might as well not have been there, for he mooched around like a silent ghost, saying nothing if she did not speak to him and snapping her nose off when she did.

He had cried too. Sophia had come down one night and found him sitting at the kitchen table, his head bent on to his folded arms, sobbing bitterly. The sight had deepened her own desolation and filled her with unreasoning resentment. Unfair, she knew — Paul had every right to his emotions — but she felt betrayed by his breakdown. He was her big brother; couldn't she expect to lean on him just a little? She had stood in the doorway for a little while, watching him and not knowing what to do, and when he looked up and saw her she was shocked by his ravaged, tear-stained face.

'Oh Sophia — I'm sorry . . .' He covered his eyes with his hands again and she saw the tension knotting his knuckles. 'I'm so sorry . . .'

'Come on, Paul, pull yourself together,' she said, aware she sounded like an echo of Lola. 'It's awful, I know, but we've just got to carry on. Going to pieces won't help anyone.'

'But I should have been here!' Paul's voice was muffled by his hands. Saliva mingled with tears and ran down his chin.

'What are you talking about?'

'When it happened — I should have been here!'

Sophia sighed. 'That's nonsense and you know it. You being here wouldn't have made the slightest bit of difference. In fact

181

it might have made things worse. They might have arrested you as well.'

Paul did not answer. She was right, he supposed, but it did not make him feel any better. For a moment the terrible, almost unreasoning guilt he was experiencing weighed on him so heavily that he almost told her exactly why it was he felt so terrible about what had happened. But he could not bring himself to. He did not want to see his blame for himself reflected in her eyes.

No, it wouldn't have made any difference, he told himself. That much was true. But he couldn't forget that almost the last words he had spoken to his parents had been lies. Whilst they were being arrested he had been practising a deception on them and also cheating on his brother. For that terrible night when the Russian had come to them for sanctuary Paul had not been spending the night with a friend as he had pretended. He had been spending it with Vivienne Moran.

He had met her one day quite by chance in town and she had come running up to him to ask if he had any news of Nicky. She must have known, of course, that he wouldn't have — contact with anyone outside the island was impossible. But she had asked all the same, because just talking to Paul gave her a vicarious contact with the man she adored and had not seen for what seemed like a lifetime.

Viv had recovered now from the injuries she had received in the bombing. The terrible recurrent headaches which had plagued her in the beginning came less often now and were not so severe and her strong young body had mended well. But although it was now four long years since Nicky's departure and her abortion there was still a yawning emptiness in Viv. In the early days she had nursed it with a fervour that was almost a religion, the pain somehow kept Nicky alive in her heart. Later, as the images began to blur so that Nicky seemed almost like a sad sweet dream, she had returned to her old ways, reaching out greedily for 'life' with the friends who had once seemed so attractive. But the pursuit of pleasure no longer held her in the same thrall, her gaiety was brittle and forced. Viv had glimpsed

182

something much deeper, much stronger, and she yearned for Nicky and what they had shared with all her heart.

At first, when she caught sight of Paul she had thought for a heart-stopping moment that it *was* Nicky. It was not the first time she had thought she had seen him and followed a stranger down the street only to discover, when he turned around that there was no similarity at all. But mostly that had occurred in the early days, when she was still obsessed. Now, the shock was different, just as stomach-lurching, but more understandable, for since she had seen him last Paul had grown up, and at the same time grown disconcertingly like his brother.

Close to, of course, the likeness was less striking. Paul's face was rounder than Nicky's, without the angles and planes that made Nicky so devastatingly attractive, his hair was straighter, falling over his forehead from the parting high on the side of his head, and his eyes were light hazel rather than Nicky's startling violet. But like Nicky he was tall and well-built and the family likeness was apparent enough to make her heart begin to beat faster.

That first day Viv had nothing in mind beyond talking about Nicky. But afterwards she found herself unable to forget Paul. That night she dreamed about him, a muddled, yearning dream and when she woke the aura of it remained with her as if in some strange way the brothers had merged and become one.

Viv made some enquiries and discovered that Paul had left school and was working as a counter clerk at the bank. One night she waylaid him as he was leaving, managing to make it look like a chance meeting. She was fully prepared this time to find herself disappointed by him. She was no fool and she realised in her aching loneliness she was using his substance as a substitute for Nicky. But when she saw him it was just the same. Paul might be three years younger than her, he might not be Nicky, but the wonderful echo of Nicky was there all the same, plucking at the deepest chords of her memories and emotions, bringing a faint elusive taste of that sweet sharp excitement.

They began to meet regularly and before long Viv was obsessed with the need to recreate what she and Nicky had shared. It was no longer enough to be with someone who looked

183

like Nicky, who was Nicky's flesh and blood, she had to go further. The need had become physical, it was a creeping ache which invaded her bones and when she was with Paul she felt as if her flesh was rising up to meet his, every muscle, every nerve, every pore crying out to be touched, to be loved. Sometimes, when their eyes met, she felt her heart flutter so hard she could scarcely breathe.

One evening, when they were walking in the soft dark she could bear it no longer. She caught at his hand, turning in to him and raising her face to his. In that moment she was both eager and afraid — afraid he would turn away, afraid that if he did kiss her the fragile shadow of glorious desire would fade. But Paul caught her arms, holding her against him, and when his mouth came down on hers she could almost have believed for a moment that he was Nicky. The scent of his skin was the same, the hard lines of his body were a dream made flesh. The dark lapping sea tipped up to meet the starless sky and Viv felt she was suspended somewhere between the two.

Such a little encounter — so little — she had to have more! She engineered, she planned, she seduced — and Paul, though he felt a little guilty, was a willing partner. Viv's sexual attraction was intoxicating in itself; somehow the knowledge that she had been his brother's girl gave an added sense of heady power so that he felt he could crush the world in the palm of his hand if he so chose.

Paul had always felt somewhat in Nicky's shadow. Perhaps that is always the fate of the younger brother, continually running to try and keep up with the older sibling, the pace setter. And Nicky had always been such a golden boy, handsome and popular, good at everything he did. He had never shut Paul out, never tried to make him feel inferior, but the very niceness of his nature had compounded Paul's insecurity. He could never be like Nicky, never do so well, never have people like him as much. He had felt clumsy, hopelessly inept, charging through childhood and floundering through puberty.

It was only when Nicky had left that Paul had begun to come into his own. His own rapid growth to manhood had coincided with his elevation to being the only Carteret son in Jersey and for the first time in his life Paul had begun to feel a certain self-

184

confidence. He had experimented with it — and with the power he seemed to have suddenly over the girls he met. They crowded round, making eyes, begging for his favours, making it clear how attractive they found him, and Paul grew in stature with every conquest.

But Vivienne Moran was something else again. She was not in the least like the girls who ran after him. In Paul's eyes she was almost a goddess. He had admired her from afar when Nicky was dating her and she had further enhanced his brother in his eyes. Now he worshipped her. But it had simply never occurred to him that he might have her.

The first time he kissed her he was shaking inside with both terror and fierce longing. Mercifully he thought he had hidden it well — she had not known of his churning emotions. And to his utter amazement she seemed to want to kiss him again — not only kiss him either! In the darkness she would press her body against his until he thought he would go crazy with desire, and even encourage him to slide his hands up under her jumper. Touching the warm firm swell of her breasts Paul could think of nothing but what it would be like to make love to her. And afterwards there was always the thought that he was following in Nicky's footsteps to keep the glow burning brightly.

Soon Paul was totally obsessed with Viv. He thought of her constantly and dreamed of being alone with her — really truly alone. But he did not tell any of the family that he was seeing her. His guilty conscience always stopped him from doing that however much he wanted to boast of their relationship because he knew that his parents, and probably Sophia too, would think that he was cheating on Nicky. And when Viv casually mentioned one evening that her mother was going to be away from home that weekend and suggested Paul might come to stay he certainly did not tell them that. Though he was beside himself with excitement he managed to keep a totally straight face as he made an excuse about staying the night with a friend from the bank and to his relief they seemed to believe him.

Like the Carterets the Morans had been turned out of their home but they had been allowed to stay on in a cottage in the grounds which had been built for a housekeeper or gardener though it had never been used as such, and Loretta and Viv had continued to use their swimming pool and tennis courts, drawing a very fine line between fraternising with the German officers who occupied the house and antagonising them. There were those islanders who branded Loretta Moran a collaborator or even a Jerry Bag, as those women who were over-friendly with the Germans were called, but neither was strictly true. Loretta was a survivor — and still beautiful enough at the age of forty-five to be able to get her own way with men without actually giving anything in return.

She did however have a 'friend' at Rozel — an artist who had been a frequent visitor to the house for the famed pool parties she and Adrian had thrown in the balmy days before the war. Now, separated from her husband by circumstances for three years, the friendship had blossomed and Loretta occasionally spent weekends at Rozel. This weekend was one of them.

By the time he arrived at Viv's home Paul was tight-strung with nervous anticipation. He knew very well what was going to happen and he was madly excited by the prospect of it but equally he was terrified that something would go wrong and he would disappoint Viv. In his pocket his perspiration-damp fingers curled around a precious packet of 'French letters' he had managed to track down – quite a feat in itself since the shortages did not stop with fuel, food and clothes. Though buying them had been horribly embarrassing the knowledge that the packet was there in his pocket made him feel manly and his confidence rose. At least Viv couldn't accuse him of being careless! And if things didn't work out as he hoped, if he had misread her intentions, then she need never know he had them.

Paul had never been to Viv's home before and he was much impressed — and almost suffered another crisis of confidence! — when he saw the vast grounds which had been kept in trim by the Germans. Their own garden would have fitted into just a corner! But the cottage Viv and her mother had been allowed to live in was delightful — a small house in its own right, with bay windows and a log fire.

'How do you manage to get the fuel?' he asked Viv, thinking of the sawdust and chippings his family were reduced to burning.

'Oh, the Jerry officers get it for us,' she replied airily. 'They feel they owe it to us because they are living in our house, I suppose.'

She was looking especially beautiful tonight in a creamy sweater and wide legged pyjama style trousers in tobacco brown. Unlike most of the islanders the privations of the war seemed to have passed her by — another point which made people glance knowingly at one another as she passed. But again the suspicion was totally unfounded. Viv was almost exactly the same size as her mother and Loretta's extensive wardrobe would easily have kept both of them well dressed for a dozen years.

'I've made supper,' Viv said. 'But perhaps I should warn you I'm not much of a cook.'

There was a little tremor in her voice and suddenly Paul found himself wondering if she was nervous too. He found it hard to believe but one never knew. After all, he was a nervous jelly inside and he was managing to cover it up. But Viv . . . it was impossible to see her as anything but totally self-confident.

He followed her into the kitchen, though eating was the last thing on his mind. A pan was simmering on the stove; Viv lifted the lid and prodded at the vegetables inside with a fork.

'Why do turnips take so long to cook?' she asked, and again the edge of nervous tension was there in her voice. 'The potatoes are done — look!' As if on cue a potato split apart and disintegrated into a gooey mess. 'Oh God!' she moaned. 'What a disaster! I told you I'm no good in the kitchen.'

'I think you're wonderful anywhere,' Paul said, amazed at his own daring.

'Oh Paul.' Her green eyes were sharp and bright suddenly, her face embued with softness. Paul felt his stomach churn.

'Come here,' he said roughly.

She came, still holding the fork. He took it from her, putting it down on the table, and pulled her into his arms, kissing her. He felt the pressure of her body against his, the yielding eagerness of her lips, and began to forget his nervousness in an all-consuming rush of desire.

God, but she was beautiful, and he wanted her so much! As her body moulded to his he slid his hands beneath the creamy cashmere of her sweater and realised with another thrill of excitement that she was not wearing a brassiere tonight. So many

187

girls seemed to encase themselves in acres of rigid elastic and rubber but Viv was wearing nothing but a silky camisole. He massaged her breasts, feeling the nipples, which were already hard and erect, rise even more beneath the touch of his fingers. She moaned, arching her back and pressing her thighs against his and he slid his hand inside her loosely cut trousers. For a moment he was puzzled; the cami top was longer than he had expected, covering her stomach and buttocks and meeting between her legs in a loose fold of silk but he was relieved to find there was still no restrictive corsetry.

Carefully, his heart beating so hard with the fear that she might still stop him that he could scarcely breathe, he slipped his fingers beneath the silk, inching across her smooth skin until they encountered the soft bush of pubic hair and the firm but yielding mound beneath. He probed gently into the moist folds and the excitement of it made his own body throb unbearably. Then, just when he thought he might climax there and then she eased away from him. Her cheeks were flushed now, her eyes still very bright. He tried to pull her back into his arms but she took him by the hand, leading him into the small cosy living room. There she took the cushions from the sofa and chairs, tossing them down in front of the fire. He tried to grab her and pull her down but she wriggled free, crossing her arms and lifting the sweater over her head. He gasped aloud as he saw her breasts for the first time, full and creamy in the flickering firelight, with the dark aureoles and thrusting nipples. He did not think he had ever seen anything so beautiful in his life.

She slipped out of her trousers, letting them and the silk cami fall to the floor, and stood there before him totally nude. Paul stood mesmerised, taking in every curve of her body, desire held for the moment in abeyance by sheer wonder. She reached for him, unbuttoning his shirt and sliding her hands inside. As her nails scratched lightly against his skin he buried his head in her breasts, kissing and sucking, scarcely aware that she was continuing to undress him until he too was naked.

Momentarily fear leaped in him again — fear of going too fast and grasping too greedily at this paradise within his reach, fear that he might hurt her, and the nagging realisation that somehow he must get out the French letters and put one on without either appearing foolish or spoiling the mood. In that instant he was once again the fumbling younger brother without Nicky's experience or expertise. Then she released him, lying down on the cushions before the fire, and holding out her arms to him, and his rush of sudden urgent desire made it all easy. Nicky faded into the shadows, there was only Viv and his own insistent need.

All too quickly it was over. Even before the after-shocks had subsided he knew that in the end he *had* rushed it — he had simply not been able to hold back. Beneath him Viv still writhed and moaned and he continued to move in her though he knew his erection had faded, praying it would be over for her soon too while the French letter was still in place. With inspiration born of desperation he withdrew, working in her instead with his finger, and felt her body arch, felt the deep spasms begin. He was sweating, perspiration pouring down his face, but his excitement had transmuted from the throes of his own demanding need to the triumphant mastery that came from knowing he was giving her pleasure. As she reached her climax, her nails raking his back, one leg fastened around the hard muscle of his thigh, she cried out, an unintelligible strangled sound. He felt her begin to relax and rolled away, clutching at the French letter. Suddenly it seemed terribly important not to make a mess on the light-coloured carpet though a few moments ago the thought would not have so much as occurred to him.

'Where is the bathroom?' he asked, feeling clumsy and anxious again, as if the glories of the last minutes had never been.

She told him. Her voice was still thick with what he imagined was passion. He reached for his shirt, taking it with him. For some reason he was embarrassed now by his nakedness and he put it on in the bathroom before returning.

Viv was lying where he had left her, her lovely body still illuminated by the firelight. He knelt down beside her, leaning over to kiss her, but she turned her face away.

'Viv?' he said tentatively. And saw the tears glistening wetly on her cheeks.

Tenderness filled him then and the strength came flooding back.

'It's all right,' he said, stroking her hair away from her face. 'It was all right, honestly. It didn't come off.'

She did not answer, just gulped deep in her throat. Another thought occurred to him.

'I didn't hurt you, did I?'

Still no answer. Just that stillness, the tears, and an occasional long shiver running through her body.

'You'd better get dressed,' he said. 'You'll get cold.'

Somehow his words seemed to release her frozen control. The tears burst in her throat and she rocked from side to side, sobbing.

'Viv!' he said, frightened. 'What is it? What's the matter?'

At first he could not make out her words. They were nothing but a low whisper, lost in her tears.

'How could I? How could I do it? Oh God, forgive me!'

'Viv, don't!' he begged. 'We wanted it, didn't we, both of us? And you enjoyed it. Viv . . .'

She sat up suddenly, her eyes blazing through her tears.

'You don't understand, do you? You don't understand what I did.'

'You made love to me. Is that so wrong?'

'Yes. Yes!'

'But why?' He was bewildered, hurt. 'Why was it wrong?'

'Oh Paul!' She buried her face in her hands. 'You just don't understand, do you?'

'Understand what?'

'It wasn't you I was making love to. It was Nicky.'

He went cold. He felt suddenly as if the ground had opened up beneath him and he was falling, falling, into a pit so deep, so dark, that he would never be able to get out of it again.

'Don't you see?' Viv was sobbing. 'I thought I could have it again, the way it was with him. I've betrayed you both. Oh Paul, I'm so sorry — don't look like that, please!'

'I thought you wanted me,' he said woodenly.

'I did. I did! Only . . . oh, it was all mixed up in my mind. You and Nicky — you're so much like him.'

'You mean you didn't want me at all,' Paul said in that same flat voice.

She looked up at him through her tears. 'No, that's not true. I *did* want you . . . I think. Only . . .'

'When it came to it I'm not Nicky.' His pain was intense. He

190

wanted to hit out, to hurt Viv as she had hurt him. But somehow he couldn't do it, even now. He loved her too much.

'No, you're not Nicky,' she said in a small wry voice.

'So what did he do that I didn't? How did I fail?' He was turning the hurt and anger in on himself instead of venting it on Viv.

'You didn't fail, Paul. It's not your fault . . .' She had stopped crying now and was looking at him sadly.

'Don't try to make it right, Viv. Don't spare my feelings. I know compared with him I must seem like a blundering . . .'

'At least you didn't make me pregnant,' she said. 'At least, I hope you didn't.'

It took a moment for her words to sink in through the haze of misery and self-condemnation. He stared at her, open-mouthed, and she laughed suddenly, a small, harsh tearing sound.

'Oh dear. I didn't mean to say that. Well, the cat's out of the bag now, isn't it?'

'Nicky . . . made you pregnant?' He was fumbling for the words. They seemed to elude him. 'When? How?'

'I should think the how was pretty obvious.' The old, wry Viv was emerging. 'As to the when, just before he went away.'

'Did he know?'

She shook her head. 'No, I told you. It was just before he went away.'

'So — what happened? If you were . . . what happened to the baby?'

'I had an abortion. Oh, don't look at me like that, Paul, there really wasn't any choice, was there? I'm not proud of what I did but there it is.'

'But I thought abortion was illegal.'

'It is. But money will buy you most things, you know. And they didn't call it abortion. They called it appendicitis, or grumbling appendix, or something. Look, I really don't want to talk about it. I shouldn't have told you. It doesn't seem right when Nicky doesn't know.'

Paul brought his fist down hard on the floor. 'Nicky — Nicky — Nicky! Nicky's not here — I am!'

'I know. And I said I'm sorry.' She got up, matter-of-fact

suddenly. 'Look, I've got to see what's happening to the stew. And I'll put the boiler on so we can have a bath.'

She went out to the kitchen. Paul finished dressing in a state of shock. He felt as if he had been bludgeoned with a ten-ton hammer. He had had such hopes of this weekend and it had all gone dreadfully wrong. And not only on a personal level either. Two of his icons had been torn down — the brother he hero-worshipped had gone off leaving his girl pregnant, his goddess had had an abortion. Paul felt sick to his stomach. He did not know how he was going to stay here now. It crossed his mind that perhaps he might go home. It was after curfew but he didn't mind running a few risks if it meant he could get some fresh air into his lungs and then shut himself away in his attic room where he could at least be alone with his thoughts. But he knew there would be questions to be answered if he did that. Charles and Lola would be bound to be suspicious if he suddenly turned up at the door.

Afterwards Paul was to wish with all his heart that he had followed his instincts that night and gone home. He couldn't have saved Lola and Charles, but at least he would have been there. Instead he had stayed with Viv though the atmosphere between them was strained and awkward. They bathed, one after the other, in the big cast iron bath that had been installed in one of the bedrooms, they ate as much as they could of the unappetising stew, and they slept one in each of the twin beds in Viv's room without so much as a goodnight kiss. Next day Paul went home, the misery still like a lead weight inside him, to find that his parents had been arrested and the guilt came rushing in, swamping him, drowning him. He felt as if he personally had condemned them by his deceit and at the same time condemned himself.

On the day that Charles and Lola were sentenced to deportation to a concentration camp in Germany, Paul demolished the entire bottle of brandy that the Russian prisoner had had just one sip of; it did nothing to make him feel better but at least for a time it gave him blessed oblivion. When he had recovered from his hangover he drank the bottle of whisky. And when there was none left he mooched around in morose silence feeling utterly, totally trapped.

When the idea first came to him he rejected it but it kept returning to haunt him and each time he thought about it, it seemed a little more possible and desirable. Jersey had become an island prison where he was trapped with his guilt and his misery; even being within a few square miles of Viv was torture to him now. Paul thought of his father's little boat which had managed the voyage to Dunkirk and knew it could provide him with an escape. If he could get away, if he could get to England, at least he would be able to join the forces and do something positive to help the war effort. It would be better than sitting out the war here, helpless and impotent, and it might do something to ease the terrible weight of guilt and make him feel a little easier with himself.

One dark moonless night Paul crept out of the cottage whilst his sisters were asleep and made for the boathouse. The thought of the voyage held no terrors for him; he had been brought up with the sea in his blood, and he did not allow himself to think of what might happen to him if he was caught trying to escape. Besides, he told himself, it would be poetic justice if he too faced deportation or even a firing squad.

But he was not caught. By the time Sophia got up next morning and found the brief note explaining what he had done, Paul was well away from Jersey and heading for England. And for the first time since that terrible day when he had left Viv and returned to find his parents had been arrested, Paul experienced a measure of peace.

When Bernard heard that Paul had escaped from Jersey he was incensed. Under normal circumstances, he supposed, he would have applauded the courage it must have taken, but these were not normal circumstances. It was only a matter of weeks since Lola and Charles had been deported. Now Sophia and Catherine were quite alone.

Since the August night when he had taken her to the theatre Bernard and Sophia had seen a good deal of one another. They went for walks, they went to the cinema, where the films were mostly German with English sub-titles, they even attended dances in the Forum's Golden Lounge, and if the romantic side of their relationship had not progressed as fast as Bernard might have hoped, he told himself he must be patient. The last thing he wanted to do was rush things and frighten her off. At least as it was he saw her two or three times a week and she seemed to enjoy his company. As long as he could sustain the relationship there was always the chance that friendship would deepen to love. She might even love him now, he thought in moments of optimism, and be too shy to let her feelings show. Yes, that must be it, otherwise why would she continue seeing him to the exclusion of any other boyfriends? But still he trod carefully because his fear of losing her was so acute. He couldn't bear it, he thought, if she should tell him she did not want to see him again. Without Sophia life would simply not be worth living.

Bernard had done his best to be supportive through the terrible days that followed Lola and Charles's arrest and deportation though he had wondered just how much help he had been. There was really nothing anyone could do or say to make it any less dreadful, and sometimes he had the feeling that she wanted nothing more than to be left alone. Just so long as she knew he was there and that he cared, that was really the extent of what he could do. Anything else seemed like an intrusion on the family grief.

On the morning that Paul sailed away from Jersey however Bernard felt he could stand on the sidelines no longer. Paul's departure changed everything.

The news was relayed to him by a roundabout source — someone from the Electricity Company had been to the bank and the whole place had been alive with it — Jersey had a brand new hero and everyone wanted to talk about him. Bernard, however, was shocked and indignant to think Paul could behave so irresponsibly towards his sisters. He informed his immediate superior that he was going out for an hour whether he was given permission or not and went round to the dentist's surgery to see Sophia. She was not there – she had taken the day off, the senior receptionist told Bernard. He got back on to his bicycle and pedalled over to St Peter only to find no one in there either.

Bernard walked right round the cottage looking in through the windows and feeling utterly helpless. Sophia would be in a terrible state, he guessed, being left all alone with Catherine, and she would not know which way to turn. Besides this she must be very worried — the fact that Paul had managed to sail out of Jersey in a little boat without being caught did not necessarily mean he had got very far. He could have been apprehended by a patrol and shot, or he could have run into bad weather — at this time of year the Channel could be very treacherous. And who was to say that he had not been bombed or machine gunned from the air or blasted back out to sea from the land when he arrived unannounced in England? Any number of things could have happened to him and Sophia, who was no fool, must be aware of that and be going out of her mind with worry.

Bernard returned to the front of the cottage, looking up at the upstairs windows and wondering what to do. Should he go looking for Sophia? But he had no idea where she might be.

As he stood there, pacing anxiously, a figure on a bicycle turned the corner, wobbling slightly on the uneven track, and dismounted at the gate.

'Hello, Bernard. What are you doing here?' asked Sophia.

Unaccountably Bernard felt slightly annoyed.

'Where have you been?' he asked. 'I've been worried about you.'

'Whatever for? I've been to the shops to get our rations, that's all. And I wasn't expecting you, was I? Shouldn't you be at work?'

'Yes, actually I should,' Bernard said, even more annoyed by what appeared to be her perfect composure. 'I took some time off because I thought you'd be in a state. It seems I was wrong.'

'Oh Bernard!' Sophia looked contrite. 'I'm sorry if I've let you down somehow. Come in and I'll put the kettle on. I've just been lucky enough to get hold of a quarter of real tea. I think Mrs Phillips at the shop felt sorry for me.'

Bernard followed her into the pokey kitchen.

'Where is Catherine?'

'At school. Oh, for heaven's sake don't look like that, Bernard. What did you expect, that we'd go to pieces just because Paul has gone off and left us? I assure you, if that had been going to happen it would have been when Mama and Papa were deported. At least Paul has gone of his own free will.'

There was a hard little note in her voice; Bernard looked at her, puzzled. This wasn't his Sophia, this strangely self-possessed young woman, getting on with running her life in the midst of terrifying adversity. It just wasn't *like* her.

She moved about the kitchen, putting away the groceries she had brought home in her bicycle basket, and boiling the kettle.

'Did you know Paul was going?' Bernard asked.

She shook her head. 'No. It was a complete shock to me, but I suppose I am getting used to shocks. I should be — I've had enough of them.'

'So . . . what will you do?'

'What do you mean, what will I do?'

'Now you're all by yourself . . .'

She laughed shortly. 'What would you expect me to do? Carry on working, I suppose, and look after myself and Catherine.'

Bernard swallowed at a lump in his throat. 'You *do* have a choice.'

She looked up at him, the kettle in her hand. 'Such as?'

'You could marry me.'

He could feel the sweat on the palms of his hands; he could scarcely believe he had actually said it. He had wanted to ask her for weeks, dreamed of it, planned for it, but been afraid to take the bull by the horns.

Now with Paul gone too he wanted nothing more than to take care of her, and the intensity of his longing somehow totally obscured all fear of rejection. Surely she wouldn't turn him down now? She had no one else; she needed him. Even the hard little note in her voice and the cold distance in her eyes did not put him off. It was a cover-up, he thought, a defence against all that had happened to her. Bernard's heart contracted with love. God alone knew what the future held for any of them. But at least he could look after Sophia and Catherine to the best of his ability. Somehow he would make certain they were all right.

Sophia was looking at him with an almost puzzled expression.

'Marry you?'

'Yes. Oh — I know we haven't been going out together very long, but I do love you, Sophia, very much, and I can't bear to think of you stuck out here all alone, responsible for Catherine, whilst the Germans . . . I could make you happy, Sophia, I'm

196

sure . . . as happy as you could ever be with all this hanging over you.'

'No,' she said, almost inaudibly. Unexpectedly the tears had come; they were filling her eyes now and running down her cheeks. She set down the kettle and raised both hands to wipe them away with her fingers, but still they were there, choking her voice and making her whole body shake. 'Bernard, it's so good of you — I don't deserve you, really I don't. But I can't marry you, not like this. It wouldn't be fair.'

'Not fair? Who wouldn't it be fair on — me? Sophia, I don't care about fair. Don't you understand — I love you and I want to take care of you. That's really all that matters to me.'

'No, no — it's not. You deserve better than I could give you. I'm all wrung out, like a rag. I have no emotions left — nothing. It's sweet of you to ask, but I'll be all right, really.'

Bernard was beginning to feel sick. It was all going wrong.

'Sophia . . .'

'Please, Bernard, don't press me. I appreciate your offer but I don't want it. Not now.'

He turned for the door. 'All right. I can see I'd better go.'

'No — please, don't go. I don't want you to feel . . . Oh God, I don't know what I mean. I'd be really sorry, Bernard, if you didn't come to see me again. I'd miss you. But I can't marry you. Not just now. Oh, please, you must understand . . .'

The tears were flowing freely now and somehow without knowing how it had happened they were in each other's arms, Bernard holding her close while she sobbed. Inexplicably it made him feel better. Tears he could understand. They were far more human than that strange hard calm. By the time she had cried herself out he was even feeling quite hopeful. She had turned him down now but she hadn't wanted him to go. Perhaps when she had come through this terrible emotional trough she would reconsider.

Sophia brewed the tea and they drank it, determined to make the most of the treat of 'real tea'.

'Well, perhaps I'd better get back to work,' Bernard said at last, standing up. 'Shall I come back this evening?' She nodded and he pulled her briefly into his arms; there was no awkwardness now as he kissed her.

'Look, love, I shan't mention it again, but don't forget if at any time you change your mind . . . well, the offer will always be open.'

Sophia nodded again. 'Thank you, Bernard. I don't deserve it but . . . I won't forget.'

When he had gone she put her head down into her hands and sobbed again as if her heart would break.

Chapter fourteen
Jersey, 1944

'Do you think it would be all right for Sylvie to come over tonight and listen to our wireless?' Catherine asked one day when she came home from school.

It was June 1944 and the island was seething with barely contained excitement for word was that an invasion of France by the Allies was imminent.

Since Lola and Charles had been arrested Sophia had been half afraid to risk listening to the crystal set, which was still hidden under the floorboards, but during the last week her anxiety for news had overcome her caution. Tuning in to the disembodied voices that crackled over the air waves had become the highlight of the day and she and Catherine took turns at keeping look-out whilst the other crouched over the radio wearing the earphones that had once been part of a telephone handset. But Sophia was all too aware of the risk they were taking. Being in possession of a radio was a serious offence that warranted heavy punishment and Sophia was afraid that if they were caught she and Catherine might even be dragged off for deportation as their parents had been. She had never so much as mentioned the existence of the 'cat's whisker', as they called it, to anyone with the exception of Bernard, much less invited friends or neighbours to listen in with them as so many islanders did.

'No, you certainly can't ask Sylvie!' she snapped now.

'But she's my very best friend and her brother is away fighting too. She would really like to know what is going on . . .'

Sophia looked at Catherine with suspicion. 'You haven't told Sylvie about our "cat's whisker" have you?' she accused.

Catherine coloured slightly. 'She wouldn't split on us. She wouldn't, Sophia, honestly . . .'

'Catherine!' Sophia exploded furiously. 'You *have* told her,

199

haven't you? How could you be so stupid! Well, I shall just have to get rid of it now. Oh Catherine, I could kill you!'

Catherine glared defiantly at her sister, wondering what had happened to the old Sophia. She was so different these days, cold and hard and very prone to flashes of temper not unlike the ones Lola had. But with Lola they had always been soon over, the memory of them eclipsed by a hug or some other gesture of loving reassurance. Catherine's throat ached with tears as she thought of it and she was overcome with longing to feel her mother's arms around her, holding her close, and to hear her murmuring that everything would be all right soon, as she had done when Catherine was a little girl.

'I can't believe you would do something like this, not after all we've been through,' Sophia went on angrily. 'What were you thinking of?'

Catherine swallowed at the knot of tears.

'I told you — Sylvie's my friend. I have to have friends — I'm not like you. And anyway, I trust her.'

'You can't trust anyone. Surely you know that?'

'That's a terrible thing to say! But it's just like you — like you are now, anyway. Well, I won't be like it — I won't! I couldn't bear it if I thought my friends could tell on me – '

'Oh Catherine, don't you understand?' Sophia was suddenly more sad than angry. 'I'm not saying Sylvie would betray you. I don't think for one moment she would, not knowingly. But one careless word is all it would take. If she tells just one more person, her mother, even, and that person tells someone else, before you know it it's common knowledge the Carterets have a "cat's whisker".'

Catherine looked a little crestfallen, but she remained defiant.

'So? Who would tell the Germans anyway? Everyone hates them.'

Sophia sighed. She did not want to tell her sister what she knew to be true — that there were all too many islanders who would be willing to inform either in the hope of gain or, worse still, out of jealousy or spite. It was not a nice thought and Sophia shrank from destroying Catherine's innocent trust in those around her, but it had to be done. Catherine must be made to realise how vulnerable they were, two girls living alone.

200

Still, the damage, if damage there was, was done now. There was no point in going on about it. 'Look — just remember, don't ever tell anyone else,' she said wearily. 'With any luck the war will be over soon and we will be able to get back to normal. But until we do, please, please don't chatter to your friends or anybody else about things like our radio.'

Catherine nodded. She didn't want to be bad friends with Sophia. Goodness knows she was all the family she had left.

'I'm sorry, Sophia, I didn't think. But . . . we don't really have to get rid of the wireless do we? I'm quite sure Sylvie won't breathe a word.'

Sophia grimaced, looking at her watch. The radio was so precious – their one link with the outside world.

'Well, all right, perhaps not tonight at any rate,' she agreed.

The Allied landings began that night, wave after wave of planes passing over Jersey on their way to the French coast, and the quiet of the night was torn apart by gunfire. For a while the two girls stood at the window watching, then when things quietened down for a while they went back to bed, but they were quite unable to sleep for excitement.

At last! Sophia kept thinking. Surely now it would soon be all over! But the war had gone on for so long now that normality seemed like a distant dream.

Will it be too late for me to go to Music College? she wondered — and then almost hated herself for thinking about something so petty while men were fighting and dying and her own parents were still in captivity. Yet no feeling of guilt could reduce the importance to her of her lost dreams for her future. A whole slice of her youth had been stolen from her. Suddenly Sophia wanted only to weep, as Catherine had earlier, without really knowing why.

Motor vehicles went racing by on the road outside, voices yelled to one another in German, and after a while the guns began again. Sophia whispered a prayer to a God she had almost forgotten how to believe in, pulled the sheets up over her head and once more, vainly, tried to sleep.

Throughout the summer months the Allies continued their

advance through France, liberating towns and villages that had been ground under the heel of the jackboot for four long years. But in Jersey things seemed to be getting worse instead of better. Hitler, determined not to give up the one little piece of the United Kingdom that he had been able to occupy, brought in even more troops and as wounded Germans were evacuated from France too there were many more mouths to feed and less to feed them on. As the French channel ports fell one by one the line of supplies was broken. Food could no longer come in from the outside world and Jersey must exist on what she could produce herself.

Sophia, struggling to feed herself and Catherine, cursed Hitler's intransigence. Didn't he know he would have to give in in the end — might it not just as well be now? But of course it wasn't *him* who was eating only husk-filled bread and being glad of it, it wasn't *him* drinking tea made from blackberry leaves and having to do without medicines and soap, it wasn't *him* who had been forced to do without every little luxury that makes life worth living for four long years and now was having to go hungry as well. And Churchill was as bad. He was determined to starve the enemy out and if it meant starving the islanders as well — so be it.

Inevitably tempers became frayed and on occasions it was not only the German occupying force that indulged in physical violence.

One afternoon in September Catherine came home from school with a long scratch mark on her cheek and a tear in her admittedly thin-as-a-bee's-wing blouse. She changed out of the blouse before Sophia arrived home from work, but try as she might she could not conceal the scratch and Sophia noticed it almost at once.

'What on earth have you been doing, Catherine?'

Catherine coloured slightly. 'Oh, it's nothing really. Just that little cat Jeanne Pinel.'

'You mean she did it deliberately? But why?' Sophia demanded.

Catherine's colour deepened. 'She thinks I've stolen her boyfriend.'

'And have you?'

'Of course not! At least, I haven't stolen him — he didn't belong to her in the first place.'

Sophia's mouth twitched. She had wondered how long it would be before Catherine began taking an interest in boys. 'Who is it then?' she asked.

'Wallace Patterson. I've liked him for ages and I *thought* he liked me, but I was afraid to hope. Then last night he was waiting for me after school. He asked me if I wanted some of his nuts and we were sharing them when Jeanne came along. She didn't say a word then but at lunchtime today she just *went* for me.'

'And what did you do?'

'Oh, not a lot. I was too surprised. But I did pull her hair — you know she's got those plaits so it was quite easy. We got hauled up before the Headmistress and she was furious when she heard there was a boy involved. She said we'd come to no good, either of us, and she kept us in for half an hour after school. But when we came out Wallace was outside, waiting. And he walked *me* home!' Catherine giggled triumphantly.

'For heaven's sake!' Sophia said sternly, but as she dished up the thin soup that was all she had been able to rustle up for supper tonight she was smiling. Her little sister was learning fast!

The following evening the girls had just finished supper when there was a loud knock at the door. They glanced at one another, fear naked in their eyes. Friends always came around to the rear of the cottage, tapping lightly and calling a greeting. But this heavy pounding was reminiscent of the morning when they had been awakened by German soldiers searching for the escaped prisoner. Sophia got up.

'Stay here,' she instructed Catherine. 'I'll see who it is.'

Her heart was beating fast as she opened the door. Outside, as she had expected, stood an officer of the Feldgendarmerie and drawn up at the gate was one of the cars they had commandeered. Sophia could see several more Germans sitting inside it.

'Yes?' she said, trying to sound cool. 'What do you want?'

The officer clicked his heels. 'We wish to make a search of your home. It has come to our notice that you have a wireless set. I am sure you are aware that is not permitted.'

For a moment Sophia thought she was going to faint. Then as suddenly, she was in control of herself once more.

203

'How dare you!' she flared. 'Who told you a lie like that?'

The German's eyes were very cold, very blue. 'I am sure you know I cannot divulge our sources. But if you do not have a wireless set then you have nothing to fear. Now, are you going to let us come in or do we have to enter uninvited?'

Sophia's mind was racing. Would they find the wireless if they searched? It was hidden, yes, but how well? The Germans must know every likely hiding place by now. And was there anything else in the house that could get them into trouble? She didn't think so, but how could one be sure? Still, she really had no choice but to bluff things out.

'All right, you'd better come in,' she said. 'You won't find anything though.'

She led the way into the kitchen where Catherine had begun washing the supper dishes. Her sister glanced up, her eyes dark with fear, and Sophia touched her arm reassuringly.

The first officer was already in the kitchen, the reinforcements marching down the path. Sophia drew herself up, determined not to let them see how afraid she was.

And then her heart seemed to stop beating. That soldier of the Feldgendarmerie, his good-looking face shockingly familiar beneath his helmet . . . it couldn't be . . . surely it *couldn't* be . . . Dieter!

But it was. Dieter had recognised her too — she knew it though his face was totally impassive, determinedly wooden. Nerves spasmed in her throat and she almost cried out his name. But his eyes seemed to be warning her: Say nothing. She glanced swiftly over her shoulder at Catherine but there was no trace of recognition on her sister's face. Perhaps Catherine had been too young to remember him clearly, and in any case, one face under a Feldgendarmerie helmet was very like another.

Unless it happened to be a face you had loved with all your heart, a face that still crept into your dreams . . . Sophia closed her eyes for a moment, trying to regain control of herself.

The soldiers fanned out and began their search. One partially disappeared up the big old chimney, another tipped the macaroni she had been saving for a pudding out of its jar on to the bare table top. Dieter, rifling through the balls of wool she had painstakingly unpicked to make a new jumper, glanced up at her and as their eyes met again, her stomach fell away. Fear, she thought. It couldn't be anything else . . . could it? But even as she formulated the thought and her own quick denial she knew it was not true. The war had not changed the way she felt about Dieter. Nothing ever would. The insistent flickering flame that was running through her now like the long slow fuse of some explosive device would ignite the self-same volcano of desire, given half a chance, as it had done in the balmy days of peace when Dieter had been a waiter and she had been no more than an innocent child.

I love him, she thought. God help me, in spite of everything I still love him.

The officer was barking commands at his men in German; because of the lessons that had been forced upon them at school she could understand what he said. Like most Jersey children she had felt it was patriotic to make a poor showing at the lessons but with her natural ear for languages a certain amount had stuck. Now, with a pang of fear, she heard the officer issue his instructions. 'Upstairs! And don't forget to look under the floorboards!'

Dieter moved towards the stairs and Sophia stood quite still, sick with terror, as she heard the thuds and creaks as drawers were thrown open and furniture pushed about. A tapping sound almost immediately above her head told her he was testing for loose floorboards. He would find the hiding place — he was bound to. A moment later she heard the familiar squeak that she normally heard every evening when she lifted the board to take out the wireless and listen to the world news and she froze, almost afraid to breathe. What would Dieter do? She waited for his shout of triumph, almost fainting with the strain of it. But instead she heard a squeak as the board was replaced, and further sounds of a search. The moments ticked by and at last Dieter reappeared.

'Did you find anything?' the officer asked.

'Nothing. There's nothing up there.'

His face was totally expressionless. Only when his eyes, narrowed and somehow full of knowledge, flicked over her, was she sure. Dieter hadn't been careless, he hadn't been blind. He had found the wireless set but he was not going to give her away.

205

Joy rushed through her like a bush fire, a joy that owed even more to knowing that he must still care something for her than to her overwhelming relief, then, close on its heels, a new fear, not for herself and Catherine, but for Dieter.

Suppose the officer wasn't satisfied? Suppose he ordered another search and one of the others rechecked the space beneath the loose floorboard? Dieter would be in even more serious trouble than they would be; with conditions deteriorating daily she felt sure the time when they could expect anything approaching normal decent human behaviour from their captors was over. Hungry, beaten and cornered they would turn on the islanders and on one another.

One of the soldiers was emptying her potato sack; she tore her eyes from Dieter's and snapped at the man angrily: 'What do you think you are doing? Don't let them roll about the floor! They are very precious to us if not to you!'

'All right, put them back,' the officer ordered. 'There's nothing here. It would seem we received a false report. Think yourselves lucky — this time anyway.'

Sophia did not dare to so much as glance at Dieter. She stood quite still, fingers laced tightly together to control her trembling. Only when the big old motor roared throatily away down the lane did she relax and when she did so her legs finally gave way and she sank to the floor, hands pressed to her face, breath coming in ragged sobs.

'They didn't find it!' Catherine shouted jubilantly. 'They didn't find it, Sophia!'

It was a long time before Sophia could trust herself to speak and when she did it was through teeth that chattered. 'Oh yes they did.'

'They did! Then why . . . ?'

'It was Dieter,' she whispered. 'Didn't you recognise him? It was Dieter. He found the radio. And he didn't give us away.'

Bernard heard of the Germans' visit to the Carteret cottage from one of his colleagues who had driven past and seen the patrol car parked outside. Beside himself with anxiety, since he was one of the few people who knew of the existence of Sophia's crystal set, he gobbled his tea, much to the disgust of his mother who had spent the best part of a day trying to put together a satisfying meal, got out his bicycle and rode over to St Peter.

Since the day he had asked her to marry him, the relationship between Sophia and Bernard had changed subtly. There was an understanding between them and a warmth; sometimes Sophia would sit in the circle of his arm and respond to his kisses with an almost desperate hunger, though that was as far as their physical union went. At other times there was an awkwardness which showed itself in small strained silences or outright coldness. They no longer went out together, for Sophia refused to leave Catherine alone, and Bernard had to be content with the shared evenings in the small cramped kitchen with Catherine never further away than her own room upstairs.

But it was not only circumstances that had changed, Bernard realised. Sophia had changed too. She was harder, more brittle, and she seemed to have lost her capacity for fun. Often he felt he did not know her at all. But he still loved her and liked to think he was of some support to her whether she showed her appreciation or not.

When he arrived at the house that evening, a little out of breath from having ridden too hard, Bernard was almost afraid of what he might find. But to his relief Sophia was in the kitchen, composed, if a little pale and drawn, and Catherine seemed almost beside herself with excitement.

'Bernard!' she squealed when she saw him. 'You'll never guess what! The Germans came, searching for our cat's whisker!'

Bernard felt the pit of his stomach drop away. 'They didn't find it?'

'Well yes, they did, but . . .'

'Catherine!' Sophia said sharply. 'Can't you ever stop babbling? I should have thought you'd have learned your lesson by now.'

'But it's only Bernard . . .'

'I know it's Bernard — and I know what you're going to say. Please don't!' Sophia ordered fiercely.

Bernard looked from one to the other of them, puzzled and disturbed.

'What happened, then?'

'They searched but must have missed it,' Sophia told him.

'Under the floorboards is obviously a good place. Though I don't know whether I ought to risk leaving it there any longer. They might come back.'

'You want me to get rid of it for you?' Bernard asked. He still could not understand Sophia's outburst but equally he felt this was not the moment to probe.

Sophia's eyes had gone far away. For a moment it seemed doubtful she had even heard him.

'Sophia?' He repeated the offer and she shook her head decisively.

'Oh no, no. You mustn't take a chance like that, Bernard. When it's dark I'll put it in a biscuit tin and bury it in the garden. There's nowhere in the house that's safe. They looked everywhere.'

Again the inconsistency struck him.

There was something here he did not understand, something that made him feel both hurt and angry without knowing why, but instinct was warning him not to question too deeply.

But at least Sophia was safe. Really, to Bernard, nothing else in the world really mattered.

Chapter fifteen

Two nights later Sophia was in the garden taking in the washing when she became aware she was being watched. She spun around, on the point of screaming because her nerves were still in tatters, to see Dieter standing there.

She knew it was him though she could not see his face, would have known him anywhere even though the uniform of the Feld-gendarmerie made him almost anonymous, and her heart seemed almost to stop beating. Somehow, deep down, she had known he would come though she had told herself not to be foolish, that he was a member of the occupying forces now, light years removed from the gentle young waiter she had fallen in love with.

She had known and she had hoped but she had also been afraid — because of who he now was and afraid of her own powerful emotions. But now as she looked towards the shadowy figure in German uniform she felt nothing but fierce joy.

'Dieter?' she said huskily.

He came towards her and the last of the fading light showed her the uncertainty in his face. 'Hello, Sophia. Forgive me but I had to come back and see you — talk to you. The other night . . . I couldn't believe it when we came into the cottage to search and I saw it was you. I mean, I wondered if you were still in Jersey and if we might meet. But I never expected . . . well, not out here in St Peter, anyway.'

'Your people took over our house, didn't you know?'

'Well yes, I did know that,' he said awkwardly. 'And I want to tell you how sorry I am for what has happened here. I couldn't let you think . . .'

'Look, it's beginning to get cold,' she interrupted him. 'Are you going to come inside?'

He hesitated and for a moment she thought he was going to

refuse. Then he said: 'You don't mind having a German in your home?'

'Oh Dieter — don't be silly! I don't think of you as a German! We know one another too well for that.'

'What about the girl who was here with you the other night? Was that your sister, grown up?'

'That was Catherine, yes. And she's here now. But there isn't anyone else. We're . . . on our own now.'

'I see.'

No, you don't, she thought. She unpegged the last of the washing and tossed it into the basket. It was necessary, some- how, to carry on with normal everyday things. When she went to lift the basket Dieter, gentlemanly as ever, took it from her and carried it into the kitchen.

Catherine was sitting at the table doing her homework. She looked up in surprise as they came in. 'Oh!' she said, faintly accusing. 'It's you!'

'Catherine!' Sophia warned. She turned to Dieter. 'Dieter, I have to thank you for what you did the other night. I . . . we . . . are very grateful.'

Dieter shrugged. 'Don't thank me. But I hope there is no longer anything in this house which could prove dangerous to you.'

'Why, you think they will come back?' Sophia asked, alarmed.

'Not this time. But someone informed against you. They may do so again.'

'Who was it?' Sophia asked. 'Do you know?'

'Does it matter? Surely all that is important is that if a search is made there is nothing to be found. Don't take chances, Sophia. Especially not now.'

'Oh I know all about the risks,' Sophia said bitterly. 'Mama took a risk and she and Papa were deported for it.'

Dieter went white. 'Deported — where to?'

'I don't know. We've never heard a word since the day they were taken. At the time it was said they were going to a concen- tration camp in Germany but I really don't know. And Nicky was wounded in the fighting, very early on, and Paul took Papa's boat and sailed for England. That was the reason I had the

210

wireless, to try and keep some sort of contact with them. I knew it could get us into trouble but I just didn't care any more.'

'I understand,' Dieter said seriously. 'Believe me, Sophia, I *do* understand. And I am sorry. Very sorry.'

'*You* are sorry?'

'Yes. Such dreams we had, but nothing has turned out the way we expected. And now it never will . . .'

Sophia looked at him sharply. She was not quite sure what he meant.

'Would you like something to drink?' she offered. 'It won't be anything very exciting, I'm afraid, just tea made of blackberry leaves, but . . .'

'Thank you. Yes.'

Catherine pushed back her chair noisily. 'Excuse me.'

'Where are you going?' Sophia asked.

'Upstairs. To my room.' She went out without a word to Dieter.

'She has a lot of homework to do,' Sophia said, trying to excuse her sister but there was no mistaking that Catherine had left her pile of books behind. Dieter smiled ruefully.

'Don't worry, Sophia. I'm used to it. I am afraid we are all looked upon as monsters.'

'It's hardly surprising, is it, considering what you've done to us? Hatred and contempt are about all we have left. They help us keep our self-respect. When we see a German uniform on the street we don't look beyond it — it means the enemy.'

'But many of these soldiers are good men — ordinary men with wives and families at home. If only you could understand that they are prisoners just as you are then perhaps it would be easier for all of us.'

'We don't want to think of them like that,' Sophia said. 'We don't want to think about them at all. But it's different with you, Dieter. You're not one of them to us. We know you.'

'But I *am* one of them. And anyway I don't suppose your sister remembers me. I would certainly never have known her. She was just a little girl when I was here.'

'You're right, of course. Oh Dieter, where is it all going to end?'

'I am very much afraid it will end with a defeat for Germany, and pretty soon, too. Things have not gone our way — I don't know why. In the beginning I was so sure victory would be ours. It seemed only right that we would prevail. And we were strong, so strong! Yet somehow we have managed to run ourselves into a corner. Perhaps if the Americans had not come in it would be different. But that is all for the history books now. And what I am wondering is this. When we hold up our hands and say "It's all over", when the world learns of the things that have been done in the name of our great Fatherland, what is to become of us?'

His blue eyes were shadowed and he had suddenly a haunted look of defeat. Looking at him Sophia found herself remembering the young man, proud and confident, who had frightened her with his unexpected outburst of blind patriotism when war had been brewing. 'France and England will not take on Germany. They know they would never win,' he had said then and his eyes had burned with fanaticism, like so many other young men and women who had been wooed by oratory and emotion into Hitler's Youth Movement. The fervour had gone now; in its place was disillusion and shame. They had been duped, all of them, hypnotised by a monster. Now their country was in ruins, their national pride severely dented. Yet still they had to fight on, for Hitler had decreed that the Channel Islands and Cherbourg must be defended to the last man.

'Once that pig Hitler is gone it will be all right,' she said. 'You will be able to begin to rebuild, you'll see.'

'But will the world forgive us? Will we be able to forgive ourselves?'

Sophia turned her attention to the kettle which was boiling at last. She didn't want to answer that.

She strained the tea into the cups and passed one to Dieter. It had a strange colour and the smell, pungent and earthy, was not appetising. I'm not getting used to it at all, Sophia thought as she sipped slowly. If anything I like it less.

'What a long time ago now it seems since I was here, working for your father,' Dieter said. 'Do you remember when we used to ride around the island on our bicycles? They were happy times, weren't they?'

She nodded without replying. They had been happy times.

212

Now they had gone forever along with her youth and innocence and so many of her dreams. Sophia felt a terrible ache of sadness as she thought of it, remembering how very young she had been, how ignorant of the fact that the long sunlit days would not last forever.

'I think of them often. Especially since I have been back here in Jersey. But it is all so changed now.'

'It's a good thing we didn't know then what was going to happen to us,' she said. 'It must be a terrible curse to be able to see into the future.'

'I suppose so. But sometimes I think, if I had known, if I had seen, could I have made it any different?'

'I doubt it. You couldn't have stayed in Jersey. Mama would still have sent you home. And what could you have done to stop what has happened? You are just as powerless as we are. We're just pawns, Dieter, little people. When it comes to something like this there's nothing we can do.'

'But our own lives, surely we can determine what happens there?'

'Oh yes,' Sophia said. 'Oh yes, I've thought about that a good deal. And I have promised myself, when this is over I am going to take control of my life, and nobody is ever going to push me around or make me drink disgusting blackberry tea ever again!'

The moment the words were out she thought they sounded so ridiculous he must laugh at her. It was true, she had promised herself those very things, lying in her bed, sleepless from hunger and anxiety, but she had never said them to anyone. Now she glanced away, embarrassed. But Dieter did not laugh. He sat in silence for a few moments, looking at her. Then, tentatively, he reached out and touched her hand, curled protectively around her mug of tea.

Sophia's heart seemed to stop beating. Such a tiny touch, and yet it seemed as if her whole world were reduced to the area where his fingers brushed hers.

'Did you think of me, Sophia?' Dieter asked.

She nodded wordlessly.

'And I thought of you. Often.'

'But you didn't write. You promised me you would write.'

'I did. And you did not reply. I wrote again and still you did not reply. I thought you had forgotten me.'

'I never got any letter,' Sophia said. 'I thought *you* had forgotten me!'

'This I do not understand . . .'

'Well, I don't suppose it matters now. You're . . .' She broke off. 'You're here,' she had been going to say, and she knew she must not. It was too soon, far too soon to be so presumptive.

Dieter shook his head slowly, looking at her. 'Oh Sophia, it is so good to see you again, even under such circumstances. You don't know.'

'Yes,' she said, 'I do.' She let go of the cup, laying her hand, palm uppermost, on the scrubbed wood table top, and he covered it with his own. She looked down at his wrist etched with tiny fair hairs and felt the love welling up in her as if time had slipped backwards, she was fourteen years old again and the intervening years had never been.

The sound of the door opening broke the spell and they jumped apart like guilty children. It was Catherine; the expression on her face told them that they had not moved fast enough — she had seen them.

'Sophia! How could you?' she flared.

Dieter leaped to his feet, clicking his heels. 'Don't be offended, *fraulein*, please!'

'He's a German!' she rushed on, ignoring him. 'They took our parents, Sophia! They turned us out of our home! I hate them — and so should you. You can't sit there with him drinking tea and holding hands. It's disgusting!'

'Catherine! It's Dieter you are talking about!'

'Yes, I know. Dieter. The German. The Nazi pig. Look at him, Sophia — look!'

'Don't be so rude, Catherine!' Sophia remonstrated, horrified at her sister's outburst.

'Why not? I feel like being rude. In fact I feel like being a good deal worse than that. I feel like killing him!'

'I am sorry if I have upset you, Catherine,' Dieter said quietly. 'This I never meant to do. And Sophia, if I have put you in a bad position then I am sorry for that also. I will go now.' He crossed to the door, nodded gravely to them and went out.

Sophia glared at Catherine and ran out after him. Dusk had fallen swiftly as it does in September and the soft air was filled with the scents of the garden, a sweet hangover from the warmth of the day. Clouds of midges moved under the trees, sign of another fine day to come tomorrow, and somewhere out in the countryside the first owl hooted mournfully.

'Don't go, Dieter, please!' she called.

He stopped, looking back at her. 'I think it is best. You don't want me here. I should not have come.'

'Catherine shouldn't have said the things she did. I'm sorry . . .'

'No, no, I understand. Truly. And Catherine, she would not be the only one to condemn if I were to visit you again. I am German, as she said, and Germans are hated here, perhaps with good reason.'

'Dieter . . . please!' Sophia, proud, strong Sophia, who never begged and never let anyone see her cry, suddenly found she was doing both. Her eyes were misty with tears, the words sprang from her lips before she could stop them. 'I don't care what anyone says or thinks, I really don't. Only please, please don't go away again!'

There was a tiny silence. Across the valley the owl hooted again, a low and haunting moan lingering in the sweet air. It sounded to Sophia like an echo of her own heartfelt plea.

Dieter touched her hand again, his fingers clasping hers briefly, and he pulled her towards him, kissing her lightly on the forehead.

'I do have to go now, *liebchen*. But I will come back tomorrow — if you are sure . . .'

Her heart rose and soared. 'Oh yes, I'm sure!'

'Very well.' His fingers squeezed hers briefly again and then he was gone, a grey shadow disappearing into the falling darkness.

Gently Sophia touched the spot on her forehead where his lips had been then she went back into the house. For the first time in years she felt truly happy.

Catherine made sure she was out the following night when Dieter came. She was furious, unable to understand in the smallest degree how her sister could fraternise with a German and determined not to be a part of it.

'Wallace has some gramophone records he wants me to hear. I shall be at his house all the evening.'

'You'll have to come home before curfew.'

'Only if *he* won't be here any more. If he is going to be I'll ask if I can stay the night at Sylvie's. Her mother won't mind.'

'And I suppose you'll tell them all the reason why you don't want to come home just like you told them about our wireless,' Sophia snapped, stung.

'I didn't! You know I only told Sylvie!'

'So you say. But if that is the case then it must have been Sylvie who informed on us.'

'She wouldn't do that.'

'You heard what Dieter said. Somebody did.'

'Perhaps it was Bernard. He knew about it.'

'Oh, don't be so ridiculous! Bernard would never . . .'

'What,' Catherine asked, 'is Bernard going to say when he finds out you're seeing a German? He has been so good to us and he is going to be so hurt.'

'Oh stop it, stop it!' Sophia cried, pressing her hands to her ears. 'Doesn't what I want matter at all? This isn't someone I've just met. I've been in love with him since I was younger than you. I *have* to see him, don't you see?'

'No, I don't,' Catherine said flatly. 'And neither will anyone else.'

'Don't tell them, please . . .'

'Why should you worry if you're not ashamed of what you're doing?'

'Because this is very special to me and I don't want it all spoiled.'

'Well you need not worry,' Catherine said haughtily. '*I* shan't tell anyone because *I* certainly am ashamed.'

Sophia was a little shaken. She had been sure Catherine would come around to understanding her point of view and her stubborn disapproval was upsetting, especially since she was effectively all the family Sophia had now. But there was something in what she had said, Sophia had to admit. People would certainly blame her if they knew she was seeing a German, and

216

Bernard would be dreadfully upset. Sophia thought that if she was discreet she might be able to keep her secret from the world at large — the cottage was fairly isolated and the nights were now drawing in so that it was dark soon after they had finished tea — but she would find it very difficult to keep it from Bernard. Though she saw him only once or twice a week he sometimes called at the cottage unannounced so there was always the possibility he might come when Dieter was there.

He would have to be told, Sophia decided — all other considerations aside she hated the thought of deceiving him — though exactly what she would tell him she was not sure. And in any case as yet there was nothing to tell. Dieter was coming back to see her tonight. That might be the end of it.

A nerve jumped in Sophia's throat. It might be the end. Perhaps that would be best all round. But Sophia knew that in spite of everything she desperately wanted it to be the beginning.

They were magic days, stolen out of time. Around them conditions deteriorated as food supplies, already severely depleted, threatened to run out altogether, and the war entered its last bloody phase with the certainty of defeat giving a bitter edge to recriminations by the occupying forces. But Sophia and Dieter scarcely noticed any more. They were too engrossed in one another, too busy recapturing some of the enchantment of their lost youth.

Their meetings were brief and discreet. Sometimes Dieter could not get away and Sophia would wait at the window in vain. When they were together there was never enough time for all they wanted to say to one another and certainly never enough time for love. But at least there was privacy in those snatched hours for Catherine was still firm in her determination to avoid any contact with Dieter. When she could she went out, when she could not she shut herself upstairs in her bedroom and stayed there until he had gone.

They became lovers almost at once and it was the most natural thing in the world. It had been the first kiss that was awkward, with Dieter not yet certain of this new, adult Sophia, and she suddenly painfully aware of the German uniform. After that everything fell into place with an ease and speed that might have

217

appeared unseemly if it had not been so totally inevitable and right. Sophia, who, if she had stopped to think about it, might have felt that her brazen behaviour was something to be ashamed of, simply gloried in every touch, every special sensual moment. There was so much time to be made up — and so little present or future to do it in!

But it was not all love making. Sometimes they talked, sitting holding hands and leaning towards one another as they explored each other's minds and beliefs, dissected the past and tried to find some hope for the future. But the subject of Nazism was left firmly alone. It was the one area where they knew they would not agree, for though he hated things that had been done in its name, Dieter still clung to the basic tenets that had first stirred him when he had been a member of the Hitler Youth Movement. It was too much, Sophia realised, to expect him to abandon them completely when his whole existence and the very lives of so many of his friends had been sacrificed at their altar. Later, perhaps, when it was all over he would allow himself to begin to believe that he — and they — had been wrong. But for now the time she and Dieter had together was too precious to be spoiled by arguments or the exposure of fundamental differences of opinion.

Sometimes they talked of the sheer chance that had brought them together again — and of the incredible stroke of good luck that had decreed it had been Dieter who had found the cat's whisker under the floorboards.

'Didn't you know how dangerous it was to have a wireless?' he asked her sternly.

'Don't lecture me, Dieter. I haven't got it now.'

'I should hope not! Don't you know that if it had been anyone but me who found it you would be in gaol by now — or on the way to Germany even, perhaps?'

'Yes, I know. But it should have been safe enough. It would have been safe enough if someone hadn't informed on us. Who was it? I'd still like to know.'

'What good would that do?'

'It would be nice to know who your enemies are. No, it's all right, Dieter, I'm not hiding anything now, honestly, but I would just like to know.'

'Very well. The people who informed on you were named Pinel.'

'*Pinel*? I don't know anyone of that name . . . no, wait a minute, Pinel! There is a girl at Catherine's school named Jeanne Pinel. She and Catherine had a fight over a boy. You don't think she . . .'

'I don't know,' Dieter said, pulling her into his arms. 'Let it go, *liebchen*, just let it go. It's all over now and you don't want to make more trouble.'

His fingers were in her hair, his mouth at her throat, and Sophia 'let it go' as he asked. But when Dieter had gone and Catherine made her appearance again, sulky and resentful, Sophia told her what Dieter had said.

'You see how dangerous it is to talk about things?' she finished. 'You said you hadn't told anyone but Sylvie but somehow it got passed from mouth to mouth and Jeanne Pinel was able to use what she knew to get her own back on you, Catherine. So let that be a lesson to you!'

Catherine looked at Sophia with utter disdain.

'I don't need you to tell me what to do,' she said heatedly. 'I don't take notice of collaborators!'

The colour rose in Sophia's cheeks and a sharp retort hovered on her lips. But she bit it back. In a way she supposed Catherine had a point. All Sophia could hope was that one day Catherine would come to understand — and forgive.

The following evening Sophia was alone in the cottage trying to alter one of Lola's dresses into a skirt for Catherine when there was a knock on the door. She looked up from her sewing, surprised. Dieter had said he had some kind of extra duty to perform and would probably be late this evening — if he could come at all.

Sophia tucked her needle safely into the material and laid it down on the table hoping desperately it wasn't Bernard at the door. She still hadn't told him about Dieter and she knew it was wrong but somehow she just had not been able to bring herself to do it. Each time she tried the words stuck in her throat and refused to come and she had made do with vague excuses to put him off coming to call on her. She told herself that her untruthfulness was because she hated the thought of hurting him; deep down she knew it was more than that —she couldn't bear him to think badly of her, couldn't bear to see the same look in his eyes that she saw in Catherine's. Now as she got up to answer the door she thought anxiously that if it was Bernard she would have to get rid of him in a hurry or he might still be here when Dieter arrived — and that would provoke a very awkward situation!

She drew the bolt, already trying to work out what she would say. But it wasn't Bernard on the doorstep. It was a German officer whom she had never seen before.

As always the sight of a German uniform made her stomach contract. In that moment two words flashed through her brain: What now?

The German, as if reading her thought, smiled slowly and leaned a hand on the doorpost just level with her head. It was casually done, and obviously intended to put her at her ease, but the gesture grated on Sophia.

'Yes?' she said shortly. 'Did you want something?'

'Oh dear! That's not a very friendly greeting!' His smile did not waver. 'I was hoping to get a warmer welcome here.'

Sophia frowned. 'I don't know what you mean by that.'

'Don't you? Oh come now, I'm sure you do! Aren't you going to ask me in?'

Sophia hesitated. It wasn't wise to cross a German officer and refuse him entry to the house. Somehow she didn't think this one was here on official business but all the same it would be very easy for him to extract revenge if he felt he had been slighted. And she could hardly slam the door because his fingers were in the way — and with squashed fingers he almost certainly would cause trouble for her!

'Why should I ask you in?' she hedged. 'I don't know why you are here.'

His smile broadened but it was not a nice smile she thought. Above that grotesquely curving mouth his cheek muscles appeared not to move and there was a fixed glassiness about his eyes.

'Oh I am sorry, *fraulein*, I did not explain. I have come with a message from Dieter.'

220

'From Dieter!' She was startled. Dieter had told her he had kept their meetings secret from his fellow officers. 'There's nothing wrong is there?'

'Don't worry, *fraulein*. Let me in and I will tell you everything.'

She moved slightly to one side. He slipped past her with a swift, almost feline movement and stood looking around the kitchen. 'This is a nice place you have here.' His eyes, like chips of blue glass, came to rest on her. 'And you, too, are very nice, *fraulein*, very pretty!'

'Just tell me why you are here,' she said shortly. 'Dieter is all right, is he?'

The sensuous lips smirked. 'Oh yes, I should say Dieter is very much all right. He has good taste, I'll say that for him.'

Sophia tossed her head. The compliments were making her even more uncomfortable.

'You have a message from him you say. What is it?'

The German was prowling round the room, picking up a photograph here, an ornament there, inspecting everything with that glassy blue stare. Then he threw himself down in the easy chair by the fire, stretching out his jack-booted legs and folding his arms behind his head.

'A message. Did I say that?'

'Yes, you did.'

'Hmm. Well, that is not strictly true.'

Sophia was beginning to be really alarmed. It wasn't just that he was a German, it was the way he was looking at her, his tongue flicking over the full lips, and the arrogance of his pose. Sophia began to wish she had slammed the door on his fingers and risked the consequences.

'If you haven't got a message for me from Dieter what are you doing here?' she demanded.

He slid down a little further in the chair, his tongue flicking again.

'Why should Dieter have all the fun?'

Sophia had begun to tremble. 'I think you had better leave.'

'Leave?' He laughed shortly. 'But I have only just arrived, *fraulein*! Surely you are going to give me a better welcome than this? I can't believe Dieter comes all this way for so little.'

'How do you know what Dieter comes here for?' she flashed. 'In fact, how do you know he comes here at all?'

'Because my dear *fraulein* we followed him. Several of us have thought it very strange that Dieter no longer seems to want our company. So we decided to find out what was claiming his attention. We followed him, and very amusing it was too. The curtains were not quite pulled — ah, but you should be more careful!' He wagged a finger, amused to see the scarlet flush explode in her cheeks. 'You were too eager, you and Dieter. You did not stop to make sure you could not be seen. So, does that answer your other question — as to how I know why Dieter comes here?'

'You're no better than a Peeping Tom!' she flared, though she was now trembling violently with outrage as well as fear.

'Perhaps. And perhaps, for some, it is enough to look. Not though for me. For me, when I have looked, then afterwards I like to . . . hmm . . . you do know, don't you, what I mean, *fraulein*?'

'Will you please go!' Sophia yelled at him. 'Dieter . . .'

'Dieter is delayed. He has extra duties to perform. Let's not worry about Dieter . . .' His hand shot out, imprisoning her wrist. 'You are not being very cooperative, *fraulein*. I can see a little persuasion is called for.'

'Let me go!'

'Not yet, *fraulein*, not yet. Don't you know how excited you can get a man when you look at him like that?' His free hand was fumbling with his trousers, then he reached out strongly pulling her down into the chair on top of him. For a moment, taken completely by surprise, Sophia found herself lying there on top of him, felt his hands rucking up her skirt and his hot breath on her neck. Then she began to struggle, trying to free herself, beating at him with her hands. His breath was coming harder, he laughed deep in his throat. 'Wild-cat!' he said in German. He swung himself out of the chair, taking her with him, so that they both fell on to the floor and his strength and the weight of his body made her helpless. One arm was twisted behind her back, wrenching painfully at her shoulder, the other spreadeagled helplessly. As he raised himself to finish undoing his trousers she got the one hand free and clawed at his face;

222

instantly the palm of his hand smashed into her chin and her head cracked back on to the floor.

The blow dazed her; she seemed to be whirling in a world of pain, scarcely aware any more what he was doing to her. Even when he had finished with her she lay for long minutes unable to move from the ungainly position into which she had fallen. Her head was throbbing and so was her body but they were not in unison, the pain jarred and danced a syncopating but totally uncoordinated rhythm. Slowly she eased herself up. The German was lying on the floor beside her, sleek and replete, and the sight of him made bile rise in her throat. She lurched into a sitting position, hatred burning in her like a cold fire.

It was then that she saw his service revolver lying on the floor. Scarcely knowing what she was doing she snatched at it, turning it in shaking sweat-damp hands to face him.

'You bastard, will you get out now?' she grated through chattering teeth.

He sat up abruptly and as she saw the alarm in his light eyes she suddenly realised just how easy it would be to kill him. One tiny movement of her index finger and she could blow that handsome hateful face apart. One tiny movement and this German would never terrify or bully or rape ever again.

'I am going to shoot you,' she said.

She saw a muscle move in his cheek and the twitch of a nerve in his throat. But his voice was very calm, very level.

'If you shoot me you too will die.'

'I don't care!' she sobbed. 'What do I care about dying?'

'You don't want to die for something so stupid. You won't shoot me. You can't do it. Now, give the gun to me.' Slowly, very slowly, his hand inched towards hers. 'Come on, give it to me.'

The cold eyes met hers unwaveringly and she felt her wrist begin to shake. He was right, she thought suddenly, she couldn't do it. With a muffled sob she let her hand, holding the gun, drop to her side and her head bowed to her chest. Oh Jesus Christ, she couldn't do it! She'd had her chance and she couldn't do it . . .

At that very moment the door opened and Dieter came in.

He stood for a moment, taking in the scene. Sophia wanted to run to him but she could not move. She was very ashamed, suddenly, as if it had all been her fault.

'What the hell is going on here?' he demanded.

The officer began to babble in German, waving his arms. Sophia could only guess at what he was saying but the thought that he might be trying to excuse himself incensed her.

'He raped me!' she cried. 'He got in here by pretending he had a message from you and then he raped me!'

'Raped? Ha! You asked for it!'

'How can you say that?' She looked down, saw the gun still in her hand, and turned to Dieter, sobbing. 'I wanted to shoot him, Dieter. I wanted to kill him. But I couldn't do it. I couldn't do it!'

'I see.' Dieter's face was white with rage. 'This is what your friends were sniggering about, was it? They knew what you had in mind.'

'They followed you here, Dieter, the other night. They were watching us . . .' She broke off, suddenly very afraid. Dieter's eyes were blazing, his nostrils flared.

'You did what?'

Sophia saw the first flicker of alarm in the other German's face. 'Oh come on, Dieter, can't you take a joke?'

'A joke? You call this a joke? All right, you bastard, you've got it coming to you.'

'Who from?' the officer sneered.

'From me.' Dieter drew his gun, levelling it at his heart.

White hot terror shot through Sophia. 'Dieter — no! Please — you mustn't!'

'Why not? I shall do what you did not have the stomach for, Sophia. I am going to kill him.'

'Dieter — please — no!'

'You are mad!' the officer blustered. 'You won't get away with this!'

'I don't care any more. I am a German, and I am proud of it. At least, I was. Not any more. These last years I have learned to feel ashamed of my birthright, ashamed of my fellow country-men. Some of the things that have been done have been inhuman. They will not be forgotten for generations. And all

224

the time I have been forced to remain quiet and do what was required of me. Sometimes I have asked myself — how can I live with this? I have tried to do only what I believed to be right but still I am ashamed. The end of the war is coming. Soon we will have to answer — all of us. And when they ask me — what did you do, Dieter? I shall tell them. I shot the man who defiled my lovely Sophia. It was not much but it was the least I could do.'

Kurt laughed harshly. 'If you shoot me you won't live to tell anyone anything. The Kommandant will see to that.'

'Then Sophia, she will tell them. She will tell my father and my mother I died because I executed a rapist. Come on, outside, you bastard.'

'Why don't you do it here?'

'And have Sophia arrested for complicity? No she has suffered enough. Outside!'

The gun was in the officer's ribs now, prodding him towards the door.

'Dieter — don't do this! I don't want you to do it for me!' Sophia caught at his arm. He shook himself free.

'Just give me his gun *liebchen*. Don't worry, no one will connect you with this.'

'Please, Dieter — no! I'm all right, really — he didn't hurt me . . .'

But Dieter was beyond the reach of reason. His gun urged the officer down the path and into the darkness.

'Go back inside and lock the door!' he called over his shoulder. 'Go on — do as I tell you!'

Sophia stood in the doorway, hands pressed against her mouth, unable to move or speak as the darkness swallowed them. He wouldn't do it, would he? And then, loud and chilling in the stillness of the night, the shot rang out.

As Sophia stood, frozen with fear and shock, Catherine came running up the path, breathless and frightened. 'Sophia, what is it? What's going on? There are Germans in the lane. There was a shot.'

Somehow Sophia pulled herself together. Protecting Catherine was all important now. 'I don't know. It's none of our business.' She grabbed the frightened child, bundled her inside and slammed the door shut. 'Draw the curtains. I have some clearing up to do and then we are going to put out the light and go to bed. And whatever we hear outside we are not going to investigate. Do you hear me?'

'But I don't understand. You know something, don't you? Something happened here tonight.'

Sophia shook her head. It was all too terrible and she did not know where to begin. Besides it was safest for Catherine if she knew nothing.

'There's no time now. I'll explain tomorrow,' was all she said.

Chapter sixteen

It was a nightmare, a nightmare from which she could not wake. It followed her around every moment of the day and disturbed what little sleep she was able to get at night. The terrible events of that evening had left her body sore and bruised and her nerves raw, and added to this was the constant terrible anxiety for Dieter. She had not heard what had happened to him, no one seemed to know anything beyond the gossip and speculation that was bound to follow the shooting of an officer of the Feldgendarmerie on a public highway, and Sophia was afraid to ask too many questions in case she aroused suspicion and put Catherine in some kind of danger.

But oh, the wondering was sheer agony. Did they know it was Dieter who had shot the officer? Had he been caught, or was he on the run? Might he turn up at the cottage seeking shelter? She didn't think so — he had been as anxious to protect her as she was to protect Catherine, but supposing he did — what would she do? The questions plagued her, running round and round inside her head until she thought she was going mad. And always the most important one of all — will I ever see him again? Will we ever be together again?

Deep down Sophia knew she could expect nothing but the worst. Yet still she hoped. And the hope seemed to be the greatest torture of all.

She heard the news at the village shop when she was queuing for what meagre rations were available. A German had given himself up in connection with the roadside shooting at St Peter — just gone to his commanding officer and given himself up. He had heard there were bound to be repercussions in the district if the culprit was not caught, it was said, so for some reason he had simply admitted it. Goodness only knew why — after all, he was bound to be executed for such a serious crime.

The words seemed to echo in her head and Sophia held tight to the handle of her shopping basket as if it were a lifeline. Execution. Dieter was going to be executed. For a moment Sophia thought she was going to faint then she thought she was going to cry. She turned and blundered out of the shop, oblivious to the curious stares that followed her, wanting nothing but to get home.

She half ran, half walked, legs trembling, breath coming in harsh uneven gasps. Out of the village, along the lane . . . and suddenly she remembered she had to pass the spot where it had happened.

It was not the first time, of course, but somehow on the other occasions she had managed to screw herself up and look the other way. Even when the Feldgendarmerie had been there examining the grass verge for clues she had managed to hold her head high and walk by. Not today. Today the dark stain on the gravel where they had not quite washed the blood away seemed to leap out at her. Here Dieter had shot the officer who had raped her. And for that Dieter was now going to be executed.

For days Sophia had felt nauseous, now it gripped her stomach with an iron hand. Tearing her eyes away from the dark stains on the roadside she began to run, but she was still within sight of the scene of the shooting when the sickness overcame her and she doubled up, vomiting into the hedgerow while the helpless tears ran down her cheeks.

'Sophia, are you pregnant?' Catherine asked. Sophia started, taken by surprise by the directness of the question. Ever since she had begun to suspect it herself she had known the moment must come, of course, but she had delayed it, dreading the look of revulsion she would see on Catherine's face, dreading the fact that talking about it would make it somehow more real. 'Well?' Catherine demanded. 'Are you?'

She was no longer a child, Sophia thought. The war had made her grow up very quickly. But even so there was no easy way to say this — and, with Catherine's eyes upon her like twin searchlights, no way to lie either.

'Yes, I think I am,' she said quietly.

'Oh Sophia!'

'I know — I know. It's a nightmare. I keep telling myself I can't be . . . but I know I am.'

The girls were silent for a moment, looking at one another. Then Catherine asked: 'What are you going to do?'

Sophia shook her head. 'I honestly don't know.'

Another silence. Then Catherine said: 'You know what they'll call you, don't you?'

'Yes. I know.'

'A Jerry Bag. My sister. How *could* you? I'll die of shame!'

'How do you think I feel?'

'You should have thought of that before you started associating with Germans. Oh yes, I know what you'll say — what you always say. It was only Dieter. But Dieter was a German and you can't trust them.'

'It wasn't Dieter's fault!' Sophia argued passionately. 'I've told you, over and over again what happened. You just don't want to listen.'

'I've listened. And it's horrible — sordid. All I can say is it's a pity you didn't shoot the officer who raped you while you had the chance. Why didn't you do it, Sophia?'

'I don't know. I just couldn't . . .'

'I would have.'

'You don't know that. You never know what you'll do until it happens to you. And if I had shot him I'd probably have been deported like Mama and Papa. What would happen to you then?'

'I'd have managed. Anyway the war's nearly over. They wouldn't have deported you now. You should have shot him, Sophia. At least then you would have some pride left.'

'All right, Catherine,' Sophia retorted, stung. 'Don't go on and on about it. Don't you think I wish I had done it? If I had then Dieter wouldn't have had to do it for me and he wouldn't be under sentence of God knows what. And if you say you don't *care* what happens to him because he's a German I swear I'll never forgive you!'

She pressed her hands to her mouth, swallowing at the lump of tears that had risen in her throat, angry with herself for seemingly being unable to control her emotions any more and angry with Catherine for her unforgiving attitude. She had been so sure her sister would understand when she explained what had happened. But all Catherine seemed to care about was what her friends would think.

'Couldn't you get rid of it?' she said now.

Sophia blinked. 'Get rid of it? Catherine . . .'

'Well you could try. Sylvie says all you need to do is to have a bath, really hot, and drink plenty of gin. Probably a whole bottle.'

'What does Sylvie know about it?' Sophia snapped. 'You haven't been talking about me to her, I hope?'

A faint colour rose in Catherine's cheeks. 'No, we were just talking generally . . .' But she sounded unconvincing.

'I see. Well, if all your friends already know it seems it's a little late for me to cover up my condition, even supposing I could get hold of a bottle of gin, and even supposing it worked, which I doubt.'

'You mean . . . you won't even try?' Catherine looked tearful suddenly.

'No,' Sophia said. 'I won't.'

'But . . .'

'Look, Catherine, if I was sure that horrible man who raped me was the father perhaps I would try. But I'm not sure. It could be Dieter's baby. Don't you see, I can't take the chance.'

Catherine went even more red. 'Dieter's baby!'

'It could be.'

'Well you are a dark horse, aren't you, Sophia?'

'Catherine, please, *please* try to understand.'

'Oh I understand all right,' Catherine said bitterly. 'I understand my sister has been going with Germans and now everybody is going to know about it. I'm not surprised that officer came here and raped you, Sophia. He'd probably heard how easy you were. And now the rest of Jersey will hear it too.'

'Catherine, please . . . you don't know how you're upsetting me talking like this.'

'I'm upsetting you! Well, that is rich! Let me tell you, Sophia,

230

I am ready to die of shame. You knew what people think about girls who go with Germans but you had to carry right on, didn't you? And you couldn't even stop at seeing him. You had to let him . . . oh, it's disgusting!'

'It is not disgusting, Catherine. I love him!'

'Love you call it? I call it being a Jerry Bag. A real, *real*, Jerry Bag. Well, I hope you are satisfied, Sophia. I just hope you are satisfied!'

Sophia turned away, sick at heart. This was only the beginning, she knew. There would be plenty more in the same vein. But it was no use thinking about it, no use letting it get to her. That was just a waste of time and energy. She couldn't allow herself to wallow in self-pity either. Now that she knew for certain that she was going to have a baby she had far too much thinking and planning to do.

There really was only one answer. She had known it, right from the beginning and tried not to think about it, not because it was such a terrible prospect but because it would mean that she had finally accepted she would never see Dieter again.

Besides, she did not know whether she could summon up the courage to do it. All very well for Bernard to have told her that whenever she needed him, and for whatever reason, he would be there. Sophia was fairly sure that he had not been thinking those circumstances might include her being pregnant by someone else. He would be terribly hurt, she knew. He might even, with complete justification, tell her in no uncertain terms that it was not his problem. But desperate situations call for desperate measures and in all her life Sophia had never been more desperate.

One night in early December when Bernard left the Electricity Works he saw a figure huddled under the wall in the gathering gloom. He did not take much notice. Although it was only four o'clock it was almost dark and he bent his head against the biting wind. Then, as he drew level, she moved out of the shadows towards him and he stopped short, staring at her in surprise.

'Sophia! What are you doing here?'

'Well — I was waiting for you actually . . .'

231

'Oh!' Nothing could stop the searing flash of love and desire that she always excited in him but nowadays he knew to treat it with caution. Sophia was not in love with him no matter how much he might wish she was and it was time he realised it and stopped behaving like a lovelorn schoolboy.

He had scarcely seen Sophia these last months. It had been back in the autumn, he remembered, when she had begun acting strangely, making all kinds of spurious excuses to put him off from visiting her, and in the end he had reluctantly come to the conclusion she did not want to see him any more and was trying to get rid of him without actually saying so. The knowledge had hurt him but he had made up his mind — he'd tried to win her, he'd given it his best shot and he had failed. Better to bow out gracefully. So he had simply stopped calling on her and when she had not made any attempt to contact him he had concluded that he must have been right in assuming she had been trying, very gently, to get rid of him.

Now, he looked at the too-thin figure shivering in an overcoat that he recognised as being one that had once belonged to Lola, and felt his heart contract. But there was no sense of rising excitement as there might have been a year ago. His confidence had taken too many knocks since then.

'Why are you waiting for me?' he asked.

She hesitated. No sign of the self-assured Sophia today.

'Can we talk?'

'Here?'

'No, not really. Could you come over?'

'When?'

She hesitated. 'Whenever.'

'Would tomorrow be all right?' he asked.

She nodded. She wanted to say that no time would really be all right for what she had to do, but that now her mind was made up she would really have preferred to get it over with sooner rather than later. But she knew she had no right to demand that he should come rushing straight over. If she wanted his help it would have to be at his convenience, not hers.

'Tomorrow then,' Bernard said. 'About seven?'

She nodded again and he mounted his bicycle and rode off

232

leaving her feeling slightly foolish and very effectively put in her place.

By the time Bernard arrived the following evening Sophia was dreadfully nervous. He had been so cool with her, he hadn't seemed in the least pleased to see her and she could not help wondering if his feelings towards her had changed. It was, after all, a long while since he had asked her to marry him and she really could not expect him to wait for her forever. Perhaps he had met someone else or perhaps — her stomach turned over at the thought — perhaps he had heard she had been seeing Dieter. She had been as discreet as possible but it was not easy to keep a thing like that quiet. The thought that Bernard might think she was a collaborator made her feel sick, but that in itself was illogical since if he was going to help her she would have to confess the truth in any case.

I can't do it! Sophia thought in panic. But she also knew she couldn't do any of the alternatives either and to do nothing at all would only make things worse in the long run. Oh God, please help me! Sophia prayed when she heard Bernard's knock at the door. Please help me!

To her surprise Bernard looked very smart. As it had been practically impossible to get new clothes since the occupation most islanders were now looking decidedly shabby and Sophia herself had wished she had something nicer to wear than the rather childish jersey and skirt that had been her 'best' in 1940, especially since she was uncomfortably aware that the skirt was beginning to strain at the waistband. But Bernard's sports jacket, although patched at the elbows, had stood up well to the test of time, as had his cavalry twill trousers and Oxford brogues. Perhaps it was because he was able to wear overalls and boots for work, Sophia thought.

They sat down by the fire — it gave out so little heat that it was necessary to sit almost on top of it to keep warm — and made small talk for a while. If only she could reach him as she used to, Sophia thought, but the barrier of reserve was still there and she did not know how to get around it.

'Well,' Bernard said at last, 'what did you want to talk about?'

Sophia swallowed at the knot of nervousness in her throat.

'You remember once upon a time you told me if ever I needed your help I could come to you?'

'Yes.'

'In fact you asked me to marry you.'

A tiny muscle moved in his cheek. 'Yes.'

'Well, I'm wondering if it's too late for me to . . . accept.'

For a moment there was nothing but total surprised silence. Even the coal-dust fire seemed to stop shifting and hissing and hold its breath.

'Well,' Bernard said at last. 'I must say this is a bit of a shock.'

'You mean you don't want to marry me any more.'

'I didn't say that. I said it was a shock. You turned me down, after all, and lately — well, we've hardly seen one another, have we?'

'I know. And it's no use my pretending I've had a sudden blinding change of heart. There is a reason, Bernard, and when you know what it is you may very well never want to see me again. But you did say any time and if ever I needed a friend I need one now.'

Bernard glanced at her flushed and rosy in the firelight. His own throat was dry. For one beautiful moment he had thought all his dreams were about to come true. But of course they weren't. Be cautious! he warned himself, but for once all his sensible steady-going will seemed to have deserted him.

'Tell me, Sophia,' he said.

She told him. She told him about Dieter and about the German officer who had raped her. She told him she was pregnant and out of her mind with worry, afraid of being an unmarried mother, afraid of being ostracised as a 'Jerry Bag', afraid of what the future would hold for her unborn child. She told him everything and the only thing she left out was that the reason she would not even consider an abortion was because she did not know for certain that her baby was not Dieter's.

'So — now you know,' she said when she had finished.

Bernard said nothing. His eyes were shadowed and narrowed and he seemed unwilling to look at her. His silence frightened her. She had expected fireworks of some kind or even, at her

234

most optimistic, a renewed declaration of his love. But this total absence of reaction was disconcerting.

'You mean you want me to pretend to be the father of your child,' he said at last.

She felt weak with shame suddenly. Put like that it sounded perfectly dreadful, cowardly and deceitful as well as presumptuous. And Catherine had been quite right — she had brought it on herself. She had no right at all to expect for a single moment that Bernard should do something like this for her. If she hadn't been at her wits' end it would never have occurred to her and she hated herself now for her weakness. But oh dear God, she had been through so much alone. And there was the baby to think of too. The stigma of illegitimacy was bad enough, but if it became known that his father had been a German, his life would not be worth living.

'I'm not asking you to marry me for ever and ever,' she said quickly. 'I realise that would be too much to ask. I couldn't expect you to want me after this and I certainly couldn't expect you to make yourself responsible for the child of a German. But if you could just . . . oh, I don't know. . .'

'Pretend the child is mine,' he said again in the same flat voice. 'That's what you want me to do, is it, Sophia?'

Wordlessly she nodded, her head bowed in abject shame.

'This has all been a bit of a shock. I honestly don't know what to say.' He stood up. 'I'll have to think.'

'Bernard . . . please don't hate me.'

'I don't hate you, Sophia. But you'll have to give me time to get used to the idea of you . . . Look, I'll be in touch. Only just now I think I want to be on my own for a bit.'

After he had gone Sophia realised she was trembling from head to foot. She closed the door and stood with her arms wrapped around herself while wave upon wave of shame flooded through her as she thought of what she had done. It had seemed such a reasonable solution when she had planned it — but then she had been desperate enough with worry for her own future and the future of her unborn child to close her mind to the worst implications of the reality. Now she could no longer do that. She had seen the look on Bernard's face when she had told him and she did not think she would ever forget it as long as she lived. It was burned forever in her memory along with the words he had spoken in that cold, flat voice: 'You want me to pretend to be the father of your child.'

Sophia bowed her head, cheeks flaming, hating the whole wide world, but most of all hating herself. How could she have thought for a single moment that Bernard might actually be prepared to overlook something so dreadful? How could she have been so arrogant as to imagine he might still want her? Well, now she knew he didn't. Oh, he hadn't refused to help her outright, of course. He was too kind for that. But there was no doubt at all how shocked he had been and how disgusted — not only by what she had done but because she had asked him to give her baby a name. A fresh wave of humiliation licked through her and she doubled up against it, wishing she could somehow disappear right inside herself and never have to face anyone — especially Bernard — ever again. She shouldn't have done it, she shouldn't, she should have looked for another way. Anything, anything would have been better than having Bernard look at her like that.

Sophia realised with a sudden sharp tug of surprise that it was Bernard's reaction that was causing her the most distress. Not because his refusal to help her would mean she had to find another way to solve her problem although, heaven knew, that was bad enough. But it was his face she couldn't forget, the way he had looked at her, that was what was beyond being borne.

I never realised how much I cared what he thought of me, she thought. I took his affection for me for granted, treated it as if it were quite worthless. Only now, when it is too late, do I realise what it meant to me. Oh dear God, what have I done?

Sophia leaned against the door weeping with pain and humiliation – and something else. A new emotion, sharp as knives, yet strangely, hauntingly bitter sweet, a longing not for what had been but what might have been. It was an emotion still tantalisingly unformed, almost ghostly, just beyond the reach of her consciousness. If Sophia had had to put a name to it she would have described it perhaps as an aching sense of loss. But this time it was not for her parents nor for Dieter. Sophia knew, in the deepest recesses of her mind, that it was for Bernard.

*

In the week before she saw Bernard again Sophia found herself thinking of him constantly.

It was ridiculous, she thought, that someone she had known so well for so long should suddenly fill her every waking thought. Perhaps it was some mechanism of self-preservation drawing her towards the man she still hoped might offer the safety of a nest for her to rear the child that was growing inside her. But she could no longer believe that for the longing was not only for the safety and security that Bernard represented, it was also physical. Each time she pictured his face, sweet sharp chords jarred somewhere deep inside her, she remembered the way his arms had once felt around her and ached with longing. It was stupid, irrational, strangely exciting and also desperately depressing since she was sure now that Bernard was out of her reach. Why couldn't she have felt this way before, when he had wanted her? But there it was, just one more crazy thing in a crazy mixed-up world.

Occasionally — usually on those mornings when she woke feeling wondrously free of the nausea that plagued her — Sophia allowed herself to think that perhaps Bernard might still care for her. He had, after all, promised to be in touch; perhaps when he had had time to get used to the idea he would give her another chance. But the moods of optimism never lasted long. Sophia had come face to face with the enormity of what she had done and she could not now imagine how Bernard could ever forgive her, much less still love her now that he knew the truth.

The best thing she could do when the war was over, she decided, was to go to England. She would get a job to support herself and her baby and there would be no one to point a finger and accuse her of collaboration. In England, she suspected, no one would know and no one would care. She only hoped the war would be over in time for her to leave before her baby was born.

The days passed, each very like the one before. Sophia lived through them mechanically, trying to plan constructively and not to think too much of the snags and problems. But they were always there in the night, accusing faces in the shadows, whispering doubts in the wind that whistled around the cottage and rattled the shutters.

Then one evening when she left the surgery she found Bernard outside waiting for her.

As she saw him standing there with his bicycle propped up beside him she felt her throat constrict with shyness.

'Bernard.'

'Sophia. I've been thinking things over.' There was a hard edge to his voice that was new. Sophia's heart sank.

'I'm sorry, Bernard, I should never have . . .'

He cut across her.

'I will marry you and give your baby a name — on the understanding that we try to make that marriage work just as we would if everything was . . . normal. To the outside world I want us to look like an ordinary happy family. But I want to make one thing clear. If ever I should find out that you have cheated on me again, in any way whatever, I shall not only leave you but I shall make damned sure everyone in Jersey knows the truth. Do you understand, Sophia?'

'Oh Bernard.'

'You do understand? I won't be messed about or made a fool of ever again.'

She nodded. Her knees were weak and she was on the verge of tears suddenly. 'I don't want anybody else. I'll be a good wife to you, I promise. I do love you, Bernard.' He laughed shortly and she laid a hand on his sleeve. 'It's true — I do. I didn't realise it until I thought I'd lost you . . .'

She broke off. He had not made even the smallest move towards her. She was frightened suddenly by this new Bernard. She had always felt before that she could twist him round her little finger — not any more. Now he was in control. He had been hurt but he had turned his pain to his own advantage, used it to form a defence. It wouldn't be easy to break down those barricades. If she wanted him to love her as well as marry her she would have to win him all over again.

Shivering in her threadbare coat, her stomach aching with hunger and the ever-present nausea rising in her throat again, Sophia felt almost as daunted by the enormity of what lay before her as she had been by the prospect of bringing her child into the world alone. But already the seeds of hope were springing. He had loved her once, she would make him love her again.

238

And she would make sure he never came to regret his decision to marry her.

Bernard and Sophia were married very quietly as soon as the necessary legalities had been observed. Scarcely an eyebrow was raised. Islanders who would normally have had a sharp eye for a thickening waistline were too concerned with their own situation and everyone was obsessed with the imminent arrival of a Red Cross ship which promised parcels of food, cigarettes and chocolate — undreamed of bliss after months of near starvation!

Bernard moved into the cottage at St Peter and he and Sophia began the long and delicate task of rebuilding a shattered relationship only this time with their roles reversed. Now it was Bernard with the whip hand, Sophia anxious and determined to please. And gradually, gradually the warmth began to return, slowly the trust began to mount, all cemented with the deep vein of physical attraction which Bernard had always felt for Sophia and which now she was beginning to reciprocate.

Her experience might, she sometimes thought, have left her frigid. On the contrary being pregnant seemed to have fostered a new sensuousness. Coupled with her gratitude and the admiration and respect she felt for the new hard-edged Bernard it made a good combination and boded well for the future.

But for all that the balance of power between them had changed. It was never to swing back again.

'Sophia — what did you do with that wireless set of Paul's?' Bernard asked one evening in May. Sophia, who was at the sink washing the supper dishes, felt a sharp sensation shoot through the pit of her stomach.

'Why?'

'I thought I might dig it up. The war is as good as over; the Germans won't harm us now. And I heard at work today that Winston Churchill is going to broadcast tomorrow. They are putting up loudspeakers in Royal Square and the Howard Davis Park for people to hear it but you're not going to feel like standing about in crowds, are you?'

'No, I don't think I am,' Sophia agreed, kneading her hands into the small of her back. She had been especially uncomfortable today, and a niggling ache low in her back had grown more and more persistent until she found herself wriggling to try and get away from it.

'I'll show you where it is,' Catherine said, throwing down her tea towel. 'Oh, isn't it just wonderful? Everyone says the troops will be here tomorrow or the next day at the very latest. And when they do I'm going down to the pier to watch them arrive. Maybe Nicky or Paul will be with them! Who knows? And Mama and Papa could be home soon too.'

She and Bernard went out into the garden and Sophia stood watching them as they dug in the little patch of earth beneath the sage bush. She felt oddly unreal. She wished she could be as excited as Catherine and Bernard about the end of the war but somehow it seemed almost unimportant. It was a relief, of course, to know that soon everything would be back to normal and they would not have to be frightened or hungry again. But as for leaping about and shrieking with delight — she just couldn't do it.

'Here we are then!' Bernard said, coming back into the kitchen with the biscuit box containing the wireless, setting it down on the table and dusting it with a piece of rag. 'Now, I'm going to fix it up to the gramophone amplifiers so you'll be able to hear it better. Three o'clock tomorrow — don't forget, will you?'

Sophia did not answer. The wireless set had awakened old memories; she was thinking that if it had not been for that Dieter would still be alive.

'Sophia?' Bernard prompted her. 'It's going to be a very historic moment. You won't want to miss it.'

'Don't worry, I won't miss it,' Sophia promised.

But she did.

Sophia's pains began in earnest during the night. At first light Bernard went to fetch the midwife, who sent for a doctor. Sophia was much further advanced than she had expected; the baby could be born very soon. The doctor, however, was less sure. He did not like the position the baby was lying in. He thought it might be some hours yet. Throughout the long morning, while crowds gathered at the pier to watch the Germans packing up, Catherine sat beside her bed, sponging her perspiring face and

240

holding her hand but eventually she could not bear to see her sister in such distress for a moment longer. She listened to Winston Churchill's speech but heard only Sophia's moans coming from upstairs as she tossed and turned and tried to escape from the all-consuming agony.

'You've got to do something!' Bernard begged the doctor when he came home from work and found the baby had still not arrived but the doctor, though looking anxious and strained himself, refused.

'I think we should wait a little longer before we do anything drastic. I still think your wife should be able to deliver her baby on her own.'

'I just want her to be out of all this pain!' Bernard yelled, uncharacteristically angry. 'How can you let it go on?'

'My dear man it's been going on for generations,' the doctor said wearily. 'Tomorrow she'll have forgotten all about it, you'll see.'

The sun set, a ball of fire, over scenes of great excitement all over the island, bathing Sophia's room in a last rosy glow, and at last — at last! — things began to happen.

Just before ten o'clock Bernard and Catherine, downstairs in the kitchen, heard Sophia's last agonised gasp and the baby's first hiccuping cries.

'You have a son,' the doctor told Sophia. 'I think in view of what's been happening today you should call him Victor — or even Winston.'

Sophia lay back on the pillows, exhausted but also exhilarated. 'Oh no, we've already decided on a name,' she said, her voice cracking with tiredness.

'And what is that?'

'We are going to call him Louis.'

Sophia cradled her baby in her arms. She looked down at the chubby face with the small button mouth which sought her breast so eagerly, the wide blue eyes and the fuzz of fair hair that covered the faintly pointed head, and a wave of love overwhelmed her. The circumstances of his conception and the terrible time that had followed were all behind her now and the thing she had feared most — that she would look at him and

241

know that he was the son of the hateful officer who had raped her — had not happened. There was nothing about the baby to indicate which of the two Germans had fathered him and in any case it did not matter to Sophia any more. He was here and she loved him, whoever his father might be. It was almost, she thought, as if he was hers alone, this soft, sweet-smelling, utterly dependent scrap of humanity.

If only she could ensure he would never grow up to suffer as they had all suffered these last five years! If only she could keep him safe with her love forever! Sophie hugged her baby fiercely and promised that nothing should ever hurt him if it were in her power to prevent it.

Chapter seventeen
Jersey, 1991

Dan Deffains pushed open the door of the pub and felt as if he had stepped back in time. If he had a pound for every pint he'd sunk here during his days on the force he would be a rich man, he thought. Add to that another pound for all the whisky chasers and he might be able to afford one of the millionaire's mansions that dotted the island. But he hadn't been inside the place from the day he'd handed in his warrant card. It held too many memories and he had had no reason to want to resurrect any of them. It had hurt too damned much, feeling that he had been discarded like a used match just when he had most needed his career to fill the barren desert of his private life now Marianne was gone. Nothing, he had thought, could ever make him forget the sight of her broken body lying at the roadside, nothing could make the raw pain of loss go away. But at least work would have been a panacea. The police force had denied him that and even when he had begun to rebuild his shattered life, finding success and even fulfilment, the bitterness had remained, rankling like a festering sore.

He had not wanted to see his old friends and not be one of them any more, he realised. That perhaps as much as anything was what had deterred him from seeking them out to pursue the Langlois case. But it was different now. With Juliet's visit the whole thing had leaped up at him, exciting his imagination and reawakening all his old enthusiasms. Dan had always believed in grasping what opportunities presented themselves; to ignore them was to kick fate in the face. This was the right moment, he had decided, to follow his instincts and try to get to the bottom of what had happened at La Grange twenty years ago. Juliet would be his contact inside the tight-knit, tight-lipped Langlois clan. This morning she had telephoned and told him she would like to go ahead with the investigation and he had

243

arranged to meet her again and talk some more. He was looking forward to hearing what she might be able to tell him. But he could not expect her to do it all for him. Some of the digging he had to do for himself. And that meant re-establishing contacts he had let slip over the last few years. With the excitement of following a trail, however cold, to egg him on he had made a telephone call or two, and now as he entered the bar of the pub he was surprised to find that it was far less painful to face the past than he had imagined it would be.

Time had moved on and he had not noticed it. He was no longer the keen young policeman whose dreams of a career in the force had been shattered. He was a different man with different ambitions. The pub, though packed with memories, was a place where he could pursue them, nothing more.

He stood for a moment in the doorway, his eyes narrowed against the fug of cigarette smoke, then made his way across to the bar to where a man was sitting on one of the high stools, instantly recognisable by the fringe of ginger hair that reached from ear to ear beneath a pink bald pate shaped like a monk's tonsure.

'Hello, Mr Gould.'

'Dan! I didn't see you come in. You're early!'

'One of my foibles, remember? I didn't think it would matter, anyway. I guessed you'd be here first.'

'I don't like wasting good drinking time, it's true. What are you having?'

'No, this one is on me. Scotch?'

'Why the hell not, if you're buying.'

'Two doubles, please,' Dan said to the barmaid, who was hovering. The girl had changed, the eagerness to serve him had not.

'So?' the older man said as the girl set the two glasses down on the counter in front of them. 'What did you want to see me about, Dan?'

Dan looked around, indicating a corner table.

'Shall we go over there where it's a bit quieter?'

'Suits me.'

Out of a sense of deference that was a hangover from the old days Dan let him lead the way. Philip Gould had been the inspector in charge of his section when he had joined the force and from the start Dan had liked him. There was an honesty about Phil Gould, it shone out of his blunt featured, rather red, face and blue eyes that were fringed by stubby colourless lashes. He was a blunt man but a fair one, hard on new recruits and old stagers alike but hot in defence of any of his men whom he felt had been wronged. Dan knew Phil Gould had fought for him and he was grateful even though Phil had failed. The man had probably sacrificed any chance of furthering his career because of his outspoken loyalty to those in his command; he had never risen above the rank of inspector and with less than five years to go to retirement was unlikely to now.

'I'll get straight to the point, Mr Gould,' Dan said when they were seated. 'Do you remember a case almost twenty years ago when a Louis Langlois was shot?'

'Louis Langlois! Now there's a name from the past!'

'You do remember.'

'How could I ever forget? It rocked the island — well what else would you expect with such a notable family involved in a murder? What's more it sticks in my mind because it was one of the first big cases I was associated with. I was a young officer at the time in the very early years of my service. I was doing an attachment with CID and not enjoying it much. The DI was a bastard by name of Ivor Fauval. You wouldn't remember him. He died not so long afterwards — cancer. They had a bloody great funeral for him, police officers acting as bearers, the full works, but I shouldn't think there were many who mourned him. He was a sod all right, the sort that gets the force a bad name.'

Dan was silent, unwilling to stop the flow, but Phil Gould looked at him suddenly, his eyes sharp behind the pale stubby lashes.

'What is your interest in this anyway, Dan?'

Dan told him about his meeting with Juliet, omitting to mention that she had given him a tailor-made excuse to investigate what he hoped might turn into a juicy story for him, and saw Phil Gould's eyes begin to twinkle beneath his thick sandy eyebrows.

'I see — there's a girl involved in this. Pretty, I suppose?'

'Very.'

'I thought so. No wonder you don't want to disappoint her. All right, what d'you want to know?'

Dan ignored the inference. 'Just a few basic details,' he said carefully. He knew he was treading a fine line. The case might be almost twenty years old but he did not want to arouse Phil Gould's suspicions that he was about to try to get it re-opened. The slightest hint of that and the inspector would bring the conversation to an end faster than he could say 'Louis Langlois'. 'Have you any idea why she did it?'

'Domestic dispute, I suppose. You know the way it is. There were all sorts of rows simmering inside the family — business and personal too. Louis was a wide boy. He had the sort of ideas that don't go down well in Jersey and he was a womaniser too. An even bigger bastard than Ivor Fauval!' He chuckled. 'He fell out with his father, Bernard, and went off God knows where. Then when Bernard died and left him a third share of all his holdings in the Langlois empire he came back and fell out with the rest of the family.'

'It must have been some falling out for his own mother to shoot him,' Dan said conversationally. 'Domestic dispute or not that's a pretty unusual scenario. She did do it, I suppose? If he was such a bastard and alienated everybody around him. . . ?'

Phil Gould laughed. 'You know that's what the centenier, John Germaine, tried to say at the time. He didn't want to believe she'd done it, even though she had confessed. I remember him and Ivor Fauval going hammer and tongs about it. Fauval wanted her arrested, Germaine was reluctant to do it. That made Fauval mad as a hatter. He said Germaine was too involved personally since he'd known Sophia Langlois since they were at school. And for once I can't say I blamed him. You know what a bloody bugbear it is having the amateurs like millstones round your neck.'

Dan nodded. 'True. But in this case he couldn't have been right, I suppose?'

Phil's eyes narrowed and for a moment Dan wondered if he had gone too far. Then the inspector said shortly: 'To tell you the truth, Dan, I've always wondered. It was too damn neat, too open and shut.'

246

'Oh come on, Mr Gould!' Dan steeled himself not to show excitement. 'If it wasn't her why should she say it was?'

'It's my guess she was protecting someone. She thought as a respected member of the community and a woman she'd be more likely to get off lightly. And by the way, drop the "Mr Gould" for Chrissakes. I'm not your inspector now. My name is Phil.'

Dan grinned. 'All right — Phil.' But he suspected the habit would be hard to break.

'Yep, that would be my guess,' the inspector continued. 'You could argue, of course, that she'd gone off her head with grief, found the body, picked up the gun in a state of shock and then convinced herself she'd fired it. I seem to remember somebody coming up with a theory on those lines at the time — David Langlois, the youngest son, if I remember rightly. There had been a lot of burglaries around the island and it was suggested Louis might have disturbed an intruder. But personally I don't think that holds water. Sophia might have acted very strangely when she gave herself up, refusing to say a word in explanation of what had happened, but I believe that was deliberate, the reaction of a woman in shock, perhaps, but certainly not the deranged behaviour of someone who had taken leave of her senses. I've rarely met anyone saner than Sophia Langlois. If she was lying she knew what she was doing all right.'

'What did the post mortem say about the time of death?'

'It did nothing to disprove Sophia's claim, if that's what you mean. But it doesn't prove anything either. You know how notoriously difficult it is to be accurate about time of death — so many factors can throw the assessment out. In any case, Louis had been out himself and would have arrived home only half an hour or so before his mother. And he was still wearing his DJ, black tie and frilly shirt when he was shot — another thing that might point to the intruder theory.'

'Nothing was taken, though, presumably? And there was no sign of forced entry?'

'None. But the housekeeper was getting old and forgetful — she quite often forgot to lock up, according to David. And of course, if it all happened just moments before Sophia came home the intruder could have panicked and fled empty-handed when he heard the car. At least, that's how the theory went.'

'But you don't believe it.'

'It's even more pat than asking us to believe Sophia did it. It was my opinion then, as now, that David came up with that one to try to take the heat off his mother. They were very close — he adored her, the way a youngest son often does. I remember the state he got in when she was sentenced . . .' he shook his head, recalling the hysterical outburst of the young David and how he had had to be removed physically from the court.

'So you think she was protecting someone,' Dan said, drawing the inspector back to the point. 'Who?'

Phil Gould laughed, a hearty guffaw that caused people sitting at the nearby tables to turn and look at him.

'Oh come on, Dan, now you're asking! If I didn't know that twenty years ago how the hell do you expect me to know now?'

'Didn't you ever have the slightest suspicion?'

'There were enough fireworks going off in that family to make Mount Etna look like a Palmatine Star nightlight,' Phil Gould said graphically. 'As far as motives go I reckon any one of them could have done it. Louis had a knack of making enemies.'

'So someone outside the family could have had a motive too?'

'True, but you know as well as I do the closest connections are always going to be the most likely, especially where a victim is killed in his own home. And besides, why should Sophie lie for an outsider?'

'Perhaps like you she thought one of the family was responsible — but perhaps she was wrong.'

'Perhaps.'

'But you don't think so.'

'No. Oh, shit, Dan, I don't know. It was a bloody long time ago. And this is now — and my glass is empty.'

Dan went to rise. 'Let me . . .'

'No, it's my turn. You might have asked to meet me but I still buy my round. Same again?'

'Better make mine a half of something long and not too alcoholic. I'm driving.'

'Shame!' But Phil Gould looked amused — until he remembered what had happened to Marianne.

Whilst he was at the bar Dan thought back over what had been said. So far everything tied in with what he had already thought but he hadn't learned a great deal that was new. Except about David trying to sell the police the burglar theory. Interesting. Had he also tried to sell it to Dan Deffains senior, his mother's advocate, and had Dan rejected it out of hand so that it did not even warrant a mention in the file? And what about the possibility that Louis had had other enemies outside the family who might have wanted him dead? Perhaps it was something he should follow up, but it wouldn't be easy after all this time and as Phil had pointed out Sophia would never have taken the blame unless she had believed someone she cared about was responsible. That meant very strong motives within the family — something Juliet could unearth if she tried.

Phil returned with the fresh round of drinks.

'So,' Dan said as Phil took the head off his own pint, 'forget motive for the moment. What about opportunity? Which of them could have done it?'

'Christ, what is this — the third degree?' Phil exploded. Beer foam had caught in his moustache and he wiped it away with the back of his hand.

'I'm just interested . . .'

'Hmm. All I can say is she must be a very attractive girl.'

'She is.'

'And you want to impress her.'

'Something like that.'

'Well it's about time you sorted yourself out a nice girlfriend. Though unless you've changed a good deal you don't need all this crap to do that. I seem to remember young ladies going weak at the knees when you were around.'

'You're exaggerating.'

'I'm bloody well not. And though I expect you'll tell me to mind my own business I'm not joking when I say it's time you sorted out your private life. It was rough on you, I know, but you can't go on grieving for ever. Marianne wouldn't expect that.'

'Perhaps not. But it's the way I want it. And we were talking about the Langlois family, not me. Which of them could have done it?'

249

'Dan, my brain is aching.'

'Mr Gould . . .'

'*Phil*, remember? Oh, all right, let me think. There were the two other sons, weren't there, Robin and David. There was Sophia's brother, Paul. There was his wife, Vivienne. And there was Robin's wife, Molly. She was having an affair with Louis — you'd better not tell your little girlfriend that. It might not go down too well and I doubt she knows anything about it. She might not even believe you, of course. It's not the easiest thing in the world to imagine your parents in flagrante delicto. As far as I can recall they were all in Jersey on the night in question and none of them had any alibi, except for the ones they gave one another.'

'There was an investigation then?'

'Not as such, though they all made statements. It's just that I looked at those statements with all the interest of a keen young copper who sees his first murder case turning out to be a damp squib.'

'So any one of them could have done it.'

'You could say that. The only close member of the family who was not in Jersey at the time was Catherine Carteret, Sophia's sister. She was teaching, in London, I believe, though she came dashing home as soon as the news broke. Yes, any one of them had the opportunity. And I reckon Sophia was enough of a family matriarch to lie for any one of them with the possible exception of Vivienne. If she *was* lying.'

'But I thought you said . . .'

'I know. That it was too neat. But there are still facts that can't be ignored.'

'Such as?'

'Number one — it was Sophia who reported Louis dead. The person discovering the body has to be a prime suspect. Number two, of all the motives hers was as strong as any and when she began talking she plugged it for all she was worth. Louis was breaking up the family by having a very indiscreet affair with his sister-in-law. Worse, he was breaking up the company. Sophia loved that company. She and Bernard had built it up together from a guest house started by her parents — she couldn't bear to see Louis destroy it. That was her story —

simple as that and every bit as devastating. Sophia is a great lady, Dan, with the emphasis on the lady. But she also has a streak of ruthlessness. She can be hard as iron and cold as steel when needs be. She could have done it. She had both motive and opportunity. You mustn't overlook the fact — she could have been telling the truth.' He raised his glass. 'Well, good luck to you, Dan, and good luck to that little girl of yours. I honestly would be very pleased to hear you had put the past behind you at last and married again.'

Dan said nothing. Phil Gould was not the first friend to try to persuade him to give it another go and he would certainly not be the last. Dan had given up being offended by the idea they seemed to have that Marianne could be replaced as his smashed motor bike had been. They meant well, he knew. But it would take one hell of a girl to make him forget Marianne. Dan doubted if he would ever meet her. And he was not sure he wanted to.

Chapter eighteen

Juliet turned her car into the pub car park, found a space and reversed into it, the squealing tyres registering their protest at her haste.

Was Dan already here, she wondered? but since she did not know what kind of car he drove she had no way of knowing. She knew very little about him at all if it came to that except that he was the son of her grandmother's advocate but then she supposed that was all she needed to know. His father had done a good job for Sophia, Aunt Catherine had said. That was recommendation in itself. Anyone who had been close to her grandmother earned an instant warm place in her heart.

What a strange thing affinity is, Juliet thought. From the first moment of meeting her grandmother it had been there between them, an unspoken bond. Although Sophia had not seen her since she was a tiny child she seemed to be able to put her finger right on her granddaughter's pulse — no, deeper than that even, Juliet thought – she could see right into her heart and had a knack of bringing to the surface deep hopes and fears, doubts and longings that Juliet scarcely acknowledged.

This morning it had happened again. Juliet had had breakfast with Sophia and they had lingered over coffee talking of Juliet's career.

'You are certain you are making the right move, are you?' Sophia had asked.

Juliet had smiled ruefully. 'I can't see how it can be wrong. Darby Grace is a very big, very well respected company and they have offered me a lot more money than I have been making at the Dream Machine.'

Sophia had nodded, her beautiful amethyst eyes thoughtful.

'Money isn't everything, you know. I suppose you'll think that's amusing, coming from me, and there's absolutely no doubt

252

that it smooths one's path and makes life a great deal more comfortable than it might otherwise be. But the fact is it can also be a trap. If you go into a company offering you an exceptionally good salary before you know where you are you'll find yourself tied to them whether you like it or not. "I can't give this up and move on," you'll find yourself saying. "It's too good a job". Especially if you have commitments at home. It's not good at any age and certainly not when you are young.'

'Grandma, I'm twenty-three.'

Sophia smiled. 'Twenty-three! If only you would appreciate just how young that really is and make the most of it! I never had the chance to be young — the war saw to that. Oh Juliet, forgive me. I shouldn't be telling you what to do. I'm an interfering old woman.'

'No you're not,' Juliet said. She was aware of a tingling in her spine as if her grandmother had inadvertently touched on some hidden nerve. How was it she could manage to make Juliet acknowledge her own doubts this way? If she had been one hundred per cent certain about joining Darby Grace why wasn't she there now? Why had she stolen a holiday which had taken her halfway round the world before starting with them? Yet she hadn't even considered refusing the job. Everyone — herself included — had said it was too good an opportunity to miss. Too good to miss. Exactly. Wasn't that what Grandma was saying? That when the advantages were stacked so heavily they made a prison from which it was almost impossible to escape.

It had been the same with Sean. Without even having set eyes on him her grandmother had somehow sensed Juliet's uncertainty, sensed that a good man had trapped her in exactly the same way she was predicting a good job would.

Juliet might have resented Sophia's instinctive knowledge of her as an invasion of her privacy but she did not. Never before had she so totally shared a wavelength with another person and the experience was more comforting than disturbing. Juliet loved her mother and father yet ever since she had been a little girl she had felt apart from them. They did not understand her and she did not understand them. It was almost, she had sometimes thought, as if she and they were looking down two different ends of a telescope. But with her grandmother the understanding was

253

total and the love that sprung from it as natural as the unspoiled countryside which stretched from La Grange to the sea. Only one thing Juliet could not understand: how Sophia could have confessed to killing her own son. But intuition — the same intuition that gave Sophia a clear insight into Juliet's deepest feelings — told Juliet that whatever Sophia had done it had not been murder.

Wouldn't it be wonderful if I could go home and tell Mum and Dad they were wrong! Juliet thought. With one stroke I could remove the barrier that has kept them apart from Grandma all these years. How worthwhile that would be!

The thought spurred her on and she hurried across the car park and through the main door of the pub into a large room set out as an informal restaurant. Although it was only just after twelve-thirty many of the tables were already occupied. 'It's as well to be early,' Dan had said to her on the telephone. 'The Windmill gets busy, even at this time of year.' Now she could see what he meant.

She looked around, unaccountably nervous. She couldn't see him amongst the jumble of people. She had got the right place, hadn't she? Oh surely! It was impossible to mistake the enormous windmill erected on the roof of the pub.

'Hello there. You got away then.'

She swung round. He was standing behind her. He was wearing a dark blue jersey and grey slacks and she thought with a slight jolt of surprise that he was taller than she had realised.

'I got away, yes,' she said. 'It wasn't as difficult as I imagined it might be.'

She did not elaborate, didn't tell him how half an hour ago she had still been chatting with her grandmother wondering how on earth she could explain dashing off at lunchtime without admitting she had someone to meet. But in the event it could not have been simpler. She had said: 'Would you mind if I went out for a bit?' and Sophia had only smiled. 'Of course not. You know I want you to treat La Grange as your home. Do exactly as you like, my dear. Will we see you for dinner?' She had nodded, glad she'd had the foresight to arrange to meet Dan for lunch. Absent for dinner would certainly have called for an explanation!

254

'If there isn't a table free down here we could always go up to the gallery,' Dan suggested.

'That sounds nice.'

'Shall we get a drink first? What will you have?'

'Beer,' Juliet said immediately, then laughed at the look of surprise he was unable to hide. 'Oh come on, I'm Australian, I'm thirsty, and it's the middle of the day. Don't Jersey girls drink beer?'

'Some do. A half or a pint?'

'Oh, a half. Though I'll probably have the other half later!' she added mischievously.

Dan bought two beers and they carried them up the open plan staircase to what he had called 'the gallery' where more tables had been set out in what reminded Juliet a little of an old-fashioned hay loft.

'At least we'll be quiet up here,' Dan said. 'If we ever get served!'

But a waitress was on hand. Dan chose steak and kidney pie and Juliet decided on scampi and salad.

'I suppose this isn't quite what you're used to,' Dan said as the waitress deposited a vinegar bottle and salt on their table.

'What do you mean?'

'Well, as a Langlois I presume you are more used to haute cuisine and a deferential head waiter placing the napkin over your knees!'

Juliet hardly knew whether to be flattered or annoyed. She was far less used to living in the lap of luxury than he seemed to imagine, but her irrepressible sense of humour came to her rescue.

'Oh, I don't mind roughing it once in a while,' she said airily. 'As long as it's in the cause of proving my grandmother's innocence!'

He laughed, admiring her for turning the tables on him so neatly. 'I take it that is an invitation to get down to business,' he said.

'You could put it like that. I won't deny I am very anxious to know if you have been able to make any progress.'

Dan hesitated. He had a journalist's — and policeman's — natural reluctance to share his information, yet he knew that if he was to retain Juliet's confidence and use her position in the family to gain inside knowledge he must give the impression that he was digging more on her behalf than on his own.

'I've talked to one or two people,' he hedged. 'What about you?'

'I'm afraid I haven't got very far,' she confessed. 'It's so difficult knowing how to bring the subject up. They're all so cagey. And I don't want to upset Grandma.'

'You are going to have to if you're going to turn up anything new.'

'I suppose so. I was hoping that you . . .'

'You were hoping I was going to do it all for you?' His voice was cold; once again the hard streak of the professional investigator had surfaced.

Juliet coloured. 'It's not that,' she said defensively. 'It's just that I really didn't know where to start. I thought maybe if you could give me some kind of lead I need not rush in treading all over people's toes unnecessarily. Who did you talk to anyway?'

'A policeman.'

'And what did he say? Did *he* think Grandma was guilty?'

'He said she might have been. Equally so might any of the rest of the members of your family.'

He heard the quick intake of her breath before it came out on a nervous little laugh.

'Do you have to put it so baldly?'

'You asked me what my contact said. I'm telling you.'

She was silent for a moment, turning her glass between her hands on the bare, ring-marked wooden table.

'I'm sorry,' she said at last. 'It's just that I find the whole thing incredible. It's almost as difficult to believe any of them were responsible as it is to believe Grandma . . . I mean, just look at them! Paul and Viv, middle-aged, no, more than that unless they are going to live to be a hundred and thirty or so, living a quiet sort of life and minding their own business; David, liked by everybody in spite of being head of the family business; Aunt Catherine, a bit eccentric but really sweet.'

'Your Aunt Catherine seems to be out of it. She was in London at the time, it would seem.'

256

'Well good. I'm glad to hear it. But I don't think any of them . . .'

'There are two others you've forgotten to mention. Your mother and father.'

For a moment he wondered if he had pushed her too far. Her head jerked up, eyes snapping with the hidden fire he had always suspected was there.

'Don't be ridiculous!'

'I'm not. They can't be excluded. They were here, remember. And they had motive and opportunity just like the others, I imagine.'

'For heaven's sake, how can you even suggest such a thing?'

'*I'm* not suggesting it. Others might. After all, if Sophia didn't kill Louis, someone else did. Statistics prove that murder is most often incestuous — victim and perpetrator are closely involved in some way. Let's face it, on that basis neither of your parents can be ruled out.'

The waitress came clattering up the stairs with the meals they had ordered and whilst she served them Dan tried to read Juliet's mind. He was taking a chance, he knew, by pushing her this far, but it was a calculated risk, based on the assumption that his suggestion that her parents might have been involved would give her an extra incentive to get to the truth. It had been one thing for her to want to prove her grandmother's innocence when she had assumed an outsider had killed Louis, now he had pointed out one of the family might have been responsible and she realised the hornet's nest she could be stirring up she might well back off. But if she thought her own parents were under suspicion then surely she would be all the more determined to uncover the culprit. Her first loyalty would be to them; the Jersey relatives couldn't mean that much to her — she had scarcely known them until a week or so ago. She would almost certainly throw them to the wolves to safeguard her parents' reputation.

Of course there was always the possibility that Robin or Molly *had* had something to do with Louis's death; they counted very much as suspects in Dan's book, but by the time such a thing occurred to Juliet, if ever it did, he hoped she would have provided him with the leads he needed.

257

'I'm sorry if I've upset you,' he said as the waitress disappeared again down the open-plan staircase. 'I just happen to think you should know what it is you're getting into.'

She rolled her knife and fork out of the paper napkin they were wrapped in.

'You haven't upset me. Annoyed me, perhaps. But not upset me. I was *upset* to discover my grandmother had served time for murder, even if they did call it manslaughter or whatever. After that, to be quite honest, everything else seems very small beer.'

Her voice was determinedly casual but he knew from the set of her face and her eyes, dangerously bright, that whatever she might say she *was* upset.

She's got guts, he thought, as well as being pretty. And beneath that veneer she is really rather vulnerable.

'Let's talk about something else while we're eating,' he suggested.

'I'd rather get it all over with at one go.' She put down her knife and fork and looked at him directly. 'What is it you want me to do?'

A nerve jumped in his throat, part triumph, part nervousness that it might still get away from him.

'Firstly I'd like to know exactly what each of them thought of Louis. They might be a good deal more truthful now than they were twenty years ago. And secondly I'd like to know where each of them claims to have been on the evening he died.'

'Don't you think they'll be a bit hazy about that after all this time?'

'I doubt it. After all everyone who was around at the time claims to be able to remember exactly what they were doing when they heard President Kennedy had been shot. When it comes to a family member their memory is bound to be that much sharper.'

'I suppose so. All right, I'll see what I can do. And what about you . . . ?'

'I'll do the same.'

She nodded, apparently satisfied, and picked up her knife and fork.

'All right. *Now* I'll talk about something different. What do you suggest?'

Jersey, Dan thought, was probably the safest subject. He would have liked to have asked Juliet something about herself — where she lived in Australia, what she did for a living — even a girl who would one day inherit the Langlois fortune must presumably do something! — whether she had a serious relationship . . . yes, he thought, he would very much like to know whether she had a serious relationship. But if he began asking her personal questions it was possible she would turn the tables and do the same to him. That could be awkward. Dan wouldn't have minded being quizzed about his private life; in his usual less-than-garrulous way he would have simply said he had no ties now and hadn't had for a very long time. Nothing, but nothing, would have drawn him on the subject of Marianne. But if Juliet began asking questions about what he did for a living it could get very awkward. Rack his brains as he might Dan had been unable to come up with a euphemism for 'journalist' which would be acceptable, neither arousing Juliet's suspicions nor her further curiosity. And he did not want to lie to her. Strange really, considering the shameless way he was using her, but there was a fine dividing line between deception by default and outright deliberate lying and Dan knew he could not bring himself to cross it.

I am like George Washington, he thought with a flash of self-derogatory humour. I go round cutting down any cherry tree that takes my fancy but I cannot tell a lie.

'So, I suppose you've been spending your time looking up old haunts,' he said, biting into his steak and kidney pie.

'Not really. I was only very young when I left, remember. Old haunts for me would be Grandma's garden, the beach, the fields near where I lived. I've driven around the lanes, of course, parked up at a few beauty spots to admire the views, but that's about all. I suppose I'm in a funny position, really, neither a tourist nor a resident, and the family seem to forget that because I've been away so long my geography of the island is limited to the hire company map and my knowledge of its history is really very sketchy indeed.'

Dan smiled, blessing his good fortune. His father, Dan senior, had been quite an amateur historian, a member of the Société Jersiaise and a wonderful raconteur into the bargain. Unconsciously Dan now borrowed something of his style as he related the old stories to Juliet, telling her how Jersey had once been part of Normandy and had remained so during the English reign of the Duke of Normandy, William the Conqueror. Later, when France and England were at war, Jersey had become an English outpost and during the French Revolution it had provided refuge for fleeing aristocracy. A beautiful island which had seen more than its fair share of conflict, his father had always said — and always been used as a pawn between international powers.

'As was proved in the last war,' he said, finishing the last of his steak and kidney pie with relish. 'Jersey under the jackboot. But I'm sure you know all about that.'

Juliet had to admit she did not. The war was yet another subject on which her family were curiously reticent.

'Well there is plenty of evidence everywhere of what happened then,' Dan said drily. 'The Jersey tourist industry is quite determined to make sure no one ever forgets we were the only part of England to be under German domination. You could be forgiven for saying we trade on it just the tiniest bit.'

'I wouldn't say that!' Juliet protested. 'Actually I want to have a look around some of the war museums but I haven't got around to it yet. I keep hoping one of the family will offer to take me but they don't and I don't like to suggest it. I don't want to impose on them too much.'

'So why don't I take you?' He said it without thinking, almost shocking himself. Juliet, too, looked surprised.

'Really? Well, that's very kind. But I didn't mean . . .'

He smiled. 'No, I'm sure you didn't. It would be my pleasure. I suggest the Underground Hospital. It was built by prisoners-of-war and it's pretty spectacular. I keep meaning to go and have another look at it myself but you know how it is when you live in a place — it takes a visitor to make you make the effort.'

'That's true. I live in Sydney but how often do I go to the Opera House?'

'I don't know. How often do you?'

'Practically never. Silly really.' She glanced at her watch. 'Good lord, is that the time? Don't you have a job to go to?'

'It's all right. I work for myself, which is why I shall be able to take you to the Underground Hospital tomorrow if that suits

260

you.' He said it smoothly but then went swiftly on before she could ask him what it was that he did: 'It might be best if I didn't pick you up though. Will you come to my house or shall I meet you there?'

She frowned slightly and he cursed himself, knowing she was wondering why he did not want her family to know he was seeing her. He should know better than to mix business with pleasure, dammit! And he still wasn't sure why he had done it. She was a very attractive girl, not a doubt of it, but he wasn't interested in girls, attractive or otherwise . . . was he?

'You think they might recognise you and ask some awkward questions?' she said thoughtfully. 'Well, transport is no problem for me. Perhaps it would be easiest if I met you at the Hospital. I'm sure I can find it from my map without too much trouble.'

'Shall we say about three?'

'Why not? I don't suppose I'll have been able to find out anything by then but . . .'

'At least we'll be keeping in touch.'

And that, he told himself, explained it. He didn't want to risk losing contact with Miss Juliet Langlois now because he didn't want to lose the chance of a rattling good story. Anything else was purely incidental.

Chapter nineteen

Dan had his key in the lock when he heard the telephone ringing. He pushed the door open and strode across the hall to snatch up the receiver.

'Hello?'

'Dan? I was just about to give up on you! Phil Gould.'

'Phil!' Dan only just stopped himself from saying 'Mr Gould'. 'I've been out to lunch.'

'Lucky for some!'

'It was business.'

'Oh yes? I'll believe you. Dan — you know what you were asking me about? And you know I said I reckoned it was purely a family affair? Well there was one thing I forgot. There's probably nothing in it, but there was a connection with Raife Pearson.'

'Raife Pearson? The Jersey Lily Nightclub man?'

'The same. Louis had been there, at the club, the night he died — and he and Raife had had a bust up. They were great pals, he and Raife, or at least they had been. You might say they were two of a kind, both flashy opportunists. At the time, of course, Raife looked the flashier. He was the one to catch the tourist trade in the early seventies with his big extravaganza varieties full of so-called star names that nobody had ever heard of — smutty comics and off-key singers, six-foot ex-Bluebell dancers in feathers and tights, second-rate magicians and even a fire-eater, you know the sort of thing. Seedy glitz. Whilst Louis, of course, represented the respectable end of the luxury market. But as I say they'd always had enough in common to be great pals — until that night.'

'So what happened?'

'Well there was some kind of almighty row. Half the staff heard it though no one seemed to know what it was about.'

'How do you know all this if the case was never investigated?'

'One of the barmen came forward after Louis was shot, thinking we might be interested. Said he'd been passing the office door and heard them yelling at one another. He thought he heard the word "blackmail" mentioned, but that seems unlikely. Raife hardly had — or has! — the sort of reputation that needs protecting. Anyway, Louis left the club soon afterwards with his bit of stuff. The barman said he heard him yell it wasn't all over yet, he'd see to that. But of course he never had the chance to see to anything. That night he was shot.'

Dan's eyes narrowed. Little hairs were standing up on the back of his neck the way they always did when he was on to something.

'This is an entirely new angle to me, Phil,' he said. 'It sounds very promising! Why was it never followed up?'

'Two reasons. One, Sophia Langlois confessed and Ivor Fauval was determined to believe she was guilty. And two, Raife had an indisputable alibi. He never left the club that evening. He watched the second performance of the floor show, he sat with some guests at one of the tables in full view of everyone in the place and he did not leave until well after the time Louis was found dead. He didn't do it, Dan. He couldn't have. But I thought you might like to know about the row. Just for the hell of it.'

'Thanks, Phil. But what made you remember now all of a sudden?'

There was a chortle at the other end of the line. Dan could imagine Phil Gould plucking at his ginger moustache as he did when he was amused.

'I have to confess I didn't remember. Not off my own bat, anyway. After talking to you I came back and got out the files, just to refresh my memory. That's where I found it. As I say, I don't think it will do you any more good than it did us twenty years ago. But I'm telling you anyway.'

'I'm grateful. Don't forget, if you think of anything else. . .'

'I know. I'll be in touch. And you can buy me another drink when you see me.'

'I certainly will.'

But there wasn't a lot in it for him, Dan thought as he put the phone down. A bit of extra colour, perhaps, the contrasting character to the suave sophisticated Langlois family. But even that scarcely applied any more. Middle age had taken the edge off Raife's flamboyance. These days the Jersey Lily Night club was as respectable a nightspot as Caesar's Palace and Swansons, booking only well known TV artistes, and Raife himself, with an extra covering of flesh beneath his well-cut dinner jackets, looked softer and less dangerous than the man Dan remembered from the impressionable days of his childhood. In those days Raife had driven around in a car with smoked glass windows, he recalled, and when he had emerged he had looked a little like a Mafia character in an American gangster film with his jutting jaw, hooded eyes and cigar. It was a wonder, Dan thought, that he hadn't been pulled in for questioning over the Louis Langlois shooting on the strength of his appearance alone! But he hadn't been and that must mean that there had been nothing there worth following up.

Dan rubbed a hand thoughtfully over his face. He was grateful to Phil Gould for taking the trouble to look up the file and phone him with the additional information but he had to admit that it certainly looked as if Ivor Fauval had been right to dismiss the quarrel as irrelevant. If Raife Pearson hadn't had such a cast iron alibi it might be a different story. But he had. Yet still Dan's intuitive antennae were buzzing. There was something here, he was sure of it, but what? Was it possible Raife had had a hit-man do his dirty work for him? He was certainly the type. But timewise it didn't really fit. It would have been too much of a coincidence if there had been someone suitably qualified on the premises — convenient chances like that simply did not happen. And there would not have been time between the quarrel and the shooting for him to have put out a contract. He could have made a phone call, of course, but it was still cutting it pretty fine — getting hold of the person he wanted, just like that, the hit-man being in just the right place to kill Louis less than an hour later — it could have been done but Dan knew hit-men liked to plan their jobs meticulously and this was all too sudden, too haphazard. Unless it had been vital Louis died that night.

Dan chewed on his thumb nail, considering, then rejecting it. By all the standards he'd ever worked to it didn't hold water.

264

Desperate people took chances, amateurs took chances. Professional hit-men did not. Pity, Dan thought. What a story it would make! And Juliet would be pleased too.

The thought caught him almost by surprise and he had a quick vision of the way her face would light up if he was able to tell her that not only had she succeeded in clearing her grandmother's name but the rest of the family were in the clear also. But he wasn't going to tell her. With Raife's innocence a more or less unassailable fact there was no point. In fact it might very well be counter-productive. She might latch on to his introduction of a diversionary character and let up on the investigation he wanted her to conduct amongst the members of her own family. That would be a great pity, for a chance like this to get inside information wouldn't come again. No, he must not do anything that might rock the boat in that direction for the sake of what was almost certainly a red herring. But it would be nice to know what Raife and Louis had quarrelled about, all the same.

Dan stood for a moment longer deep in thought. He could always ask Raife, but it wasn't likely he'd get a straight answer. And if the staff had said at the time that they didn't know what it was all about then there was very little chance of learning anything from them now, even if he could find them, which he doubted. Hotel and club workers in Jersey were a notoriously transient lot.

But there was one favourite avenue of investigation he had not yet started down — the archives of the Jersey Post. In the past Dan had found the archives to be a rich vein of information, indisputable black and white reporting of events as they had appeared at the time, not coloured by a witness's personal recollection some years on. There might be nothing there, of course. It was hardly likely that the Post, excellent newspaper though it was, had printed information which the police had been unable to unearth — except, of course, that the Jersey Post would probably have been trying where the police, it seemed, had not. But scouring the columns of news at about the time Louis had died might uncover some valuable clues, titbits which could slot into place like pieces of a jigsaw puzzle though at the time they had seemed unimportant or irrelevant. At the moment Dan did

265

not know what it was he was looking for but he was sure he would know it when he saw it.

Dan smiled to himself. He was feeling very good about this investigation. As yet there was nothing to go on, nothing new or different from anything that had been public knowledge twenty years ago. But if he knew anything about it there soon would be. The feeling of standing on the very brink of an exciting unknown tickled Dan's nerve endings again.

He reset his answering machine and fetched a new pad and pencil from his office. Then he retrieved his keys from the hall table where he had dropped them as he came rushing in, and went out, locking the door behind him.

In the long low attic room at La Grange Juliet was sitting on the boarded-in floor working her way methodically through an old wooden box of mementos. It was fascinating stuff — everything from old photographs to yellowing theatre programmes, postcards to school reports — and although she had not yet found anything with any obvious bearing on Louis's death she was enjoying herself immensely.

Perhaps, she thought, her parents had had her welfare in mind when they had whisked her away to a new life in a new country. No, no perhaps about it, she was sure that they had. But at the same time they had deprived her of the rest of her family and a hung chunk of her heritage. Now, though her main purpose in asking to go through some of the old photographs and memorabilia in the attic was to try to build up a picture of Louis, yet at the same time the faded scraps in the dusty boxes were a treasure trove of collected family memories and Juliet felt a little as she had done when as a child she had been given her first magic painting book. That same sense of wonder she had experienced as she brushed water on to the page and saw the black and white picture take on softly muted colour was with her now as she leafed through the long-forgotten mementos.

Some teased, posing more questions than they answered, like the Valentine's card signed only by a question mark and three kisses, others were clues to the growing-up years of Louis, Robin and David.

Even as a child it was obvious Louis had been the wild one —

the sporting mementos were all his and almost without exception his school reports read: 'Could do better if he tried', 'Should learn to take discipline' and, most revealing of all: 'If Louis applied himself to his work with as much enthusiasm as he does to getting into mischief he would be an excellent pupil'. Her own father's reports, on the other hand, spoke of his day dreaming, whilst David's depicted a less than brilliant boy who achieved good results through hard work. The photographs, too, told their story — Louis always ready, it seemed, to pose for the camera, the other two more interested in whatever it was they were doing. There was also a photograph of Louis and Robin with a young girl who Juliet recognised as her mother. They were in a field, all three of them, Molly between the two boys, her arms linked through theirs, but once again it was Louis who had stolen the shot. What a handsome boy he had been! Juliet thought, and tried to ignore the fact that Molly was standing a little closer to Louis than to Robin, leaning her head towards him as she laughed for the camera.

Juliet stacked the papers she had already sorted into a neat pile and delved into the trunk again. At the bottom was a box file, bulging at the edges. Carefully she lifted it out. Something had been written on it, not on a label but straight on to the grey cardboard with a thick black pen. Juliet held it to the light and read: 'Louis Langlois. Private Papers.' Her skin prickled with excitement and she opened the box eagerly. Then disappointment set in. The box appeared to be full of nothing but bank statements and receipted bills, 'Private' as opposed to pertaining to business, and a small red-covered petty cash book. Nothing there. She was on the point of putting it back when something made her flip the cash book open, reading a few of the entries at random.

At first she did not understand them. Just names and sums of money. Enormous sums of money. Then, as she pored over Louis' flamboyant scrawl light began to dawn. The accounts were connected with gambling — Louis's winnings and losses at a couple of London casinos. But there were individual names too — presumably Louis had also gambled privately and recorded the results with enormous precision. Juliet's immediate reaction was one of disgust but she read on in almost morbid

267

fascination. And as she did so one name leaped at her from the page, and then reappeared with shocking regularity.

Paul Carteret.

The dates beside the amounts were all in 1970 and 1971; totalling them Juliet realised they came to thousands of pounds. Sums like that wouldn't mean as much to a Langlois or a Carteret as it would to many people, of course, but it was a lot of money all the same. And none of it appeared to have been paid off. Whilst lines had been drawn through most of the other transactions, Paul's debts to Louis stood out with startling clarity. The last one was dated November 1971 — just days before Louis's death.

Carefully Juliet replaced the cash book beneath the bank statements and put the whole lot back in the box where it had lain neglected for almost twenty years. She felt slightly sick — so Dan had probably not been far out when he had said that some of her family had motives for killing Louis — she had just unearthed Paul's. Eight thousand pounds worth.

Juliet got up, realising her feet had gone numb from sitting on them so long. She had, she thought, done more than enough investigating for one afternoon.

Of all the wartime museums in Jersey perhaps the most unforgettable is the German Underground Hospital at Meadowbank, St Lawrence. From a cave-like entrance at the foot of a steep hillside the tunnels and caverns burrow into the solid wall of rock, each perfectly symmetrical, each with its own specific purpose, each hewn by the sweat of a prisoner-of-war.

As a child Juliet had left Jersey long before she was old enough to be taken to the Hospital, so now she stared almost in disbelief at the monument to the terrible times her grandmother and the other islanders had lived through.

Dan had paid for them to go in and Juliet walked slightly ahead of him through the turnstile and down the first echoing tunnel, chill and dark after the bright sunshine outside. She wanted time to read each and every one of the pieces of information on the display boards, to look into the half-shored up unfinished passages and soak up the atmosphere that emanated

268

from every inch of bare rock face. It was, after all, part of her heritage, a heritage which she had lost without even realising it.

Dan obviously knew the Hospital well; he pointed out the pipes for central heating and air conditioning and the rooms behind their protective grilles laid out as hospital wards, operating theatre and officers' mess rooms. Here, in the honeycomb of passages, Juliet forgot for the time being the twenty-year-old mystery that dominated her thoughts and wondered what it had been like living here in the knowledge that human beings were dying like slaves of old as they constructed an impregnable fortress for the invaders. They were Polish and Spanish, Russian and Belgian, the plaques on the walls said, and Juliet found herself remembering that her great grandparents, Charles and Lola, had been prisoners-of-war themselves. When their children saw the mistreatment of the poor men who had built the hospital they must have known that their parents were suffering a similar fate. How terrible it must have been for them! Yet somehow they had survived it and Paul had even managed to escape to England in his father's boat.

Paul. Her stomach lurched as she thought of him, catapulting her back to the present and her own dilemma. Should she tell Dan what she had discovered? Yesterday afternoon, sitting on her heels in the attic she had decided against it, for the moment anyway. She would talk to Paul first and see what he had to say — tonight she was having dinner with him and Viv, and it might give her the opportunity to raise the subject of Louis, she had thought. Now, however, she found herself wondering if perhaps it was wrong to stay silent. She had, after all, asked for Dan's help and he had been good enough to give it. Wasn't she being just a little dishonest — and unfair — keeping to herself the one piece of information that, when put together with whatever he was able to find out, might at least begin to solve the puzzle?

But it really wasn't that clear cut. Juliet had not realised how protective she would feel of her family's secrets. However indebted she might be to Dan Deffains she was not ready to trust him completely.

She glanced quickly at him, half afraid suddenly that he might somehow have been able to read her mind and know she was keeping something from him. He was looking at a display set up on the wall of the tunnel and the electric strip lighting threw his face into sharp relief — the jutting lines and planes that could be so hard and uncompromising, the full mouth and creases at the corners of his eyes that worked such a transformation when he smiled — and with a shock she realised for the first time what a very attractive man he was. How could she have failed to notice it? Because she had been so bound up in herself, she supposed, able to think of nothing but getting to the bottom of the family mystery. Now, quite suddenly, she was startlingly aware of him as a man and the awareness made her awkward, especially when he turned unexpectedly.

'You saw this? Violette Szabo, the British Agent? Her daughter lived in Jersey. She was just a little girl when her mother was shot.'

'Yes. Her father was killed in the war too, wasn't he? Etienne Szabo.'

'You've obviously heard of them before.'

'Yes.'

There was a poem she had once read, which Etienne had written to Violette. She couldn't remember where she had seen it but it had stuck in her memory as being quite beautiful: 'The life that I have is all that I have; And the life that I have is yours; The love that I have of the life that I have; Is yours and yours and yours. A rest I shall have, and a peace I shall have, But death will be but a pause; For the peace of my years in the long green grass Is yours and yours and yours . . .'

They were almost back at the entrance to the Hospital. Outside the sun was shining, early summer bright in a cloudless blue sky, but none of it reached into the cold grey passages. Juliet shivered suddenly. She had got cold almost without realising it; now she wanted to be outside in the fresh air and the warmth.

'Can we go now?'

'Of course, if you're ready.'

'I'm ready.'

'Well, did you enjoy it?' he asked as they emerged into the sunshine.

'I don't think enjoy is quite the right word.'

'An experience, then.'

270

'Oh, certainly that.' But she wasn't only thinking of the museum pieces. She was thinking of the sharp thrill of awareness she had experienced when she had seen him, quite literally, in a different light.

'What do you say we look for somewhere doing cream teas?' he suggested.

She looked back at him. His eyes were on her, his mouth half-smiling. Nothing hard about that face now, just a strength that made her stomach lurch suddenly. But the unexpectedness of the emotion, twice repeated in such a short space of time, panicked her.

'I think I ought to be getting back.'

Even as she said it she knew she was perversely half-hoping he would try to persuade her to stay. She had the unmistakeable feeling she would not take much persuading. But pressure was not Dan Deffains's style.

'I guess you know best.'

'Yes. Thank you for a lovely afternoon.'

'And you'll be in touch.'

'Yes.' She hesitated, wondering again if she should tell him at least that she was going to dinner with Paul and Viv tonight. But again she decided against it. Better to keep her own counsel for the moment. Later, when she had heard what Paul had to say, she would decide what to do. 'I'll phone you tomorrow,' she said and walked away across the car park to where she had left her hire car.

Dan watched her go, watched the scarlet Metro streak out of the car park in the opposite direction to St Helier, and rubbed his chin thoughtfully.

Was he going soft or what? *Cream tea?* He hadn't had a cream tea since . . . He broke the thought mid-stream and waited for the pain to come rushing in. Marianne had loved cream teas. They'd used to stop off on summer afternoons at one of the little cafés that served them, and he'd always been amused at her childlike enjoyment, scraping the last bit of strawberry jam from the pot, licking her lips like a little cat until the very last taste of cream had gone. He'd never been that keen on cream teas himself, give him a good juicy steak any time, but he'd eaten

271

them to please her. Now . . . He narrowed his eyes against the glare of the sun, surprised to discover that he was remembering without wanting to bury himself in a deep dark hole, without wanting to get his hands around the neck of the bastard who killed her, without burning up with love and anger and grief. He felt sad, yes, but it was a sweet sadness, nostalgic almost rather than ravaging.

And oddly he knew that part of the sadness was regret that Juliet had not accepted his invitation.

Chapter twenty

Dinner at Paul and Vivienne Carteret's was always a patchy affair. Viv had never been much of a cook and left to her own devices the food she served up ranged from the unappetising to the inedible. When entertaining she invariably hired someone in to prepare the meal and see to the clearing up afterwards, but tonight she had been badly let down — Fenny le Grove's son had telephoned during the afternoon to say his mother had gone down with a stomach bug and Viv had had no option but to roll up her sleeves and take over.

'I'd never have decided on coq-au-vin if I'd known I had to do it myself,' she complained to Paul when he arrived home from the office to find her in the kitchen hacking away at a chicken in an effort to cut it into joints. 'I do think it's very inconsiderate of Fenny to be ill today just when I need her.'

'Never mind, Friday would be even more inconvenient,' Paul comforted her. 'You haven't forgotten half the Tourist Board are coming to dinner then?'

'Oh my God, I had forgotten! Well, if Fenny's not better we shall have to have something sent over from one of the hotel kitchens.'

'We could do that tonight if you like,' Paul said hopefully. Even had Viv been completely sober he doubted the chicken would be worth eating and as it was she had been fortifying herself with gin and tonic during her lengthy preparations and was beginning to get decidedly slap-dash.

To his disappointment, however, Viv dismissed the idea.

'No, it's only Juliet, and it would be a pity to waste the things I've bought for the coq-au-vin. The mushrooms won't keep, the chicken is a fresh one and there's a bottle of red wine I got especially.'

'I can't imagine the red wine going to waste when you're

around,' Paul said, and Viv snorted indignantly, pulling at chicken skin with her long red nails.

'It's only plonk! That's why I bought it — I thought you'd object to my using good stuff in a casserole.'

'Very true,' Paul said, resigning himself to a less-than-Cordon Bleu meal.

When Juliet arrived at seven Viv was still wearing her old slacks and struggling to prepare a salad while the potatoes boiled over onto the hob.

'Don't worry, Viv,' Juliet said when her aunt apologised. 'You go and get changed — I'll take over here.'

'Really?' Viv sounded relieved but amazed that anyone should actually volunteer for such a chore.

'I don't mind at all,' Juliet said, handing Viv her gin and tonic. 'I do quite a bit of cooking at home.'

'All right. I'll be as quick as I can.'

'No hurry. Have a nice long soak,' Juliet said. 'The chicken will be at least another half hour if we're not all to risk getting salmonella.'

'Bless you!' Viv sipped her gin and disappeared out the door. 'You're a good girl, Juliet!'

Juliet smiled wanly. She wondered if Viv would think she was quite so wonderful if she knew what was in her mind — half an hour with Viv out of the way meant half an hour alone with Paul, perhaps the best chance she would have to ask him a few pertinent questions.

'A glass of sherry, Juliet — or would you rather have a g and t?' Paul asked when Viv had gone.

'A g and t I think.' Juliet was not looking forward to what she had to do; a gin might, she thought, help her through it. She adjusted the heat under the potatoes — they would be more than done by the time the chicken was ready — and cut the French bread into thick slices for the croûtes. But it was an effort to keep her hand steady and when Paul returned with the gin she sipped it gratefully, wondering how best to broach the subject. Thankfully he made it easy for her.

'How is your grandmother today? Better?'

'Better than she was. I'm still concerned about her . . .' Juliet hesitated then plunged in. 'Paul — there are a few things I was hoping to ask her about but obviously if she's poorly I really can't. I don't want to upset her.'

'Oh and what are they?' Paul asked, but Juliet could tell from his expression and the way he took a gulp of his Glenfiddich that he knew already.

'Louis,' she said.

'Louis? You mean my nephew Louis?'

'Well of course. I'm curious about him. What was he like?'

For a moment Paul looked startled. That wasn't the question he had been expecting.

'What was he like? Well, he had a lot of charm. No one could deny that. The ladies certainly fell for him. You could say he had a devilish streak they found irresistible. And he liked them. A little too much.'

'He never married though.'

'Oh no, not Louis. Sensible man, he knew how to love 'em and leave 'em. But then he knew how to make the most of all life's little pleasures. He was fond of good food, good wine, good living generally.'

'And gambling? Did he gamble?'

'He was a bit of a one in that direction, yes. He used to go over to London and even the States to the casinos. He couldn't gamble here, of course. It's illegal — though if he had his way he'd have had the law changed. He'd have liked to open a casino or gambling club of his own as an extension to one of the hotels.'

'You talked about it then?'

'Well yes. But I couldn't see that he'd ever get anywhere with something like that. Jersey can be pretty set in its ways and even Louis wouldn't have stood much chance of getting the law changed so drastically.'

'If he was so keen I expect he found ways to gamble himself,' she persisted and from the corner of her eye noticed that Paul had begun to sweat a little.

'There's nothing to stop anyone gambling in the privacy of their own home, obviously,' he said shortly. 'Good God, plenty of people do that.'

'I suppose they do.' Juliet hesitated, unsure how to go on. She could hardly ask Paul outright about the money he had

275

owed Louis and whether Louis's death had saved him from having to pay it. Judging by the fact that the entries had never been ruled out in Louis's little account book she rather suspected it had. But so what? Juliet was suddenly overcome with repugnance for what she was doing. Standing here in her uncle's kitchen pretending to cook his dinner and asking questions with a view to proving that he had had the motive, and perhaps the opportunity, to kill Louis. All very well to argue that her original intention had been good, to clear her grandmother's name, but the road to hell, they say, is paved with good intentions. Suddenly Juliet felt very strongly that she had somehow inadvertently taken that road.

'You're right, of course,' she said, shifting the subject. 'It certainly sounds as if Louis enjoyed life. I should imagine he was very popular.'

A short laugh from the doorway made her look up. Viv was standing there, holding her glass high so that it almost looked as though she was about to drink a toast. She had changed into a bright green dress; the colour reflected in her eyes and vied with the scarlet of her lips.

'Did I hear you say Louis was popular?' she asked loudly. 'If so I have to tell you you are very much mistaken.'

Her voice was slightly slurred; Juliet, embarrassed, wondered just how much gin she had drunk.

'Come on now, Viv, let's not speak ill of the dead,' Paul urged her, mock jovial. 'We were just saying Louis liked the good things in life, and so he did.'

'You can say that again!' Viv shrieked. 'But *this* good thing didn't like him — and neither did anyone else much. Louis made plenty of enemies inside the family and out. It was his way, you know that. He loved being top dog. Loved making others look small. Loved taking from them what little they had. Loved creating mayhem. Cuckolding, boozing, greedy, mean-spirited Louis — God bless him!'

'Viv!' Paul said sharply. 'That's enough. You don't mean what you are saying. Louis wasn't that bad.'

Viv giggled. In a younger woman her demeanour would have been unpleasant. At her age it was quite grotesque.

'You're a fine one to talk, Paul! Louis wasn't that bad, was

276

he? You hated his guts! No one was more pleased than you when he . . .'

'Viv, that will do!' Paul thundered. A pulse was beating at his temple, and Juliet, guilty and embarrassed, leaped in:

'Viv — I've cut the bread for croûtes. Would you like me to fry them? Where's the oil?'

'Croûtes? For a minute I thought you said . . . Oops, sorry! Never mind bloody fried bread. Let's just eat. If you want to, that is. I'm not sure that I do.'

Juliet tried to smile but her lips felt stiff.

'Just go and sit down, Viv. I'll serve in a moment.'

'Sit down before I fall down, you mean? That's not such a bad idea, except that I think I'll sit here so we can talk while you're doing . . . whatever it is you're doing. Now, you were asking about Louis. What was it you wanted to know?'

'Nothing really,' Juliet said and for the first time she meant it. The emerging picture of the uncle who had met his death when she was only four years old was not a pleasant one. Just at the moment she did not think she could face any more of it.

As soon as she decently could Juliet pleaded a headache and left, telling herself that Viv and Paul would probably be only too glad to see her go.

Dinner had been one of the most uncomfortable meals she could ever remember having to sit through. There had been no further mention of Louis — between them she and Paul had managed to steer the conversation towards less controversial topics and Viv had subsided into a mellower mood. But the awkward atmosphere had persisted and Juliet knew she was responsible.

'I'm sorry, really sorry,' she said to Paul when Viv went to the bathroom between courses.

Paul served himself to an extra slice of Black Forest Gateau — straight from the hotel kitchens, Juliet guessed.

'It wasn't your fault. Viv can be pretty explosive when she's been drinking. I'm just sorry you had to witness it.'

'I know but . . .' She wanted to say that if she hadn't raised the subject of Louis it would never have happened but she could not bring herself to mention his name again.

'In case you hadn't realised it Louis is a rather touchy subject in this family,' Paul said, as if reading her mind. 'In life as in death. Viv put things pretty baldly but most of what she said was true. We sometimes used to joke that the only person who didn't hate him was his mother — rather ironic, as it turned out.' He pulled a face as he heard Viv coming back down the stairs. 'Better change the subject. How about coffee?'

Juliet had agreed to the coffee and even offered to help wash up, an offer Viv had swiftly refused. The daily woman would be in in the morning, she could deal with the clearing-up then. Imagining her face when she saw the state of the cooker hob, the burned saucepans and the plates and cutlery which Viv had not even bothered to load into the dishwasher gave Juliet a brief moment's wry amusement, though it was tempered with sympathy. Any daily woman who could stand working for Viv for long must be sorely in need of a job!

When she left Viv kissed her warmly and said she hoped she would come again, as if she had totally forgotten the earlier scene. But Juliet found it less easy to put the incident — and her own sense of guilt concerning it — out of her mind. As she started up the engine of her hire car she had already more or less decided what she was going to do; by the time she had turned, not into the road leading to La Grange but towards St Helier, she acknowledged she was more or less on auto-pilot. Her curiosity had caused more than enough trouble already, creating far more problems than it had solved. Time to put a stop to it. She would see Dan Deffains and tell him she was not prepared to continue interfering with the ghosts of the past and she would tell him right now.

The lights were burning in the downstairs windows of the tall old house on the outskirts of St Helier. Juliet glanced at her watch. Ten o'clock. Late, but not too late. She couldn't imagine Dan being an early bird and in any case what she had to say would not take more than ten minutes.

She rang the bell and waited. No reply. Perhaps it *was* too late to come calling. Perhaps he was in the shower or engrossed in watching something on television. Or perhaps he just hadn't heard her. Juliet was just hesitating between ringing the bell again and going home and leaving what she had to say until the

278

morning, when a light came on in the hall and the door was opened.

He was — thank heavens — fully dressed in shirt and slacks.

'Juliet! What are you doing here?'

'I wanted to talk to you.' She felt foolish suddenly. There really had been no need to come rushing round to see him tonight. The morning would have been quite soon enough.

'I see. You'd better come in then.' As she walked past him into the hall she caught the fleeting gleam of quickening interest in his eyes.

'I know it's late but I was practically passing,' she lied. 'I thought maybe it would be better to come now rather than disturb you tomorrow when you may be working.'

Her voice tailed away suddenly. A woman had emerged from the sitting room, a petite dark-haired woman a few years older than Juliet herself.

'I think it's time I was going, Dan. I'll see you again.' The woman stood on tiptoe, kissing him lightly on the cheek. 'Take care now.'

'Yes, and you, love. I'll see you soon.'

'All right. Bye now.' She smiled at Juliet as she passed but it was a guarded smile, without warmth, and Juliet wished heartily that she had not come. Stupid, really, but it had never crossed her mind Dan might have a woman with him. She wondered why the very idea of it made her feel irritated and depressed. A man as attractive as he was was bound to have women friends for heaven's sake!

'I'm sorry,' she said awkwardly, 'I didn't mean to interrupt.'

'It's all right. You didn't. Fran was just leaving.'

Fran. Yes, she looked like a Fran. Self-assured and pretty. Just the sort he would go for. Juliet's stomach tightened another notch.

'Look, I realise I should have waited until tomorrow,' she said hastily. 'It was a hell of an imposition, turning up like this. I'll go again.'

'No need. I'm going to have a nightcap. Why don't you join me?'

His hand was under her elbow, steering her into the sitting-

279

room. Fran's perfume lingered faintly. Juliet tried not to notice it.

'What would you like?' he asked.

'Oh, something soft. I've already had a couple of glasses of wine this evening and I'm driving.'

'Mineral water?'

'Fine.'

'It seems awfully unexciting,' he said, passing her the glass.

'No, really, I don't want anything else.' She didn't add that after seeing Viv's drunken performance this evening she thought she might very well give up alcoholic liquor completely and for ever.

'So,' he said, pouring himself a good measure of whisky. 'What brings you here at this time of night? Interesting developments?'

'No. I'm sorry, Dan, but I've had second thoughts. I don't think I want to go on with this.'

'Oh really?' Not for a moment did he allow his expression to betray his dismay. 'Why is that?'

'Because I think I'm stirring up a hornet's nest.'

'That might mean you are getting somewhere.'

'I suppose so but I'm beginning to wonder if I have any right to do that. My family must have suffered a great deal over what happened. What right do I have to rake it all up again?'

'I thought you were anxious to establish your grandmother's innocence.'

'She claimed responsibility. Nobody forced her to do that.'

'How do you know?'

'Oh come on! I've had a couple of weeks in which to get to know her but I think I can safely say she is not the sort of woman anyone can force to do anything. In her own quiet way she is a very determined lady. No one forced her and no one framed her. The decision to confess was hers. Right or wrong, who am I to interfere after all this time?'

'Hmm.' He looked at her steadily. 'What brought on this change of heart?'

Juliet sipped her mineral water. 'What do you mean?'

'The last time I saw you you were absolutely dedicated to investigating the past. Now you turn up at — well, rather a late

280

hour for a social visit, saying you don't want to go on with it. Something must have happened to change your mind.'

'Not necessarily,' she hedged. 'I just don't like interrogating my relatives, that's all.'

His pulses quickened. 'I see. And which of them was it you were interrogating when you suddenly developed a prickly conscience?'

The colour flamed in her cheeks. 'I don't think that is any of your business.'

'Really? Then let me remind you that you came to me asking me for my help. I have invested quite a bit of time and effort into helping you with your enquiries. I would have said that makes it my business.'

She bit her lip, embarrassed. Put like that it didn't sound too good.

'Look, Dan, I don't really expect you to understand but I just feel terribly disloyal to my family. In the beginning I didn't really know them. My only loyalty was to my grandmother. I even thought in a naive sort of way that if I could prove she had been wrongly convicted my parents would make things up with her. They went to Australia because of what happened you see and they've really had nothing to do with her ever since. I thought maybe I could bring them together again. But now I feel like some kind of spy. I've got to know the others and to like them and I can't do this to them. When Viv blew her top tonight about Louis I realised for the first time just what a dislikeable person he must have been and I realised something else too. What on earth would happen if I discovered one of them had a hand in his death? It would start the whole nightmare up for them all over again. I can't do it, really I can't.'

Dan sipped his drink. He was sitting in one of the faded wing-chairs, long legs splayed, apparently very relaxed. But his eyes were narrowed and he tapped thoughtfully on the rim of his glass with his forefinger.

'You think then that someone else in your family might be implicated,' he said after a moment.

'Isn't that what *you* suggested when I first talked to you about it?'

'Well, yes. Yes, I did, it's true. But now I'm beginning to wonder if I might have been wrong.'

'How come?'

He turned his glass between his hands, regarding her steadily.

'Suppose I told you I have uncovered at least one angle that has nothing whatever to do with any of your family, Louis excluded of course. Would that make any difference to the way you feel about going on with your enquiries?'

Juliet sat forward eagerly. Her eyes were suddenly very bright.

'Say that again!'

'What?'

'That you think there's a chance someone else might be implicated — someone outside the family.'

'I didn't exactly say that. Don't put words in my mouth.'

'Who?' Juliet demanded.

He hesitated. He was still not certain whether he should be telling her what Phil Gould had told him. For one thing it was breaking a confidence, for another he was no nearer knowing what it was Louis and Raife Pearson had quarrelled about that night, and certainly he had not the least reason to suppose it had any bearing on the shooting. But in a way the second reason negated the first. Raife was not and never had been under suspicion. It was no secret — at the time plenty of people at his club had known about the quarrel, but no one had ever been able to point the finger at Raife. Now Dan felt the one way to make Juliet keep on digging was to dangle an incentive under her nose. And besides . . . she was obviously very worried and unhappy about this whole affair. He would have liked to be able to reassure her that none of her family were involved.

'All right, I'll tell you as much as I know,' he said.

He watched her as he talked, watched the expressions flicker across her face, and found his attention wandering.

What was it about her that made him feel this way? It was so long since any woman had reached him on any level at all, let alone stirred this cocktail of tenderness and, yes, desire, that he was experiencing now when he looked at her, listening intently as he talked about Raife Pearson and the possible connection between him and Louis. He was, he thought, beginning to want her and the emotion was disturbing. Angry with himself, feeling

282

oddly that he was somehow betraying Marianne, he dragged his full attention back to Louis Langlois.

'So, there you have it,' he said at last. 'Raife Pearson is just one man outside the family who had quarrelled with Louis.'

'Hmm.' She was looking thoughtful, her earlier hopefulness overshadowed a little as if she too had seen through the thinness of the story. 'Did he hate him enough to kill him though? I mean, if he'd been going to shoot Louis wouldn't he have done it there and then, not waited until he got home and shot him down in cold blood?'

'Raife didn't shoot him. He couldn't have. It would have had to be a hired gun.'

'It sounds awfully far-fetched to me. He would have had to have a pretty strong motive to go to all that trouble — or take the risk if it comes to that. I'd like to think it might have been him, of course. I've just got my doubts, that's all.'

Dan drained his glass and got up to pour himself a refill, wondering just how much he should say.

'There were plenty of others who had good reason to hate Louis by all accounts.'

'Hate him enough to kill him? Do you really think people go around killing other people because they hate them? Isn't it far more likely to be because they love them — well, love them too much, or for all the wrong reasons . . .' She broke off, realising what she had said — made out yet another argument as to why Louis should have been killed by someone close to him. 'Oh shit!' she said softly and suddenly all the traumas of the evening came together, gathering into a knot of tears in her throat. She lowered her head, blinking fiercely in the hope that he would not notice. But the tears escaped anyway, rolling down her cheeks. She fumbled in her bag for a handkerchief. 'Dammit, what's the matter with me?'

He pulled a clean handkerchief out of his own pocket. 'Is this what you're looking for?'

'Yes. Thanks.' She took it gratefully. 'I'm sorry. I'm being very silly.'

He dropped to his haunches beside her, covering her hands with his. 'Come on, cheer up. Nothing is that bad. It's all very old history, remember.'

'Not to me.'

'No, I suppose not.' He put his arm around her more by instinct than design and after a moment she looked up at him. Her eyes were still slightly muzzy with tears which lent a soft focus to the outlines of his face, blurring them a little so that she was reminded of the way he had looked in the Underground Hospital, still strong, but with the edges knocked off somehow so that she could glimpse the man underneath. She laid her face against his shoulder and at the touch something sharp and sweet stirred within her, something so powerful and surprising it took her breath away. For a moment she remained motionless, afraid of the surge of feeling that was setting her on fire, more aware than she had ever been before of the nearness of another human being. It was so little, that contact, just her head against his shoulder and his arm lying lightly around her, yet it was as if she could feel him with every nerve ending in her body, as if the whole of her being was alive suddenly with desire and expectation.

Very gently he took her chin in his hand, tipping her face up towards his. Mesmerised she watched his face come closer, closer, until she could no longer see those outlines, even muzzily, and his lips were on hers. A shudder ran through her then, as every bit of the tension in her body was jarred by the contact and after a moment's hesitation she was kissing him back with a fervour that made her senses swim. Oh God, she wanted him, she wanted him! But as the thought edged her consciousness it seemed somehow to trip a switch deep within her and shock her back into reality.

'For heaven's sake . . .' She pushed him away, laughing shakily.

'What's wrong?' His voice was rough, grating.

'Well, you're quite a man, aren't you? Two women in one night . . .' She didn't really know why she'd said it, the moment it was out she knew that she had somehow betrayed the jealousy she had felt, but to her surprise he only tried to pull her close again.

'What are you talking about?'

She wriggled away. 'Your lady friend — the one who was here when I arrived. What would she say if she knew that you . . .'

He released her. She saw his eyes darken.

'That wasn't a lady friend. That was my wife's sister.'

She went cold. 'Your *wife*! I didn't know you had a wife!'

He swallowed, turning away. 'I haven't. She's dead. Fran comes to see me sometimes, just keeps in touch . . .' He didn't add that seeing Fran hurt him sometimes more than helped. She was so much like an older, more sophisticated version of Marianne that it drove daggers into his heart.

'Dead! Oh dear, I had no idea . . .' Juliet said. She should be sorry for him she knew — she *was* sorry — and embarrassed too at her gaffe. But neither regret could erase the soaring relief. Oh, for one horrible moment to have thought he had a *wife*!

He was pouring himself another drink, tossing it back.

'Is it . . . ? Was it . . . ?' She faltered, not sure whether she ought to pursue the subject.

'It was a motor cycle accident,' Dan said without turning round. 'A drunken driver hit us on Christmas Eve three years ago. She was in a coma for almost a month before she died. I used to go and sit with her, looking at her lying there — it was just as if she was asleep. I expected her to wake up at any minute. But she didn't. She died. And I was driving the damned bloody motor cycle and I'm here.' He put down his whisky tumbler with exaggerated care then balled his fists and drove them into the table top.

Juliet's stomach contracted. 'Oh, I'm so sorry! But you mustn't blame yourself. It wasn't your fault, I'm sure . . .' Instinctively she went to him, putting her arms around him, but this time there was no response. He stood bowed, seemingly oblivious to her being there even and suddenly she felt foolish and awkward again. 'Dan . . . I'd better go . . .' She turned away.

'Don't go.' He said it so softly she wasn't sure she'd heard him right.

She hesitated. 'I must. They'll be wondering where I am.'

He straightened as if trying to throw off his mood of despair. 'Yes, I suppose they will.' His voice was almost normal now, matter-of-fact. Only the slight note of uncertainty betrayed the emotions that had been tearing him apart moments before. 'I'm sorry about all this.'

'Don't be silly. There's nothing to be sorry about. I'm the one who should be sorry for reminding you.'

'You didn't remind me. I never bloody forget. But perhaps I should try to. Perhaps it's time to stop looking back. It's just not that easy, that's all.'

'No. Dan, I must go.'

'OK.' He was looking at her, his brows drawn together so that his eyes were almost shadowed. 'Juliet, I want to see you again.'

A pulse jumped in her throat. 'I thought I'd explained — I can't go on with it,' she said, deliberately misunderstanding him because she did not know how else to deal with the sudden rush of conflicting emotions. 'If you can prove someone else was responsible I'd be over the moon. But I'm not playing detective any more if it means taking advantage of my family's hospitality.'

'I know. I wasn't talking about that. Forget your grandmother, forget this whole damned business. I want to see *you*.'

The pulse jumped again, again she experienced something close to panic. She hadn't expected such intensity of emotion, especially on his side. He had seemed so cool, cold almost, and self-contained, it was disturbing to see what went on under the surface. She wasn't sure she could cope. And besides . . .

What about Sean? Dear Sean, waiting for her at home in Australia, trusting her, expecting her to get engaged as soon as she got back. How could she have forgotten him so easily? One kiss and she was ready to turn her back on the years of loving. Was this what they meant by holiday romance? Swept off one's feet by a different man in a different place?

'I'm sorry,' she said, 'but I really do think it would be better if we just left it. I don't know if I mentioned it but I have a fiancé back home. I suppose I should have said but it didn't really seem relevant.'

His eyes narrowed. All emotion was hidden again.

'Oh I see. Well in that case I suppose there's no more to be said.'

'Not really.' But she felt like crying again and in the privacy of her car, driving home in the soft darkness she let the tears come, sliding down her cheek though she did not make a sound.

Oh Sean, why don't I feel that way about you? What the hell is wrong with me? But I won't be unfaithful to you, don't worry.

I wouldn't do that to you. I couldn't . . . however much I might want to.

When Juliet had gone Dan Deffains poured himself yet another whisky. He was drinking too much, he knew, but what the hell? He needed it!

What a night, he thought ruefully. First Fran, doing her duty call, then Juliet with her double bombshell — no more investigation into the death of Louis Langlois, and 'no thanks, I don't want to see you again'. It was difficult to decide which was worse. No — he knew that all right. There would be other jobs. Something always turned up. But Juliet was the first girl since Marianne died to stir him at all. He had thought his emotions had been embalmed along with her. Tonight, for the first time in three years he had wanted a woman, and on more than a physical level too. Yes, it was a mixed emotion. Yes, it made him feel faintly guilty, as if he was somehow cheating on Marianne. In spite of that he had still wanted Juliet — and he had thought briefly that she wanted him. But his judgement was way off key. She had a fiancé back home, blast his eyes, so that, presumably, was the end of that.

Dan drained the last of the whisky from the tumbler and hurled it across the room. He had the feeling it was going to be a long night.

'What a bloody life!' Viv said vehemently. 'What a bloody, bloody life!'

It was an hour since Juliet had left and Viv had now worked her way through all the stages which inevitably followed one after the other when she drank too much. The desire to shock had gone now and the feeling of invincibility and the euphoria. Now she was merely maudlin — and very wide awake.

Paul, on the other hand, was ready for bed and did not relish the thought of one of Viv's long discourses just now.

'Oh I don't think you can say we've done so badly,' he said placatingly, but Viv was not to be sidetracked.

'You really think that?'

'Yes, I do. Things were a little dicey for a while twenty years ago, I admit, but that all sorted itself out after Louis died. We have everything we could wish for now.'

'Have we.'

'Yes, Viv, we have, and we should count our blessings. We have a decent home, enough money to live in the style to which you have always been accustomed and I am looked on as an elder statesman in the company. What more could you want?'

Viv was silent. A family, she wanted to cry. I wanted a family. But she could not bring herself to say it. On most subjects she was outspoken, garrulous even, but this one she hugged to herself, a terrible emptiness within her that sometimes erupted to a pain too sharp almost to bear.

Once, long ago, when they had first realised there would be no children for them there had been the shared sadness and the recriminations. Blame had been bandied about between them as a weapon whenever they had a row, although they had never dared to seek a final and definitive answer to the question — which of them was actually unable to deliver? Was it Paul who was infertile? Or had Viv been somehow damaged in that long ago abortion? Each shrank from discovering a truth about themselves which they could not face, each pretended, for the most part, indifference. Viv never knew how inferior Paul was made to feel by the knowledge that she had once been pregnant by his brother. Paul never saw Viv in the extremities of grief which sometimes overcame her so that she doubled up against the excruciating pain as the sobs wrenched her guts and she stretched out her arms in an agony of longing for the child she had lost. Those spasms came less often now. Old age had muted them. But somehow, strangely, the past seemed very close these days. The distant past, when they had been young, and the more recent past too, when Viv had watched her nephew Louis grow into a man and thought that if she had had the courage and conviction of Sophia she, too, would have a son or a daughter of similar age. How the bitterness had rankled in her then! Jealousy of Sophia and a hatred of Louis that had grown, unseen, to almost manic proportions.

When he had been a child she had looked at his beauty and wept silently for her own child, denied the chance of life; when he grew into a thoroughly dislikeable young man the unfairness

288

of it made her evil. Louis was a German's brat, no wonder he was such a pig. Her child would have been a young Nicky. She always saw him in her mind's eye as Nicky had been before the war had robbed him of his manhood — young, strong, handsome, with the power to reduce her to a jelly of wanting. No one else had ever done that. Now no one else ever would. But by some monstrous trick of fate the despicable Louis was alive and her own child, Nicky's child, was dead. Viv had been consumed by rage every time she thought of it, so much so that for a time, when he was destroying their lives with his ruthlessness, she had been obsessed with hatred for him.

Even now, twenty years later, the echo of that hatred remained and she could feel nothing but triumph when she remembered that he, too, like her child, was dead. Because of her extrovert nature few people realised the depth of emotion Viv was capable of. Only Paul had had an insight from time to time into the recesses of her soul and he, copying the ostrich traits of his father, had chosen not to acknowledge it.

There was one thing, however, that he could not ignore. The older Viv grew the more, it seemed, she harked back to Nicky. Paul found it hurtful in the extreme but there was little he could do about it. When Viv wanted to talk about Nicky there was no way to stop her — and she wanted to talk about him now.

'Perhaps it hasn't been so bad for us,' Viv was saying, plucking at her lips with scarlet painted nails, 'but what about Nicky? Life wasn't very fair to him, was it? Maimed as he was, dead before his twenty-fifth birthday — Christ, Paul, what did he do to deserve that?'

Paul got up. He really had had enough for one day.

'Come on, Viv, time for bed.' He took the glass from her hand and eased her to her feet. She let him, too sunk in depression to protest. On the stairs she stumbled and he supported her. At least we're still together, he thought. In spite of everything, after all these years, still together.

'Can you undress yourself?' he asked her. She nodded. 'I'll be back in a minute,' he said. 'I'm going down to turn off the lights.'

When he came back Viv was standing in the middle of the

289

room. She had undone her dress and stepped out of it. In her silk underslip she looked curiously vulnerable.

'I killed him,' she said.

'Killed who, Viv?'

'Nicky, of course.' She laughed shortly. 'Who did you think I meant?'

'Come on, Viv. Into bed.'

'Oh Paul, why is it all so bloody?'

'It's not, Viv. We've been over all this. Go to sleep now.'

'I can't. They are there. All of them . . .'

'Go to sleep, I tell you. I don't want to dwell on the past if you do.'

But as he left her, pulling the door closed behind him and making for his own room, Paul thought that it was not so easy to leave the past behind even if one wanted to. Viv was right. There were some things it was impossible to forget.

Chapter twenty-one
Jersey and Surrey, England 1943–1945

Though he still felt thoroughly ashamed of what had happened between him and Viv, Paul could not wait to see Nicky again and after making his escape to England in his father's boat, the very first thing he did was to find out the whereabouts of his brother. All he knew was that Nicky had been wounded in France, taken to hospital in Weymouth and then moved again. But apart from the initial correspondence there had been nothing. With the occupation lines of communication had been cut and Paul had no idea where Nicky would be now or how to set about finding him. It was possible, of course, that he had made a full recovery and was back with his unit. In that case he could be anywhere in the world, or he could be right here in England.

Paul began checking up. The powers-that-be were more concerned with waging war than they were with answering his queries but eventually he learned what he needed to know — Nicky was now being cared for in a nursing home in the depths of the Surrey countryside. Paul was puzzled. It was nearly three years since Dunkirk. What was Nicky doing still in a nursing home after all this time?

Paul did not write or telephone to let Nicky know he was coming to see him. With boyish glee he decided to surprise him — after all, Nicky would know that the Channel Islands were still occupied and would never guess that his brother had managed to escape.

'I'll be down on Friday afternoon,' he told the Matron on the telephone. 'But don't tell Nicky I'm coming, please. I may not make it and I'd hate him to be disappointed.'

'You do know the situation, don't you?' the Matron said.

The seriousness of her tone should have warned Paul but he

was too excited at the prospect of seeing Nicky again to even wonder about it.

'I know all I need to know — the address and how to get there.'

'Very well. Come to reception when you arrive and we'll take it from there.'

Paul arrived at the nursing home early in the afternoon. It was a huge place which might in peacetime have been a stately home with acres of grounds and manicured lawns, a rose garden and a flight of steps flanked with stone lions leading to an impressive front door. In his haste Paul failed to notice the ramp running alongside the steps. He took them two at a time and found himself in an airy entrance hall. A pretty young nurse approached him.

'Can I help?'

'Paul Carteret. I've come to visit my brother Nicholas.'

'Oh Nicky, yes. He will be pleased! I thought his family were all in Jersey and unable to make any contact.'

'Well this one isn't in Jersey any more,' Paul said cheerfully.

The nurse showed Paul into a big cosy room equipped with comfortable chairs, a large table and a wireless set. A fire was blazing in the open grate and an enormous jigsaw puzzle partly completed, was laid out on the table. There were three young men in the lounge; whilst he waited Paul passed the time of day with two of them, who were playing a game of draughts, but he could not bring himself to speak to the third, who sat all alone, his face heavily swathed in bandages. To his shame, Paul realised he simply did not know what to say to him. He picked up a magazine, flicking through it, and as the door opened he looked up eagerly. Nicky? No. The nurse was manoeuvring in a wheelchair. Paul glanced back at his magazine then did a double take. The guy in the wheelchair . . . it *was* Nicky!

For a moment he stared at his brother, totally stunned and bewildered. He hadn't changed at all, a little older maybe, but . . . what was he doing in a *wheelchair*?

'Paul! Is that really you? What the hell are you doing here?' Nicky was yelling, his voice overjoyed, and Paul ran to him, falling to his knees beside his brother's wheelchair. 'Why are

292

you in that thing?' he asked when they had finished hugging one another. 'Have you broken your leg or something?'

Nicky snorted. 'Something like that. Tell me about you. How did you get here? I thought that Jersey . . .'

'It is. I got out in Papa's boat.'

'Did Papa come too?'

'No.' Paul rubbed a hand across his face. He didn't want anyone to see that he was crying. 'What is it you've done to your legs, Nicky? You will be all right, won't you? It isn't serious?'

And then Nicky told him and after the first few sentences all Paul could hear was a roaring in his ears. It wasn't just some temporary problem with Nicky's legs. As a result of being wounded on the beaches he was paralysed from the waist down. There was no hope he would ever recover.

Afterwards Paul found he could remember very little about the rest of that first visit. The shock of finding Nicky in a wheelchair and learning that he would never walk again was so great it seemed to wipe him clean of all coherent thought. Only later, at the country pub where he had booked in for bed and breakfast, did his mind begin to function again. But he could still scarcely believe it — his brother, his hero, with whom he had shared so many adventures and pranks — a total cripple! It couldn't be true!

The next time he visited he pressed Nicky for a glimmer of hope.

'You'll be all right in the end though won't you?'

'I don't think so, Paul.'

'Of course you will! Don't be so defeatist! You can do anything you want to — remember?'

'Not this time.'

'Why not? Because the doctors say so? Don't take any notice of them! You're going to be all right. I know you are!'

'Paul, my spinal cord was damaged — there's no connection any more between my brain and my legs. It's like a telephone line that's been cut. Only it can't be repaired.'

Paul was angry then. He was so angry he could not bring himself to stay in the same room with Nicky a moment longer.

293

He stormed out and put as much distance as he could between himself and the nursing home, with its stench of sickness that not even antiseptic could dispel, and the aura of oppression that came with wheelchairs, wounds and scars. He was angry at the injustice of it all, angry with the whole world of sickness and maimed bodies and insoluble human problems, angry because he felt so utterly helpless.

It was several days before he could bring himself to go back and when he did he was full of dread. But to his surprise, once he had broken the ice, it was not as difficult as he had expected. Nicky had already come to terms to a certain extent with his disability; it was he, Paul, who had to adjust.

On fine days he would push Nicky's wheelchair around the grounds of the home looking not for corners where nature was at her most beautiful but short slopes out of view of the windows where the chair could be released to run wildly out of control for a few moments. Nicky was sick of being pushed out for staid outings on the gravelled paths only, and he whooped with delight when the chair gathered speed down a grassy slope even though on more than one occasion he was deposited unceremoniously on to the ground when the wheel hit a concealed tree root and Paul had to manhandle him back into position. Sometimes they sat in Nicky's room and talked and Paul found this fraught with difficulties.

He told Nicky the truth about Lola and Charles because he thought it only fair to do so and he saw, in Nicky's impotent anger, a mirror image of the anger he had felt over his brother's disability.

'Couldn't you have stopped them?' he demanded.

'You don't understand. The Germans are in complete control over there. You can't argue with them.'

'No — I mean couldn't you have stopped Mama and Papa from doing something so dangerous?'

A dull red flush crept up Paul's neck. He certainly did not want to tell Nicky that he had been with Viv that night. That was taking honesty too far — and besides the thought of it still made him cringe.

But there was no avoiding the subject altogether. When Nicky asked about Viv, as it was inevitable he should, Paul answered truthfully that he thought she and her mother were coping fairly well though they had been forced to move out of their house and into the gardener's cottage, but he did not say he had been there and he did not pass on the information that Viv had had an abortion to get rid of Nicky's child. Did Nicky suspect he might have left her pregnant? he wondered, looking at his brother and trying to read his mind. But Nicky gave no indication that he might and Paul was relieved he was not going to be forced into divulging what he knew. That was something between the two of them, he thought. He certainly did not want to be dragged into it!

Sometimes Paul talked to Nicky about what he should do now that he was in England. Although the government had not yet caught up with him to conscript him into the armed services he knew it was only a matter of time before they did and in any case he was anxious to do his bit. As an ex-soldier Nicky favoured the army but somehow it did not appeal to Paul, and though he was used to boats and the son of a sailor he did not think he wanted to join the navy either.

But he did rather fancy the idea of flying. After discussing it with Nicky at some length Paul decided to take the bull by the horns. He presented himself at an RAF recruiting station and to his delight his high standard of education and physical fitness meant that he was accepted to train as air crew.

Paul was sorry to have to leave Nicky again, though in some ways it was a relief not to have to continue to push the wheelchair around the grounds trying to find ways of avoiding talking about either Vivienne or the future. After his initial training he was posted to one of the fighter squadrons stationed in the south east and so he was able to visit Nicky more often than he had dared hope. In spite of a few hairy moments Paul spent a fairly uneventful war. On two separate occasions his plane limped home, damaged; once he had to eject and watch it spiral down in a plume of black smoke. But Paul himself seemed charmed. He earned the nickname 'Lucky' and the cheerful confidence that was a façade with many of the young men reflected Paul's true attitude very accurately.

During his service he met a great many girls, both WRAFS and civilians, and most of them were only too eager to take up with the good-looking young man in the light blue uniform. But though he dated quite a few of them he thought they all compared unfavourably to Viv. Perhaps the night they had spent together had been something less than a spectacular success, perhaps Viv was a sharp-tongued tease — a pretty lethal combination when one considered it reasonably. But somehow where she was concerned reason did not get a look-in. Just what her attraction was Paul was not sure; he only knew she was the most desirable woman he had ever met.

Paul put Viv out of his mind, concentrating on flying and staying alive, and on having a good time whenever and wherever he could. And when the end of the war came and Jersey was freed it was Nicky who went home first because, for all his good intentions, he could not bear to stay away any longer.

When he had first been told he was going to spend the rest of his life in a wheelchair Nicky had made up his mind that he would never see Viv again. The decision was not entirely selfless though the fact that he did not think it would be fair to expect Viv to lumber herself with a cripple did come into it. To a greater extent, however, it was a matter of pride. He had had to be the master with Viv in order to interest her; he was very much afraid it would be impossible to keep her respect as things were. Nicky felt illogically ashamed of the fact that his legs now refused to obey him; even worse was the knowledge that he would never again be the lover Viv remembered, a prospect he found unbearable. What he and Viv had shared had been the best; he was no more prepared to settle for less than he imagined she would be.

Weighed down by the terrible depression that refused to lift for even a moment in those first weeks, Nicky had decided a clean break would be best for both of them. He steadfastly refused to write to Viv, even to let her know that he was safe, and by the time he had begun to have second thoughts it was too late. Jersey was occupied; no mail could get through.

As time passed Nicky had begun to accept his situation. The bouts of depression came less often and did not last so long and he even began to plan what he might do when the war was over.

But he still refused to allow himself to include marriage to Viv, or anyone, in those plans.

'Who would want damaged goods?' he said lightly to the therapist whose job it was to teach him how to lead as normal a life as possible, and took no notice at all of her when she told him he was talking nonsense. Perhaps there were women who would still fancy him, but he was certainly not prepared to present any of them with the pathetic parody of the physique of which he had once been so proud.

After Paul arrived on the scene, however, he had begun to be aware of a change in his attitude. Although his own situation was highlighted by Paul's health and strength, he enjoyed his company so much that Viv and the old life became very real to him and he sometimes almost forgot that things had changed for ever. Suddenly all his deepest feelings which had been imprisoned for so long escaped and he found himself yearning for Viv with an overpowering longing.

The moment the war was over and he was free to return to Jersey he knew he could not bear to stay away a moment longer. But he wanted to avoid giving Viv the same shock that he had given Paul, and in any case, the practicalities had to be considered — he simply could not breeze in unaided.

When telephone communications were restored Nicky put through two calls to the island. The first, to La Maison Blanche, was fruitless, there was no reply. Knowing how the family had been turned out by the Germans Nicky realised it probably meant only that they had not yet returned or maybe that at the moment the place was uninhabitable.

The second call was to Viv. She answered the telephone herself; he knew it was her the moment her slightly husky voice came down the line, as dear and familiar to him as if he had last heard it just yesterday, not five years ago.

'Viv?' he said. And she knew him instantly.

'Nicky! Nicky — is that you?'

'Yes.'

'Oh Nicky!' He knew she was crying, he could hear it in her voice, and his own face was wet with tears. 'Nicky, where are you?'

'In England,' he said. 'But I'm coming home!'

'When — when?'

'As soon as I can.'

'Oh — I can't wait! It's been so long! I thought . . .'

'Viv,' he said, 'there is something I have to tell you and if you don't want to see me I shall quite understand. I am in a wheelchair.'

He felt her moment of shock. 'A wheelchair!'

'Yes. So if you don't want . . .'

She did not let him finish. 'Don't be so bloody silly! It doesn't matter, Nicky. Just as long as you are coming home. It doesn't matter at all!'

But of course it did matter. Not at first, maybe, because their euphoria at being together again was so complete there was no room for doubts. Those first weeks Viv was like a child with a new toy, insisting Nicky move in with her and her mother since Sophia already had her hands full looking after Bernard, Catherine and baby Louis. She waited on him hand and foot, there was so much to talk about, so much catching up to do, so much touching and kissing. They even found ways of making love, partly from Nicky's therapy lessons ('She must have been quite a lady, your therapist!' Viv teased), partly from instinct and imagination.

It was only when the novelty started to wear off that Viv began to realise she no longer felt the same. At first she did not want to admit it, even to herself. She had Nicky back, as she had said to him that first day on the telephone, that was all that mattered. The trouble was he wasn't the same Nicky. He looked the same — well, more or less the same. A little thinner in the face and his legs were horribly wasted — Viv thought with a pang of the muscular tanned limbs that had been part of Nicky's attraction. He was kind. He was courageous — God, how she admired his courage! He had even managed to retain something of his sense of humour. But he wasn't dashing any more, he wasn't young and strong and invincible. People felt sorry for him now and although they might admire him too that admiration was for different qualities than the ones that she had found so devastatingly attractive.

On the surface Viv kept up the façade of sheer delight at

having Nicky home again. Privately, to her own distress, she was beginning to have serious doubts.

Sophia, on the other hand, was very happy. It was almost as if the birth of baby Louis had marked the end of one chapter of her life and the beginning of a quite different one.

There were times when she still thought of Dieter — useless to pretend there were not — but he had become unreal to her now, a distant dream that had happened to someone else and not to her at all. Bernard was the reality now, not the old easygoing Bernard whom she had treated so badly, but a man who had grown in stature since the day he had laid down his ultimatum to her and was now very much master in his own home. Sophia respected him and was a little afraid of him though she would not let him see it. And she found that the uncertainty she still felt about him heightened the attraction he now had for her in a way that his earlier consideration never had.

Not that he was inconsiderate now — on the contrary he was a kind and generous husband — but always there was that edge and Sophia was in no doubt that if she ever deceived or let him down there would be no more second chances.

When the soldiers moved out of La Maison Blanche Bernard and Sophia went over to assess the damage. To their relief they found it was not nearly as bad as it might have been — some places, like The Pomme d'Or, were in a dreadful state. The main hotel where the soldiers had been billeted was in need of decoration and some of the furniture and fittings had been damaged or looted, but the officers who had used the cottage annexe had treated it with respect. Even Sophia's precious piano seemed little the worse for wear. Sophia played a few notes on it, listening critically to the pitch and feeling the joy that always came from making music mingled with regrets for her lost dreams. What a long time ago it seemed now since the days when she had hoped to win a place at music college and perhaps make a career on the concert platform! Such a thing was out of the question now, of course; with all her new responsibilities it was an ambition destined to remain unfulfilled. But at least she would still be able to play the piano for her own pleasure. That was

299

something she could look forward to once they were back at La Maison Blanche.

'We must get the decorations done as soon as possible,' she said, retracing her steps through the rooms and assessing them with a critical eye. 'I think we should start with Mama's room. I want to have everything ready for her and Papa. They could be coming home any day and I want it to be nice for her. What colour do you think she would like, Bernard? Rose pink? That's a warm colour. Or yellow? Like sunshine?'

Bernard said nothing. Privately he thought she was taking a rather over-optimistic view but looking at her shining face he did not have the heart to disillusion her.

'I'm sure they'll be so glad to be back in their own home they won't care what colour the walls are!' was all he said.

As the weeks passed with no news, however, even Sophia was hard put to it to remain optimistic. At first she was too busy with the preparations to move back to La Maison Blanche to have any energy left over for worrying, but as the gates of the prisoner-of-war camps began to be opened and the horror stories of the way the prisoners had been treated began to emerge, she was overtaken by a gnawing dread. Desperately she tried to discover the whereabouts of Charles and Lola but every effort seemed destined to end with stone-walling by the authorities and ultimate failure.

For a long while she kept her worst fears to herself, feeling almost superstitiously that to talk about them made them more real and Bernard, though he was growing daily more concerned as to Charles and Lola's likely fate shrank from suggesting to Sophia that it was his opinion that her beloved parents might very well be dead. She was going to take it very badly, he thought. She had put so much effort into preparing for their return. And he wondered and worried about his own ability to help her come to terms with yet another crushing blow.

One evening in September Sophia took Louis into the garden to feed him. Although it was late the air was balmy and from the window Bernard could just see her sitting on the wooden bench, her back towards the house, completely screened from curious eyes. His heart contracted with love and the desire to

300

protect her but he held back from joining her. He knew she liked this time alone with Louis.

As darkness began to fall, however, and Sophia still had not returned to the house, Bernard began to wonder what was keeping her. Surely Louis was satisfied by now? He was a quick, efficient feeder who did not take up hours of his mother's time as Bernard had heard many babies did. He waited a little longer, glancing occasionally out of the window at Sophia's motionless figure, then pushed open the door and went down the garden.

During their occupation the Germans had tended the vegetable patch but this year it had not been replanted and weeds now rioted where Charles's cabbages and beans had once stood in neat rows. The fruit trees had done well, however, producing barrow loads of apples and pears and Bernard trod on the odd fallen one as he crossed the rough grass.

Sophia glanced up as she heard him approach. As he had thought, Louis had finished feeding and Sophia was holding him against her shoulder, one hand supporting his fair downy head. Bernard felt something sharp and painful twist inside him. Why the hell couldn't Louis have been his baby? He was a beautiful child, and very good, but Bernard could never quite bring himself to forget that his father had been a German soldier — a man prepared to rape if the desire took him. Perhaps, he thought, it would be different when Louis was older, a boy with a personality of his own. He never had been able to understand what people saw in babies and this one, good as he was, much as Sophia obviously loved him, merely reminded Bernard of things he would rather forget.

There was no moon yet it was far from dark, a soft ethereal dusk. Sitting there in the shadows Sophia looked very soft and very beautiful.

'Are you all right, sweetheart?' Bernard asked, going up to her.

She was silent for a moment.

'Mm. I've been thinking. About Mama and Papa. Do you remember when Papa went to Dunkirk? We were terribly worried about him but somehow I never doubted he'd come back.'

'You were young then,' he said gently. 'Terrible things weren't real to you.'

'It wasn't just that. It was a sort of certainty inside even though my imagination was working overtime. But now it's different. I know it sounds dreadfully morbid, but I don't think they are going to come back. At least . . . I don't think Papa is. I'm not sure about Mama.'

Bernard, who had been wondering how to prepare Sophia for the worst, found himself hedging now that the moment had come.

'You mustn't give up hope.'

'No, it's not a question of not hoping — more a question of *knowing*. And anyway, to be honest, we should have heard something by now, surely? The camps are all being liberated. And when you think of what the Allies are finding . . .' She broke off, swallowing hard. It was almost beyond being borne, knowing that her parents might have been starved to skeletons, gassed or gunned down. 'A lot of people have died in p.o.w. camps,' she went on when she had collected herself. 'I think it might be sensible to assume Mama and Papa were amongst them. Don't you?'

'I . . . don't know . . .'

'I shall still continue to write letters, of course, to the Red Cross and anyone else I can think of. I won't give up until every last camp has been liberated and every living prisoner named. But it's no use going on in limbo. They wouldn't want that. I think we should plan our lives as if they were never coming back. And then if by chance they do it will be all the more wonderful.'

Bernard was so surprised by this strangely philosophical Sophia that he hardly knew what to say.

'I suppose that is the sensible way to look at it,' he said.

'Of course it is. Maybe I would have found it more difficult to say this if it hadn't been for the business, but I do have this very strong feeling that they would want us to get it going again, Bernard. It meant so much to them, they would be very sad if we just let it all go because they hadn't come home. Now the war is over I expect the visitors will start coming back — more than ever, perhaps, because they will be so fed up with no holidays and nothing nice happening for five years — and I think we should be ready for them. Don't you?'

302

'Well — yes . . .' Bernard said, even more surprised. He had had similar thoughts himself about the likelihood of a tourist boom and wondered how he could suggest resurrecting the business without upsetting Sophia. The opportunities, he had thought, could turn out to be far too good to be missed, particularly for someone as eager to be his own boss as he was. But with Charles's fate so uncertain he thought that to do anything about it was in rather dubious taste. It smacked of opportunism and of stepping into dead men's shoes and keen though his ambitions were Sophia's feelings were more important to him than any advancement.

'The guest house is almost respectable again,' Sophia went on. 'We could be open to visitors next summer with no trouble. And you worked for Papa at the Agency. Would you be willing to run it now — for him — as a sort of memorial?'

'Well, yes . . .' he said again.

'There's only one thing. Papa would have given Paul a job in the company if he had wanted one — when he gets out of the RAF you must talk that over with him. And Nicky — well, Nicky will have to be provided for too. Maybe there will be something he can do, in the office or something. He's very good with people, of course, but I'm not sure what guests would think of him being in a wheelchair. It shouldn't make any difference, I know, and he's a hero. But will people want to be reminded now the war is over?'

Bernard shook his head. 'I don't know, I really don't know. I need to think about all this. But I'm glad it's in the open.'

Sophia nodded. 'So am I.' But he noticed she was shivering a little and he put his arm around her.

'Come on, now, sweetheart, I think it's time we went inside. And it wouldn't be such a bad idea to get to bed before that little alarm clock you've got there decides it's time to wake up again and start demanding breakfast.'

With his arm still around her shoulders he guided her back across the apple-strewn lawn to the house.

The letter from the Red Cross arrived the very next week, so vague they were almost afraid to hope, let alone believe, and then, just when they were least expecting it, came the telephone call.

Sophia, who answered it listened in almost total silence to what was being said and then set down the receiver with exaggerated care.

Feeling almost numb she turned to Catherine, who was rolling on the floor tickling Louis.

'Mama is coming home.' Her voice was flat, dazed.

Catherine froze. 'Mama? What about Papa?'

'I don't know. They didn't mention him. She's been very ill — too ill to be able to tell anyone who she was, and she had no papers on her.'

'When? When is she coming?'

'Today. They are flying her in — we have to meet her at the airport.'

'Oh Sophia!'

'Oh Catherine!'

'I'm scared!'

'So am I! Will she have changed much, do you think? She may still be really ill. They didn't say. Her old room is all ready for her, but do you think if Papa's not coming would it be better to put her somewhere else? I don't know!'

'Give her her old room, of course. She may have been ill, she may be changed, but it's still Mama. She'd hate to be treated like a visitor.'

'Yes, you're right.' Sophia snatched up Louis, who had begun to wail. 'Hush, Louis, hush! Your grandmama is coming home! Do you know what I'm saying? Your grandmama is coming home!' And suddenly she and Catherine were laughing and crying, hugging one another and dancing with Louis squeezed tightly between them.

The Lola who arrived on the Red Cross plane was a very different Lola to the one who had showed her defiance as the German soldiers took her away. Had there been other passengers Sophia thought she might not have known her at all. Her high cheekbones were accentuated now above the hollows of her cheeks, her face pallid, smudged with grey shadows and etched with lines. Her teeth appeared more prominent because her lips had somehow drawn away from them and her hair, though drawn back into its familiar knot, was sparse and dull. She looked not three years older but thirty, a parody of her former self. Even worse was the haunted expression in her eyes. Lola had been to hell and back and it showed.

They could understand now how it was that she had been unable for so long to tell anyone who she was. They asked nothing about her ordeal; she would tell them in her own good time — perhaps. And they certainly did not ask what had happened to Charles.

But Lola told them anyway, though with the directness and simplicity they might have expected of a child.

'Papa died, you know. He had no coat. They made him go without his coat and it was very cold. I think he must have caught pneumonia.'

'Mama, don't try to talk about it!' Sophia cried in distress.

But Lola seemed almost as unaffected now as if the whole nightmare had happened to someone else.

'Oh it was a very long time ago. I missed him, of course. But at least he didn't suffer like some of the others. No, at least he didn't suffer much.'

Dear God she has lost her mind! Sophia thought. But it wasn't quite that.

From the very beginning Lola was very taken with Louis. She had far more patience with him than she had ever had with her own children, playing with him, feeding him egg yolk and mashed up rusks on a spoon, rocking his cot when he cried. Once, when he was teething, Sophia caught her mother rubbing whisky on to his gums with her little finger. Sophia was horrified. But it was impossible to be angry with Lola.

Sophia kept waiting for one of her outbursts to come but they never did though she was prone to fits of anxiety when her whole body became jittery, her mouth would work and the horror in her eyes was frightening to see. She was frail, too, and often ill that first winter, she who had scarcely had a day's illness in her life.

'How could anyone do this to her?' Sophia cried to Bernard one night when she had settled Lola back to sleep after a distressing nightmare. 'My God, how I hate the Germans!'

305

Bernard agreed with her — he hated them too. But he could not help wondering whether Sophia, when she made such sweeping statements, had forgotten that one of Hitler's robotic monsters had fathered her child. With all his heart he hoped that nothing would ever happen to give her cause to remember that.

Chapter twenty-two
1947

Viv knew something was seriously amiss with her father's affairs. Although they had never been close, yet at the same time they shared an instinctive understanding and she had noticed over the years that the more jovial and laid-back his manner the more likely he was to be hiding something. She knew now that something was wrong and she hardly needed to be a genius to guess what it was. Only two things really mattered to her father – her mother and money. Since Loretta had been behaving herself extremely well since her artist friend had unexpectedly married a very young and very pretty girl who had modelled for him, that left money as the explanation for the shadow behind his eyes.

Not that there was the slightest indication of it yet in any material way or any noticeable change in his lifestyle. But then, Viv knew, there wouldn't be. It was terribly important to keep up the image of affluence and Adrian would continue to fly in and out of Jersey, drink fine wine and drive one or other of his fancy cars whatever the restrictions his long suffering bank manager tried to impose. 'I have funds, it's only a temporary blip,' he would explain, airily dismissing an overdraft that would have kept many people in luxury for a year and it was certainly true that over the years no matter how many times he had appeared to be on the very brink of ruin something had turned up to put things right.

This time, however, Viv was afraid it might be different – and she was right. As a result of the war the whole of the economy was in a mess. During the dark years the only firms that had boomed were those that had ridden the wave of essential war goods – steel and munitions and the industries associated with them – and in his position Adrian had managed to do some cunning juggling with their shares and keep a reasonable income.

Now he hoped to do the same with those companies whose products would be needed to rebuild the shattered towns and cities. But in the summer of 1947 he made an error of judgement. Laconic as ever he had bid heavily for shares in a construction company whose performance he was convinced would rival that of the big munition firms during the crisis. Greig International, with its building division and associated cement, timber and quarrying interests seemed a sure-fire bet for success. But something had gone wrong. Just a week after he had put down an option on the shares, word leaked out of dirty dealings and the price of Greig plummetted. By the end of the month when Adrian was due to settle up they were virtually worthless.

Adrian knew he was finished – a bankrupt stockbroker cannot be tolerated. For as long as he could he hung on, trying to clear his debts by one method or another, but in the end it was no use. There was nothing for it – the house in Jersey would have to go and with it practically everything of value which they owned.

When the news broke Loretta was hysterical but Viv was oddly philosophical. She was so used to having everything she wanted she simply could not visualise what it would be like to have no money at all. It was only when she had to face the harsh reality that she became first indignant, then incensed, at the unfairness of it.

One day in the summer of 1947 Adrian called the family together and announced that he thought they would have to leave Jersey altogether. Viv was horrified. Jersey was her home – she could not imagine living anywhere else. Then, as she thought about it, she began to think that perhaps it was not such a bad thing after all.

For some time now Viv had been feeling restless and the chief reason, she knew, was Nicky. She still loved him dearly – yes, she *did* – but it wasn't a great deal of fun being tied to a man in a wheelchair. They couldn't go dancing any more, he couldn't swim properly, they couldn't ramble along the cliff paths, even making love had become a big boring effort. In the beginning they had talked about getting married but as time passed and the first delight of having him back began to pall under the constant burden of monotony, the idea appealed to Viv less and less. Selfish she might be, impatient she knew she was, but however shameful, the fact of the matter was she simply did not want to marry a man with his disability. Worse, she did not want to marry Nicky, because he was no longer the man she had fallen in love with. All the things about him that had most attracted her were no more.

There were even times when Viv had regretted offering Nicky a home. It was such a strain, having him there all the time, and secretly Viv had wondered how she could change things. Well – here was the solution! As her father explained that they would have to live in a small suburban house from which he could commute to his new job in an estate agency, and even that might have to be rented for the time being, Viv's brain began working overtime.

'There is something else, Vivienne,' her father said miserably. 'I'm afraid we won't be able to afford to support you any longer. You are going to have to get a job.'

This might have been an even greater shock to Viv than losing her home. At twenty-seven she had never done a serious hand's turn in her life. She had helped out at a jewellery shop in St Helier, owned by a friend of Loretta before the war had closed it down, she had done a little modelling and promotion work. She had even, on occasions, posed for some of the artist friends of Loretta's former lover and played at being a receptionist at La Maison Blanche during the busy season. But all these things had been undertaken on an almost social basis. Now, without a moment's hesitation, she heard herself saying: 'I know exactly what I'd like to do. I'd like to be an actress like Mummy!'

Under different circumstances Adrian might have argued. As things were he was only relieved not to have Viv making a scene. And Loretta looked positively delighted.

'I'm sure I could get you started, Vivienne. Blake Cooper – you remember Blake? I used to play with him – has a repertory company of his own nowadays. He'd train you I know and it could lead to all kinds of success.' She broke off, radiant as she remembered her own glory days and imagined how she could relive them vicariously through Viv. Besides, Blake had been one of the most handsome of her leading men; already she was looking forward with excitement to seeing him again. 'I'll write to Blake tomorrow,' Loretta promised and Adrian sighed with relief.

Only one member of the household remained to be told and that was Nicky. But by putting a roof over his head for so long Adrian felt he had already more than done his bit to help rehabilitate the wounded. Now he did not owe him a thing.

It was almost two years now since the evening when Sophia and Bernard had discussed the future in the garden of La Maison Blanche. Throughout that first winter they had worked on plans for the re-opening of the hotel and the tourist agency and in the spring Bernard had given notice to the electricity company and thrown himself whole-heartedly into the new venture. Soon bookings were rolling in again and the whole family, with the exception of Paul, who had decided to stay on in the RAF for the time being at least, were involved. Sophia took over the tasks that had once been Lola's domain, Lola pottered a little in the kitchen, and Nicky worked part time in the agency office. It was, Bernard admitted privately, about all Nicky could do – his debilitating injuries meant he became overtired if he worked too long at a stretch. But the office was all on one level with a flap-up counter that he was able to negotiate in his chair and Viv was perfectly willing to drive him into town each day so the arrangement served both to give Nicky an interest and a modicum of self-respect and to save Bernard having to employ a lad as Charles had employed him.

Sophia's early fears that the sight of a disabled clerk might deter potential clients had proved groundless – on the whole people were still kindly disposed towards the young men they referred to as 'our gallant lads, the wounded soldiers', but nevertheless Nicky was not particularly happy. Whereas in the early days he had managed to look on his wheelchair as a challenge to be overcome, now it was becoming a trap from which he could not escape and he hated being forced to work indoors in a sedentary occupation. But he could see no way out and so he went on taking each day as it came and trying to do his best for the family business. At least, he thought, he still had Viv – though sometimes in black moments he even felt that she was slipping away from him. He wondered if he should tell her that she must not feel she was tied to him in any way but somehow he could not bring himself to do it. She was his whole life. Without her he did not think he could find the will to go on.

Like Viv Nicky had realised all was not well with Adrian Moran's affairs but he had assumed that they would sort themselves out just as she had. Men like Viv's father always landed on their feet, didn't they? It was only poor fools like him who started out with dreams of being invincible and ended up being tolerated and pitied. He closed his mind to any thoughts that Adrian might be in serious financial trouble, and it came as a total and terrible shock to him when one day in the summer of 1947 Viv broke the news to him that the house he had come to look upon as his home was being sold, and she and her mother were going to England.

'I'm very, very sorry,' she said in a voice full of forced brightness, 'but I'm afraid that's the way the cookie crumbles. We are broke, darling, absolutely totally skint.'

'But why England?' Nicky asked. He felt stunned. 'Why do you have to go to England?'

'To work, of course. What on earth could I do here? And besides, it would be really rather horrid having all my old friends seeing me in my straitened circumstances. It was different in the war, we were all in the same boat, but now . . .'

'What about me?' Nicky said. The moment the words were out he thought how pathetic they sounded and he began to feel angry.

'You will be all right, won't you?' Viv said in that same bright voice. 'You can live at La Maison Blanche. There's a lift there now, isn't there, quite big enough to take your chair and the place is practically just around the corner from the tourist agency.'

For a moment Nicky was unable to reply. The anger had become a roaring in his head, a sort of black rage which was the culmination of all the bitterness and resentment and humiliation that had been fermenting away inside him for months now. For the first time in his life he wanted to strike Viv, to hit out at her pretty, well made-up face and wipe the smile off her scarlet lips. He wanted to hurt her as she was hurting him but he couldn't

311

do it. He was in his wheelchair and she was out of reach. He couldn't even do that.

'I'll come over to see you as often as I can,' Viv was saying. 'It will be quite fun. In fact it might even be good for us, being apart for a bit. We have been living in one another's pockets rather. You don't mind too much, do you, darling?'

Nicky brought his fists down hard on the arms of his chair making it rattle and jump.

'Does it matter whether I mind or not? You're going anyway, I suppose. And I can't say I blame you. Who in their right mind would want to stay with half a man?'

Viv coloured. 'Nicky, you're not . . .'

'How else would you describe me then? No – you go, Viv, and good luck to you. I should have had the guts to tell you to get off and leave me long ago.'

'That's just stupid!' Viv flashed, her own underlying guilt making her voice sharp. 'You're twisting it. You know I care for you. I waited for you, didn't I? All those years?'

'Did you? Are you sure about that?'

Her colour heightened. 'Of course I'm sure!'

'Well I'm not. I never have been. You weren't cut out to be a nun, Viv. I never said anything. I didn't think I had the right. Only don't pretend to be a bloody vestal virgin. It doesn't suit you.'

'I've had enough of this.'

'You mean you've had enough of me.'

'Stop it, Nicky, please! I can't bear it.'

'*You* can't bear it!' he said bitterly. 'Well that really is tragic.'

She swallowed hard. 'Don't be like this, darling, please. Look, I've said I'll come back just as often as I can. And it will be fun. We'll have lots of things to talk about . . .'

'You might. What am I likely to have? Oh, I suppose I could always regale you with the exciting happenings in a tourist office or update you on the latest thing in wheelchairs.'

Viv felt sick. When Nicky had first come home he had seemed so brave and well adjusted. Now he was bitter and in a permanent state of depression. Somehow she had failed him and now she was about to walk out and leave him altogether. But perhaps that was the best thing for both of them. Perhaps she was too much of a reminder to him of the past, the days when things had been so different. He was upset now, but later he would be free to meet someone else, someone who would accept him just as he now was. With her there would be no echoes of what had once been, with her he would be able to build a new life based only on the reality of the present. It was what she had told herself whilst she had been planning what she was going to do and the sentiments had salved her conscience. Now, however, faced with Nicky's anger and distress, it seemed a hollow and rather selfish deception.

I still love him, Viv thought. But the way things are it is quite impossible. I have to make a new life for myself and allow Nicky to do the same.

'You'll have lots of other things to talk about, Nicky,' she said. 'You have to look on, not back, and you'll do it better when I'm not around.' He did not answer. She went towards him intending to kiss him but he turned his head away and instead she trailed her fingers around his neck and lightly brushed his hair. Nicky sat stiff and unresponsive. Viv crossed to the door and went out. Nicky did not turn to see her go.

'Poor old Nicky is in a pretty state about Viv going isn't he?' Paul said.

He had some leave from the RAF and had come to spend it in Jersey. He, Catherine, and Sophia – who was pregnant again – were relaxing in the garden before the rush to put on the evening meal began.

'It's understandable,' Sophia said, shifting a little in her chair to relieve the discomfort that she was experiencing. At least this time she did not feel nauseous all the time as she had when she was expecting Louis, but she had grown much bigger and was carrying her baby very low, and the recent hot weather had added to her discomfort. 'I only wish there were something I could do to help but there isn't. There's nothing anyone can do except be there for him and at the moment that seems to be the last thing he wants.'

'I can't understand it,' Paul said. 'When he was in hospital in England he seemed to have taken it all so well. I was the one

313

in shock. Now it's as though there's a black cloud surrounding him. He's a different bloke.'

'It's all Viv Moran's fault,' Catherine said venomously. 'I never liked her. How can she just go off like that and leave him? It's cruel!'

'You can't blame her entirely,' Sophia said. 'She has done her best for him as far as I can see and it's not her fault her father has lost all his money.'

'But if she loved him . . .'

'I wonder if she ever told him about the baby,' Paul said thoughtfully.

They both looked at him.

'What do you mean?' Sophia asked. 'What baby?'

Paul flushed. He had never mentioned to a soul the conversation he had had with Viv and he knew he should not have done so now but it was too late, the damage was done.

'She was pregnant,' he said awkwardly. 'When Nicky went off to join the army he left her pregnant. He didn't know, of course, and Viv had an abortion. That's all.'

For a moment they gazed at him open-mouthed.

'An abortion? Viv was expecting Nicky's baby and she had an abortion?' Catherine said. 'I don't believe it!'

'How do you know about this?' Sophia asked.

'She told me. I never said anything. I didn't think it was my place.'

'And Nicky doesn't know?'

'I don't know. She's probably told him by now. Look – just forget it. It's none of our business. What we should be thinking about now is what we can do for Nicky. Maybe one of his old friends could help – do you remember that chap Jeff McCauley? He and Nicky had been in hospital together and he came over once when Nicky first came home. Perhaps he could get through to him.'

'You're right,' Sophia said, trying to pull herself together. 'What he needs is someone who has been through a similar experience, someone he would feel could understand. I think I've got Jeff McCauley's address in the visitors' book. I'll write to him.'

She and Paul went on discussing ways to help Nicky, successfully silencing Catherine who was thoroughly disappointed at not being able to find out more about Viv's abortion.

But that night, as she put pen to paper to Jeff McCauley Sophia sat for a long while thinking about what Paul had said, and wondering how different things might have been if Viv had borne Nicky's baby, instead of taking what she could not help thinking of as a coward's way out.

In the September of 1947 Sophia was heavily pregnant but according to her doctor not due to give birth for another two weeks. Since Louis had been almost three weeks late Sophia assumed, quite wrongly, that the same thing would probably happen again and one warm afternoon she set out with Louis in the pushchair and with Lola in tow for a walk and a picnic.

Bernard, when he heard her plans, had tried his best to dissuade her, but Sophia with her mind made up was not for turning.

'The exercise will do me good,' she argued, strapping Louis into his pushchair. 'Sitting cramps me up and gives me heartburn. And besides I want to get Mama out of the kitchen before the chef gives notice.'

'Well, if you think you'll be all right,' Bernard said. He was still doubtful about the wisdom of the excursion but getting Lola out from under the feet of the new chef he had hired was a powerful argument. Stefan Polanski produced dishes that were truly inspired and were beginning to attract just the kind of reputation Bernard wanted for the hotel, but he was also temperamental and resented what he considered Lola's interference.

'Of course I'll be all right!' Sophia said impatiently as she set out.

It was the most pleasant of afternoons, the sky that deep rich blue that is like an accumulation of all the lighter blues of summer pasted layer on layer, the sun low and bright and there was enough breeze going to keep the air pleasantly fresh. Though there was still an almost childlike quality about Lola she had recovered well physically. She could stride out with a resolve that almost surprised Sophia each time they took a walk together, and now she set a cracking pace along the coast road. As she struggled to keep pace Sophia felt, but ignored, a niggling pain like a toothache somewhere in the depths of her body. It felt quite different to the pains she had experienced when Louis was born and it did not occur to her that one labour is rarely exactly like another.

Sophia was sitting on a rug on the beach, watching Lola digging happily with Louis when she experienced a sudden hot rush between her legs. Oh God! she thought in panic. Either her waters had broken or she was having a haemmorhage. Trying to conceal her anxiety from her mother Sophia struggled to her feet, squinting over her shoulder at the wet patch on the back of her skirt. At least it wasn't blood – Sophia supposed she should be grateful for small mercies. But the thought of walking all the way home with this sticky fluid dripping down her legs was not a pleasant one. And besides she had no way of knowing how long it would be before she went into labour proper.

'I think we should be going, Mama,' she said briskly.

'Oh, but we have only just arrived!' Lola protested, disappointed as a child. 'It's such a lovely afternoon! Can't we stay a little longer?'

'Not now. We'll come back another day.'

'But soon it will be winter. You know how cold it is in winter when the snow comes.'

'You're thinking of Russia, Mama.'

'Am I? Oh, perhaps I am. I get so muddled sometimes. I had a beautiful fur hat and a muff. Did I tell you, Sophia? We would go skating and sometimes we would go whooshing over the snow in the sledge drawn by horses. It was wonderful. Except when we heard the wolves. They make such a mournful sound, you know, when they call to one another.'

'Yes, Mama.' Another rush of fluid trickled down Sophia's leg. Oh God, she thought, I am going to die of embarrassment!

She bent over, folding up the rug and putting it into the carrier on the pushchair. Lola was still chattering and it was only when she straightened up again that Sophia realised that Louis was missing.

'Louis!' She looked round anxiously. 'Where is he?'

'He was here a moment ago. He can't have gone far.'

There were a couple of families on the beach but no sign of a small fair-haired boy in a white blouse and blue shorts.

'Louis!' Everything else forgotten Sophia ran to and fro, a few steps in one direction, a few in the other. Louis seemed to have disappeared off the face of the earth. Someone had kidnapped him, she thought in panic. Or else he'd run down to the sea and drowned! She would never see him again! 'Louis! Louis!' she called frantically. 'Where are you?

'Excuse me!' a voice called. 'Have you lost your little boy?'

'Yes!' Sophia called back. 'Did you see what happened to him?'

'He's here, playing with my daughter.'

Sophia looked. She could see nothing. 'Where?'

'Here – behind my pushchair.'

'Oh!' Sophia wanted to weep with relief. She ran across the beach. Sure enough Louis was squatting on the sand hidden by the pushchair and completely engrossed in a baby, about six months old, who was lying gurgling on a rug. 'I though I'd lost him!' she gasped.

She bent over to scoop him up and as she did so the first pain caught her, almost taking her breath. As it passed she straightened to see the young mother gazing at her anxiously.

'Are you all right?'

'No, not really. I think . . . my baby's started.'

'Oh Lord! Is there anything I can do? Call an ambulance or . . . ?'

Sophia was overcome with longing for Bernard and the aura of safety he always engendered. 'Perhaps if you could phone my husband . . .'

'Of course.' The young woman got up, lifting her own child into her pushchair. 'Look, you wait here, or make your way slowly up to the road. I'll get help for you if you give me your husband's number. I'm Susan Feraud, by the way. And this is Molly.'

Sophia nodded, too engrossed in her own situation to take much notice. Another pain gripped her as she watched the young woman struggle across the beach with her pushchair and child. And she little realised that as a result of this chance encounter she and Susan would become firm friends and the reverberations would continue for another generation.

*

Thanks to Susan a very worried Bernard was soon on the scene with his newly acquired car and was rushing Sophia, Louis and a very confused Lola, home. Then he called the doctor and sat holding Sophia's hand and rubbing her back until he arrived.

'Off you go and have a cigarette or a stiff whisky while you wait,' the doctor told him. 'It won't be long and she's in safe hands now.'

'I'd rather stay,' Bernard said.

The doctor shot him a glance. A father present at the birth – unheard of! But everything was happening so fast he was too busy to argue. So it was that Bernard was there, a little pale, but very excited, when Robin Charles Bernard Langlois made his hasty and quite unexpected appearance, crying lustily and looking very pink and fresh and also very hurt at being thrust into the world a little before he was ready for it. As Bernard afterwards told everyone who would listen, he would not have missed it for the world!

Chapter twenty-three
1948

In the spring of 1948 Bernard called a family conference.

'I want to talk to you, Nicky and Catherine,' he said to Sophia, who was in the middle of bathing Robin. She looked up in surprise, supporting Robin with one hand and lathering soap with the other.

'What do you mean, you want to talk to us? You see Nicky practically every day and I'm here. Talk to me now.'

'No, I want to talk to all three of you together,' Bernard said. 'Really Paul should be there as well but since he is in Germany that's obviously out of the question.'

'Is something wrong then?' Sophia asked, slightly alarmed. 'The hotel isn't in trouble, is it? It's been doing so well!'

'Everything is fine,' Bernard said. 'It's no use you ferretting away, Sophia. As I said, I want the three of you together.'

'Well that sounds pretty silly to me,' Sophia replied, needled. 'I am your wife, after all. I hope you're not going to become pompous in your old age, Bernard.'

Bernard smiled. 'With you to keep me in line, Sophia, I should think there's very little danger of that. Now, how does three o'clock tomorrow afternoon sound to you?'

'All right I suppose.' Sophia was still irritated at not being taken into Bernard's confidence. 'If you are being so businesslike I'm surprised you haven't sent out formal agendas. I'll take the minutes if you like.'

Bernard, who was quite used to Sophia's sarcasm, only smiled. 'That's not such a bad idea. You could say this is our first board meeting.'

'I expect you are wondering why I've called you all together,' Bernard said. He was standing beside the fireplace in the sitting-room of the annexe. Clutched to his chest was a brown manilla folder but the label, if there was one, was hidden in his deep-blue Guernsey sweater, and his expression gave nothing away.

'We are wondering, yes,' Nicky said from his wheelchair which was positioned in the convenient gangway between table and door.

'It's quite exciting isn't it?' Catherine settled into the big soft armchair, curling her legs up beneath her and hugging them.

But Sophia, who was expecting Robin to start crying at any moment — he had seemed to have colic when she had given him his last feed — merely shifted impatiently.

'Oh do get on with it, Bernard. Tell us what it's about and we can all get on.'

'All right, I'll put it in one sentence. I want to buy another hotel.'

He looked from one to the other of them, a faint smile on his lips, his eyes direct. After a moment Nicky laughed.

'That was short and sweet. Come on, Bernard, elaborate. Tell us what you have in mind.'

'Very well. The Summerton in St Clements Bay is up for sale. It's in a prime position, right on the coast road and facing out to sea with its verandah practically on the beach. I knew it as a boy — I always thought it must seem like a little bit of heaven to mainland visitors staying there. But it was occupied by the Germans during the war. They made a pretty mess of it and obviously the owners haven't had the heart to go in and do anything about it. It's been empty — and falling into a worse state of repair — ever since. Now they've decided to put it on the market and I would like to buy it.'

'What with?' Sophia asked.

'That's the whole point, really. Although we've been doing very nicely, both with the guest house and the tourist agency, I don't actually have the wherewithal. We would have to remortgage La Maison Blanche as collateral. And La Maison Blanche isn't mine to use in that way. It belongs to the three of you — and to Paul.'

'And Mama,' Catherine said.

'No,' Sophia told her. 'Strictly speaking Papa's will left everything to be divided equally between the four of us with the proviso that we should always afford Mama a place to live. He

320

was thinking of simplifying matters, I expect, when he did it, though he could never have guessed that when we inherited, Mama would be quite incapable of making any decisions anyway.'

'Right. And since Catherine is still under twenty-one her share is a trust. But she's an intelligent young woman and I feel it is only morally right to ask her opinion too.'

Catherine smiled at him. She liked Bernard. He never treated her like a child and she sometimes thought Sophia gave him an awfully rough deal.

'If you think it's a good idea then I expect it is, Bernard,' she said.

'Thank you for your confidence, Catherine,' he said seriously. 'What about you, Nicky? And Sophia?'

'What exactly do you have in mind for the Summerton?' Sophia asked.

'I'd like to see it become a good class hotel, medium to top end of the market. I'd like to include on the premises all the facilities that people staying at other hotels come to the agency for and more — a private swimming pool, a ballroom with dancing and a cabaret nightly, a beauty shop where the ladies can be pampered. I am quite certain Jersey is just coming into its own as a holiday island — if the Tourist Board promote it properly I can foresee the day when visitors will come flooding in, and who could blame them? Now the war is over everyone wants a good time and to make up a little for what they have been forced to miss. I want to make the most of the boom I know is coming — and to do that we have to expand.'

'But suppose it doesn't work out?' Sophia said. 'We could lose everything, couldn't we, if we put La Maison Blanche up as security?'

'It's a possibility,' Bernard said gravely. 'That is why I felt I needed to talk to all of you together. I don't happen to think it is very likely — if I did I would never be suggesting it. I'm not a fool. But actually I did want to talk about La Maison Blanche too. I think the time has come to upgrade it. "Guest house" is not really the right image any more. I want to turn it into a hotel.'

'What's the difference?' Catherine asked.

'A fine dividing line. When we installed the lift that was a step in the right direction and so is the new chef, temperamental though he might be. But I have a few more plans in mind — a cocktail bar, for one, where guests can enjoy a pre-dinner drink, and perhaps a night porter so we don't have to lock the doors at night.'

'It all sounds very ambitious,' Nicky said. 'Where would you find the space for a cocktail bar? La Maison Blanche isn't very big.'

'Exactly.' Bernard was beginning to enjoy himself. 'I think what we should do is buy a house for us to live in and make the annexe part of the hotel.'

'More money,' said Sophia.

'Yes, I'm afraid so. But if we ever want to get this off the ground we have to be prepared to speculate.' Bernard's eyes were shining with enthusiasm. He tapped the manilla folder. 'Here I have various sets of details from the estate agents. The Summerton is amongst them, of course, but you'll also find particulars of some of the houses I thought might be suitable, too. I'd like you all to have a look at them.'

'Just a minute, Bernard,' Nicky said. 'This all seems very cut and dried to me and I don't care for it. It's my mother's home you are talking about. She might not be very compos mentis these days but that's no reason to disregard her.'

'I'm not disregarding her. It will benefit Lola just as much as the rest of us if I can lift us into another league.'

'And if it fails and we end up without a business and without a roof over our heads either?'

'It won't fail,' Bernard said shortly.

'How can you be sure of that?'

'I don't know. I just am.' Bernard spoke with a zeal that was also quietly confident. 'Anyway as regards the house I am quite willing to take that on as a purely personal thing. Sophia and I have a growing family; we need a home we can call our own. Catherine, of course, would be welcome to live with us, though I dare say before long she'll be off to college and then getting married. And of course that invitation extends to you too, Nicky.'

Nicky nodded. 'Thank you, Benard, that's kind, but I think I

322

shall stay where I am if it's all the same to you. The lift and the wide doorways are convenient for my chair. A small house probably wouldn't be. And I'd be on hand during the winter months to act as a sort of live-in caretaker.'

Bernard nodded. 'I take your point. But I hope we won't need a winter caretaker. I intend to push the image of Jersey as an all-the-year-round resort. The holidaymakers won't come, of course — at least not the ones who want to worship the sun — but business people might. What better place for a conference when mainland Britain is in the throes of a dreary November or February?'

'Good heavens, Bernard,' Sophia said. 'You have got some ambitious ideas!'

Bernard smiled. 'I've always believed in setting my sights high, Sophia, and generally speaking I have to say it works. Now, I'll put these property details on the table so you can all have a look at them. And when we've come to some agreement amongst ourselves I'll write to Paul, tell him what we plan and ask for his blessing.'

'I don't suppose Paul will mind much one way or the other,' Sophia said. 'And I for one think you are right, anyway. I don't care much for the thought of all the upheaval but I know that's a very negative point of view. On balance I'm all for pressing ahead and trying for real success.'

'I agree.' Nicky wheeled himself over, holding out his hand for the manilla folder containing the property details. 'I take my hat off to you, Bernard, you've done a great deal more than I would have been able to do even if I still had all my faculties. Go ahead, I say. Make an offer for this other hotel and raise whatever cash you need to put it in order. I'm right behind you.'

'Catherine?'

'Oh — yes.'

'That's it, then,' Sophia said. 'Seventy-five per cent backing for your plans, and the other twenty-five per cent almost certain. Now I must get on. Louis will be waking up from his afternoon nap and I think I can hear Robin crying.'

She got up, hurrying upstairs to the big sunny room that served as a nursery.

How things had changed! she thought — and Bernard with

them. These days he was so positive and powerful it was difficult to remember the quiet and rather diffident young man he had once been. But perhaps the strength and ambition had always been there concealed beneath his unprepossessing manner. It was just that she had never been able to see it until that night when he had asked her to marry him and laid down the ultimatum that had changed the balance of power between them for ever.

Sophia smiled to herself. Good for you, Bernard! she thought. And was warmed by a glow of love and pride.

That summer was one of the busiest Sophia had ever known. As she supervised the loading of all their possessions into tea chests and spring cleaned the new house they were moving into, as she went over the interior decorators' suggestions for colour schemes at the Summerton, which Bernard had been successful in buying, and which he intended to rename the Belville, as she chatted to guests and took charge of a hundred and one household arrangements and all with her 'three babies' as she referred to Louis, Robin and her mother, to look after, Sophia wondered how on earth Lola had managed to run a guest house with four small children under her feet.

Looking at her now it was almost impossible to believe she had ever been such a strong and driving force. The sleek hair had turned dove grey and her severe hairstyle did nothing to hide the gauntness of her once-handsome face. She had put back on some of the weight she had lost in the concentration camp but it seemed to have gone on in the wrong places — it was her stomach now that protruded rather than her breasts and she would never recover the good health she had once taken for granted. Every germ that was going seemed to find her, she went down constantly with colds and influenza and all too often they turned to bronchitis and even, on one occasion, to pneumonia. Sophia had thought then that she was going to lose her but somehow she had pulled through. Even more disturbing was what had happened to her mind — sometimes she was perfectly lucid, at others she seemed to forget Charles was dead and wandered about in distress looking for him. Once Sophia had found her in the garden in her nightdress and she had become quite abusive when Sophia tried to persuade her back indoors.

'I have to find your father! Don't you care about him? How could you take this attitude, Sophia? It's not the way I brought you up! Now if Paul was here things would be different. Paul would make sure his father was all right . . .'

'Yes, Mama, I know, but he's not here.' Sophia had learned it was best not to argue. She also realised nothing she did would ever really satisfy Lola. But there it was. She was glad that at least she could do something for her mother. If only she had had the opportunity to do the same for her father!

The new house they were buying was very close to where Susan Feraud lived and when she had a spare minute she was able to see her for a chat. Sometimes Susan called at the house and she and Sophia had become firm friends. Since Molly was only a few months older than Robin there was always plenty for them to talk about.

'You are lucky, having a little girl,' Sophia confided to Susan, looking at Molly who was round and pretty and always pink-and-white clean in her smocked dresses and little gathered sun-bonnet. 'Not that I'd swop Robin of course — or either of them for that matter — but I should love a little girl! They are so little trouble compared with boys, aren't they?'

'I don't know about that,' Susan said sagely. 'I'm sure there will be all sorts of problems later on that we haven't even thought of yet — like boyfriends for instance. I can't say I'm looking forward to that. I remember accusing my mother of having forgotten what it was like to be young — now I'm beginning to think the trouble was she remembered only too well!'

Sophia laughed. 'Perhaps Molly will fall in love with Robin. It would be nice, wouldn't it, if they got married?'

'Mm. Though of course she may prefer Louis. He's that bit older than she is and he really is a very handsome little boy.'

'Yes he is, isn't he?' Sophia said, pleased. She did not add that he was also too often a very naughty one, or that bringing him up was beginning to be a bone of contention between her and Bernard that threatened to disrupt their family life. To say that, even to as close a friend as Susan, was getting too close for comfort to things Sophia preferred not to think about, but which she was unable to ignore all the same.

'Why are you always so hard on him?' she had yelled at Bernard one evening when he had spanked Louis and put him to bed for systematically ripping holes in every one of Robin's soft toys and pulling the stuffing out. 'He's only a child, for goodness' sake!'

'He has to learn he can't go around being deliberately destructive.'

'He's not. Really he's not. I expect he's just jealous. Children often do odd things when a new baby comes along.'

'He's had plenty of time to adjust. Robin is nearly a year old! And anyway, there's no reason for him to feel jealous. You make more than enough fuss of Louis.'

'Are you saying I favour him?'

'Actually yes, I think you do.'

'Well somebody has to! You certainly don't! In fact you make it perfectly obvious he comes second with you. Though I suppose that's inevitable when he isn't your own son.'

'That's not true, Sophia!' Bernard said angrily.

'Isn't it?' Sophia knew she was being unfair. She had not the slightest grounds for thinking Bernard favoured Robin — he was, after all, still a baby and certainly not old enough to be spanked, yet she could not rid herself of the feeling that it was so. She couldn't see how Bernard could possibly not feel more loving towards his own flesh and blood and sooner or later it was bound to show up. It was one of the reasons, she knew, why she would have liked Robin to have been a girl — it had very little to do with dressing a baby in ribbons and lace, and a great deal to do with the fact that Bernard's feelings would have been quite different towards children of a different sex anyway — they would not have been in direct competition. But Robin was a boy and he was Bernard's son whilst Louis was not.

Somehow she had to make up for that, she thought, act as a buffer between them. It wasn't Louis's fault that he was the child of a German; he hadn't asked to be born.

As soon as she could she slipped up to the boys' bedroom. Robin was sleeping soundly but Louis was sniffling into his pillow. She knelt down beside his bed pulling him into her arms.

326

'Don't cry any more, Louis. Mummy knows you didn't mean to hurt Robin's toys. Mummy loves you.'

And Louis opened his eyes and looked at her. It wasn't easy to be sure in the half light but for a moment Sophia felt quite certain she could see something of Dieter in that look and her heart contracted with love. She leaned over and kissed the soft cheek and smoothed back the lick of blond hair. Then she sat beside the bed holding Louis's hand until he fell asleep.

When she went back downstairs Bernard said nothing, but she was sure he knew where she had been and what she had been doing all the same. And the barrier was there between them, unjustified resentment on the one side, a determination to run his house in the way he saw fit on the other.

For an hour Sophia banged pots in the kitchen, cleaning shelves, cupboards and even the stove, though it did not need doing. At last Bernard appeared in the doorway.

'Come on now, this is silly when you are tired.'

'Why? I'm just cleaning up the pots that have got dust on them.'

'It's got nothing to do with the pots and you know it. It's because I spanked Louis. He's got to be disciplined, Sophia. I'd do the same if it were Robin. And whatever you may think I *do* look on Louis as my own. Now come and make up, eh?'

She poured away the water, made a great show of rinsing out her cloths, but he was still there in the doorway waiting when she had finished and she went to him, a feeling of guilt beginning to replace the resentment. Bernard was good and kind, perhaps he would do the same if Robin was the offender. But it was easy for him, he saw everything in black and white, not the million shades of grey that coloured her own reactions.

'I'm sorry,' she whispered. 'I know you were only doing what you thought was right. It's just that I'm a bit, well — touchy where Louis is concerned.'

'Let's forget it,' Bernard said. He came up behind her, putting his arms around her and she relaxed against him, feeling the tension easing out of her body as he held her.

But somewhere in the back of her mind a small voice that refused to be silenced was whispering that this same confrontation was going to be acted out many more times before the boys were grown. It was inevitable the way things were. And it would take all her efforts to ensure that it did nothing to damage the precious relationship she and Bernard now shared.

Chapter twenty-four

Vivienne was utterly and completely fed up. She was fed up with the miserable English weather, fed up with having very little money to spend on herself and most of all fed up with the theatre.

Why, she asked herself, had she ever imagined that a career as a repertory actress would be glamorous? It wasn't. It was sheer bloody hard work, monotonous, tedious and tiring.

Perhaps, she thought gloomily, it wouldn't be so bad if she were the leading lady. At least the leading lady got to wear pretty clothes on stage — even if she was expected to provide them herself — and she was in the centre of the curtain call line-up, blowing kisses to the audiences who were, in the main, noisily appreciative of the repertory company's efforts. But she was not the leading lady. A good deal of the time she was not on stage at all. She was blessed with the insulting title of Assistant Stage Manager and the reason for her existence was to be a general dogsbody. She made tea and coffee, she swept the stage, she called the cast, and occasionally she got to play bit parts, maids mostly, with nothing to say but 'Yes M'm' and nothing to do but carry on the trays of glasses or cups that she herself had laid up in the wings.

If she had been seventeen years old, as the other ASM was, Viv thought it might have been bearable as a start to a career. But she was twenty-seven, long past the age of being prepared to put up with such indignities. How Loretta had stood it she could not imagine, yet she had always spoken of her days on the stage in such glowing terms. And certainly Blake seemed to remember her fondly. But then he addressed everyone, even the very butch stage hands, as 'darling' — when he wasn't yelling at them and telling them that never, ever, would they work in the theatre again!

Blake had a wife, a busty little character actress with a cleaned-up Cockney accent who brought a bow-bedecked Yorkshire terrier to the theatre each day, but it did not take Viv long to realise he also had something going with Belinda Grey, the leading lady. Intimate little looks passed between them and sometimes in the gloomy passage between dressing rooms and stage Viv saw him patting Belinda's bottom or fondling her rather underdeveloped breasts. Was that how she had got to play leads? Viv wondered. After all, she was hardly Peggy Ashcroft! Well, two could play at that game!

The moment she had met him Viv had known Blake was interested in her but she had frozen off his advances — Blake might once have been attractive but now he had gone to seed, faintly ridiculous in the plum velvet smoking jacket, frilled shirts and cummerbund which strained over his pot belly. Now, however, she set to work on him, flashing a smile, teasing with her eyes, brushing her thigh against his with just enough pressure for him to feel the tantalising knub of her suspender.

It was not long before she saw results; she could tell from the little beads of perspiration that broke out on Blake's forehead when she looked at him in a certain way that he was falling into her trap. At first he would turn abruptly and walk away as if by ignoring her he could deny the lust that was burning him up, but she persisted, amused at how easy it was to first fluster and then manipulate the man who could terrorise whole companies of professionals with his histrionic bawlings, and eventually he made his move, just as she had known he would.

They were sharing an after-the-show drink in the lounge bar of the Smugglers' Hole, the pub which was just across the road from the theatre.

'I'm thinking of trying you out in a bigger part, Viv, but you will need some extra coaching. How would you feel about that?'

Viv smiled, tossing her hair. Did he really think she was too naive to see through that one? Men! They were such children! Viv ran her tongue around her heavily glossed lips.

'Extra coaching? At the theatre, you mean?'

'Possibly. But it might be embarrassing for you in front of other members of the company. Why not come to my digs? The Clairmont Hotel. Thursday afternoon, 2.30 sharp.'

Viv smiled again. He really was so transparent! Everyone knew that Dee-Dee, his wife, went to the hairdressers' on Thursday afternoons for a shampoo-and-set and to have her 'roots done' — quite a lengthy process.

Promptly at 2.30 on the Thursday afternoon Viv went to the Clairmont Hotel. It was a small seedy looking place in one of the backstreets and hardly warranted the name of 'hotel', but Viv supposed it was one step better than the digs she and the other members of the company had to endure. At least Blake and Dee-Dee would not have to give twenty-four hours notice of wanting a bath as she had to, or get locked out by a landlady who refused to hand over a front door key 'in case it falls into wrong hands'!

Blake himself was on the pavement outside waiting for her and he hurried her through the dingy lobby and up the stairs. The smell of stale cooked cabbage and boiled fish went with them. The bedroom was small and cheerless — dark, old-fashioned furniture, a threadbare carpet and a bed covered with a quilt which might once have been described as 'old rose'. But the dressing table was cluttered with Dee-Dee's make-up jars and perfume bottles and a faded silk dressing gown which might have belonged to either of them hung behind the door.

'Now the part I have in mind for you calls for a little more experience than I believe you have,' Blake announced, slicking back what little hair he had left from a forehead beaded with perspiration. 'I've taught you to turn, haven't I? But I think perhaps we might practise that first. Now, imagine I am the audience. You come on from stage left — over there by the window — walk across and *turn*. That's the way. Facing me at all times. Good. Now. Sitting. Remember never to cross your legs. If you do the people in the front row will be able to look right up your skirt. Hands. On stage actors often become very conscious of their hands and wonder what to do with them. Well what do we normally do?'

I know what you do with yours! Viv thought. Aloud, she said: 'I suppose we forget them.'

'Good. And that's the way it should be on stage. Let them move naturally — definitely no flapping. Then, most difficult of all, the stage kiss.'

Viv was keeping one eye on the clock. She had no desire to be in the room when Dee-Dee returned from the hairdressers.

'For heaven's sake, Blake, do we have to go through with this charade?' she asked coolly. 'If you want to make love to me why don't you just get on and do it?'

Blake stared at her, shocked. In all his years as an actor-manager not one of the girls he had seduced had spoken to him like that. Some had been shy and modest and he had had to lead them (though they were, he had to admit, in the minority); others were bold, flirtatious and downright sexy. But none had ever been quite so blunt.

'Well?' Viv said, smiling. 'That is what this is all about, isn't it? I want some decent roles, you want me. It seems a fairly straightforward arrangement.'

Blake suddenly laughed in delight as the initial shock subsided. It was positively erotic seeing her standing there, hands on hips, head thrown back, issuing her challenge. Blake loved power games. He loved to conquer but most of his conquests had been too easy. Not this one. She might be offering him her body on a plate but the power struggle was not really about bodies — unless they were doing something very different and exciting.

'You think I'll give you better roles after this, do you?' he asked.

'I know you will,' Viv replied sweetly, going to him and undoing the buttons of his frilled shirt. 'You won't be able to refuse me anything.'

That afternoon was the first of many Viv spent at the Clairmont Hotel. She always arrived promptly and left well before Dee-Dee returned and the only thing that worried her slightly was wondering if her mother had been here before her.

Repercussions at the theatre were not long in coming. Belinda, realising she had been usurped in Blake's affections, became impossibly bitchy, blaming Viv for every little thing that went wrong and bawling her out in front of everyone, and the rest of the company, who were fond of Dee-Dee and hated to see her made a fool of, ostracised Viv as they had ostracised Belinda before her. The improved roles Blake had promised her meant free cigarettes (supplied by du Maurier as props), her photograph in the glass fronted display case outside the theatre, and her Equity card. But Viv soon discovered they were not as much fun as she had imagined; learning lines and rehearsing a new play each week was incredibly hard work, especially since she still had to do all her old backstage jobs.

One evening towards the end of August Joe the stage-door keeper came looking for Viv during the interval.

'There's a young man out front says he's a friend of yours,' he told Viv in his soft Dorset burr. 'Wants to see you after the show.'

'Really? What's his name?'

'He wouldn't say. Said he wanted to surprise you. It could be just a take-in, I suppose, but I don't think so. I've seen most of the tricks in my time and I think he's genuine.'

'What did he look like?' Viv asked.

'Oh, a good looking chap. In uniform.'

'What sort of uniform?'

'RAF.'

Paul! thought Viv. It must be Paul.

'I think I know who it is,' she said to Joe. 'Tell him I'll be out just as soon as I've taken off my make-up.'

For the rest of the show Viv was in sparkling form, making the most of her role — Elvira in Blythe Spirit. It gave her an extra kick of excitement to know Paul was in the audience and afterwards as she wiped the greasepaint off her face with wads of cotton wool her hands trembled a little with excitement at the thought of seeing him again. She slipped into the cotton trousers and shirt she had worn to the theatre and calling a quick good-night to anyone in earshot she hurried along the narrow dusty passageway to the stage door.

The moment she emerged she saw him, standing under the wall, smoking. His back was towards her and she crept up behind him, reaching up to cover his eyes with her hands.

'Hi Paul! Guess who!'

'Viv!' He turned, taking her hands in his. 'How did you know it was me?'

'How many men do I know in the RAF?' she countered. 'Oh, it's so good to see you!'

And that was no lie, she thought. The years since she had last seen him had matured Paul. Both his face and his frame had filled out and the extra weight suited him; in uniform — always an attraction Viv had to admit — he looked quite startlingly handsome and she found herself wondering why she had thought of him as nothing but a substitute for Nicky. Of course the truth was that in the old days he had been a boy and now he was a man — and a very personable man at that.

'Did you enjoy the show?' she asked.

'The show was very good, though I have to admit I only came to see it because you were in it. I'm not a great theatregoer, as you know.'

'I'm flattered! But how did you know I was in it? What are you doing here in this part of the world?'

'I'm stationed nearby. I was in town with some friends and saw your photograph. So I decided to come in on my first free evening and see how you were doing.'

'And was it worth it? Was I all right?'

'Stop angling for compliments, Viv! But yes, you were terrific. Though I'm not sure I like the idea of you as a ghost. I have to say I prefer you in the flesh.'

'Paul – you are wicked.'

'I'm trying! Now, how about a drink or something to eat. Have you eaten?'

'No, I never eat until after the show.'

'Where would you like to go then?'

'Well I'm not dressed for anything grand, that's for sure. I usually grab sausage and beans or something similar at the Lyons on the corner. But I tell you what, since it's such a nice evening, let's go and get fish and chips and eat them on the beach.'

'Fish and chips!' Paul laughed. 'Well if that's what you want, that's what you shall have. Do you know a good chip shop?'

'I do. Come on, I'll show you.'

They took their fish and chips, liberally sprinkled with salt and vinegar and wrapped in newspaper, down to the promenade. They sat on the sea wall to eat it, and Viv thought every mouthful was ambrosial. What was it about this night that was so magical? She couldn't put her finger on it but it was there all the same, a tingling excitement and anticipation, something crackling in the air between her and Paul.

334

'I heard you were treading the boards,' Paul said.

'Oh yes – how?'

'From home of course.' But neither of them mentioned Nicky.

'I thought I'd follow in my mother's footsteps but it's not nearly as glam as I imagined. To be honest I think I'd chuck it all in tomorrow if I had the chance.'

'Why don't you then?'

'Necessity, my dear Paul. No doubt you have heard of the Fall of the House of Moran?'

'Well . . .'

'I'll bet you have! I'll bet people are glorying in it. Not that I care very much what people say.'

'Good for you.'

'And what about your family? Are they all well?'

'As far as I know. Except for Mama, of course. You know she's . . . well, a bit peculiar?'

'Hardly surprising. God, I wish that monster Hitler had lived to be captured! He should have been hung drawn and quartered for what he did! A bullet was far too quick and easy for him.'

'They're all pretty busy,' Paul said, changing the subject. 'They are expanding the business. In fact when I get out of this outfit I might just join them.'

'You!'

'Why not? After all, a quarter of La Maison Blanche and the Agency are mine by right and since they were used as collateral then I should think that morally I have a right to be counted in on the rest. And a pretty big rest it looks like being. Bernard is very ambitious and he's good at spotting the main chance too.'

'Really?' Viv said thoughtfully.

'Really. Now, if you've finished your fish and chips do you want me to see you back to your digs or shall we go for a walk first?'

'Oh a walk!' Viv said. The excitement was singing in her veins again. 'Definitely a walk!'

Nicky pulled down the blinds at the front of the Tourist Agency, locked the door and wheeled himself back into the office. Once there he retrieved the letter which had come with the eleven o'clock delivery from where he had pushed it down the side of

335

his chair between seat and arm and spread it out on his knee. He didn't want to read it again. He wished he'd never read it at all. Yet it held a kind of awful fascination for him, a twisting of the knife so painful yet so strangely addictive that he knew he would read it again not just once but many times until it was imprinted on his heart.

Paul and Viv. Viv and Paul. They were together now. God, how it hurt!

He'd known, of course, when she had left for England, that he had lost her. He had known it would not be long before she found someone else and he had made himself think about it over and over hoping that the pain would be blunted by familiarity. And it had been a little. He had almost come to accept the inevitability of it. She would find someone else. But he had not expected that someone to be Paul.

Nicky's face darkened. A nameless unknown lover – yes, he could just about take that. But Paul! Christ, no! That he could not stand.

Nicky screwed the letter into a ball and hurled it across the room. Then he clenched his fists, striking at the arms of his chair, his face contorted with agony.

He'll bring her here, I suppose, home to Jersey. I'll have to watch them together, know he's taking my girl to bed, hear her called 'Mrs Carteret' and know it's not my name but his . . . I don't believe she could do this to me . . . I don't believe it!

A rapping at the door cut through his misery. A customer? He didn't want to see anyone just now. 'I'm sorry, we're closed!' he called. His voice was thick and blurred.

'Nicky?' It was Sophia's voice, anxious-sounding. 'Are you there? What's the matter?'

Nicky swore. He couldn't just send Sophia away. He wheeled his chair over to the door. The moment he turned the key, she opened it and put her head round.

'Nicky? Why did you have the door locked?'

His eyes, haunted, slid over her. 'Where are the children?'

'Catherine is looking after them. Why? What's the matter, Nicky? You look dreadful, as if you'd seen a ghost!'

'Maybe I have.' He laughed shortly. 'Have you heard from Paul lately?'

'No. I expect he's kept pretty busy.'

'Not too busy to get off with Viv.'

'What are you talking about?'

'My brother and my girl. Priceless, isn't it?'

'Oh Nicky, I'm sure you're wrong . . .'

'I'm not wrong. Read it for yourself – that's the letter – over there, screwed up. Why did he write to me here I'd like to know? Why *here*?'

Sophia retrieved the letter, smoothed it out and read, her face setting grimly.

'You see?' he said when she had finished. 'I didn't imagine it, did I? Paul and Viv. What do you think of that?'

'What can I say? I'm as shocked as you are.'

'Are you? Well I can't say I am. Not really. I've been half expecting something of the sort. But it doesn't make it any damned easier, especially when it's my own brother.' He buried his head in his hands. 'Oh Sophia, I really love her. I know I've got nothing to offer her now but I did really love her. I'd do anything for her – anything she asked. Except watch her with Paul.'

'Oh Nicky, I'm sure it won't come to that. Paul would have more tact than to bring her here . . .'

The outer door opened and Catherine came in holding Louis by the hand.

'What on earth is the matter?' she asked.

'Nicky has had a letter from Paul. He and Viv are together. Nicky is very upset.'

'Oh pooh!' Catherine said with rude exuberance. 'Who cares about her? She's not worth upsetting yourself over, Nicky. I should say Paul is welcome to her, and more fool he! After all he knows all about it. He knows what she did . . . what sort of a girl she is.'

'What are you talking about, Catherine?'

'Well Viv of course, and the abortion. I think it was a terrible thing to do under the circumstances. I mean, supposing you'd never come home? I know it would have been difficult for her but at least she'd have had something of you left.' She broke off, staring in horror at Nicky's stricken face. 'You didn't know.'

'Catherine!' Sophia groaned.

337

'Know what?' Nicky demanded tersely. 'What didn't I know? I think you'd better explain yourself.'

'Oh Nicky . . . I . . .' Catherine faltered.

'Go on. An abortion, I think you said.'

'Well – yes . . . it was after you went away, right at the beginning of the war . . . at least, that's what Paul said . . .'

'*Paul* told you this?' he demanded.

'Well, yes . . . he said . . .'

'You're telling me Viv had had an abortion and he knew? He knew about my baby and I didn't . . . it was my baby, I take it?'

'I suppose so,' Catherine said miserably. 'I honestly thought you knew, Nicky. Paul said she would have told you. I'd never have said anything if I'd thought for a moment . . .'

'But you never do think do you?' Sophia interjected angrily. 'How could you be so stupid, Catherine?'

'A conspiracy of silence.' Nicky's voice was low and bitter. 'I take it you knew too, Sophia?'

'Well . . . yes. Paul mentioned something about it when Viv went away but we don't know any details.'

'I see. Wonderful, isn't it? Everybody, it seems, knew except me – and it was my baby! What else don't I know? And why did she tell Paul? Was there something going on between them then? Has he been making a fool of me all these years?'

'Nicky, please – no one has made a fool of you!' Sophia said, distressed. 'Certainly not Paul.'

'Then why didn't he tell *me* what he knew? And how did he know about it anyway?'

'Obviously she must have told him,' Sophia said. 'And I suppose he didn't tell you because he didn't think it was his place to tell you. One would have expected Viv to do that herself. You were living at her house after all. I can't understand why she didn't tell you if she'd told Paul.'

'Clearly she felt closer to him than she did to me,' Nicky said bitterly. 'What a bloody fool I've been!'

There was a strained silence, then Catherine blurted: 'I've got to go. I'm due at the dentist's in ten minutes.' She was flushed and flustered, close to tears.

Sophia nodded. 'Yes, you go on Catherine. Is Robin . . .'

'In his pram, outside. I'm really sorry, Nicky . . .'

Nicky did not answer. Sophia followed Catherine to the door, checking on Robin, who was fast asleep. Louis was busily turning out a drawer in the outer office, playing with the paper clips and rubber bands he found there and she left him to it.

'I don't know what to say, Nicky. Catherine . . . oh, she's such a blabbermouth! Will she never learn?'

'Don't blame her. She was only telling the truth. More than the rest of you have done.' He looked up, his face cold and blank. 'I suggest you go too, Sophia. I'm sure you've got plenty of things you should be doing.'

'But I can't leave you like this . . .'

'Why not? I'm quite capable of running this office. Good God, I have to be fit for something!'

'But . . .'

'Oh go on, Sophia, leave me alone! Can't you see I just want to be left alone?'

'Come on, Louis,' Sophia said quietly, thinking that perhaps for the moment it was the best thing. But in the doorway she looked back at him, sitting there hunched in his chair, not looking at her, not looking at anything, and her heart contracted with pain and anger.

Damn Catherine and her loose tongue! Damn the war that had done this to her beloved brother! And most of all damn Viv Moran! If she had ever loved him at all how could she possibly have hurt him like this?

After they had gone Nicky locked the office door again. For a long while he sat staring into space and thinking about what his sisters had told him. Viv had been pregnant with his baby and she had got rid of it. The only child he would ever father. The only woman he would ever love. The pain was a roaring wind inside him, devouring him. He rode it for as long as he could bear it but there was a darkness closing in from the edges of his mind. Ever since Dunkirk he had lived in a far from satisfactory present with no real hope for a future, now the one thing left to him – his memories of the past – had been raped and looted. The darkness closed in still further and with it a strange stillness. Nicky wheeled himself over to the filing cabinet and took out

339

the bottle of whisky he kept hidden there. His pain killing tablets were in the top drawer of his desk; he got out the bottle and tipped it out on to the blotter. A whole new prescription and more . . . the ones he had saved just in case a day like this ever came when he could not bear to go on any longer. Nicky wheeled himself over to the window and pulled down the blind. Then he poured a full tumblerful of whisky, put the first tablets into his mouth and swallowed them.

Sophia and Bernard found him late that evening. Worried when he did not come home, they went down town to the office and found it apparently locked up for the night. But when they opened the door with a spare key and went inside they found Nicky there. His wheelchair was drawn up to his desk and he had slumped forward across it. When she saw the whisky bottle and glass Sophia almost sobbed with relief – he had been drinking to drown his sorrows.

'Nicky! What a state to get in!'

But Bernard had seen the empty tablet bottle; he grabbed Nicky's wrist, feeling for a pulse, and yelling at Sophia to phone for an ambulance.

'Why?' She was trembling uncontrollably. 'He's only drunk, isn't he? Bernard . . .'

'No. I think he's gone.'

'Oh my God!' She tried to take a step towards him and could not. She was frozen, repelled by the thought that he was dead, afraid of the change that even she could now see had come over him. She didn't want to touch him, didn't want to feel his flesh cool and stiff – not her brother, not Nicky!

But when she had phoned for the ambulance she crept back into the room drawn to him now by love and pity that were stronger than the revulsion had been. She ran to her brother, dropping to her knees beside him and burying her face in his useless legs. And her tears were for all of them – and for the shadow that it seemed would never leave them.

Chapter twenty-five

Of all the Carteret family it was Catherine who was most deeply affected by Nicky's death.

Lola was scarcely able to grasp what had happened — she tended to shut out everything but her immediate concerns — and Sophia had become almost philosophical about the cruelty of fate. It was not that she did not care that Nicky was dead, she did, very much, and at first she felt that she could simply not bear yet more sorrow. But she no longer had the capacity for the total grief that had overwhelmed her when she had known Dieter was dead, she had been through too much and for the time being at least her sensibilities were blunted. Besides, she had Bernard to support her now, and two babies dependent on her. She could not afford to go to pieces. `

Paul was shocked by the news of his brother's death and at first suffered the agonies of guilt that came from knowing it must have been his letter which had pushed Nicky over the edge. But soon his strong instinct for self-preservation took over. He had had nothing to do with Viv leaving Nicky, he told himself, their romance had been over long before he had met up with her again, so he could hardly be held to blame. And, although he was rather ashamed of it, there was also an element of relief tangled up with the other emotions. For one thing he had not been looking forward to facing Nicky with Viv at his side, for another Nicky's death removed for ever the dread he had never been quite able to banish that Viv might choose to leave him and go back to her former love. He had never forgotten his hurt and humiliation that long-ago night when she had confessed after their love-making that she had been using him as a substitute for Nicky. The fear that something similar might still happen again had hung over him like the sword of Damocles so that although he grieved for the brother who had been his hero, at

341

the same time a small part of him gloried in knowing that never again would he have to fear him as a rival.

Catherine, on the other hand, was inconsolable. She had adored Nicky; to her he had been a hero, the big brother who had spoiled her and teased her. And whilst Paul managed to suppress his guilt, Catherine was overwhelmed by it, holding herself entirely responsible for what had happened.

'You mustn't blame yourself, Catherine,' Sophia had said kindly. 'It wasn't your fault.'

But Catherine had shaken her head. 'It's no use you saying that, Sophia. It *was* my fault. If I hadn't told him about the baby . . .'

'That wouldn't have been enough to make him take his own life.'

'Not on its own, maybe, but it was the last straw. Oh yes, it was. And nothing will ever convince me otherwise.'

'We all have to share the blame,' Sophia said. 'I shouldn't have left him that afternoon. And I should have realised the state of mind he was in and made sure he didn't have the chance to store up his pain killers, but I didn't. That in itself absolves you — he must have considered it before otherwise he would never have had that many tablets in his possession. He must have been repeating his prescription far more often than he needed to in order to build up a store like that — he had them tucked away as a sort of insurance against the day when he simply could not go on any longer.'

'But it was me who drove him to that point,' Catherine said. In spite of her terrible grief she was dry-eyed. In the beginning she had not allowed herself to cry because she had thought that once she began she would never be able to stop and now, though her whole body felt heavy with the weight of tears, they simply refused to come. Catherine went about in a daze of wretchedness which etched the whole of her world in darkness and destroyed all coherence of thought.

On the day before the funeral the guilt and grief built up to such a pressure inside her that Catherine felt she was going to explode. She could hear Sophia on the telephone making yet more arrangements and unable to bear being in the house a moment longer she walked out without a word.

Although it was now October the air still held an echo of the warmth of summer. Catherine walked steadily, her head bent against the stiff breeze from the sea, without any clear idea of where she was going, and it was only when she found herself on the esplanade that she realised; she had wanted to go back to La Maison Blanche where they had been so happy, all of them, in the old days.

The hotel was no longer at full stretch now it was the end of the season. The annexe, which had been their home, had been shut up, and those guests requiring a late holiday were being catered for in the main building. At this time of day the lobby was quiet, with only Brenda, the clerk/receptionist, sitting behind the desk and surreptitiously reading a paper novelette. She looked up as Catherine came in, embarrassed to be caught reading and also uncertain what to say to someone so recently bereaved.

'Oh, Miss Carteret, I'm sorry, I . . .'

'It's all right,' Catherine said. 'I don't want anything. I just . . .'

She wandered on without completing the sentence and Brenda stared after her anxiously. Catherine was usually so ready to chat!

Catherine walked straight through the hotel and out of the back door, left open because it led now to the small swimming pool that had been installed in what had once been the kitchen garden. There was no one in the pool; the water looked very cold and very blue in the October sunshine. Catherine walked across the lawn heading for the end of the garden. It was planted now with flowers and shrubs, but the apple tree was still there — the tree Nicky and Paul used to shin up, and which Charles had often threatened to cut down because it drained all the goodness out of the soil. She looked up, remembering how they had picked the last remaining apples to take with them when the Germans had turned them out of their home and feeling that the events of that year had somehow marked the end of her childhood. Until then everything has seemed to be bathed in sunshine like the endless Jersey summers and what problems they had were solved as easily as a kiss had taken the sting out of a grazed knee. Catherine went to the tree, throwing her arms around its gnarled trunk and pressing her face into the cool rough bark. But still the tears would not come, only the bitter-sweet rush of memories and the pain of her own guilt.

The snap of a dry twig invaded her thoughts and Catherine looked up accusingly to see a young man, casually dressed, on the lawn behind her. So lost in memories was she that she forgot for a moment that hotel guests now had access to the garden, so startled that she demanded angrily: 'Who are you? What are you doing here?'

'I'm sorry, I . . .' He broke off, looking at her. 'It's Catherine, isn't it? I'm Jeff McCauley. I was a friend of Nicky's. I've come over for the funeral.'

Jeff McCauley — who had been in hospital with Nicky. Sophia had written to ask him to visit in the hope of pulling Nicky out of his depression but he had not come. Catherine felt a rush of animosity, as if he was personally responsible for Nicky's death.

'It's a bit late now isn't it?' she said bitterly.

Jeff McCauley looked shocked. 'Yes,' he said quietly. 'I suppose it is. Look, I'm really sorry about what has happened. I didn't mean to intrude. I'll leave you in peace.'

He turned to go but suddenly she did not want him to. He was a link with Nicky, someone who had known her brother in the years she had managed to miss. 'I shouldn't have said that,' she apologised. 'Please don't go. Tell me about Nicky — when he was in the army. Talk about him — please!'

'Well, there's not a lot to tell,' he said a little awkwardly. 'I didn't know him in the army, just in hospital. I knew it had hit him pretty hard, being paralysed. I guess it's one of the things we were all afraid of, and I was one of the lucky ones. But all the same I never thought that Nicky would . . . he had such guts. It just goes to show you can never tell . . .' He broke off but she was silent, waiting, and after a moment he went on: 'I had a spinal injury too but mine wasn't permanent, thank God. When I was in my chair Nicky and I used to have races, round and round the grounds'

'Who won?'

'Oh he did usually. His arms were so strong. He said it came from all the rowing he used to do and the swimming. Christ, I can't believe he's gone.'

344

'No,' Catherine said. 'Neither can I.' The bursting sensation was there in her head again but this time the pressure was hot and hard behind her eyes.

'He was a good bloke, a really good bloke,' Jeff went on. 'And he thought the world of you, well, all of you really, but he never stopped talking about his little sister . . .'

Catherine barely heard him. I'm going to cry, she thought. All this time the tears refused to come and now in front of a stranger I am going to cry.

'Excuse me,' she tried to say, intending to run and hide somewhere but all that came out was a sob and she clapped her hands over her face, turning away as the tears escaped from her eyes and her nose in an unstoppable torrent. The pain inside her creased her like a stomach cramp and she doubled up against it whilst he stood helplessly by.

At last the great tearing sobs began to quieten though her shoulders still shook and her hands still covered her face.

'I'm sorry,' he said. 'I didn't mean to upset you.'

She shook her head wordlessly, still not looking at him, then after a moment she fumbled unsuccessfully for a handkerchief. Jeff took out his own, clean and unused, and passed it to her. She took it without speaking, blowing her nose, sobbing some more, then blowing it again.

'I'm really sorry,' he said again.

'No, *I'm* sorry.' She turned, looking at him with red and swollen eyes. 'I don't normally burst into tears in front of someone I don't know.'

'This is pretty exceptional.'

'More than you know. That's the first time I've cried since it happened.'

'Has it helped? Do you feel a bit better?'

'Not yet.' She blew her nose again. 'But perhaps I will.'

'I hope so. Look, I'm staying at La Maison Blanche, but I don't want to intrude . . .'

'You're not,' she said and she meant it. It was like a breath of fresh air to talk to someone who had known Nicky well, yet was not family, who cared, but not with the same overwhelming emotional involvement, and his vitality seemed to compensate a little for the terrible emptiness that Nicky's passing had left inside her.

'Don't go,' she said. 'Unless you really want to. At least, not yet.'

Miraculously he seemed to comprehend her need.

'I'm not in any hurry,' he said.

He told her that he came from Yorkshire and like Nicky he had been wounded in the last ditch fighting before the fall of France. Since the war he had done all kinds of jobs because he seemed unable to settle to anything and now he was in London, servicing office machinery.

'I don't know how long I'll stick it,' he said. 'I'm an open-air man really but I still have problems with my back and at least it's a living. What about you? What do you do?'

'I'm still at school but I shall be leaving soon and I hope to go to college and train to be a teacher.'

'Clever, eh?'

She flushed. 'No, not really. But I like children and it's what I've always wanted to do.'

'I wish I was clever. I was never much good at school. Always in trouble.'

She smiled. Being clever is really not so very important, she wanted to say, but she was afraid it might sound patronising. And then the conversation was back, inevitably, to Nicky.

'I wish I'd come to see him when Sophia wrote to me,' Jeff said. 'I feel dreadful about it but I was so tied up with my own problems. Maybe if I'd come to see him, I could have helped. After all, I've been there. I'd have understood. I'll never forgive myself for not making the effort.'

'It's no use thinking like that,' Catherine said forgetting that she had hated him a moment ago for the self-same reason. 'I've been blaming myself too, terribly, for something I said. But I expect the ones who are left behind always feel like that when someone dies. That if you'd done or said something different then perhaps they would still be alive. I doubt if it's true. No person is to blame.'

'Maybe you're right.'

'I'm sure I am, though I didn't realise it until just now. And

346

I've been so angry. Angry with myself for what I said, angry with Paul and Viv, angry with God for letting it happen, even angry with Nicky.'

'And now you're not angry any more.'

'Not at the moment. At the moment I feel kind of released. Maybe I'll be angry again tomorrow.'

'At the funeral.'

She nodded. 'Jeff — thanks for being here. I don't know what I'd have done without you.'

'That's OK.' He looked awkward suddenly. 'I didn't do anything. Look, Catherine, if you come over to England to teacher training college, you will look me up, won't you? I'd like to see you again, only . . .'

He broke off. She knew exactly what he meant. They could be friends, very good friends, but this was not the time nor the place to pursue it.

'I'd like that, Jeff,' she said. 'And thanks again.'

He smiled briefly, nodded, and left her there. Catherine cried a little more but now the tears were softer and healing. Then she went home.

Viv did not know whether or not she should go to the funeral. She wanted to go and yet she didn't want to. She was afraid of seeing the rest of Nicky's family, afraid of what people would say and, most of all, afraid of her own emotions.

In the end she decided she could not stay away but neither could she go with Paul.

'Why not?' he asked curtly when she told him this, because suddenly he felt secondary to Nicky again, and was ashamed of it. 'Why shouldn't you come with . . .' he broke off. He had been going to say 'with me'. Instead he substituted 'the family'.

'I don't think they would want me.'

'Rubbish.'

'It's not rubbish. They've never liked me. Now they will hate me.'

'I'm sure that's not true. I don't hate you.'

She looked at him coldly. 'That's different, isn't it? No, I can't come with the family mourners, Paul. I don't have the right.

And the last thing I want is to cause an atmosphere and make it all worse than it is already bound to be.'

'If you feel like that I don't suppose there is much I can do about it.'

'That's right.'

'And afterwards?'

'We'll see.'

Paul experienced stirrings of the old familiar panic.

'If you are going to marry me sometime or other the family is going to have to get used to seeing us together.'

'Perhaps but this is not the time.'

'You are still going to marry me, I presume?'

He had first asked her two weeks ago, just before he had written to Nicky. The letter had been by way of breaking the news gradually. He had asked her and she had said yes, seemed actually to want to marry him, but now this had happened and she was behaving oddly again so that all his old doubts were resurfacing – had she only accepted because he was the best prospect she had? She didn't appear to be very happy in the theatre — she had been 'resting', waiting, without much enthusiasm, for the pantomime season — and it certainly was not keeping her in the manner to which she was accustomed. Her father, though he was apparently picking himself up from his crashing fall on the stock market, was not able to support her and on a limited income Viv the extravagant, who had never had to give a second thought to budgeting or economising, was a hopeless manager. Paul did not like to think about it but it was after he had told her of the planned expansion of the family business that she had begun to sit up and take him seriously. Though he hardly liked to admit it even to himself he had held off mentioning marriage until after he had told her of the plans he had made for his own future — when he left the RAF he would go back to Jersey and involve himself in the chain of luxury hotels that Bernard planned.

'I think old Bernard might have something there,' he had said to Viv. 'Holidaymakers are going to begin flocking to Jersey now that transport is so much cheaper and easier and we might as well think big and make the most of it.'

'What would you do?' Viv had asked.

'Help run the show, of course. I own a quarter share of everything there is, remember, and at the moment Nicky and Bernard are running everything between them. I'm not sure how able Nicky is these days and Bernard doesn't have the know-how to aim the hotels at the really top class bracket. I mean, look where he was brought up, for God's sake. I'm amazed he even knows which knife and fork to use. But if I went in with them I could organise the best of everything.' He had given her a sly glance. 'With your help, of course.'

'Mine?'

'There's nothing you don't know about socialising and society, Viv. You'd be an asset in every way.'

'Are you offering me a job?'

'I suppose I am. Unless of course . . .'

'Unless what?'

'Unless you would consider marrying me.'

'Yes.'

'Yes?'

'Yes, I would consider marrying you.'

'Good lord!'

'I'm twenty-eight years old, Paul, and I doubt I'll get a better offer now. I like the idea of overseeing interior decor for a chain of hotels, if that's the job you're offering me, and besides . . . I quite fancy you. There's only one thing bothering me — will I still fancy you when you are in civvy street or is it the uniform that sets me all a-tingle?'

He had laughed, not quite sure how much of what she said she meant and how much was a joke, but too delighted by her acceptance to worry over much. It was only later that he had begun to wonder. He didn't know what to make of Viv, he'd never known, that was part of her attraction. The only damn thing he was certain of was that he loved her so much it hurt. He wanted to show her off to the world as his but he had the awful sick feeling in his stomach that she never would be as completely his as she had been Nicky's.

And in any case what good had it done Nicky in the end? When the chips had been down, when Nicky had ceased to be her golden hero, she had left him. Viv had no time for tarnished

349

dreams. When the time came she would treat him just as ruthlessly.

The knowledge sickened him but it made no difference. She was an obsession with him; somehow he had to prove to himself that she would stay with him where she had not stayed with Nicky. And he had to begin proving it now. By having her by his side at Nicky's funeral. Only she wouldn't play ball.

The night before Nicky's funeral Paul went out drinking. He had discovered during the war that temporary oblivion came out of a bottle, that it was possible to relax stressed nerves and forget the loss of a friend and fear for one's own future when enough alcohol was running in one's bloodstream, and that night he set out to put the solution to the test on his peacetime problems. Not only did he drink, he also played a few hands of poker and pontoon with some old friends. Paul started off with just a few pounds and won handsomely. And he found that what problems the whisky bottle could not obliterate, the exhilaration of winning a card game did.

It was the first time in his life that he had taken such measures to ease his nagging feeling of insecurity. It certainly was not to be the last.

Chapter twenty-six
Jersey, 1991

Juliet had been awake a good deal of the night. She was too hyped up to sleep, she supposed, her body roused, her senses swimming, confused and yearning, her conscience nagging her that she had betrayed — still was betraying — Sean. Then, as the responses Dan had awakened in her began to cool down, all the other events of the evening were waiting in the wings to pop into her mind like jumping beans and with them the unstoppable questions.

Viv's reaction to the mention of Louis's name was one of the unforgettable moments, Juliet thought — drunk as Viv had been there had been no mistaking the shocking strength of feeling that lay behind her outburst. She had hated Louis — still hated him almost twenty years after his death — with a passion that verged on obsession. Might *Viv* have had something to do with Louis's death? Paul had owed Louis a great deal of money, might possibly have been ruined if he had had to settle his debts, and Louis's death had saved him from that. Was one of them capable of killing him? Juliet shuddered. At least her grandmother had claimed the shooting was an accident. If Paul or Viv had been responsible it would have been cold-blooded murder.

But then there had been others who had hated him — this Raife Pearson, with whom he had quarrelled on the night he died, for one. Dan had said it was impossible for Raife to have killed Louis and Juliet herself had pooh-poohed the idea that he might have hired someone else to do the job for him. It sounded so ridiculously far-fetched. But if it *were* true, what a wonderful relief it would be! And the coincidence was enormous, a quarrel on the very night he died. If only I could find a link! Juliet thought. If only, after all this time, I could clear not only my grandmother's name, but that of the whole family.

Towards dawn she dozed, dreaming muddled but strangely

vivid dreams, and when she woke full sunlight was streaming into her room. The clock beside her bed said almost nine o'clock; worried, Juliet leaped out of bed and dressed — she'd shower later.

Deborah was the only one in the breakfast room — David had already left for the office and Sophia, as usual, was having a light breakfast on a tray in her room. As Juliet came in she looked up from the morning papers, smiling, and Juliet thought again what a beautiful woman she was. With no make-up to distract and with her hair pulled back in a loose bunch and tied with a chiffon scarf, the perfect bone structure of her face was more evident than ever and beneath her silk wrap the lines of her body were revealed as equally perfect.

'You look tired,' she said. 'Sit down and have some coffee.'

'Oh yes please! I only just woke up and I do feel pretty grim!'

'You were late home last night,' Deborah said, pouring the coffee and passing it to Juliet. 'Did you have a good time with Paul and Viv?'

'Lovely.' Juliet put a little milk into her coffee and hoped Deborah and Paul would not compare notes about what time she had left. Viv, she thought, had probably been too sozzled to know what time it had been. 'They're fun, aren't they?' she added.

'Mm. Well, Paul is. I'm not so sure I'd call Viv *fun* actually, although I understand she was quite a girl in her day.'

'She's quite a girl now! It's hard to believe she is as old as Grandma.'

'Older, I think. But of course in spite of all that has happened to her, Sophia is ageless.'

'You are very fond of Grandma, aren't you?' Juliet said, buttering a piece of toast.

'I adore her,' Deborah said simply. 'If there was one person in the whole world I wish I could be like it would be Sophia.'

Then won't you help me clear her name? Juliet almost said before she remembered. No more questions. No more probing. Except, perhaps, one visit to one man to try and discover what he and Louis had quarrelled about on the night Louis died . . .

'More coffee?' Deborah enquired. 'There's still some left in the pot, I think.'

352

'Thanks.' Juliet passed her cup and swallowed a mouthful of buttery toast. 'Do you know the Jersey Lily Nightclub?'

For a fleeting second Deborah seemed to freeze. Her eyes widened with what might almost have been shock or fear, the expression caught as if by a camera, then as quickly it was gone and Deborah was her usual calm and smiling self.

'Why on earth do you want to know that?'

'Oh, I heard it mentioned somewhere. I thought it sounded interesting,' Juliet said evasively and thought: Shit, I'm lying again!

Deborah relaxed visibly. 'Yes, it does sound glamorous, I agree. It's quite tame though as nightclubs go — Jersey nightspots always are. We're very staid here. But I think it puts on some good floor shows — it's very popular with the summer visitors.'

'Where is it?'

'On the outskirts of St Helier. You practically pass it driving into town from here. It's got an enormous Jersey Lily in neon lights on the side. Appalling taste, but it seems to attract the customers.'

'It's no competition to the Langlois empire then?'

'Heavens no! It's in a totally different class. Though you may very well have heard that Louis was keen to move into that kind of thing. It was one of the bones of contention between him and the rest of the family.'

She said it very lightly but Juliet could see the wariness still there in her eyes and the tiny tremble in her hand as she set down the coffee jug and knew that she had only made the point about Louis as a defensive measure. She had realised Juliet had been told something about Louis's connection with the club and had come in quickly to scotch any speculation. But her very defensiveness proved one thing — there *was* something she wanted to keep hidden.

'You mean Louis wanted to open up a nightclub?' Juliet asked.

'Heaven knows what he wanted!' She glanced at her watch. 'Juliet, you are going to have to excuse me. I'm due at the hairdressers in just under an hour.' She stood up, slim and elegant in a peach silk wrap and matching high heeled mules

353

that might have escaped from a thirties Hollywood movie. 'Will you have time to look in on your grandma later?'

'Well of course.' Juliet felt a momentary irritation. Wasn't that the reason she had come halfway round the world — to spend some time with her grandmother and the rest of the family? But the flash of annoyance passed as swiftly as it had come. Deborah meant no harm. She shared a special relationship with Sophia and felt responsible for her. It was nice to know that one of her daughters-in-law cared so deeply, nice to know that Deborah and David, at least, had stood by her when she most needed them.

'Don't worry, I'll make sure she's all right,' Juliet assured her.

'Good morning, Grandma.'

'Juliet! Good morning!' Sophia, like Deborah, had not dressed yet, but her full length housecoat was of rich blue velvet and she was seated at the window in her room sorting through the day's mail, making notes in a huge leather-bound desk diary and consigning the envelopes to the wastepaper basket. She looked perfectly well now with no sign of the pallor that had followed her 'heart turn'. 'We missed you at dinner last night. I'm dreading you going home to Australia, you know.'

'I shall come back to visit really often,' Juliet promised. 'It certainly won't be another nineteen years. I'll make sure of that.'

Sophia smiled sadly. 'It's easy to say that when you are actually here. When you get home it will be a different matter. You'll have your job for one thing. And your young man for another. He may have something to say about you jetting off around the world too often.'

'He won't mind. We don't have that kind of a relationship,' Juliet said but her heart had sunk at the very thought of being tied down by Sean. He wouldn't run her life, of course, she wouldn't let him, but the very idea of being with him permanently made her feel claustrophobic.

'How were Paul and Viv?' Sophia asked, changing the subject, and as they chatted the age gap, as always, seemed to disappear.

'Have you any plans for today?' Sophia asked after a while.

'I thought I'd drive into St Helier and do some window shopping.' Juliet hesitated, then added: 'I have been looking at the

354

names of places. It all sounds so exotic. French and yet not French.'

'Your island heritage, my dear.'

'And there are the names that sort of cash in on the island, aren't there? I've seen goodness knows how many Bergerac guest houses and hotels, named after the TV detective Jim or whatever his name is, someone said. And I noticed a Jersey Lily Nightclub the other day. That's an allusion to Lily Langtry, I presume.'

She was watching Sophia closely as she said it, waiting to see if she got the same sort of reaction from her as she had done from Deborah. Sure enough there it was — a small shadow for a moment in the startling amethyst eyes, a little tightening of the muscles in her cheek — before she said: 'Lily Langtry. Yes, it could be named after her. But our lovely island flower is also called the Jersey Lily, of course.'

'Of course.' Juliet felt guilty, suddenly, for having mentioned it. There was nothing of Deborah's evasiveness in her grandmother's reaction, only recognition and sadness, the reaction of a mother whose son had been at the Jersey Lily the night he died.

But her mind was made up. Before she tried to put the whole business to the back of her mind she would certainly visit the Jersey Lily and try to discover just what connection it had with Louis's death.

The Jersey Lily Nightclub stood on the main road into St Helier, just as Deborah had said. Juliet wondered why she had not noticed it before — because she had been concentrating on her driving, presumably. Now she pulled into the big asphalted car park and looked it over — stuccoed, with blue paintwork and that enormous neon sign — every inch the holidaymakers' Jersey. No wonder Louis had wanted to emulate it — and no wonder the rest of the conservative Langlois clan, with their penchant for luxury and taste, had been totally against such an idea.

But had Louis wanted to emulate it — or had it been more than that? Had he perhaps wanted to muscle in on his friend's very profitable enterprise? And had Raife Pearson objected to such a thing — objected so strongly that there had been a terrible falling out between the two men? It was a possibility, very real for all that Dan had dismissed any suggestion that Raife might be implicated in Louis's death.

Or am I simply thinking on those lines because it suits me to? Juliet wondered. And if Raife was involved in Louis's murder and Deborah knows it, why has she never spoken out?

She left the car and went towards the club. The main doors, flanked by enormous photographs of the TV stars who were appearing in the nightly floor show, were firmly closed and Juliet walked around the building looking for another entrance. She found one at the rear, a narrow blue-painted door wedged ajar, and went inside.

After the brightness of the late spring morning the passage beyond the narrow door was dim and a smell of stale tobacco smoke hung in the air. A small office to the left was empty — the stage doorkeeper's domain? — but from somewhere within the building came the intermittent sounds of music. Juliet followed the passage past a number of doors, all closed, whilst the percussion sounds grew louder. Baize covered a doorway to her right; she pushed it aside and found herself in the main bar of the club — a large empty area which obviously served as a stage, tables and chairs covering two thirds of the room and a long, well-stocked bar. The harsh electric lighting gave the place an air of slight seediness. In a corner a young man with shoulder length hair and dark glasses — dark glasses, in here? — was fiddling with a drum kit. Juliet approached him.

'I'm looking for Raife Pearson.'

'Raife? Try the office. D'you know where it is? Back the way you've come, first on the right.' From behind the dark glasses he looked her up and down. 'Are you auditioning?'

'No.'

'Oh — right.' He returned to his drum kit, brushing softly.

Following his instructions Juliet retraced her steps. There was no plate on the door the drummer had described, nothing to make it different to the others, but she tapped at it anyway and after a moment a man's voice called: 'Come in.'

She pushed open the door. He was sitting behind a large oak desk, a dark swarthy man with the look of the Mediterranean

356

about him. He was on the telephone; he waved to her to wait with a well-manicured and beringed hand on which the small dark hairs grew thickly from wrist to knuckles.

Juliet looked around the office while she waited. Posters, glamour photographs, a couple of big bound directories, everything exactly as one would imagine the office of a nightclub owner to be.

'The job's gone, I'm afraid.'

She jumped. He was looking directly at her, telephone still cradled in his shoulder, hand covering the mouthpiece.

'Sorry, are you talking to me?'

'You've come about the job, have you? Bar staff?'

'No. I'm not looking for a job.'

'Pity.' He was eyeing her up and down with a professional but not lascivious eye. 'I could have found you something, I expect . . .' He broke off as a voice crackled down the telephone, finishing his conversation before replacing the receiver and swinging his chair up on to its back legs. 'What can I do for you then?'

'I wanted to talk to you.' Juliet was nervous now but determined not to show it.

'Oh yes. What about?'

'Louis Langlois.'

The hooded eyes beneath the heavy dark brows narrowed. 'Louis Langlois? But he's been dead for the last twenty years.'

'Yes. I know.'

'His mother did time for killing him.'

'Yes. Look, let me introduce myself. I'm Juliet Langlois, Robin's daughter. Louis was my uncle.'

Raife Pearson laughed shortly. 'Robin's daughter, eh? Who'd have thought it! Didn't he push off somewhere after Louis was killed? The States, was it?'

'Australia.'

'And now you're back in Jersey. The old girl is pleased, I expect. I must say I'm highly honoured myself. I didn't know I was on the list for social calls from the Langloises.' The note of sarcasm in his voice was evident: Juliet guessed there was little love lost on his side either but refused to rise to the bait.

'You knew Louis, I understand,' she said.

'What of it?'

'He was a friend of yours?'

'I wouldn't call him a friend exactly. We were drinking partners. And we would have been business acquaintances if Louis had had his way.'

'He wanted to go into partnership with you, is that right?' Juliet asked, backing her earlier hunch.

'How did you know that? Yes, Louis had some big ideas, too big for Jersey. It's a staid sort of place, this.'

The words rang bells in Juliet's head. Someone else had used that word to describe Jersey. Who was it? Deborah, this morning. She too had said Jersey was staid.

'Of course in those days we were young and optimistic.' Raife found a half-smoked cigar in the ashtray on his desk and puffed it to life as he spoke. 'Louis and I wanted to get into casinos. I'd just started the Jersey Lily, he had control of the Langlois hotels — well, more or less. His father had died leaving him and his two brothers equal shares and he could run rings around 'em. Robin, your father, always followed where Louis led and David was too young to argue. We thought, Louis and me, we could make our fortunes if we could turn Jersey into Las Vegas.'

'But gambling isn't allowed here is it?' Juliet said.

'I told you, we were young and optimistic. We thought we could get that changed and be in at the start of something new and very profitable. It would never have worked, of course, but we had our dreams.'

He smiled at her, but in spite of his apparent frankness there was something shifty in the way his hooded eyes darted and held, and the cigar, still clamped between his teeth, managed to make the smile look more like a grimace.

'Have I told you what you wanted to know — Juliet, is it?'

'Juliet, yes. You've been helpful but there is one other thing. I understand Louis was here the night that he died.'

She sensed rather than saw the instant withdrawal. His expression did not change but his tone became frosty.

'What's that supposed to mean?'

'I've been told you and Louis quarrelled that night. Was it about the casinos?'

Raife had lowered his chair close to the ground; there was something vaguely uncomfortable in his demeanour.

'How the hell am I supposed to remember twenty years later what we quarrelled about? And why do you want to know anyway?'

'I am trying to find out the truth about my uncle's death,' she aid directly. 'And I can't believe you'd forget what you quarrelled about. Under the circumstances that is the sort of thing that would stick in your memory.'

Raife scraped back his chair. He was not a tall man but there was something powerful and threatening about the bulk of him and the sheer force of his personality.

'I suggest, Juliet Langlois, that you go home to Australia and mind your own business.'

Adrenalin was pouring through Juliet's veins now, making her hands and fingers tingle. There *was* something here. There had to be.

'My grandmother served time for my Uncle Louis's killing, Mr Pearson,' she said steadily. 'My family split up as a result of it. So you can see it is my business.'

He laughed suddenly. 'So you've come here to accuse me of shooting Louis, is that it? I'm sorry, my dear, but you're barking up the wrong tree. I did quarrel with Louis and because of that I was interviewed by the police at the time, even though Sophia had confessed. But there was never any question of me being under suspicion. I was here the whole evening with a club full of witnesses to prove it if necessary. As for motive, I didn't have one. Louis and I were friends.'

'You said just now you weren't friends.'

'Well we certainly weren't enemies. As I told you, we had plans for the future. The only reason we quarrelled that night was because we disagreed about how best to make them operational. But if you were looking for someone with a motive I can provide you with the name of someone who had a very good motive indeed. Frank de Val.'

'Who?'

'Frank de Val. He was a senator in the States — the Island Parliament. Louis was trying to get him to support us and bring about a change in the law.'

'The law on gambling?'

'Of course. Louis thought de Val would be . . . persuadable, shall we say. Only he was proving difficult.'

Suddenly Juliet was remembering what Dan had told her that the employee had overheard that night, and the pieces of the jigsaw began to fit together. 'You mean Louis was going to blackmail this Frank de Val?'

Raife nodded. 'Clever girl. Yes, de Val had been a little unwise at some time. Louis knew about it and wanted to put the pressure on. I thought he was going too far. I said so in very plain terms. So you see, unfortunately for you I really had no reason to kill Louis, as well as no opportunity. I'm afraid you will have to look elsewhere if you want to pin Louis's death on someone other than your very accommodating grandmother.' He opened the door and stood waiting for Juliet to leave. 'It's been a pleasure but now I do have work to do. Remember, if you want a job . . . But I suppose that's a vain hope — that I should have the Langlois heiress working for me.'

Juliet went out into the corridor and the cigar smoke followed her.

'Juliet Langlois . . .' She turned. He was standing in the doorway watching her go. 'Just remember, everyone might not be quite what they seem.'

Something about the way he was looking at her, those strange eyes, the curling mouth beneath the dark grey-streaked moustache, made a sharp dart of fear streak inside her.

'What do you mean?' she asked.

But he only returned his cigar to his mouth, smiled at her through the smoke and went back into his office, closing the door behind him.

Dan was working in his office when he heard the doorbell. The office was cluttered — a huge old civil service desk housed a word processor and wire baskets; newspaper cuttings, scribbled notes and open files littered the floor. The window looked out over the Howard Davis Park, a mass of late spring colour, but it was days since Dan had stopped to notice it. He was too bound up in the story about Louis Langlois's death to appreciate anything that had no direct bearing on it.

360

He swore to himself as the doorbell shrilled and glanced at his watch. Dammit, Mrs Ozouf the daily woman would have gone by now. He'd either have to answer it himself or let it ring. Even as the thought crossed his mind the bell shrilled again. Dan pushed back his coffee cup to make a little room on the desk, put down the newspaper cutting he had been studying, and went down to answer it.

'Juliet!'

After her abrupt departure the previous evening she was the last person he expected to see. She was wearing a gold-buttoned navy blazer over a striped top and narrow-legged white trousers; a navy blue yachting cap sat on her sleek fair hair at a jaunty angle. But Juliet did not look jaunty. Far from it.

'Dan — thank goodness. I didn't know if you'd be here or not.'

'What's happened?' he asked.

'I have to talk to you. Can I come in, please?'

'Well of course,' he said, cursing himself for behaving like a dummy. He pushed open the living-room door and followed her in.

'Have you got anything to drink?' she asked.

'Coffee? I expect there's some in the pot.'

'No, not coffee. Something stronger. Oh, I know it's a bit early in the day but I need it.'

'Scotch?'

'Anything. I'll have it neat. No! — I suppose I'd better not. Put some water in it.'

He handed her the glass and watched her gulp at it as if her life depended on it. Then he said: 'Sit down, Juliet, and tell me all about it.'

She refused the invitation to sit, crossing to the window then turning abruptly. 'I went to see Raife Pearson.'

'You did what?'

'Went to see Raife Pearson. To ask him what he and Louis quarrelled about the night Louis died.'

'Good lord!' Dan was staggered. Even he, seasoned investigator, had hesitated to take such a rash step. Raife could be a dangerous man. Not that Dan was afraid of him, but he had felt too blunt a line of questioning could well be counter-productive.

361

Up would go the defences, out would come the minders and a promising line of enquiry could be totally lost in the smokescreen Raife would throw up. And if Raife did have something to hide it could be more than that. Raife sailed very close to the wind. He stayed on the right side of the law — just. But he was the sort of man who could very easily step over the dividing line. And when he did anything could happen. Dan had wanted to have a good deal more to go on before he asked any questions of Raife Pearson. Now, it seemed, Juliet had beaten him to it — and judging by the look of her she had got some answers.

'What did he say?' he demanded.

'Do you know a Senator Frank de Val? Well, he may not be a senator now, but he was then.'

'De Val. Yes.' Dan was suddenly doubly alert.

'According to Raife Louis was blackmailing him. He wanted his assistance . . .'

'To get the law on gambling changed,' Dan finished for her. 'Blackmail, eh! So that was it.'

'You knew?'

'Not about the blackmail, no. I knew de Val was agitating in the States for a change in the law on gambling.' He did not add that the newspaper cuttings strewn over his desk right now were on that very subject. He'd picked it up going through back numbers of the Jersey Post and wondered if there could be a connection — Louis and Raife with their ambitions to open a casino, de Val speaking out against the strictness of the gaming laws. But this was better than he had dared hope.

'What was he blackmailing de Val about?'

'I don't really know. Raife didn't say, except that Senator de Val had been "a bit unwise" and Louis knew about it.'

'Hmm.' Dan laughed grimly. 'I can guess what that means. Louis lived a pretty wild life — my guess is his path and de Val's crossed at some time and he knew something de Val wanted kept quiet. It could be girlies, it could be drugs, probably a mixture of a lot of sordid revelations that would have seen de Val booted out of the States if ever they came to light. Well, well!'

Juliet tossed back the last of the whisky and put the glass down.

362

'It's strange,' she said, 'all this time I've been asking questions I've been hoping I might uncover something like this and now it's happened it's — well, to be honest, it's a bit of a shock! I mean, all of a sudden there's someone with a real reason for wanting Louis dead.'

Her face was flushed with eagerness. Dan felt something sharp and sweet twist within him.

'Listen, Juliet,' he said gently. 'I can understand you being excited about this. But you must realise it may be nothing. It could be a red herring.'

'Do you really think so? It sounds highly suspicious to me. What's more, it could be the reason the shooting was never investigated properly. It's been bothering me, the way everyone simply accepted Grandma's confession without really questioning it at all. At first I thought someone had slipped up somewhere, or been very lazy. Now I'm beginning to think they didn't *want* to investigate too deeply. It must have been bad enough, someone like Grandma shooting her son. Imagine if it had come out that a public figure was responsible! And it wouldn't stop there. The reason for the blackmail would come out too.'

'But just a minute — why, if this was the case, did your grandmother confess?'

'I know it's odd. I can only think she found him dead and went kind of crazy. Dan, you have to admit this is pretty startling stuff.'

Dan pulled a wry face. 'Dynamite.'

'Exactly. That's why I came straight on to see you. I didn't know what else to do.'

'You did the right thing.'

'What are you going to do about it?'

'First I am going to get you another drink and one for myself. Then we'll think.'

He poured more drinks and handed one to her. She sat down at last, perching on the edge of the over-stuffed sofa, cradling her glass between her hands. She felt shaky now that she was allowing herself to relax, all the excitement and the stress and strain bubbling to the surface like the lava of an erupting volcano.

'Raife said something very odd when I was leaving,' she said

363

reflectively. 'He said I shouldn't take everyone on trust. No, not quite that. What he actually said was "remember everyone might not be quite what they seem". What do you suppose he meant by that?'

Dan's eyes narrowed. For a moment he wondered if Raife knew about his alter ego and felt a flash of guilt that he had not told her about it himself. But he thought his secret was pretty well kept, there was no reason Raife should know, and as far as Juliet was concerned this did not seem the right moment to come clean. He'd managed to let her know in conversation that he was a writer — step one to the truth. But at the moment she seemed to be under the impression he wrote books about Jersey — he had his extensive knowledge of the island to thank for that, he supposed.

'It sounds as if he was trying to warn you about somebody,' he said thoughtfully.

'I know. That's what I thought. Who, though?'

Again he thought: should he tell her? She'd have to know some time and he hated deceiving her. There was no reason for her to mind now, thinking as she did that she was on the point of proving a perfect stranger had been responsible for Louis's death. But supposing she did mind? The whole thing could still come crashing down around his ears. And worse . . . he couldn't stand the thought of the look that might come into her eyes. Coward! he thought, angry with himself. You want her to think well of you for just a little longer. Well, perhaps she need never know. Perhaps nothing would resolve itself and she would go back to Australia without ever discovering the truth about him.

Back to Australia. Back to that damned fiancé of hers. Jealousy flooded through Dan, confused somehow with the pain of losing Marianne. It was so damned ironic, the first woman who had meant anything to him in three years and he was deceiving her. The first woman to touch his heart and she had a bloke waiting for her.

What the hell is the matter with you? he wondered suddenly. Are you a man or a mouse? Fight for her, for Christ's sake. If you want her, fight for her!

He set down his glass, sat down on the sofa beside her and covered her hand with his. It was a small move, yet a very

364

decisive one. She looked up at him questioningly and he held her glance, saying nothing, letting his look say it all, and after a moment he felt her hand move beneath his, turning over so that their fingers clasped. Slowly he drew her towards him, until their lips met, kissing her lightly at first and then more deeply, smelling the faint flowery scent of her perfume, feeling the firm yielding pressure of her breasts against him. God, how he wanted her, and the wanting was somehow like being born again, coming out of the darkness of the last years into sunlight and warmth. He put his hand on the nape of her neck, twisting his fingers in her hair, feeling the desire spiral within him, tenderness and passion all rolled into one. He would have made love to her there and then if he could but he knew it was too soon; the last thing he wanted to do was frighten her off again.

He released her lips, looking down at her, still holding her hand, still caressing her neck.

'You shouldn't have gone to see Raife Pearson, you know.'

'Why not?' She seemed to come back from a long way off.

'He's a strange man. If he had something to hide . . . I don't know. But I wouldn't trust him any further than I could throw him. You shouldn't get mixed up with people like that.'

He was feeling very protective. God, if anything had happened to her, as it had happened to Marianne. . .

'It was all right,' she said. Her voice was soft, muzzy. 'He was fine really.'

'You were lucky.' He paused, smiled ruefully. 'Still, I'm glad you did. If you hadn't you probably wouldn't have come back to see me.'

She did not reply and he said: 'Let's forget about Raife Pearson, Frank de Val and all. I still want to see you again. I hope you are not going to refuse me this time.'

'No,' she said softly, a little shakily. 'I don't think I am.'

'Good. What about this evening?'

'Not this evening. I'll be expected in for dinner this evening.'

'Tomorrow evening then? You can make your excuses by then, can't you?'

'Yes, I expect so.'

'That's not good enough. I want a firm promise.'

'All right. I promise.'

Even as she said it she was wondering: what am I doing? What about the promise I made to Sean? But somehow it did not seem important any more. Nothing mattered except seeing Dan again. Tomorrow evening could not come soon enough for her, Juliet thought.

David was in a meeting when Deborah telephoned. At her insistence his secretary interrupted.

'What's wrong, darling?' he asked anxiously when he came to the phone. 'It's not Mother, is it?'

'No — no, nothing like that.' But there was an edge to Deborah's voice all the same. 'It's just that I'm thinking of flying to London tomorrow. I'm about due for another lot of collagen injections — it's a good six months since I had the last ones — but I wanted to check with you before I phone Harley Street to make the appointment, just to make sure you didn't have anything planned.'

'It's fine as far as I am concerned, but won't Juliet think it a bit strange, you taking off for London?'

'I don't see why. She goes out quite a bit and it isn't as if she arrived only yesterday. Besides, I thought it was as good an opportunity as any for me to go while she is here. She can keep an eye on Sophia.'

'Debs, I appreciate the way you look after Mother but I really don't think there's any need for you to play nursemaid to quite the extent you do.'

'David, your mother has been through an awful lot in her life. I intend to make sure she has an easy passage from here on in.'

'Well, you've certainly done your best in that direction,' David said with feeling. 'No one could have been sweeter than you have been to Mother. So if you feel happier going to London knowing Juliet will be on hand to keep her company then I'm not going to argue.'

'Thanks, darling. You won't be late home tonight?'

'Certainly not, if you are going jetting off tomorrow.'

Deborah blew a kiss down the phone, then held the receiver for a moment cradled against her chest. There was warmth within her, a warmth that was always there when she spoke to David, even at the end of a telephone line, and also a small hard

366

edge of determination that had begun when Juliet had begun asking questions this morning about the Jersey Lily Nightclub.

She loved them both so much, Sophia and David. Between them they had given her the chance to be what she was today. When anything happened to threaten either of them she reacted with the ferocity of a tiger with her cubs. Nothing must be allowed to hurt Sophia again. And nothing must be allowed to hurt David.

Especially not David.

But she did not know how to prevent it. There was only one person she could think of who could help her. Deborah put a call through to the airport and booked herself on an early flight to London. But she did not call her beautician in Harley Street.

Chapter twenty-seven

When she left Dan's home it seemed to Juliet she was floating a foot above the pavement. How could she possibly feel like this? she wondered. She should be riddled with guilt at her betrayal of Sean and worried by the knowledge that without a doubt, before this was over, someone was going to get badly hurt. But she wasn't worried and she did not feel guilty — well, perhaps just a little, but not enough to matter. Instead she was soaring, full of anticipation, happier than she could ever remember being in the whole of her life. Strangely not even the interview with Raife, which had seemed so momentous an hour or so ago, was important now. She had moved, for a while at least, into a whole new dimension and she and Dan might have been the only members of the human race.

A car horn honked and Juliet swung round, startled. A Metro was pulling up on the other side of the road and to her surprise Juliet recognised Catherine behind the wheel. She waved and Catherine wound down the window.

'Hello there! What are you doing in this part of town? Have you come over to see the Howard David Park? I wouldn't stop there if I were you. Take your next left, keep straight on, and you'll see the sign for the Belle Visage car park. There's always plenty of room there.'

'The Belle Visage?' Juliet crossed the road to her. 'That's not one of our hotels is it?'

Catherine laughed. 'No, but who's to know the difference? With over four hundred rooms in the hotel they can't possibly know for sure if you're staying there or not.'

Juliet laughed too. 'Aunt Catherine, you are wicked! I can just imagine how cross David would be if *our* car parking was abused that way.'

'Well, if you're squeamish about it, forget the Howard Davis Park for today and let's go into town for a cup of tea.'

Juliet had wanted nothing more than to be alone to explore her new found emotions but she did not have the heart to turn Catherine's invitation down. She had become very fond of her great aunt.

'That sounds a lovely idea. Where do you suggest?'

'I know just the place. You'd never find it though unless you follow me and then you'd probably get lost in the traffic. Look, leave your car where it is after all, hop in mine, and I'll bring you back for it later.'

Juliet hesitated. Wouldn't Dan think it odd if her car was still outside his house in half an hour's time? But Catherine was opening the passenger door.

'Jump in. Between us we're blocking the road. And if I get booked for yet another traffic offence I expect I shall lose my licence.'

Juliet smiled. 'You are the limit!'

Catherine smiled back and the wicked twinkle in her eyes was totally infectious.

'Yes,' she said mischievously. 'I know!'

The Copper Kettle was an old-fashioned tea room with lace table cloths, potted parlour palms and a three-tier trolley laden with tiny delicious French pastries.

'So, tell me how you are enjoying Jersey,' Catherine said, pouring tea into the bone china cups. 'I know your grandmother is delighted to have you. She feels she has missed out on so much where you are concerned and of course she is right.' Her gaze was direct — and also shrewd. 'There's no chance, I suppose, that you might decide to stay on?'

Juliet coloured slightly. It was almost, she thought, as if her aunt had been able to read the innermost hopes and dreams she had as yet scarcely acknowledged, even to herself.

'It's far too early to be thinking on those lines but Jersey does have its attractions,' she admitted.

'Ah!'

Juliet laughed, a trifle embarrassed. 'I expect you were wondering where I had been just now. Well, I have to admit it wasn't the Howard Davis Park.'

'No.' Catherine's mouth twisted with wry amusement. 'Somehow I didn't think it was.'

'I've met someone. You remember you told me when I first arrived about Grandma's advocate, Dan Deffains? Well, this is his son. He's a writer and he's widowed . . .' She broke off. Catherine's face was alight, a picture of pleasure and disbelief.

'Dan Deffains! Really? Oh Juliet!' It was Catherine who was blushing now, her small round face rosy beneath the mop of soft grey curls. 'I suppose I shouldn't be telling you this, but once upon a time Dan Deffains and I . . . well, we were rather fond of one another.'

'Aunt Catherine! You dark horse! Come on, now, you must tell me about it!'

'Oh Juliet, there's really not much to tell. And I haven't thought about it for years . . .'

She broke off, remembering the attraction that had sparked between her and Sophia's lawyer twenty years ago. She had come dashing home to Jersey when she had heard of her sister's arrest and practically her first port of call had been to Dan's office. Across the years she pictured him, a slimly-built man with gold-rimmed glasses perched on a hooked nose and hair that receded slightly above each temple. He had been slightly disconcerted that morning, not only because he was horrified at finding himself in the position of having to defend Sophia, whom he had known socially for many years, but also because Catherine had more or less forced her way past his secretary and caught him unawares. But that slightly ruffled air had not detracted from the impression of strength and competence and it had, in Catherine's eyes, only made him more attractive.

Catherine, to the surprise of all the family, had never married. She had had her boyfriends, of course, in her youth, one of them Jeff McCauley, whom she had met when he had come to Jersey for Nicky's funeral. When she had gone to London she had looked him up as she had promised that day in the garden of La Maison Blanche and for a while they had seen a good deal of one another. But Jeff was too footloose to settle down and similarly none of the other young men she met ever seemed to be just right for her. Unwilling to settle for anything but the perfect relationship, always optimistic that her 'Mr Right' was just around the next corner, Catherine had pressed on with her career and her single life until one day she had woken up and realised it suited her very well and she was unlikely ever to want to give up her independence for anyone.

And then, just when she had least expected ever to fall in love again, she had met Dan.

She had not realised what was about to happen at that first meeting, of course. She had been far too concerned with the terrible thing that had overtaken Sophia and how best she could support her. The realisation that he was the one man for whom she would have given up her job, her life in London and her much-prized independence had come later, nurtured during the many inevitable meetings, and striking her one day with the suddenness of a bombshell.

Catherine had, of course, known Dan when they were young but the age gap between them had been enormous — she had still been a child when he was a young man. Now it had closed to the point where it was non-existent and they were simply a man and a woman working to a common end and finding they shared that comfortable unity of mind and spirit that is the basis of so many enduring relationships.

The trouble was that it was too late for them. Catherine might be free but Dan was not. He was married with a young family, a boy of eleven and a girl two years younger. Although briefly Dan almost succumbed to what might have been the great passion of his life, he loved his wife and children too much to cause them pain and Catherine, who had seen the tragic results of too many shattered families amongst her East End pupils had known her conscience would not allow her to fight for him. The flame had flared brightly but briefly, illuminating her life for a time with a brilliance she would never forget, but when the trial was over she had returned to London and her old life. For a long while the sense of loss had been almost more than she could bear — to touch such happiness and then deliberately walk away left her in a state of depression that came close to desperation. But Catherine was a survivor. She refused to indulge her pain, burying herself once more in the work she loved and gradually

371

it had begun to hurt less. Over the years Dan Deffains had become a sweet poignant memory.

When she had heard Dan's wife had died it had occurred to her to wonder if perhaps when she retired and returned to Jersey they might have the opportunity to finish what they had begun, but ironically Dan himself had died during her last year in London. Catherine had been sad — very sad — when she heard of it but she was too sensible to cry for long for what might have been. Obviously it had not been meant to be. Catherine tucked Dan away in her closet of memories and made the most of what she had.

Now, however, it all came flooding back; the old excitement quirked deep inside her as she looked at her great-niece and saw only the reincarnation of a dream.

'What a small world it is! Juliet,' she said softly. 'How on earth did you come to meet him?'

'Well . . .' Juliet hesitated. 'You remember I told you I would really like to know the truth about Grandma and Uncle Louis? I thought maybe if I spoke to her advocate he would put me in the picture. I looked him up in the phone,book and went to see him.'

'But my dear, Dan has been dead for more than a year.'

'I didn't know that. You didn't say he was dead. So I asked for Dan Deffains — and met a young man who turned out to be his son — also named Dan. It could have been embarrassing. As it was . . . well, it turned out rather well.'

'I see.' Catherine smiled. 'So you gave up asking questions in favour of romance.'

'Not exactly. At least, not at first. Dan was interested too. Like you he said he was almost certain his father had believed Grandma innocent and he seemed to think that between us we could get at the truth.'

Catherine shook her head. 'Oh Juliet, I hoped you would have the good sense to leave well alone. I did warn you.'

'I know you did. And I must say I was beginning to think you were right. I asked Paul some questions about Louis and really stirred up a hornet's nest. I thought Viv was going to have a fit she was so angry.'

'I'm not surprised. She hated Louis. He was undermining Paul's position, you see, making it quite untenable.'

'Wasn't Paul senior to Louis in the company?'

'Senior in experience, yes, but he had no say in the running of it. Bernard had bought out his share years earlier, just as he bought out mine. I spent what I got on a nice little flat and a car, and I invested enough to give me a comfortable income for the rest of my life. Paul, I am afraid, was not so wise.'

'But surely your share should have been worth a great deal more than that?' Juliet said, a little shocked.

Catherine smiled ruefully. 'In those days, no. Oh, I'd have been a wealthy woman if I hadn't sold out when I did, it's true, but equally Bernard might not have worked so hard if the whole shooting match hadn't been his and Langlois Hotels might not be what they are today. I don't bear any grudges. I have all I want to live on — I don't know that I'd want more — it certainly hasn't bought Sophia happiness. But Paul and Viv are different. Viv was used to money — her parents were seriously rich at one time, until her father lost it all on the stock market. So it was the supreme irony that she married Paul — another gambler in his own way.'

'Paul?' Juliet echoed, remembering the cash book she had found in the attic at La Grange.

'Oh my dear, yes. In his heyday Paul would gamble on anything that moved. His share of the money Bernard parted with to buy him out went that way — in fact I think he may already have been heavily in debt and that is why he didn't take much persuading to sell. I'm sure it must have been that — after all, he continued to work for the company. For me it was quite different — I was in London, I had no interest in it really. Anyway, to get back to Paul. He was always a gambler and in later years Louis encouraged him, I'm afraid. They spent a good deal of time in one another's company when Louis was in Jersey and sometimes they flew off together on one of their wild weekends. But this mateyness didn't do Paul any good when it came to business. Louis had the upper hand and he made the most of it.'

'I see.' Juliet was very thankful she had a different line of enquiry to pursue regarding Louis's death. There was no doubt about it, what with the gambling debts she had uncovered and the position Louis had placed him in within the company Paul would have made a prime suspect! she thought.

'Have you ever met anyone called Frank de Val?' she asked aloud.

Catherine looked genuinely puzzled. 'Frank de Val. I know the name. Well, it's an old Jersey one, so I suppose I would. Frank de Val. Who is he?'

'He used to be a senator in the Island Parliament.'

'The States.'

'Yes.' Juliet lowered her voice. 'I think he may have been involved in Louis's death.'

'A senator? Oh no, I don't think so.'

'Why not?'

'My dear, I can tell you don't know senators and justices de greffe. They're a stuffy bunch. They might bore you to death of course,' she added with a wicked twinkle.

Juliet pushed her cup to one side, leaning forward on the table on her elbows.

'This one was being blackmailed by Louis.'

'Blackmailed? Are you sure? Goodness me, how very melodramatic!'

'But it would be a marvellous motive for wanting Louis dead, wouldn't it?'

'Oh my dear!' Catherine shook her head. 'I do wish you'd take my advice and stop all this nonsense. I don't think you understand the harm you may be doing.'

'By trying to prove Grandma's innocence?'

'By raking up a whole lot of things that are best left alone. I don't know how to make you understand but I'm quite sure your parents would tell you the same if they were here.'

'I expect they would. They never told me anything about what happened at all, remember.'

'No, and they may well have had their reasons. Think about that, Juliet.'

Quite unaccountably Juliet shivered. What the hell was this? Why was everyone so determined to keep the subject a closed book even when she was suggesting a totally new theory which had no unpleasant implications for the family? Only Louis came out of it in a bad light and that hardly mattered any more.

'This is all a novelty to you at the moment, Juliet,' Catherine went on. 'Please remember it is no novelty to us. We want to forget what happened. And I think you would be wise to do the same.' Her voice was sharper than Juliet had ever before heard it, the voice of a teacher controlling a class of unruly seven-year-olds. 'I'm very glad you've met Dan Deffains' son. I would be more happy than you could possibly know to see you fall in love with him. But don't let him lead you down this path, please.'

Juliet wrinkled her nose, puzzled. 'He's not leading me anywhere.'

'That's all right then. And now,' Catherine said with her wonderful capacity for changing the subject, 'shall we ask for another of those delicious pastries? Or do you think it is time I started considering my figure?'

Dan tapped a final sentence into his word processor, checked it on the screen and sat back, rubbing his eyes. He had worked too long, not even stopping to eat. Now he was hungry and his eyes ached but it had been, in his opinion, well worth while. Tomorrow he had an appointment with Centenier John Germaine and he wanted to be well prepared for it. His father and the centenier had been good friends, he knew, despite the fact that they had been on opposing sides of the courtroom on more than one occasion. But he could not rely on that for goodwill any more than he could rely on their mutual respect. It was vitally important that he correlate all the bits of information he had so far gathered so that he could judge how best to approach the centenier. Now a simple print out would give him the main points in one concise list — might even trigger his brain into spotting some new connection that had escaped him before.

Dan put the word processor into print mode and sat back, stretching his arms above his head. He felt good, pleased with himself from almost any angle you cared to name. The investigation into the Langlois case was progressing and the same antennae that had made him a good policeman and which now monitored his journalistic progress told him that things were beginning to move and there was much more just waiting to be uncovered. On the personal front too things were looking definitely promising. Only yesterday it had looked as if Juliet was a lost cause, now, suddenly it was very much all systems go again, and the knowledge gave his spirits the sort of lift he had not expected to experience ever again.

The word processor clattered to a stop. Dan ripped out the finished sheet, heaved himself out of his swivel chair and went in search of a beer. Apart from the array of cans the fridge looked depressingly empty; he'd have to go out later on for a pizza or a Chinese if he wanted to eat, but for now the beer would satisfy him nicely. He yanked at the ringpull and threw himself down on the sofa, propping his feet up on the low table. Then he drank direct from the can, at the same time studying the print out.

LOUIS LANGLOIS KILLING
Possible suspects

Family: Brothers Robin and David Langlois
Sister-in-law Molly Langlois
Uncle Paul Carteret
Aunt Catherine Carteret (supposedly out of Jersey at the time)
Mother Sophia Langlois (always possible she was telling the truth!)

Others: Raife Pearson (alibi but had v. seedy contacts)
Frank de Val (reputation on the line — powerful motive)
Louis's lady loves (more investigation needed. Louis was a known womaniser)

Dan raised the can again, swigging thoughtfully. The women in Louis's life had been one area on which the Jersey Post had thrown nothing up. It was, after all, a local newspaper, not a scandal sheet. But there had been a photograph, a group at some gala or other, which had showed Louis, handsome and well-groomed, in evening dress, with a young lady on his arm. In newsprint the photograph had not been sufficiently good for Dan to identify her though he felt there was something vaguely familiar about the pretty face beneath the tumbling hair, but he

376

was working on it. A photographer friend — also ex-police — had promised to work on an enlargement though whether it would be any clearer was doubtful and Dan had also persuaded the girl at the Jersey Post to plumb the archives in the hope of discovering a copy of the original. Meantime he could exercise his imagination — what might that young lady look like twenty years on — always supposing she was still in Jersey, of course. By now she could be anywhere in the world.

The telephone shrilled suddenly almost startling Dan and he dumped the print out on the low table and went to answer it.

'Dan Deffains.'

'Mr Deffains. My name is Catherine Carteret. You won't know me but I used to be a friend of your father's. And I believe you know my niece, Juliet Langlois.'

'Yes.'

'You've been seeing her in fact.'

'I have, yes, but . . .'

'This may sound like the most dreadful cheek but are you . . . fond of her?'

Dan shook his head in disbelief. 'Miss Carteret, I can't see what business that is of yours.'

'No, I know. I knew it would come out all wrong, but I can see she is very taken with you and I was hoping . . . What I am trying to say, very badly, is that I am concerned about her and I was very much hoping you might help me.'

'Help you? In what way?'

'Oh dear, this is so dreadfully difficult. I'm quite sure at this moment in time you think I am just an interfering old woman. But it's not that, I promise you — at least, not in the way you think. Mr Deffains — Dan — it really is very important. I must talk to you.'

Those warning prickles were rising once more on the back of Dan's neck. He hooked out a chair with his foot and sat down.

'Very well, Miss Carteret, fire away. I'm all ears.'

By the time she had finished Dan had almost unconsciously crushed the empty beer can in his hand. He replaced the receiver, returned to the computer print out and wrote on it in biro, a mass of almost illegible scribble and some bold underlining of the printed script. Then he went over to the drinks cabinet and poured himself a whisky. Beer was all very well — at this moment he felt he needed something a good deal stronger!

Chapter twenty-eight

Juliet looked at Dan across the table in the candlelit bistro, puzzled and slightly hurt. Yesterday she had been so sure he had felt as she did, so excited by the attraction that had flared between them; today there was something different about him and she did not know what it was.

'What's wrong?' she asked eventually. 'You seem very far away.'

'What do you mean?'

'You're . . . preoccupied. It's not very flattering.'

'I'm sorry. I've had a heavy day.'

'Heavy how? You were going to see the centenier, weren't you? Did you find out anything interesting?'

'No.'

His abruptness shocked her. 'Sorry for asking!' she said shortly. 'If you're so tired out perhaps you'd like to go home.'

'Oh hell, Juliet . . .' He reached across the table, covering her hand with his. 'I didn't mean to upset you. But I thought you wanted to drop this post mortem examination of the past.'

'That was before I found out this senator man was involved. It throws a whole new light on everything.'

'I'm not sure that it does. I'm not sure he was involved. I asked John Germaine, the centenier, point blank whether any pressure was exerted on him to leave well alone where de Val was concerned. He denied it and I believe him.'

'But . . .'

'De Val had something to hide, that's true, and it could make an interesting story. But I doubt very much if he had anything to do with Louis's death.'

A tiny frown creased her forehead. 'What do you mean, an interesting story?'

'I think he was involved in some very un-Senator-like junketings. But that doesn't make him a murderer,' Dan said, cursing himself for his carelessness. Though he knew the time was coming when he would have to tell her what he did for a living, a public bistro was not the place for it.

'But it's a really good motive,' she protested.

'I think half Jersey probably had a really good motive. It doesn't mean they killed him. And even if they did, how likely is it we'd be able to prove anything after all this time?'

She stared at him, bemused. 'That's not what you said before. You were really keen to get to the bottom of it. What's changed?'

'Oh . . .' He toyed with a bread stick. 'I've been thinking, looking at it rationally. If an outsider killed Louis they must have followed him home. He'd been out that evening, remember — he was often out — and Sophia was often in. No one in their right mind would have gone to La Grange with the intention of murdering Louis. They simply wouldn't have known when to find him there.'

'But if it was done in the heat of the moment . . . Suppose Louis was blackmailing this Frank de Val and de Val went to see him to try and get him to lay off. They could have quarrelled and he could have shot him.'

'With Louis's gun? The one that nobody but his close family knew he had? And no witnesses ever came forward, remember. The housekeeper was asleep in bed and heard nothing. Neither did David, who was suffering from influenza and had gone to bed early with a hot toddy and a bottle of aspirin. Nobody came forward to say they'd seen a strange car on the road or someone in the area who shouldn't have been there. It was November, remember, the island wouldn't have been full of tourists, it would have gone back to being parochial Jersey where practically everyone knows everyone else. That would have been even more true twenty years ago than it is today.'

Juliet was trembling. She pressed her hands down hard on the chequered table cloth.

'Are you saying what I think you are saying — that my grandmother was guilty after all?'

'No, I'm not saying that. I'm saying I don't know. But I think maybe that after so long it would be best to forget the whole thing — leave it alone. Ah!' he looked up as the waiter

380

approached with the desserts they had ordered, 'at last! Service is very slow here tonight. Do you want coffee, or shall we go home and have it there?'

'Let's go home.' There was something claustrophobic about the bistro suddenly and Juliet had no appetite whatsoever for her zabaglione. She did not understand the change in Dan's attitude, nor why when he was puzzling and annoying her she should still find him so devastatingly attractive. When she fell out with Sean she didn't want him near her, couldn't bear the thought of him touching her. Yet even now a glance at Dan's face, shadowed because it was just out of the circle of light cast by the candle, was making her weak at the knees.

'What's up?' he asked. 'Is there something wrong with your sweet?'

'No, it's fine. A bit rich that's all . . .' She put her spoon down. 'I'm sorry, I don't really think I want it after all.'

'Don't look so worried! Leave it!' He finished his cassata very quickly and put down his spoon. 'Let's go then, shall we?'

He paid the bill and they climbed the winding staircase to street level. It had been a pleasantly warm day and Juliet had decided not to wear a coat over her soft cotton jersey trousers-and-tunic. Now the evening air struck cool after the mugginess of the cellar bistro and she shivered.

'Cold?' he asked.

'No. I'm fine.' She said it impatiently to cover her confused emotions.

'Would you like my jacket?'

'No, really. Honestly I'm all right.'

He put an arm around her shoulders. 'Come here.'

She wanted to protest, wanted to pull away and make her annoyance doubly plain but somehow she could not. His arm felt good around her and suddenly all the awareness was sparking again, powerful as an unexpected electric storm. She turned her head slightly towards him and as she did so he pulled her close, kissing her. As their lips touched she felt her knees go weak so that she stopped walking for a moment, the whole of her body sensitised, wanting nothing but to cling to him.

Crazy! How could it happen so instantly? With Sean she had to work at it, but with Dan one kiss, one touch, could affect her so rapidly it was like bare wires crossing. His mouth was hard yet at the same time deliciously malleable. When he lifted it from hers she felt bereft.

'You are cold.' He slipped out of his jacket and draped it around her shoulders. She snuggled her face into it as if it were him. A minute or two ago she had wanted to punish him for suggesting her grandmother might after all have been guilty, now, quite suddenly and almost against her will, she wanted nothing but to be close to him.

He had his arm around her again, holding his jacket in place. She leaned against him lightly as they walked a little haltingly up the hill towards the Fort Regent car park, but he did not kiss her again until they were inside the echoing concrete framework and there was no one else to see.

His car was parked on one of the upper storeys; it took them some time to reach it and by the time they did Juliet was not thinking about Sophia or Louis any more.

His car was an old but beautifully restored soft-topped TR6. The low slung bucket seats made it impossible for him to do anything but concentrate on driving, but the electricity was still there sparking between them so violently that she could almost feel his touch on her skin and she held his jacket around her, enjoying the faint male smell of it. The journey was accomplished in minutes but time had lost all meaning for Juliet. She felt deliciously unreal and it was almost a shock to see her car parked outside Dan's house where she had left it. But the shock was not enough to return her to reality.

Dan parked and she stood beside him waiting while he unlocked the door. The spell almost broke as she followed him into the house, then, as he kicked the door shut and pulled her into his arms again it surrounded her once more, powerful as ever.

'You want that coffee?' he whispered against her ear.

She shook her head. There was nothing she wanted but him.

I've taken leave of my senses, she thought. And I don't care. It's wonderful!

He was kissing her there in the hallway over and over again, and his jacket slid off her shoulders and fell to the floor. Freed, she wriggled closer, her own hands exploring the hard lines of

382

his shoulder blades, the muscular ridges and lean hollows beneath the crisp cool cotton of his shirt. His nearness was intoxicating — she had drunk very little this evening yet she felt as if she had indulged in a whole bottle of champagne which was now bubbling on her tongue and effervescing in her veins.

He ran a line of kisses from her mouth down her throat and her inner thighs tingled, spreading a weakness through her legs. Then just as she thought she was going to collapse on to the floor she felt his arm go behind her knees and he swept her up into his arms as easily as if she were a child, carrying her into the living-room.

The curtains had not been drawn as it had still been daylight when he had gone out. Now the glow of the streetlamps bathed the room in soft illumination lending a muzzy romance to the worn leather suite and the plain functional furnishings. He left the curtains open, setting her down on the sofa and leaning over to kiss her again. She wound her arms round his neck, pulling him down, and a moment later they were undressing one another with urgency and tenderness. She shuddered at the touch of his body on hers, arching towards him. This was the moment when everything began to fall apart when making love with Sean, the moment when what desire she had seemed to drain away leaving her cold and disinterested yet vaguely yearning for what she had lost. For a brief moment she was afraid it would be the same — if it were she would die of disappointment and despair, she thought. But she need not have worried; with Dan it was quite different. The ebbs and flows were exhilarating, each one lifting her to a higher plane, and when at last it was over there was no feeling of terrible let down or frustration. Instead she felt totally relaxed, confident and happier than she could ever remember.

The irritation she had felt for him earlier had all gone now and for practically the first time since she had come to Jersey she was not sparing a single thought for the long shadow of the past.

'How about that coffee?' Dan said, untangling himself and getting up.

She nodded. 'Sounds lovely.'

But to be honest anything he suggested would have sounded

383

lovely to her in her present mood. It was as rare as it was beautiful and Juliet wished it could last forever.

It was well past midnight when she arrived home. Dan had tried to persuade her to stay the night but she had refused.

'I don't know what you must think of me now, letting you make love to me the very first time we go out together properly!'

'What do I think? I think you are a very special lady. We share a very special something. Whatever happens I want you to remember that.'

For a moment she had sensed something unsaid, something he was perhaps on the point of saying, but she refused to allow it to spoil the happiness that was glowing in her.

'I can't possibly stay the night, Dan. The family will wonder what has become of me.'

'I thought you said Deborah was away.'

'She is. Until tomorrow anyway. But David is there. And Grandma.'

'They'd never know you weren't in. Stay, Juliet.'

'No.' She shook her head. 'Really, I can't. It would be the most appalling bad manners.'

'Let me take you home then. I can't let you just drive off into the night all alone.'

'Why ever not?'

'It doesn't seem a very chivalrous thing to do.' He did not add that he was terrified of losing her.

She laughed, not with scorn but with pleasure. 'Oh, you do know how to make a girl feel wanted! But I'm going to refuse, Dan. I don't want to leave my car parked outside your house all night. I'll be all right, really I will.'

Reluctantly he had given in and as she turned into the drive of La Grange Juliet was glad she had insisted — there was a light burning in Sophia's window. It would have been embarrassing as well as inconsiderate if she had stayed out all night and Sophia had known about it.

The house was very quiet. In the stillness the tick of the long case grandfather clock in the hall sounded very loud and the light over the door crept in through the stained glass fanlight and made shadows on the polished floor. Juliet crossed the hall stealthily, then stopped abruptly, gasping in shock.

There was a dark shape on the floor in the doorway to the drawing-room. A dark shape in the very place Louis had died. Juliet's blood seemed to turn to ice and her first thought was that she was seeing a ghost. For a moment she could not move, she stood quite still, heart pounding, then common sense came rushing in and she reached out and snapped on the hall light.

It was Sophia lying there in a crumpled heap. Juliet dropped to her knees, turning Sophia over and feeling for her pulse. In her panic she could not find one. Then Sophia moaned, low in her throat. 'Grandma!' Juliet called. 'Grandma — can you hear me?'

Again Sophia moaned softly. Juliet ran into the room, snatched up a brocade cushion and placed it under Sophia's head. Her grandmother was wearing a housecoat over her night-dress but she felt quite cold and Juliet grabbed a Burberry that was hanging on the hall stand and tucked it around her.

'Stay there, Grandma. I'll fetch David.'

Sophia's eyelids flickered. 'No . . . no . . .. not David!' Her voice was slurred but urgent.

'Deborah is away, Grandma. David will know what to do.'

Sophia's eyes were wide open now, though their usually spark-ling amethyst looked oddly faded and Juliet was not sure her grandmother was hearing what she was saying.

'Not David!' Sophia repeated. Then, after a pause when Juliet hesitated, unnerved by her insistence: 'I couldn't let him take the blame! I couldn't . . . I couldn't . . .'

'It's all right, Grandma. Just lie still. I'll be right back.' Juliet ran up the stairs on shaking legs, then up again to David and Deborah's apartment on the top floor. All very well for Sophia to insist she did not want David bothered — there really was no alternative. Juliet banged frantically on the bedroom door and after a moment David opened it, rumpled from sleep, wearing nothing but a pair of pyjama trousers.

'What's going on?'

'Grandma has collapsed in the hall.'

'Oh my God!' Stopping only to pull on a silk dressing gown

David tore downstairs, Juliet following. 'Get her bag!' he shouted to Juliet over his shoulder. 'Her tablets should be in it.'

By the time Juliet had located Sophia's bag and found the little pillbox she had seen Deborah use in the restaurant David was on the telephone to Dr Clavell.

'Put one under her tongue,' he instructed Juliet, tucking the receiver beneath his chin and raising Sophia's head as he waited for the doctor to answer. 'Hurry! I wonder how long she's been here.'

'I don't know. I only just got in.'

David looked at her strangely, taking in the fact that she was fully dressed, but before he could comment the doctor, finally awakened from a deep sleep, came on the line.

To Juliet's relief the tablet seemed to have an almost instantaneous effect. Sophia could not have been lying there for very long, she imagined — and thanked her lucky stars she had come home when she did. By the time Dr Clavell scorched up the drive in his high powered GTi they had managed to make her comfortable on the sofa, covered by a blanket which David fetched from her room, and she was almost back to normal.

'What happened, Sophia?' Dr Clavell asked her, checking her pulse against his watch.

Sophia shook her head. 'I don't know. Another of my attacks. You know what they're like, Damon. A terrible pressure in my chest so I feel I can't breathe and then everything seems to get dark.'

'What happened to bring it on?'

'I don't know what you mean.'

'Did something upset you?'

'Upset me?' She laughed, rather bitterly. 'No.'

'Then why were you wandering about down here at this time of night?'

'Oh, I don't know. I couldn't sleep. Does it matter? I had an attack, that's all . . .' But her eyes were opaque and the doctor knew he was not going to get any more out of her.

'I'm going to give you something to help you sleep, Sophia. But I think it might be wise if you avoided using the stairs tonight. Can you sleep down here?'

'Nonsense! I want to be in my own bed.'

'If you had been in your bed, Mother, and not wandering about none of this would have happened,' David said sternly. Their eyes met and briefly Juliet saw some kind of clash of wills flare between them. David broke away first, shrugging helplessly.

'You see the problem, Doctor? My mother is a very stubborn woman.'

'And it's lucky for some that I am!' Sophia's voice was sharp.

'We'll have to get a lift installed,' David said, ignoring her. 'The staircase is quite big enough to take one.'

'I don't want a lift!' Sophia snapped. 'You'd make me an invalid, David, if you had your way.'

'It might be a sensible idea, Sophia, but let's not worry about that tonight.' Dr Clavell turned to Juliet. 'Can you make up a bed down here?'

'For the last time, I don't want a bed down here! If you help me and I take it steadily I can get back to my own room.'

The doctor exchanged glances with David. We are doing more harm than good by getting her excited, that look seemed to say.

'Very well, Sophia, on your own head be it. But don't blame me if you collapse again.'

'When, Damon, have I ever blamed you for anything?'

'I think she is feeling better,' David said drily.

Between them he and Damon Clavell helped Sophia up the broad staircase and into bed while Juliet looked on anxiously.

'I'll come in and see if you are asleep in a minute, Grandma,' she promised before switching the light out.

'For heaven's sake, don't fuss!' Sophia returned with asperity but she sounded a little muzzy. Obviously Dr Clavell's pills were beginning to work.

'What I want to know is why she was wandering about downstairs at this hour,' David said when the doctor had gone and Juliet was warming some milk to make cups of Ovaltine.

Juliet coloured a little. 'I think I might be to blame. I was very late home. I wonder if Grandma was worried about me.'

'I doubt it. Your grandmother was never one for keeping tabs. She may react differently with you, I suppose, than she did with us. We were boys, you are a girl. And she may feel responsible for you in a different way. But it's not really like her. And there's one very odd thing and I don't like it at all.' He hesitated.

'The place where she was lying is practically the exact same spot where Louis was shot.'

Juliet shivered — and not just because of the spooky coincidence. She had known it without being told! Well, perhaps she had been told and not remembered, and certainly the totally different style of floor covering in the drawing-room had indicated it had been changed in the not-too-distant past and probably chosen by a different person to the one who had been responsible for the furnishings in the rest of the house – Deborah, possibly. Juliet could imagine that she might have preferred wall-to-wall fitted carpeting to rugs, however rich and beautiful they might be. But the doorway! Juliet thought. How did I know it was the doorway? She shivered again. Weird!

'I can't help feeling this whole thing has been playing on her mind lately,' David said. 'Why suddenly it should I don't understand. God knows it was a terrible business but she always seemed to cope with it so well. Mother has always been expert at hiding her feelings, of course. But perhaps as she grows older they are beginning to surface. I don't know. But she has certainly been behaving very oddly.' He unhooked two mugs from the dresser and set them down. 'Two attacks in as many weeks and we know stress is one of the things that brings them on. What have you been doing to her, Juliet?'

His tone told her he was teasing but it hit home anyway, a huge hot wave of guilt.

'Me? Nothing!' she replied quickly, but she was glad she was busy with the milk pan and David had not been able to see her face.

Was it possible that she was the cause of her grandmother's attacks? Had she somehow managed to resurrect something Sophia desperately wanted buried? She had done it with the best of intentions in the beginning but Viv's reaction had shown her in no uncertain way that she was playing with fire and Catherine had issued a stern warning to leave well alone. Now it seemed there was a possibility Sophia too was being upset by her interest.

For goodness' sake I have to stop this, Juliet thought, disturbed. Perhaps Grandma really did shoot Louis accidentally and she just wants to forget. Or perhaps she had a reason for taking the blame and she sees it as being just as valid today as it was twenty years ago.

'I think I'll take my Ovaltine to bed with me and try to get back to sleep,' David said. 'I have a couple of very important meetings tomorrow.'

'I'll look in on Grandma once more and then get to bed myself,' Juliet agreed.

The shock of finding Sophia collapsed had totally dispelled the lovely warm glow she had brought back with her from her evening with Dan. Perhaps, she thought, tucked up in bed with her Ovaltine she would be able to resurrect it. She certainly hoped so! Goodness knows this relationship itself would cause enough problems if it became serious — and she rather thought it was going to. For the moment she wanted to savour its special magic for just a little longer.

Sophia was sleeping peacefully. In repose her face looked very young — far too young for someone who had experienced all the traumas she had experienced, Juliet thought. But she knew it was only an illusion. Without a doubt all that had happened to Sophia had taken its toll on her health and strength.

'Goodnight, Grandma,' Juliet whispered. 'Don't worry, I won't upset you any more.'

In the half-light it seemed Sophia smiled.

Juliet was almost asleep when it came to her. What the hell had Sophia meant by what she had said when she was lying in a state of semi-consciousness in the hall. 'I couldn't let him take the blame . . . I couldn't . . .' Who was it she had not been prepared to allow to take the blame?

Juliet drifted, trying to grasp the answer she felt sure was there, hiding just out of reach. Then it came to her and suddenly she was wide awake again and trembling.

'I'll fetch David,' she had said to Sophia moments before and Sophia had replied: 'No, no . . . not David.' At the time Juliet had assumed she had meant it was Deborah she wanted, not David; Deborah, who always cared for her when she needed it. But now Juliet realised with a shock she might not have meant that at all.

'No, no . . . not David' and 'I couldn't let him take the blame, I couldn't!' spoken almost as a single sentence — a single thought maybe.

Suppose it had been *David* Sophia had been protecting all these years? David, nineteen years old in 1971, too young to do anything to prevent his brother ruining his birthright but certainly old enough to realise what was going on. He had been at La Grange at the time of Louis's death, Juliet remembered, confined to bed with influenza. Like the housekeeper he had claimed to have heard nothing of what happened in the hall. But supposing in fact he had been the one who had pulled the trigger! What would have been more natural than for Sophia to want to protect him? If he had been charged with shooting Louis his whole future would have been in jeopardy. And he was her youngest son, her baby. Had Sophia followed her maternal instincts and laid down her life, metaphorically speaking, for her child?

My God, how can he live with himself if that is the way it was! Juliet thought. But no wonder Sophia was so utterly paranoid about too many questions! No wonder if she thought her secret was about to be discovered, she was becoming so stressed she was suffering too-frequent recurrences of her heart trouble.

David! Juliet thought, and shivered. Had her parents known the truth — was that why they had run out on Jersey and Sophia, because they could not stay there knowing David had allowed his mother to take the punishment that should have been his? And did Deborah know?

Juliet, her skin crawling, got out of bed and crossed to the window. She would never sleep now, she knew. Outside the night was soft and dark, somewhere along the long narrow valley that ran down to the sea an owl hooted. A beautiful place that was her heritage, populated by people she had grown to love too easily for they were her kin. But at that moment Juliet found herself wishing she had never come.

Chapter twenty-nine

Deborah's plane touched down at Jersey Airport just after eleven a.m. She collected the small overnight bag that was her only luggage, walked through the 'Nothing to Declare' channel in the Customs Hall and across to the car park where she had left her Mercedes, every step a silent sigh of relief. It was not much more than twenty-four hours since she had left the island but how glad she was to be back! Once Deborah had thought Jersey dreadfully dull and staid. Not any more. Now it was her haven. Here she was safe; nothing could touch her; nobody would wrench her away from the life that was hers now. Here she was Mrs David Langlois, here she wanted for nothing and never would again. At least, that was what she had thought — until Juliet had arrived and started asking awkward questions!

Damn her! Deborah thought with a flash of uncharacteristic anger. Why did she have to come? But the anger soon passed. Juliet was David's niece, a nice kid — she wouldn't intentionally do anything to hurt him. It was the unintentional that was worrying Deborah.

Her visit to London had not thrown up any answers to the problems. She had been to see one of her oldest friends, one of the few people who knew everything there was to know about the past and what had happened. Between them, Deborah had thought, they might be able to work out some plan to avert disaster. But this time Grace had been unable to help. They had shared a bottle of Brut, talking deep into the night, and for a while, mellowed by the champagne, Deborah had almost managed to convince herself that it would be all right. But the morning had found the problem still there, as insoluble as ever, and Deborah, with a sense of mounting panic, could see no way out of the long dark tunnel of anxiety into which she had plunged when Juliet had come to Jersey and begun her destructive investigations into the past.

'She won't find out, darling, not after all this time,' Grace had said soothingly when the champagne had done its work, and Deborah had wanted to believe her. But with the light of day her fear and dread were as great as ever. Juliet, with her quick enquiring mind, was a danger. She might be very young and casual-looking, her deceptively lazy Sydneyside drawl might lull one into a sense of false security, but beneath it all she was a Langlois and a Carteret, very much a descendant of her grandparents.

Carterets and Langloises were stickers, Deborah knew. Carterets and Langloises never let go — never. Deborah was very much afraid Juliet would be the same.

She bit her lip now, fighting the claustrophobic feeling of inevitability that was smothering her. There was really nothing she could do. Grace had only confirmed that. She could try to head Juliet off and she could hope and pray. Deborah had never been religious. But like most people faced with something beyond their control which they fear she discovered a fervent hope that there might indeed be Someone Up There — and if there was that He would come to her assistance.

Juliet saw Deborah's car turn into the drive from Sophia's bedroom window.

'Deborah is home, Grandma,' she said conversationally and saw Sophia's face light up.

'Oh good!'

She was looking surprisingly well this morning for someone who had been so ill only last night, Juliet thought, intensely relieved. She could so easily have died — and almost certainly would have had Juliet not come home and found her in time. But as before her recovery was little short of miraculous. Sophia was clearly very strong despite the weakness that caused her heart problems but Juliet had taken no chances. Sophia always had breakfast in bed — as soon as it was over Juliet had gone to sit and talk to her to make sure she did not try to get up and over exert herself. It had meant passing up the arrangement she had made to go to Dan's this morning and that, admittedly, had caused her a pang of regret. The time they would have together before she had to leave was all too short. But Juliet had no intention of letting anything stand in the way of her concern for Sophia's welfare. She felt guilty enough already. So she had phoned Dan to explain, then gone upstairs to Sophia's room.

Typically, Sophia was very interested to know about Juliet's evening. Going out for dinner Juliet had had to break the news that she was seeing Dan, and Sophia had shaken her head: 'Well, well, Dan's son! If he's like his father I'm sure he's a very nice boy.' But she had said nothing about Catherine and Dan Senior and Juliet guessed that was Catherine's secret. 'Hardly a boy! He must be about thirty,' she had laughed, and Sophia had laughed with her. 'I suppose he must. But at my age anything less than forty seems very young indeed!'

Now she listened with interest as Juliet described their meal and tactfully refrained from mentioning the fact that it seemed to have lasted rather a long time!

'You haven't given up any plans to stay here with me, have you?' she asked after a while. 'If you have I shall be very cross because there is absolutely no need. I shall be perfectly all right. I have all the mail to attend to and if I don't feel like doing that I can read the papers and cudgel my brains over the crosswords. You get out and enjoy the sunshine.'

'I see quite a bit of sunshine in Australia,' Juliet hedged. 'It's not really a novelty to me.'

'I suppose not. Your parents certainly knew what they were doing when they chose Australia,' Sophia said, smiling, and Juliet registered mild surprise. Sophia so rarely mentioned her middle son and his wife and more than once Juliet had thought how odd her silence was — one would have expected her to be full of questions about what they were doing and so on, but she was not. It was almost as if she had cut them out of her life and her mind. But then of course in twenty years she had not visited them and they had not visited her. Perhaps she harboured some deep resentment that they had gone off leaving the rest of the family in a time of crisis, perhaps they had their own reasons, such as being unwilling to go along with what they knew to be a charade. Whatever the reason the division was there and was seldom breached. That Sophia was voluntarily mentioning Robin

393

and Molly now might have given Juliet an opening to ask what it was that had caused the split but she was determined not to do so. She did not want to risk upsetting her grandmother again. To her surprise, however, Sophia continued with the same line of conversation.

'Of course Molly was always a sunworshipper,' she said with a reflective smile. 'When she was a little girl she was brown as a berry all summer long. The boys had such fair skin, they burnt very easily. I remember once Robin stayed out in it longer than he should, and ended up so red and sore he couldn't even bear the sheet over him in bed at night. I had to dab him all over with Calomine lotion but he still couldn't sleep. Not Molly though. No, not Molly.'

She was silent and Juliet knew she was seeing them as children — those same children in the faded photographs in the attic; her mother, hair in beribboned pigtails, dressed in short flouncy cotton frocks, her father a little too thin and gangly in shorts and white cotton ankle socks, and Louis, so good looking even as a child, standing hands on hips, master of all he surveyed.

'We have to be a little more careful these days,' Juliet said, wanting to change the subject without really knowing why. 'Skin cancer is a real threat and nobody soaks up the sun the way they used to — at least, not if they have any sense.'

Sophia shook her head. 'Skin cancer. Oh dear, dear. It seems these days there's a Government health warning attached to anything the least bit enjoyable. I think I'm glad I've had my day. We might have lived through some dreadful times but at least when they were over we were allowed to enjoy the simple pleasures of life without dire predictions to spoil them.'

'I think I enjoy life,' Juliet said.

'Make sure you do, my dear. It's too short for anything else. Oh, I'm not encouraging you to be rash, of course, but don't be afraid either. There's nothing more debilitating than fear.'

Juliet nodded. Somehow it was impossible to imagine her grandmother ever being afraid. No — that was not true. She would be afraid sometimes, of course, only a fool was never afraid and Sophia was certainly not a fool. But she would not allow it to rule her. Never that.

They chatted on but the subject of Robin and Molly was

allowed to lapse once more. At eleven Juliet went down to the kitchen and fetched a freshly perked jug of coffee. She was just setting the empty cups back on the tray to take back downstairs when she saw Deborah's car turn into the drive.

'Why on earth does she have collagen injections?' she asked conversationally. 'She really doesn't need them.'

'Perhaps the end result is so good you think she doesn't need them!' Sophia smiled. 'But no, I have to admit, I think Deborah is far too young to be worrying about that sort of thing. And quite honestly I can never tell any difference when she gets back. You may be able to but I can't. Still, I suppose when one is as attractive as Deborah it's very easy to get paranoid about losing one's looks. Quite a nightmare really, looking into the mirror and seeing that perfect image becoming less than perfect. Most of us mere mortals are used to that from very early on. But Deborah is such a darling we must allow her one or two little foibles.'

Her tone was indulgent and her face soft with love.

'You're very close to Deborah aren't you, Grandma?' Juliet said.

'She's the daughter I never had. I couldn't wish for more.' It was said so simply and with such feeling that Juliet felt quite humble.

'Whenever I have needed her, Deborah has been there,' Sophia went on very softly. 'She took care of things for me when I wasn't able to and when I came back we became very dear friends. I owe Deborah a debt I can never repay.'

Juliet said nothing. She turned away so that Sophia should not see the thought that flashed across her mind. David. Was that what Sophia had been referring to when she said Deborah had 'taken care of things when she had been unable to'? That Deborah had looked after David, nineteen years old, totally out of his depth, horrified at what he had done and the chain of events he had unleashed? But it had to remain speculation. She could not ask. Not now.

'I'm going to take the coffee cups back downstairs, Grandma,' she said. 'I'll tell Deborah what has happened and I'm sure she'll be right up to see you.'

Sophia smiled, the serene smile of a woman whose world has once more come right.

'Yes,' she said. 'I am sure she will.'

Deborah had left her small suitcase in the hall and gone through to the kitchen.

'Is there any coffee left?' she asked as Juliet came in. 'It smells divine after the dishwater in plastic cups they serve on the plane.'

She was looking coolly elegant as ever in navy gaucho pants and an emerald green cropped jacket. Juliet examined her face for signs of any change the collagen injections might have wrought and was disappointed. Deborah looked exactly as she had when she left, no better and no worse. But still, it had to be admitted, pretty good!

'I think Grandma and I finished off the first lot but it won't take long to make more.' Juliet set down the tray. 'Deborah — I need to talk to you. Grandma had another turn last night.'

'Oh my goodness! Is she..?'

'She's not too bad this morning all things considered but I must say it was pretty alarming at the time.'

'What happened?'

'We don't really know. I found her collapsed in the drawing-room doorway at around midnight. We called Dr Clavell but by the time he got here she was already beginning to recover.'

'I must go straight up and see her.' Deborah hurried to the door. Her face was ashen.

'She's much better this morning, I promise,' Juliet said quickly. 'There is no need to worry now.'

Deborah, her hand on the door, half-turned, speaking more to herself than to Juliet. 'No need to worry? Oh, it's easy to say that! I should never have gone — I should never have left her.'

'Deborah, for goodness' sake, you have to have some life of your own! I was here, David was here.'

For a moment Deborah's beautiful face seemed to express anxiety, guilt and love all at the same time, together with some other even deeper and more powerful emotion. Then she was gone, her footsteps flying up the stairs.

Frowning Juliet set the coffee to perk once more. Presumably Deborah was blaming herself for not being here when Sophia was taken ill, but surely her reaction had been a little excessive? No one could have foreseen her attack and Deborah had been gone for one night only. When the coffee was ready Juliet laid the tray up again and carried it upstairs.

Deborah was sitting beside Sophia's bed, leaning over to hold her hands. The closeness between them had never been more apparent and Juliet felt a pang of envy. If her parents had not emigrated perhaps she might have had a relationship such as this with her grandmother. Perhaps, if she stayed in Jersey, she still could.

'Coffee!' she said.

Deborah straightened. She looked more relaxed now, as if seeing Sophia for herself had set her mind at rest.

'Wonderful! Are you having some, Sophia?'

'No thank you, dear. Juliet and I just drank one pot dry and I'm not sure too much coffee is good for me. I'm afraid I'm going to have to start being very careful about a lot of things and coffee may well be one of them. I gave my granddaughter a terrible fright last night, didn't I, Juliet?'

'You certainly did!'

'If she hadn't come in when she did I don't know what would have happened. Or, in fact, if she had been in bed and asleep. Juliet went out last night, you see, Deborah. She's met . . . someone. And I must say I for one am hoping perhaps she's going to fall in love and decide to stay in Jersey. I wouldn't expect her to do it for an old woman like me but if there's a young man involved it could be a very different story.'

'Yes.' But Deborah didn't look as pleased as she might at the prospect of her niece remaining in Jersey permanently. 'So who's the lucky lad, Juliet?'

'Well, his name is Dan Deffains.'

'Daniel Deffains' son,' Sophia put in. 'My advocate, remember? He dealt with all the Langlois business for years. It's a small world, isn't it?'

There was a pregnant pause when the atmosphere in the room was suddenly charged with something Juliet could not understand. Then Deborah said: 'Dan Deffains? Really — how very strange!'

'Isn't it just?' Sophia smiled at Juliet, seemingly unaware of anything wrong. 'I was always terribly fond of Dan and I know Catherine was too. You must invite his son for dinner, Juliet — unless I'm being too presumptive, of course. But I really would love to meet him.'

Deborah said nothing but her lips were tight. Why doesn't she like him, Juliet wondered. What could she possibly have against him?

But she was filled with a sense of foreboding. Something about Dan had set Deborah on her guard. Juliet very much wanted to know what it was.

She did not have long to wait. When she went downstairs Deborah followed.

'How did you come to meet Dan Deffains?'

'What do you mean?' Juliet hedged.

'It seems a tremendous coincidence with a whole islandful of eligible men you should have run into the son and namesake of Sophia's one-time advocate.'

'Life is full of coincidences,' Juliet said uncomfortably. 'But I rather get the impression you don't approve. Don't you like him?'

'I wouldn't know. I've actually never met him.' Deborah took a packet of cigarettes from her bag and lit one. Juliet noticed her hand was trembling slightly.

'Then what have you got against him?' Juliet asked directly. 'There is something, I can see that.'

Deborah drew smoke nervously, her eyes meeting Juliet's briefly then flicking away again as if she was uncertain how to respond and Juliet waited, inexplicably apprehensive.

'Did he contact you?' Deborah asked at last.

'No . . . I . . .' Juliet broke off. 'Deborah, what is this? So far you seem to be firing one question after another at me and giving me no answers. Can't you just tell me straight out what it is you are hinting at?'

'All right.' Deborah stubbed out her half-smoked cigarette and faced Juliet directly. 'I'll tell you. The reason I asked if he contacted you is because about a year ago he contacted *me*. He telephoned and asked if I would be prepared to talk to him about Louis's death, said he was very interested in it and thought

398

that as a member of the family by marriage it might be less painful for me to talk to him about it than someone more closely connected. I asked him the reason for his interest. He told me he'd come across the file while clearing out his father's things and that it had always been a case very close to his father's heart. I told him I didn't think I could help — I didn't marry David until two years after Louis died. But it wasn't easy to get him to take no for an answer and I couldn't really understand why he should be so interested. I mean, curiosity is all very well, but this did seem a bit excessive. So I made a few enquiries of my own.' She paused, extracting another cigarette from the pack and gesticulating with it at Juliet as she spoke. 'Has he told you what he does for a living, Juliet?'

'He's a writer, isn't he.'

'And do you know what he writes?'

'Books about Jersey, I think. He's very knowledgeable about the history of the island and the occupation and everything.'

'Oh — is he really? Well, I suppose he has to have a sideline. Perhaps business in the sewers is none too good.'

'Deborah, you are talking in riddles again,' Juliet said, but she had begun to tremble a little too as if she already somehow knew what Deborah was going to say.

'I'm sorry, Juliet but if you really don't know what Dan Deffains's main source of income is I can tell you you are not going to like it.' She flicked her lighter, let the flame burn for a moment and extinguished it again. 'He used to be a policeman, did he tell you that?'

'Yes.'

'And after he got thrown out of the force he turned his talents to investigative reporting. He followed up a drugs story that he'd had a sniff of when he was in the force and made a lot of money out of selling it. After that he honed in on an English businessman who was trying to buy a property over here. Dan wondered how he had made so much money so fast. The result was a case of insider dealing that rocked a well-established British company, caused a scandal in the City and put two men in gaol. Now, it would seem, looking for a new story to help him earn a crust by dishing dirt, Mr Dan Deffains had lightened upon Louis's death. He remembers hearing his father talk at the

399

time, expressing doubts that Sophia was really guilty and decided to try to rewrite history. Yet another scoop in the bag.'

'I can't believe it.' Juliet didn't really know why she had said that. Shocked she might be, yet the facts held together all too well — Dan's willingness to help her, the way he had tried to persuade her to question her family about where they had been that night twenty years ago, the way he had drawn her gently back to the subject again and again. Besides which there was no reason on earth why Deborah should be making this story up. But Sophia hadn't raised the slightest objection to her seeing Dan and neither had Catherine; in fact Catherine had positively encouraged her!

'Do the others know?' she asked. 'I mean . . . I told Grandma and Aunt Catherine I was seeing Dan and they didn't say anything.'

'He uses a pen name.' Deborah lit her cigarette at last. 'His position in Jersey would be quite untenable if it was common knowledge that Harry Porter was really Dan Deffains.'

'I see.' Juliet felt very cold, shocked and hurt. How could he have misled her this way? She didn't usually smoke but just now the thought of a cigarette seemed comforting. 'Could I have one do you think?'

Deborah passed her the packet and lit the cigarette for her. Juliet coughed slightly on the smoke; it tasted vile.

'I'm sorry if you liked him, Juliet,' Deborah was saying. 'I understand he's very charming. That of course is what makes him so dangerous. But I had to tell you. He didn't get his story out of me and I suppose he thought he stood a better chance with you. I don't know what you'll do about it — I know what I'd like to do — throttle him! Especially when I think what it would do to Sophia having it all raked up again.' A young woman in tee-shirt and jeans passed the window, laden with plastic carrier bags and a basket of salad, and Deborah put a finger to her lips. 'Oh, here's Margot coming to prepare lunch. I won't say any more now. But be warned, Juliet. And for God's sake if you do see him again be very, very careful what you say to him.'

'Don't worry, I won't be seeing him again,' Juliet said. Suddenly she was not simply shocked and disbelieving — she was furiously angry. How could he have deceived her this way? He must have thought it was his birthday when she had turned up asking him questions! And she'd thought . . . she'd actually thought . . . Her face burned as she remembered the way things had been between them last night. Christ, how could she have been so naive!

Leaving Deborah to greet the perspiring Margot she stubbed out her cigarette and slammed out of the kitchen. There was a telephone in the study; no one would be there at this time of day. She grabbed it up and dialled Dan's number.

'Dan? It's Juliet,' she said shortly when he answered.

'Juliet! This is a nice surprise!' Clearly he had not registered the ten degrees of frost in her voice.

'No, it's not nice. Not at all. In fact I'm spitting mad! I have just discovered your nasty secret, Dan — or should I say *Harry*? That's who I've been keeping company with, isn't it? Harry Porter the investigator.'

'Juliet . . . hang on . . .'

'No, you hang on! If I'd had any idea of the real reason why you were so-called helping me I'd never have talked to you at all. You knew that, I suppose. That's why you deceived me. I should have been warned, of course. Raife Pearson tried to tell me, didn't he? He said everyone was not quite what they seemed to be. And to think I even let you make love to me! Was that part of the investigation too?'

'Juliet — you've got it all wrong . . .'

'Have I? Have I really? You must think I am very stupid, Dan, if you think I can't see through you. I wanted to stop probing the past. I realised the damage I might be doing and I told you I wanted to stop. So what did you do? You found another way of keeping on seeing me — in the hope I would change my mind, presumably, or even if I didn't you would still have a link to your next meal ticket. Well let me tell you I think it was a despicable thing to do!' She broke off, trembling.

'Juliet, will you listen a minute.'

'No! I didn't ring you to listen. I rang to tell you what I think of you. And also to warn you that if you print one word — *one word* — about my family I will personally tell the world just what sort of man you are.'

401

'Juliet!'

'Goodbye, Dan.' She slammed the phone down. She was shaking now from head to foot and for a moment she stood, fists clenched, as the anger slowly died and a flood of misery began to creep in.

Oh Dan, Dan, why did it all have to be a charade? How could I have been such a fool as to believe, even for a minute, that we had something special?

Too late. It was over now. Please God she hadn't given him anything he could use for his despicable exposé or whatever he called it. Please God the only person she had hurt was herself.

Deborah carried her small overnight case to her top-floor apartment, closed the door after her and leaned heavily against it.

She had hated having to tell Juliet about Dan Deffains but there really had been no alternative. The man was a menace, worming his way into her confidence, and Deborah was worried as to what he might already have managed to find out.

She pressed her hands to her face, closing her eyes behind her fingers. She had known, the moment Juliet had mentioned the Jersey Lily Nightclub, that someone had been talking to her. It was not the sort of place Juliet would have been likely to visit alone. She was too well brought up, discriminating without even realising she was doing so because of her breeding. With Juliet the veneer was not skin-deep, she had been born into affluence, raised to have confidence in her own worth and her God-given right to certain privileges. Deborah felt a thrust of envy. She had lived the grand life now for almost twenty years and still, deep down, she was insecure. She didn't make stupid mistakes of etiquette any more, she always said and did the right things, she appeared poised, elegant, sophisticated and totally self-assured. But she had always been an actress though she had never set foot on a stage; always been able to hide her true feelings. These days her insecurities were buried deep; living the part she had been playing all these years had helped her almost to become it. But scratch deep enough and the old fears of rejection were still there as real as ever, and perhaps the more sharp because now she had more to lose.

Deborah shivered. After all this time she had come to believe the secrets of her past were safe; now she could see how really very easy it would be to blow away the layers of illusion and reveal the truth beneath. Dan, helped by Juliet, was digging into the past to try to solve a murder. In doing so he might very easily unearth the secrets of a past that Deborah had tried so hard to conceal, secrets that would shock a parochial Jersey and embarrass the family of which she was now a part.

She straightened, slipping out of her jacket and hanging it up in one of the wardrobes that ran the full length of one wall. The door was mirrored; as she closed it she caught sight of herself and the haunted, hunted look in her eyes. She had to pull herself together — that look alone was enough to announce to the world that something was very wrong — but she really did not know how any more.

A sense of utter helplessness powerful and fluid as a tidal wave was threatening to engulf her and carry her back through the years. The image looking back at her from the mirror seemed to mutate and change, the features becoming younger and sharper, the eyes more wary, not smudged with soft pinks and browns as they were nowadays but outlined in black and fringed with spiky lashes, the mouth softer and fuller but palest pink not warm peach. She touched her hair, seeming to feel the brittleness that comes from constant peroxiding instead of the salon-induced conditioning, and half-expected to see her expensive couture designer clothes turn, like Cinderella's at midnight, to a cheap mini skirt or pants in the psychedelic prints of the early seventies.

In that moment it seemed Deborah Langlois ceased to exist. In her place was Debbie Swift, seventeen years old, frightened and alone. She had thought she knew everything, that girl, been quite certain she was grown up enough to handle life in the fast lane. How wrong she had been! And now it was all beginning again, whirling past her like a hurricane and dragging her, helpless and afraid, with it.

Deborah closed her eyes, trying to shut out the images, but it was too late. The past that she had tried so hard to forget was all around her. And she was as much a part of it now as she had been then.

Chapter thirty
London — 1971

'Hey there, you wake up now! You can't go to sleep in here!'

The hand on her shoulder was insistent though not unkind, the voice world-weary with an accent part West Indian, part Cockney.

Debbie opened her eyes and lifted her head carefully from the coffee-stained formica counter. Her neck felt stiff and achy and there was a stale taste in her mouth. The hand shook her shoulder again.

'Come on, now, you either have another coffee or you got to go. That's the way it is round here.'

Debbie looked up into the black face beneath the tightly pinned down black hair and the incongruous little starched gingham cap that went with the uniform of main line station buffet attendant.

'Couldn't I stay just a bit longer — please? I won't go to sleep again, I promise.'

'You want another coffee?'

Debbie cudgelled her sleep-fogged brain trying to decide if she could afford such a luxury. She had a little money in the cheap plastic shoulder bag that she had slung around her neck for safety and the rest of her savings tucked away in her shabby hold-all, but she did not know how long it was going to have to last her. If she was able to get a job straight away maybe it would be all right, but she couldn't be sure of getting a job straight away. No, better not spend any more of it now, on her very first night in London.

She slid down from the stool and picked up her hold-all.

The waitress shrugged and watched her cross to the door, a slender waif-like girl in an imitation leather jacket and mini skirt, teetering slightly on three inch heeled sandals, just another of the runaways come to London in search of the glamorous life.

Fools, she thought scornfully, silly empty-headed little fools. God alone knew what became of them — she did not want to. She shrugged again and turned to load the dirty coffee cup and used ashtray from the counter.

On the station concourse Debbie stood for a moment uncertain what to do next. There were not many people about at this time of night and the display boards announcing arrivals and departures above the platform approach were still. Out here, away from the claustrophobic heat of the buffet, it was cold, a chill wind blowing the odd paper cup or cellophane food wrapper. Debbie crossed to a wedge of plastic bucket seats and curled up in one, pulling her imitation leather jacket around her.

If only she had arrived earlier she might at least have been able to find somewhere to sleep, but she had not really planned to come today. Perhaps she hadn't really intended to come at all — it had all just been a lovely dream, something to make life at home in Plymouth a little more bearable. Debbie had read every article and feature she could lay her hands on describing high life in London — the clubs and the restaurants, the shows and the parties. London was where 'it was ,at' and she wanted to be part of it. She had fantasised and dreamed and planned, imagining she was the girl on the arm of this pop-star or that celebrity, dressed in Mary Quant or Biba, with the flash bulbs popping all around. She was as pretty as any of them, she knew — her looks were the one thing Debbie was sure of — and sometimes she stood in front of the fly-blown mirror in her bedroom wearing nothing but her bra and panties, holding her hair away from her lovely heart shaped face and imagining she was posing for a glamour photographer or charming a minor Royal. One day she would leave her sordid existence behind forever, Debbie promised herself. One day she would have wonderful clothes and real gold jewellery, have her hair styled by John Frieda or Vidal Sassoon, drink champagne and dance until dawn at Annabels. One day, one day . . . But she had not expected that day to come quite so soon. Only this morning when Barry, her mother's boorish live-in lover, had made yet another pass at her had she decided: that was it. Enough.

She had been in the kitchen making herself a late breakfast and he had come in, grabbing her from behind, sliding his hands beneath her cotton wrap and groping for her breasts. Her heart had sunk and she had twisted away, glowering at him and muttering angrily at him to leave her alone. But he had followed her, trapping her against the sink, smothering her with his huge hairy body and those awful groping hands. Debbie had struggled with him, sickened by the stale beer and tobacco smell of his breath, and the pervasive sweaty odour that emanated from the singlet and shorts she knew he had been sleeping in, alarmed by the hot pressure of his aroused body against her bare legs where he had yanked her wrap open. But she was afraid to scream or even shout at him, because if she did she knew her mother would hear and come in and find them. She would blame Debbie. That was the worst of it — well, almost the worst.

'Come on, baby, you know what to do.' Barry's voice was rough and he was forcing her head down, forcing her on to her knees with one hand while with the other he opened his shorts. The body odour smell was overpowering now, filling her nose and mouth, and she twisted her head, desperate to get away from him, desperate to take in only clean fresh air. She knew what he felt like in her mouth, thrusting at the back of her throat until she gagged, because he had made her do it before, not once, but many times, whenever he could get her alone. Once he had climbed into her bed when she was asleep and she had woken to find him lying on top of her forcing himself into her, but that had been the only time he had actually raped her and she thought that then he had been so drunk he did not know what he was doing. Mostly, in his rather thick-headed way, he had too much sense for that. He didn't want to make her pregnant. He was too afraid of finding himself hauled up before the court for having sex with a girl below the age of consent, so he preferred it this way. Besides, it had other advantages. She could not scream with her mouth full.

'Come on, come on you silly little bitch!' His hands were one each side of her head, pressing, so that she felt he was going to crack her skull between them like a nut. He forced himself against her tight closed lips and tears of helplessness stung her eyes. 'I don't want to!' she wanted to say but she knew the moment she opened her mouth he would be in it. Already she could practically taste him, the taste that meant she could never eat fish these days without wanting to be sick.

He thrust himself at her harder and as her lips parted she imagined herself biting him, biting with all the savagery of a cornered animal, but she knew she could not do it. Instead she went on to auto-pilot, distancing herself so that it was as if she had flown up to the top corner of the kitchen, high above the dingy green-painted wall cupboard, floating somewhere just beneath the flaking ceiling that was sticky from the residue of chip-pan grease and discoloured by the smoke of too many cigarettes, and looking down on the clumsy uncouth man and the girl on her knees in front of him.

All she wanted now was for it to be over so she could crawl away, wash herself in the rust stained bath, clean her teeth, get rid of the smell and the taste and the feel of him, but he was slow this morning, too much beer the previous night stunting the performance his lust demanded. On and on it went, disgusting, interminable. And then, quite suddenly, there was a voice screaming above the roaring in her head — her mother's voice.

'What the fucking hell are you doing?'

Barry jerked away from her so abruptly Debbie fell forward on to her hands. She looked up, terrified, to see her mother in the doorway, still wearing the off-white nylon slip she had slept in, her face raddled, hair mussed. Her eyes, dark-smudged from mascara, were ablaze with fury, her scarlet-stained mouth screamed abuse. Debbie hardly knew what she was saying; she was too dazed, too shocked and afraid. She tried to get to her feet, pulling her robe around her with trembling hands.

'Mum — I didn't — it wasn't my fault . . .'

Her mother's hand lashed out, catching her in the mouth. Debbie fell back jarring her shoulder against the cupboard. Something inside fell from the shelf with a clatter.

'You filthy little slut!' She lashed out at Debbie again but this time Debbie managed to avoid the blow, slipping past her to the doorway.

'I couldn't help it! I couldn't! He makes me!'

'You love it — you know you do!' That was Barry.

'I don't! I hate it! I hate you . . .'

'You can't get enough of it!'

407

'I hate it!'

'Always parading about with nothing on! She asks for it —
bloody begs!'

'I don't! It's not true! You make me! He makes me!'

'Liar!'

'Shut up! Shut up,' her mother screamed. 'You filthy two-
timing bastard! And you . . .' She swung round on Debbie again,
'get out of my sight! Go on — get out — get out!'

Debbie backed away. When she was in the hall she turned
and ran up the stairs, her bare feet rasping against the worn-out
stair carpet. She half fell into her room and slammed the door.
She was shaking violently, her breath coming in harsh dry sobs,
and when the tears began they ran down her cheeks in scalding
rivers. She could still hear the raised voices downstairs but they
sounded a long way off.

It wasn't fair — it wasn't fair! She had never done anything
to encourage that lout — as if she would! But her mother
wouldn't believe her. She worshipped the ground the bastard
walked on.

Debbie fell back on her bed, sobbing bitterly, curled up with
her wrap pulled tightly around her and the pillow over her head
to shut out the angry voices downstairs, and when the spasms
eventually passed she knew what she was going to do. She would
not stay here under the same roof with them a day longer. She'd
leave — go to London as she had always promised herself —
and she would go now.

She got up and dressed in a mini skirt and cotton polo-neck,
slung a few chains around her neck and clipped on her big dangly
ear-rings. Then she yanked her old school hold-all down from
the top of the wardrobe and began throwing things into it. She
didn't own much, a few items of cheap clothing, some tinny
jewellery from Salisburys, her make-up — Miners and Outdoor
Girl — her hot brush, and a couple of tapes of the Partridge
Family and the Carpenters. She searched through her odds-and-
ends drawer for the old sunglasses case that she used to hide her
savings — her mother was not above robbing her if she was skint
and desperate for a drink or a packet of cigarettes — took out
enough money to cover her train fare to London, and tucked
the sunglasses case into the hold-all beneath her clothes and her

favourite white plastic boots. One much loved soft toy went on top — a furry koala bear she had had since she was a little girl — and a well-thumbed paperback copy of The Dragon Book of Verse which she had managed to avoid handing back in at school because she loved the poems in it. Then Debbie zipped up the hold-all, slipped on her imitation leather jacket and picked up her handbag.

She opened the bedroom door and crept out on to the landing, listening. The raised voices were silent now but she could hear certain unmistakeable sounds coming from her mother's bedroom. Her mother and Barry were making up. Bile rose in Debbie's throat at the thought of it. She went swiftly and quietly past the bedroom door and down the stairs, half expecting to hear her mother's sharp voice asking where she thought she was going, though she knew they were far too busy to take notice of a creaking board.

In the kitchen she wrapped the bread-and-marmalade sandwich she had been making for her breakfast in a piece of cling film and stuffed it into her handbag. At the moment she did not feel she ever wanted to eat again but common sense told her she would be hungry before long. Then she let herself out of the back door and closed it after her.

It was chilly outside but the fresh air tasted good and when Debbie shivered it was more from nervous excitement than from the cold. She glanced back once at the house, curtains still drawn at the windows though it was almost midday, and felt an exhilarating tingle of freedom. She turned into the street, hurrying as fast as her high-heeled sandals would let her and she did not look back again.

She was leaving, she was going to London to *be* somebody and she was never coming back. Never!

Only that had been this morning. Now, hours later, as she hunched into the bucket seat on Paddington Station, cold, hungry and a little afraid, Debbie almost wished for a moment that she was back home where at least she would be warm and could make herself a hot drink without wondering if she could afford it. It wasn't too late to change her mind. She had her train fare back to Plymouth. Her mother would scream at her, ask her where the hell she thought she'd been, but in a day or two it would be forgotten and everything would be as it had been before.

Everything. As she thought of it Debbie's resolve hardened. She couldn't go back to being trapped in that life with her mother resenting her and blaming her for everything, including having grown up into a beautiful young woman whilst she herself was fast becoming a haggard old has-been. She couldn't go back to Barry and his disgusting demands. He'd start on her again before long she knew, just as soon as her mother's back was turned. She couldn't go back — she wouldn't. She had made the break now. All she had to do was stick it out.

'Hello there, darlin', all by yourself then?'

Debbie looked up, startled.

'Are you talking to me?'

'Well I don't see anybody else around, do you?'

The man was youngish with a thin weasely face and shoulder-length hair tied back in a bunch at the nape of his neck. He was wearing flared jeans, platform soled shoes and a great deal of jewellery.

'There's no need to look so scared!' He laughed, pulled out a packet of cigarettes and thrust them towards her. 'Want one?'

Debbie shook her head.

He lit a cigarette himself and flicked the spent match away.

'Just got here, have you?'

Debbie nodded.

'Left home and got nowhere to go. I know — it's the old story. D'you want a bed for the night?'

A bed. He might have been offering her heaven. For a moment Debbie hesitated — but only for a moment. She knew what he was, she'd heard about men like him — a pimp, touring the stations and streets to look for new girls, runaways to London with nowhere to go. If she went with him now it would be just the beginning of a new sort of degradation. She hadn't escaped from Barry to end up working the streets. She clutched her bag tightly and looked away from the weasely face.

'No thank you.'

'It's a decent room, not a squat. Come on, darlin'.'

'I said no.'

His lip curled and she experienced a flash of fear realising just how vulnerable she was, how alone. Then he shrugged. 'Suit yourself.'

She watched him walk away then she got up, making for the station entrance. She had to get out, get away. There might be others like him, scouting the platforms, or the police might come around and start asking questions. They might send her home or, worse, take her into care. Debbie had been in care once, a long time ago, but she had never forgotten how she had hated it. The smell of that children's home, disinfectant mingled with cooking cabbage and steamed fish, and the urine smells of the children who wet their beds, had pervaded her nightmares for long afterwards. She was fifteen now but she knew she was still not too old to be taken into care if the authorities decided she should be.

She walked along the street until she came to an alley. In the alley was a doorway stacked high with black plastic rubbish bags. They made an effective barrier. Debbie crawled into the doorway behind them and sat down on her hold-all.

This would have to do for tonight. Tomorrow she would find a job and somewhere to stay. Tomorrow she would begin a new life. Tomorrow everything would be different.

When dawn broke Debbie moved on. She was stiff and cold but when she had drunk two cups of coffee and eaten a burger in the station buffet she began to feel better. The attendants there were all different — they did not spare her a second glance though she knew she must look dreadful. The most important thing was to have a wash and brush-up — no-one would consider giving a job to a girl who had so obviously been sleeping rough.

Debbie was on her way to the station cloakroom when she noticed the entrance leading to the Great Western Hotel. It looked wonderfully plush — just the sort of place she hoped to be frequenting soon. Well — why not begin now? Debbie gave her hair a quick comb, licked her finger and removed any smudged eye make-up, then walked boldly up the steps and in through the impressive doorway, past an entrance leading to a restaurant with a foreign-sounding name. On her right was the hotel reception, on her left a broad staircase. Trying to look for all the world as if she had every right to be there she turned up

411

the stairs, following the sign marked 'Bathrooms'. At every moment she expected someone to call out and ask where she thought she was going but no one did. The Ladies' Bathroom at the top of the stairs was very big, very grand — and deserted. Debbie washed in a huge china basin — big enough to bath a baby in, she thought — and made up in front of the mirror. She changed her cotton polo for a black halter top and her sandals for the high white plastic boots. Then, head held high, she went back down the stairs and on to the station. Again no one challenged her.

At a news stand she bought a London paper and sat down to scan the small ads, circling in biro one or two accommodation addresses. But there was no point flat-hunting until she had a job to pay the rent. Filled with a sense of purpose Debbie flicked through the pages to find the situations vacant, and one leaped out at her almost at once — a club advertising for hostesses.

Debbie circled that too in biro and looked in her purse for small change for the telephone. Then she changed her mind. She wouldn't telephone — she'd leave it until nearer lunchtime and then just go there. What was more, she would arrive in style. A taxi fare would use quite a bit of her precious store of money, but so what? She wanted to impress. Start as you mean to go on, Debbie told herself.

She waited a couple of hours, watching the trains come and go, while excitement built up inside her. Then she crossed to the line of taxis waiting for fares and went boldly up to the one at the front of the queue.

'Benny's Club, please,' she said.

Afterwards, when she knew a great deal more about London and its clubland, Debbie came to realise just how fortunate she had been to pick on Benny's Club.

Benny's was prestigious — the rich, the famous and the titled came here as well as the lonely far-from-home businessman. It was also respectable and Benny himself was a charming aristocratic man who reminded Debbie of a Scottish laird — certainly not in the least what she had expected in a nightclub owner. He interviewed her with perfect courtesy, his shrewd eyes looking beyond the waif-like appearance and the cheap clothes and seeing a classically beautiful young face half hidden by a cloud of bleached and backcombed hair, and a figure that was lissom and shapely beneath the inelegant halter top and psychedelic mini skirt. He was also impressed by her demeanour, calm and apparently confident, though not brassy like some he saw, in spite of her youth.

'How old are you?' he asked.

Debbie had expected this question and was ready for it.

'I'm eighteen,' she lied. 'I shall be nineteen in the spring.'

Benny nodded. He was not sure whether he believed her or not. It was difficult to tell when girls were made-up whether they were adding a year or two to their ages. But certainly this one would pass for nineteen — especially by the time he had finished with her.

Benny made his decision and hired her on the spot.

'You'll have to have new clothes,' he told her. 'And do something about your hair. It looks as though you have been dragged through a bush backwards. Now — where do you live?'

'I don't have anywhere to stay yet. I only arrived . . .' (she just managed to stop herself saying 'yesterday') 'today.'

'Right. I am going to place you in Grace's hands. Grace is one of my dancers. She has been here a good while and knows the ropes. She will tell you how to behave, give you advice about your appearance and help you find a room. Do as Grace says and I think you'll do very nicely. Now, I'd better give you something in advance of your wages so that you can get yourself kitted out, hadn't I? It's a small flat rate wage, the rest you make up in commission and tips, but you understand that I expect.'

'Yes,' Debbie lied. She did not have the faintest idea what he was talking about.

Grace was an elegant ebony-skinned beauty, nearly six feet tall and lissom. At first she was a little impatient of having to take the new girl under her wing but after they had visited a hairdressing salon, where Debbie's bleached frizz was turned into a tumble of blonde curls, and shopped for clothes together they had established a rapport, and Grace was even suggesting Debbie should move into her flat rather than looking for a room elsewhere.

'I could do with someone to help me pay the rent but I wouldn't ask any of those other bitches at the club. Most of them have it in for me because I'm a dancer.'

Debbie looked puzzled and Grace explained — the hierarchy at Benny's was quite explicit — dancers were definitely 'top of the heap' as she put it, on the next rung down were the showgirls who posed, scantily clad, in the cabaret, beneath them came the hostesses. Dancers and showgirls earned a good deal more than hostesses and their earnings were also supplemented by the same perks because invariably a patron would request that the dancer or showgirl who had taken his fancy should join him at his table between performances. There was a good commission on any drink a girl could persuade her benefactor to buy for her, understandably so, since the girls were forbidden to order anything other than champagne or Bucks Fizz.

'I always seem to be short of money though,' Grace wailed. 'It runs through my fingers like water. Are you any good at keeping a check on bills and things? I'm hopeless. I've had the electricity and telephone cut off more times than I care to mention. I just forget to pay the damned things and when I do remember I'm skint. Will you help me keep an eye on that sort of thing?'

Debbie nodded. Personally she hated not knowing exactly how she stood financially and she was not naturally extravagant. The taxi had been more of an investment than a luxury — and it seemed to have paid off!

'We might even be able to turn a trick or two together,' Grace added speculatively, watching Debbie strip off to try on a white halter-necked evening gown. 'We'd make a good pair — you small and fair, me big and black. Men like variety in bed.'

Debbie was shocked. 'But I thought . . .'

'That we weren't supposed to do things like that?'

'Yes.' Benny had been quite explicit in his instructions. No encouraging amorous advances from the clientele and definitely no selling sexual favours or she would find herself out of a job — fast.

Grace laughed. 'Look, sweetie, what Benny doesn't know won't harm him. A girl has to make a living for God's sake! Besides, he soon enough turns a blind eye if one of his best customers takes a fancy to a girl. Just don't make it too obvious and you'll be all right. My gentlemen are "friends" not clients — get it?'

Debbie did. But she was determined not to 'turn any tricks' if she could avoid it. What Grace was suggesting might be a vast improvement on what the pimp on Paddington station had had to offer but it wasn't the way she saw her future. She had come to London to make something of herself — and call girl, high class or not, was definitely not on the agenda!

Six weeks later and Debbie had still managed to avoid becoming part of one of Grace's 'threesomes' though sometimes, she had to admit, the temptation to earn a little extra money was very strong. There had been an Arab prince, very handsome and very rich, who had taken a fancy to her and who had had a fine fit of pique when she declined his advances, and a well-known TV personality who had suggested she visit him at his Maidenhead home when his wife was away, but Debbie had resisted him too. Grace had called her all kinds of fool and asked what was wrong about having a good time and getting paid for it — in kind if not in cash — but Debbie remained stubborn. She could not explain to Grace the revulsion she felt at the thought of going to bed with a man, particularly one she scarcely knew. She did not want to talk about the disgusting Barry and the things he had made her do, she wanted to forget them and she thought that if she never had to let a man lay a finger on her again she would be happy. Besides, she was fairly sure Grace would not understand. Grace loved sex and everything about it, she loved men, she loved 'getting laid'. If there were also financial inducements and expensive presents they were just the icing on the cake. Grace was, Debbie thought, the most sensual woman imaginable, proud of her beautiful black body and the response it could excite in men, gloriously voluptuously uninhibited about her own enjoyment. But the pleasures of the sexual romps which she recounted in graphic detail, licking her full red lips and running her hands over her own shapely body as the memory excited her, only made Debbie feel slightly sick, though she managed to hide her reaction from Grace. Sometime, she supposed, she would have to succumb. But not yet . . . not yet! For the moment her plans were working out very nicely — and they required every bit of her energies.

From the moment she had realised the hostesses were the lowest order in club life Debbie had made up her mind to better herself. She was not statuesque enough for a show girl, she knew, but there was no reason why she should not be a dancer. She had a good sense of rhythm and as far as she could see the routines performed by the girls at Benny's were scarcely demanding. Once the rent and her share of the electricity and telephone bills were paid Debbie put every penny she could save towards dancing classes and a modelling course, which had been Grace's idea.

'You'd be wonderful in glamour,' she had said. 'You've got just the right face — and shape. But you need a portfolio to get going. I can give you the name of a marvellous photographer if you like. He's a doll and he loves women — that's why he photographs them so well.' She grinned. 'He might even break your ice-maiden's heart!'

Debbie said nothing. She knew that good photographs could be a horrendous expense even if she avoided the rip-off merchants but if Grace was implying 'her' photographer would do the job cheaply, or even free, in exchange for a tumble in the dark room, then tough! The photographs would just have to wait until she had saved up enough to get them done legitimately.

As for having her heart broken — Debbie was quite determined that should not happen. Perhaps one of these days she was going to have to loosen up a little for the sake of ambition if nothing else. But just at the moment she could not imagine what the circumstances would be. She was not going to prostitute herself and she was not going to fall headlong in love with the wrong man. It would be far too distracting, she decided.

And then she met Louis Langlois and overnight everything changed — her values, her resolutions, her plans. She met Louis Langlois and fell in love and knew that nothing in her life would ever be the same again.

What was it about Louis, she sometimes wondered in later years, that had had such a devastating effect? He was handsome, yes, heart-stoppingly so, especially dressed as he had been the night

416

she had met him, in DJ and black tie, his frilly-fronted shirt somehow only accentuating the absolute maleness of him. But plenty of the men who came to Benny's were handsome — film stars and pop singers, peacocks every one — and the Arab prince had possibly been more handsome than any of them. Louis was obviously well off — the cut of his suit and the solid gold cuff links and rings he wore announced serious money, even if Debbie was not yet experienced enough to recognise a Cartier watch or handmade shoes. But again this was no novelty. Every man who came to Benny's had money to spend — if he had not he would not be there. No, it was something else, something quite indefinable and quite devastating, charm and power and the most potent brand of animal sex appeal all rolled into one and spiced with something else. For a long time Debbie could never make out what that something was. Only years afterwards did she come to realise. It was evil.

The night she met Louis had been a trying one. Debbie had been assigned to a visiting Swiss businessman who spoke little English, and since she had lied to Benny about her linguistic ability the man had been led to believe, quite wrongly, that she spoke — or at least understood — both French and German. Luckily for Debbie the man liked the sound of his own voice and Debbie had been able to keep her side of the conversation to the occasional 'oui' and 'non', smiling sweetly all the while, but by the time the second cabaret show was over he was beginning to want to do more than talk, pressing his leg against hers under the table and brushing her breast with the back of his hand.

Debbie thought she could handle him but it had to be done diplomatically. Benny hated scenes. He felt, and rightly so, that they were degrading and damaged the good name of the club. There were always a couple of 'heavies' on hand in case a customer became troublesome, but they were intended to blend into the background and Benny was always furious when they had to break cover. Two men — a client and a jealous ex-fiancé — had almost come to blows over one of the girls last week but although the heavies had escorted them off the premises with the utmost discretion the girl had been fired on the spot.

'Another drink?' the Swiss asked.

417

Debbie nodded, thinking gratefully of the extra commission every round he bought would bring her, then, as he turned away to signal to a waitress she surreptitiously poured the remains of her current Bucks Fizz into the enormous cheese plant conveniently positioned near the table.

A waitress brought fresh drinks. Beneath the table the man's thigh pressed against Debbie's more insistently and his hand hovered over her knee.

'We go now?' he asked in French when he had demolished his drink.

'Non,' Debbie smiled brightly. 'It's early yet. I am enjoying myself.'

The man was beginning to look inebriated, his face flushed, beads of perspiration standing out on his bald head. His hand, also hot and sweaty, closed over her bare arm.

'I enjoy myself too but it will be better when we are alone. My hotel room is very nice, you will like it.' He moved closer, brushing her ear with his thick rubbery whisky-smelling lips and sliding his hand right inside the boned bodice of her dress to squeeze her breast.

His touch sparked something in Debbie. For a moment she was back in the kitchen in Plymouth with Barry groping for her beneath her cotton wrap. Without a thought for the consequences she reacted against the memory, kicking the Swiss sharply on the shin. He let out a yell and withdrew his hand, glaring at her in pained outrage.

'You are not supposed to do that,' she hissed.

'Mais j'ai acheté les boissons tout le soirée . . .'

'But you have not bought me. Je ne suis pas une . . . oh what's the word?'

'You are nothing but a little tease! I have been cheated!' The Swiss started to his feet. To her horror Debbie realised people were beginning to stare.

'Please . . . sit down!' she begged.

'Can I be of help?' The voice was smooth, baritone, upper crust.

Debbie looked up, desperately trying to regain her composure. 'It's all right, really . . .'

'It sounded to me as if you were having trouble.'

418

'I'm just trying to explain that I don't come free with the drinks but I don't speak much French and he doesn't speak much English.'

'Leave it to me.' He spoke to the Swiss in rapid French, scribbled something on a business card and handed it to the man. To her intense relief Debbie saw his expression begin to lighten and he rose, actually kissing her hand and bowing slightly before leaving the table and making his way towards the exit.

She turned to her saviour, realising, now that the moment of danger was over, just how attractive he was. A few inches taller than she, slimly built yet somehow powerful, the fairness of his skin and hair complimented by the stark black and white of his dinner suit.

'Thank you so much. I could have lost my job if he had turned awkward. What did you say to him?'

'I explained you were not the sort of girl he thought — and gave him an address where he can find someone who is. Now — can I buy you a drink?'

Debbie hesitated. This was against all the rules. But in her relief at being rid of the awful Swiss and faced with the devastating charm of the man who had rescued her she found it difficult to care.

'Thank you. I'd like that.'

He signalled to the waitress. 'What are you drinking?'

'Bucks Fizz.'

Amusement sparked in his light blue eyes. 'I'll rephrase that. What would you like to drink as opposed to what it is you are pouring into those poor tipsy pot plants?'

She giggled — he actually knew the fate of those endless free drinks!

'We're only allowed to order champagne or Bucks Fizz.'

'But if you could choose . . . ?'

'I'd have a lovely long glass of orange squash. It's so hot in here and I never dare have more than a few sips of any alcohol.'

'Orange squash it is then.'

'No — I can't I tell you!'

'A very long orange squash,' he said to the waitress. 'And if there is any query about that you can tell Benny it's for Louis Langlois.'

*

419

She was in love and it was wonderful. She was in love and suddenly everything was changed. He was the most incredible man she had ever met and unbelievably he seemed to want her too.

Two weeks after first meeting they became lovers and Debbie revised all her ideas about physical contact with a man. She actually wanted Louis to touch her, loved the feel and the smell of him, felt her body respond to his lightest caress, ached with the need to have him in her. To taste his flesh and experience delight, not revulsion, was a wonderful revelation to her, to lie in his arms was like finding the home she had never known, safe and warm and utterly satisfying.

Not that she was completely sure of him. When she was not with him she suffered agonies of uncertainty, for she could not believe that she could be anything but a passing fancy to a man like him. He called her Kitten and she liked that — it made her feel small and cuddly and playful and loved — but she also wondered if it meant that she was just a toy to him. Each time the moment came to leave him she held her breath wondering if he was going to suggest seeing her again or if this time would be the last. But less than a month after that first meeting Louis suggested she should move in with him, and thrilled beyond words at this evidence of her permanence in his life she agreed without hesitation.

Louis owned a fully modernised town house near the river in the east end of London. At first Debbie was quite shocked to learn he lived 'south of the river' — to her Wapping and Bermondsey, Catford and Peckham were not much better than the poor area of Plymouth where she had hailed from. But when she saw his home for the first time, she was impressed as well as surprised.

Louis had anticipated the trend that would soon make the docklands fashionable and his house with its stuccoed walls stood out against the crumbling grey stone like flowers clinging to a cliff face. To step through the elegant dove grey front door was to enter a world that bore no resemblance to the slum dwelling the house had once been — everywhere was stark minimal design, but minimalism that smacked of money.

Since coming to London Louis had made a great deal of money

from gambling — he was both lucky and daring at the tables — and he also dabbled in property. Some men who got rich quick as he had done elected for obvious Regency-style luxury epitomised by Adam fireplaces and ceilings, William Morris wallpaper, French furniture, Old Masters and silk drapes. Not Louis. He had had enough of that sort of thing at home and it stifled him, just as his father with his courteous olde-worlde ideas of running a hotel business stifled him. When he and Bernard had fallen out and Louis had left Jersey for the wider — and more cut-throat — world in London he had also left — for ever, he hoped — the trappings that reminded him of home. He had furnished his dockland home with stark ebony and sparkling crystal, with gleaming stainless steel and wall-to-wall carpeting in soft dove grey the exact same shade as his front door. The enormous picture windows were fitted with dove grey Venetian blinds but left uncurtained, a starkly simple ebony table held nothing but a glass ashtray in the shape of a large but slightly twisted cube. The only flowers were Dartington glass — Louis had an aversion to real ones, another throwback perhaps to his youth when his Jersey home had been filled with freesias and lilies, carnations and Christmas roses in season.

It was the bedroom however which Debbie found especially intriguing. It was furnished in the same colour scheme as the rest of the house, black white and grey, the vast futon-style bed covered with black and white striped silk and scattered with cushions and pillows in geometric designs. But the ceiling was mirrored and so were three of the walls and if the scene they reflected had not been so aggressively modern, they would have seemed better suited to the bordello than to Japanese minimalism.

At first Debbie found it unnerving to continually catch sight of herself from every conceivable angle. But as she grew more used to the experience she began to like it especially since she was usually such a pretty sight. Debbie was not vain in the accepted sense but she did enjoy her own good looks and since her appearance was the principal tool of her trade, it was useful to be able to see at a glance that her hair was not flattened at the back nor her skirt creased.

Debbie was aware that the mirrors were not there for the

purposes of her grooming, of course, but she did not mind that. After all it was not as though Louis was like Barry, with his bull neck, dirty singlet and beer gut. Louis's body was beautiful, smooth and lithe with muscles that rippled across his shoulders and bunched strongly at the back of his thighs. The mirrors enabled her to see them when they were making love and she found it exciting. This, she supposed, was what Grace went on and on about, this wonderful intoxicating feeling, this impulsion to repeat the experience again and again and again. But Grace seemed able to capture it with almost anyone. She could find it only with Louis.

When Louis asked her to move in with him Debbie wondered if he would want her to give up working at Benny's, but he did not. He was quite happy for her to continue just as long as she came home by taxi when he was not there to collect her in person, and he positively encouraged her to continue with her dancing and modelling classes. To these he added — and paid for — elocution lessons to eliminate the last traces of her West Country accent. Debbie scarcely needed them. A born mimic, she was already hanging on his every word and copying the way he spoke. Heavens, hadn't she already begun to pick up Grace's West Indian-inspired drawl? Imitating Louis's clipped accent and open vowels came much more naturally.

Besides the classes there were shopping sprees. The cheap chain store dresses she had chosen with such delight only a few short weeks ago were parcelled up for Oxfam, and Louis dressed her from head to toe in Mary Quant and Biba, young, zingy and highly fashionable. No woman of his was going to be seen wearing C & A or Richard Shops. Debbie might not be able to tell the difference – he certainly could. For shoes he took her to Annello and Davide, known principally for stage shoes; her hair was styled at Vidal Sassoon. Benny was furious when one day she arrived for work with her blonde hair shorn into a sleek bob — to him the shoulder-length and wavy Barbie-doll curtain epitomised everything a hostess should be. And when he saw the jewellery she was wearing he was almost alarmed. Gold chains, a solid gold slave-girl bangle, sapphire ear-rings, a Cartier watch.

'I hope you know what you are doing,' he grumbled to Louis

one day. 'I hope you are well insured, letting her wear that stuff. Because I certainly do not have cover for my girls in the sum of thousands of pounds for personal effects.'

'Don't worry about it, old son. There's plenty more where that came from,' Louis said with a smile.

He was enjoying himself, enjoying playing Santa Claus to his Kitten. He was only twenty-five years old yet he seemed to have everything — a ready supply of money from the gaming tables, a nice home, good looks and a girl so beautiful and young and luscious she made men's mouths water — considerably younger than she admitted to, in his opinion. Louis was very glad now that he had fallen out with his father and decided to leave Jersey. His father was a stick-in-the-mud and Jersey was such a staid and boring place, bogged down by carefully invested wealth and self-importance. He was far better off here — for the time being anyway — making money hand over fist and having a good time into the bargain. Perhaps one day when his father began to lose his touch he'd go back, like the young lion looking to lead the pride when he knows the old one can no longer fight. But for the moment he was happy enough where he was.

And Debbie was happy too.

'Haven't you got any family, Kitten?' Louis asked Debbie one night.

They were lying on the futon, carelessly wrapped in the black and white silk sheets after having made love. Debbie nestled her head against his shoulder, squinting up at their reflection in the huge mirrors above the bed and wondering how much she dare tell him. Not about Barry, that was for sure. She was still so ashamed about the things he had done to her, she knew she would never share them with anyone. They were her secret — she would take them to her grave with her. She was also still irrationally afraid that if Louis knew the truth about her background he would no longer want her but tonight she wished she could tell him, reach out for him on an emotional level as well as a physical one. If he knew everything and still wanted her she would feel completely safe; she would have nothing else to fear.

'There's only my mother,' she said hesitantly.

'Don't you ever go to see her?'

423

'No. She wouldn't want me to. She was really glad to see me go. I've never been anything but a nuisance to her.'

Louis laughed. In his experience mothers weren't like that at all. His own mother certainly had always been fierce in his defence; he knew he had caused endless friction between her and his father and had quite enjoyed the sense of power it gave him. The idea that Debbie's mother simply should not want her seemed like fantasy to him. It was Debbie's excuse to herself, he decided, to square her conscience for having ducked out of the family scene.

'Come on, Debs,' he said lightly, 'I'm sure that's not true.'

He felt her draw away from him slightly.

'What would you know about it?'

'Well I don't, I suppose, but . . .'

'I was nothing but a nuisance to her from the day I was born,' Debbie said, the urge to tell him suddenly very strong. 'I'm not making it up, Louis, she really truly didn't want me. Not as a baby — well, I suppose I can understand that in a way, babies are a bit of a nuisance, aren't they? — and not as a child either. I was always being shunted from pillar to post. I was taken into care once because she used to go out and leave me alone. It was really scary. One night I thought a burglar had broken in and I ran out into the street screaming. The neighbours told the police then that I was often by myself all night and the social workers came and took me away.'

She broke off, shivering even now at the memory.

'Were you in the home for long?' Louis asked.

'No. Thank goodness. Mum promised not to leave me alone again and they let me go home.'

'Well there you are then!' Louis said. 'If she really hadn't wanted you she would have left you there, wouldn't she?'

Debbie sighed. Put like that it certainly sounded as if her mother must have wanted her. But she knew better.

'No, you don't understand. Having me taken away was a kind of insult to her. When she got me home she gave me a good hiding for getting her into trouble, that's all. She never kissed me or put her arms round me or anything. Just hit me for being a nuisance.'

'And did she ever leave you alone again?'

424

'Oh yes. She stayed in for a few weeks but she was really bad tempered all the time, telling me I was a pain in the ass and threatening to send me back if I did anything she didn't like. And then she went back to her old ways. I didn't really mind. After all, she was my mum.'

She broke off again, unexpected tears aching in her throat. In those days she had so much wanted her mother to notice her, approve of her, love her. There had been times when her whole existence had seemed to revolve around that desperate aching longing.

She had done everything in her power to try to win her mother's love. Once, she remembered, she had cleaned the house from top to bottom and filled jam jars with celandines to brighten every corner. But her mother hadn't said one word of praise. 'What the hell are those smelly weeds doing in the house?' was all she had said. 'Go and tip them in the dustbin, for crying out loud!' On another occasion when she had had a man friend to stay Debbie had taken them breakfast in bed, cutting slabs of bread and marmalade with infinite care, and making a pot of tea in the silver plated teapot that normally graced the sideboard. Her efforts had been rewarded by a shriek of anger. 'That teapot's not for *using*, you stupid bitch! Surely you ought to know that! Are you fucking thick or something?' Debbie had felt tears of injustice prick her eyes as she had stood mutely trying to blink them away, until her mother had suddenly become coy about the hulking great stranger hunched beneath the sheets beside her and yelled at Debbie: 'Oh just get out, will you, you nosy little cow!'

Across the years Debbie remembered all too clearly how she had been hurt, hurt and hurt again. In those days, as a child, she had not been able to understand her mother's attitude — she had only known she was a dreadful nuisance to her. But later, when Barry had begun taking an interest in her, she had recognised the jealousy that had taken the place of mere irritation.

Debbie's heart ached even now thinking of the empty place inside her that only a mother's love could fill.

'What about your father?' Louis asked. 'What happened to him?'

'I don't know,' Debbie said truthfully. 'There was only ever me and Mum. I never knew my father. I'm not sure my mother even knew who he was.'

There was a moment's silence when Louis lay completely still. She felt the rigidity in his body and experienced a moment's fear.

'I'm sorry, Louis, but that's the way it was,' she said miserably. 'I don't suppose you want me any more now you know the truth about me.'

And Louis laughed, a short mirthless chuckle that bubbled up from somewhere inside him.

'Don't be silly, Kitten. You shouldn't let something like that worry you. He was probably a complete bastard anyway.'

'Do you think so?'

'Yes. Why not?' He reached for her, cupping her breast and playing with the nipple until it grew firm and erect between his fingers. 'All men are bastards.'

'You're not.'

'Don't be too sure of that. Now come here and make one bastard happy — OK?'

'OK,' she whispered, forgetting her doubts in a rush of love and turning to love him again.

Chapter thirty-one

When she had been living with him for about two months Louis decided it was time Debbie gave up being a hostess and started being a full-time mistress. At first she argued — though there was a certain appeal to the prospect of being a lady of leisure she liked the sense of at least a little independence which having a job gave her — but Louis was adamant. He did not want her being eyed up by other men, he wanted her to be free to spend her evenings with him when he so wished it and he did not like her sleeping half the day away. He was quite happy for her to continue with her dancing and modelling classes. The elocution lessons were no longer necessary but they had done their job well, Debbie's voice was now low and musical and a pleasure to listen to. But the job at Benny's had to go.

Debbie gave in gracefully. She was flattered that Louis cared enough about her to want her at his beck and call all the time and it did not cross her mind that in reality she was nothing more or less than his plaything. She settled happily into her new routines and went along with all Louis's wishes — with one exception. That exception was Grace.

For some reason Louis did not approve of Debbie's friendship with the beautiful ebony-skinned girl with whom she had once shared a flat and had in fact gone so far as to forbid Debbie to see her. When Debbie asked him the reason he was evasive but Debbie thought it might be because Grace was a bit of a wild child. Whereas Debbie had never been terribly interested in sex, Grace undoubtedly was. She had had so many lovers Debbie thought she must have lost count, but she seemed to enjoy them all. Debbie had once said to Louis that she envied Grace's lusty appetite — it must be nice to get such fun out of each and every encounter. Debbie thought that Louis had remembered this and was perhaps afraid Grace might lead her astray — he could be extremely possessive where his Kitten was concerned.

This attitude pleased Debbie as much as his insistence she should give up working had done but in this case she was not prepared to be quite so obedient. Grace was the first friend she had made in London, perhaps her only real friend, and she was determined not to give that up so easily. On afternoons when Louis was tied up with business Debbie sneaked out for an hour's shopping with Grace, the two of them would 'do' Harrods or Harvey Nicholls, chat and laugh over coffee and pastries, and stagger home laden with lingerie, perfume and make-up all bought with the credit card Louis had given Debbie. She never told Louis who she had been with for she had learned that beneath the suave exterior Louis possessed a wicked temper. The shared trips were her secret – hers and Grace's.

One weekend Louis had to go away on business leaving her alone. It happened occasionally and Debbie hated it, hated the feeling of being left behind which was somehow reminiscent of the times when her mother had left her, as a child, in the dark empty house in Plymouth. She met Grace for one of their shopping sprees on the Thursday afternoon before he was due to go, and when she told her about it Grace's black eyes lit up with a wicked sparkle.

'When the cat's away the mouse can play! Simon Chambers is having a party on Saturday night. Why don't we go to it?'

'Oh I don't know if I dare. Louis would be furious if he knew I'd snuck out — especially to Simon Chambers'.'

'What's wrong with Simon?'

Debbie laughed. 'Well he is a bit . . .'

'. . . more fun than most!' Grace finished for her. 'He's harmless, Debs. He's gay — didn't you know? And he really is very sweet. Oh come on! Don't be a dodo. Louis will never know.'

'Oh all right!' Debbie agreed, throwing caution to the winds. She was not looking forward to spending Saturday evening all alone and an outing with Grace promised to be nothing if not fun.

By the time Grace picked her up in her nippy little Sunbeam Alpine, however, Debbie's conscience was troubling her a little. She wished the Sunbeam was not so conspicuous, but at least

428

Louis was not on friendly terms with any of the neighbours — they were unlikely to tell him she had driven off in it! But every time they had to stop at traffic lights or for some kind of jam Debbie slid well down in her seat, convinced that someone who knew her and Louis would be in the car beside them.

'Relax, honey!' Grace laughed. 'Have a smoke — I'm going to.'

Debbie shook her head. She'd have a cigarette later — but she knew that Grace did not mean ordinary tobacco and sure enough when they had found a parking space outside Simon's impressive Mayfair home out came Grace's 'smokes' and the car was soon filled with the sweet smell of cannabis. Debbie waited uncomfortably while Grace smoked, hoping the smell was not impregnating her clothes. Louis had a sharp nose for such things.

When Grace was ready they climbed the flight of steps to the front door. The sounds of music and laughter came floating out and moments later the door was opened by Simon himself wearing nothing but a sheet draped around him and pinned on the shoulder with a brooch to make a Roman toga.

'Welcome! Two more beautiful ladies for the festivities!' he greeted them, kissing Grace warmly.

'Simon — I didn't know it was fancy dress . . .' Grace demurred.

'Fancy dress? What's fancy dress? At my parties you wear what you choose. And if you don't want to wear anything at all then you don't! Leave your dresses on the hat-stand, my darlings!'

'Thanks but I'll keep it on if it's all the same to you,' Grace laughed.

'Pity. Still it's probably just as well. That is a divine creation, my sweetheart, and Philip or Bruce would probably be quite unable to resist slipping into it! Now, come in and say hello to the gang.'

Debbie followed Grace into the elegant hallway, her feeling of discomfort growing and as she saw a naked couple chase one another up the stairs, shrieking with laughter, she began to wonder just what she had let herself in for. For 'party' read 'orgy' she thought, fascinated in spite of herself but quite determined that no one, but no one, was going to persuade her to take her clothes off!

The elegant drawing-room was full of people in various stages of undress cavorting on the sofas and dancing sensuously to the music of the Beach Boys and the Beatles. Debbie saw a man she recognised as a prominent member of parliament wearing nothing but a garland of laurel leaves lying back on a chaise, and being fed grapes by one near-naked young lady whilst another sat at his feet massaging them gently. What would his constituents think if they could see him now, she wondered, partly amused, partly repelled and partly embarrassed for both herself and the so-called respectable men who were making such a spectacle of themselves.

'Jimmy!' Grace shrieked, falling into the arms of an aristocratic man in a Tarzan-style loin cloth and Debbie picked her way between the gyrating bodies towards a tall parlour palm, intending to hide behind it.

'Would you like some champagne, my love?' Clearly she wasn't hiding herself very successfully, Debbie thought as a man's hand touched her arm. She swung round and almost laughed out loud when she saw that he was wearing nothing but a frilly white French maid's apron and a pair of sheer black hold-up stockings. Above the starched muslin his chest was pale and smooth, his balding head and gold rimmed spectacles completed the totally bizarre picture. Debbie took a glass from the silver tray, sipping gratefully, and the plump little man wiggled away on his high heels, buttocks wobbling.

Oh dear God I have to get out of here! Debbie thought. This is definitely not for me! She looked around for Grace, but her friend was otherwise engaged with the tall lean aristocrat she had called 'Jimmy'. Debbie drank her glass of champagne and edged back towards the door.

'Not going so soon are you, my angel?' Simon called, bearing down on her.

'I'm afraid so. I've got a terrible headache. Tell Grace, will you?'

She slipped past him and into the hall. The door was on the latch, Debbie escaped out into the cool evening air and took two or three deep breaths of it, overcome with a fierce longing for Louis. Why had he had to go away? Why couldn't he be there all the time?

A taxi turned into the street. Debbie ran down the steps and hailed it. At that moment she wanted nothing more in the world than to get home.

One morning when Debbie had been with Louis for six months she was awoken by the sound of the telephone shrilling. Beside her Louis was still dead to the world — he had, she thought, had rather more to drink last night than was good for him. She got up quickly, slipping on a silk wrap and hoping she could reach the telephone and answer it before it disturbed Louis; the rude awakening would probably give him a headache — if he didn't already have one. She thought the clock in the living-room said twenty past seven but she decided she must be mistaken. She always had trouble telling the time with that clock — it was nothing but two black hands on a lump of lead crystal and it was very easy to be an hour out or even muddle the minute and hour hands — and who in the world would telephone at twenty past seven in the morning? It would be hours yet before any of their friends or acquaintances surfaced. Debbie rubbed the sleep — and the stale mascara — out of her eyes and lifted the receiver.

'Hello?'

'Who the hell is that?' It was a man's voice, not one she knew.

'Debbie Swift. Who are you?'

'I'm trying to get hold of Louis Langlois. Do I have the right number?'

'Yes, you do, but he's asleep.'

'I'm afraid you'll have to wake him.'

Debbie began to feel alarmed. 'Who is this? What do you want him for?'

'I'm Robin Langlois, his brother. Would you get him to the phone, please? It's very urgent.'

She went back into the bedroom, pulled the sheet back and shook Louis by the shoulder. He stirred, mumbled and hunched the sheet over him again.

'Leave me alone.'

'Louis — please — you must wake up. Your brother is on the telephone. I think it's important. Louis, *please!*'

431

After a tug of war with the sheet and some more grumbles she thought she had won but a moment later she could see Louis was fast asleep again. In desperation she went back to the telephone.

'I'm sorry, I just can't seem to wake him. He's like a zombie. Can I give him a message or get him to ring you back or something?'

'He doesn't change, does he?' A loud sigh. Then: 'Perhaps he might just wake up if you tell him his father is dead. And will he please call me back without delay.'

'His father . . . ?' Debbie repeated, shaken, but the click at the other end told her the line had been disconnected.

She stood for a moment holding her wrapper tightly around her while her mind chased in panicky circles. She had never had to break bad news to anyone before; she didn't know how to go about it and the prospect was scaring her to death. It wasn't fair of his brother — Robin, did he say his name was? — to expect her to do it. She wasn't a policewoman. At least he could have told her to have another go at waking Louis and stayed on the line whilst she did. But it was too late now. The brother had gone and the ball was very firmly in her court.

Debbie went back to the bedroom. Louis was fast asleep again, blissfully unaware. She bent over the bed, shaking him.

'Louis, please! You must wake up!'

He stirred, reaching for her.

'What's wrong, Kitten? Come here and shut up.'

'No! Louis, there is something I have to tell you. Didn't you hear the phone?'

'No. Do you know you have the most beautiful tits . . .'

'Louis!' She dragged his hand out from inside her wrap. 'Will you please listen to me! It was your brother on the phone. Your father is dead!'

The minute she had said it she could have kicked herself. She hadn't meant to say it like that. His fingers froze half way back inside her wrap, his face seemed to have turned to stone.

'I'm sorry, Louis,' she half-sobbed. 'I didn't mean to tell you like that. But you wouldn't listen.'

For a moment he lay unmoving and she wanted to cry for him.

432

'I'm really sorry. Oh, Louis . . .'

He pushed the sheets aside. Her first thought was that he was going to get up and swing into action the way she imagined people did when told a close relative had died. He would have to phone his brother back, call the airport to check up on flights home to Jersey — there would be a million things to do. But Louis just lay there, lithe and unclothed, his body taking on a golden glow from the early sun that was streaming in through the enormous picture windows.

'It doesn't matter,' he said.

'What do you mean, it doesn't matter?'

'Would it matter to you if someone told you that your father was dead?'

'Louis, I never knew my father.'

'No,' he said, and there was a strange hard note in his voice, 'and I never knew mine. Now, are you coming back to bed or do I have to come up there and get you?'

If Louis's unconcerned reaction to the news of his father's death led Debbie to believe that it would make no difference to their lives she could hardly have been more wrong.

When he eventually stirred himself to get out of bed Louis booked himself on the earliest available flight to Jersey and he was gone for more than a week. Debbie paced the house, bored, lonely and unaccountably anxious and when Louis returned she was able to get very little out of him. His father had died of an embolism, he said, it had been very sudden and totally unexpected. His mother and brother, together with his Uncle Paul, were coping with things but the situation might mean he would have to spend more time in Jersey than he had done before.

At first Debbie was excited at the prospect of going with him — her world had been so narrow Jersey seemed to her like an island paradise — but Louis soon made it clear he had no intention of taking her along. Debbie was to stay in London. He didn't want her along on 'business trips' and anyway, didn't she have some modelling commitments?

Debbie did, and although they were far less important to her than being with Louis she knew all the same that she could not afford to show herself as unreliable. And so, whilst Louis made his frequent trips across the water, Debbie presented herself at photographic studios all over London to model lingerie for catalogues and make-up for the brochures of a well-known mass market cosmetics firm. She even did a TV commercial for a chocolate bar, shivering in a summer dress in a punt on a bright but freezingly cold winter day and trying to devour the chocolate bar with the kind of sensuousness to make viewers lick their lips with her.

Sometimes when Louis came home he spoiled her, as if to make up for his absence, bringing her luxurious presents and once taking her away for the weekend to a cottage on a grand country estate which he said he had access to. The weather had been crisp and cool and they had a real log fire in the grate and the guests at the big house, mostly titled, except for a film actor and his model wife, had called in for drinks at lunchtime and in the evening. Louis had taken her round the grounds and had almost made love to her in a deep drift of bone dry dead leaves — almost, but not quite, they had gone back to the cottage and done it on the rug in front of the roaring log fire instead. Louis had also shown her the swimming pool, empty now, with the covers on for winter, and told her about the pool parties that were held there in the summer. When he promised to borrow the cottage and bring her back again then Debbie had been delighted, thinking that it must mean that Louis still planned to be with her next summer.

At other times though he was curt and ill-tempered with her, refusing to explain what he did during those long weeks when he was absent.

'It's business,' he said shortly when she complained one day that after only a few days at home he was off again.

'But your business is here,' she protested.

'And in Jersey. Look, I can't stay talking now. I'll miss my plane. I'll see you when I get back.'

He kissed her and she clung to him, wanting to beg him not to go but knowing it would do no good. Louis liked her to be his little girl, his kitten, but he hated it when she became clinging or cramped his style. 'Just remember it's my business that keeps you in silk knickers,' he had said once, rather unpleasantly, and the words had wounded her and resurrected all her feelings of

434

insecurity. Debbie was still not quite seventeen and the scars of her mother's rejection had gone deep.

She loved Louis, she couldn't imagine life without him. He was her sun, her moon, her stars. Perhaps that was the reason she was so afraid, so chillingly shakingly terrified that he would leave her and she would be alone again with nothing but her memories.

Debbie thought that if that happened she might as well be dead.

One day when Louis was away and she could bear the emptiness of the London house no longer Debbie telephoned Grace.

She had seen less of her friend since that disastrous orgy/party as she was afraid that if Louis got to hear about it he would be very angry and his anger would spoil the precious little time they now had together. Now, however, Debbie was so lonely and bored that she decided to take the risk.

'It's me, Debbie,' she said when Grace answered her telephone. 'Are you doing anything?'

'Now?'

'Yes. I'm all alone and fed up with myself. Why don't you come over? Or we could go out — have tea at Harvey Nicholls like we used to and do a bit of shopping. All the summer things are coming in now.'

'All right. I'll meet you in the restaurant there. Half an hour?'

'Yes,' Debbie said, smiling. She knew it would take Grace at least an hour, she was a terrible time-keeper, but at least saying half an hour would give her something to aim at.

Whilst she waited for Grace, Debbie wandered round the lingerie department and bought a boned ivory basque and a dainty camisole in pale apricot silk. It was lovely to have money to spend on such luxuries — whatever else he might be, Louis was certainly not mean — and Debbie found herself remembering the days when she had been an underprivileged youngster in Plymouth, able to do no more than window shop and dream. She really should stop crying for the moon and be content with what she had, she told herself.

When Grace arrived the two girls greeted one another with an enthusiastic hug and went into the restaurant oblivious for once to the attention they were attracting — the one glossy black and beautiful in a glorious suit of hot pink, the other the perfect English rose in a simple shift dress of cornflower blue.

'So what have you been doing? I want to know all the gory details!' Debbie demanded, biting into a Danish pastry without the slightest thought for her figure.

'Well, I've got myself a new man. Handsome and titled, no less.'

'Titled!' Debbie thought of the aristocratic man in the Tarzan loin cloth and wondered if it might be him. 'Are you going to marry him? Grace — you could end up as Lady Something or other!'

Debbie smiled, her mobile cherry red mouth lifting engagingly.

'I suppose I could! What a thought! Still at least it makes a nice change to find someone single. Most of the bastards have a wife at home, don't they? They think they can have it all ways.' She sipped her lemon tea. 'How is Louis?'

'Fine, as far as I know. The trouble is he's away so much these days and it's driving me crazy.'

'Why? Freedom is not to be sneezed at, my dear. All this and freedom too . . .' She spread her hands with their white-pearl painted nails. 'But why is he away so much more than he used to be? Fill me in.'

'Didn't I tell you? His father died and left Louis a big chunk of shares in his Leisure Group — hotels and an entertainment agency of some sort I think. As the oldest son Louis seems to be taking on an awful lot of the responsibility. I suppose he's doing very well but I don't like it. He seems to be in Jersey more often than he's here these days.'

'Oh yes, I'd forgotten he's from Jersey. Why doesn't he take you with him?'

'I don't know. He likes me to be here, waiting for him.' Debbie did not add her private fear that Louis was ashamed of her.

'I know somebody from Jersey,' Grace said reflectively, getting out a packet of Marlboro and lighting one. 'Frank de Val. He's some sort of politician over there. Funny, they're often the worst, aren't they, politicians? They are so busy trying to pretend they're something they're not, I suppose. And mostly their wives are really boring, solid sensible middle-class types in twin set and pearls, ideal wife, mother and committee member. Or else they're earnest feminist left-wingers too busy trying to run round looking after everyone else to consider the needs of their own fella. Not a lot of fun either way really. No wonder the men go astray. I don't know what Mrs de Val is like, of course, I never met her. She's always left in Jersey — where no doubt Frank is respected as a sober senior political figure. Lord knows what the people who elected him would think if they knew what he gets up to when he's over here!'

'What does he get up to?'

'What doesn't he get up to would be more to the point! If ever there was a man with more fetishes than Frank I'd like to meet him! Black leather and bondage is one but he also likes to dress up . . . wait a minute, you've met him. He was at Simon Chambers' party. He was prancing about serving drinks wearing nothing but a little white pinny and long black stockings. Do you remember him?'

'How could I forget? That man looked absolutely ridiculous! And you say he's a Jersey politician?'

'Uh-huh.'

'I wonder if I dare tell Louis?' Debbie murmured reflectively, thinking what a marvellous imitation of the little fat man she could do to amuse Louis.

'Why not?' Grace asked.

'You know very well why not! Because he wouldn't approve at all of the company I keep!' Debbie teased and went back to the counter for another Danish pastry.

Chapter thirty-two

Debbie might never have told Louis about Frank de Val if one night she had not had a little too much to drink.

They had spent a quiet evening in with a Chinese take-away and a bottle of Chablis listening to Vivaldi. Louis was uncharacteristically quiet and Debbie, who had been getting steadily more and more tiddly, was wondering how to liven him up.

'What's wrong, darling?' she asked, sitting on his lap and winding her arms round his neck.

'Nothing. I'm just tired.'

'Oh, I see. It's the high life you're living in Jersey, I suppose.'

'You couldn't be more wrong about that,' Louis said. 'There isn't any high life in Jersey. It's too damned quiet and staid. All right if you happen to be a sea gull, I suppose, but otherwise deadly. They're just a lot of stuffed shirts.'

'Not all of them, surely.'

'All of them.'

Debbie giggled. 'I could tell you about one who isn't. I could tell you about one who is quite a lad when he gets away from the island.'

'Me?'

'No — well, yes, you too, I suppose. But you're quite tame compared to him.'

'Oh? Who is it then?'

'I'm not sure I should tell you,' Debbie said. 'If I told you you'd probably be very cross with me.'

'Why should I be cross?'

'Because . . .' Debbie hesitated, half afraid to go on. But having started she could hardly stop now — Louis would probably think she had something much worse to hide. Besides the temptation was almost irresistible and if Louis was cross — well, she knew how to get around him again. 'All right, I'll tell you,

438

just as long as you promise not to tell me off. Once, when you were away, I was really fed up with myself and I went to one of Simon Chambers' parties with Grace. I know you don't like me seeing her but I was very good, I promise. In fact the party was so wild I only stayed a little while and then I made my excuses and left, as the News of the World reporters used to say.'

'Kitten! You know what that girl is like . . .'

'Yes. I know. Hush, or I won't tell you. There was this man there, dressed up in a French maid's outfit — I mean *really* — a little white pinny and high heeled shoes, stockings and nothing else.' She giggled again. 'He looked ridiculous, Louis, and he wobbled when he walked — like this.' She jumped up off his lap and demonstrated.

Louis laughed. Debbie could be a born comedienne when she tried.

'Very amusing! Doesn't sound much like anyone from Jersey though. And now you know why I warned you off Grace. I hope you won't do anything so stupid again.'

'I won't. But he *was* from Jersey, Louis. Grace told me his name. She said he was a politician there — Frank de Val.'

Louis's eyes narrowed. For a moment Debbie thought he really was angry, then a slow smile curled his lip.

'Frank de Val, eh? Are you sure?'

'Quite sure. Do you know him?'

Louis did not answer that. 'Well, well, Frank de Val one of Simon Chambers' party boys! What a turn-up for the books! I'm only surprised I've never heard it before.'

'Why would you? They're a whole different set. I don't think Benny would even have them in his club.'

'No, they do keep themselves pretty much to themselves,' Louis agreed. 'Now I can see why. They're a load of perverts.' His tone was so scornful that Debbie was quite taken aback. She had never visualised Louis as a champion of moral standards though certainly for all his profligate ways there was nothing quirky about his sexual appetites.

'I don't think I could ever fancy you again if you dressed up in a French maid's outfit,' she said, nestling her head against his shoulder.

'I'm very glad to hear it,' Louis said, pulling her close.

439

But although he began making love to her his mind was already busy.

Since coming into his share of the Langlois empire Louis had had all kinds of ideas to extend the hotel chain. He was greedy for the rich pickings that were there for the taking from well-to-do locals and holidaymakers alike, and his ideas included the gaming clubs and casinos of which he himself was so fond. But his plans had come up against a seemingly unmovable stumbling block — the ancient and very strict laws forbidding such a development. Louis had begun to think, regretfully, that there was no way he could get around them. Now he turned over in his mind what Debbie had told him and thought that perhaps he had found a chink in the defences. Frank de Val was a senator. He was, perhaps, only one voice in the States — the island parliament — but he was much respected and well-liked. If anyone could talk his fellow senators around, it was Frank. And Debbie had presented Louis with a way of getting Frank on his side.

Louis kissed Debbie hard and long. Her lips were soft and sweet from the lip gel she had used this evening. But Louis tasted only the heady flavour of anticipated success.

Sometimes in the long and lonely days when he was away Debbie wondered if Louis was true to her. Somehow she could not imagine that he was. Louis was too physical a person to be satisfied with just one lover for very long, particularly when they were separated so much of the time. The very thought of Louis with someone else made Debbie feel physically sick, but when she could not put it out of her mind all together she tried to rationalise her suspicions.

At least she was the one steady relationship in his life. She was his kitten, installed in his London house. She was the one he came home to.

What Debbie had forgotten however was that whilst Louis had lived in London for the five years since he had crossed swords with his father, Jersey was also his home. His roots there went very deep — and so did his attachments. And one weekend, one of their lovely precious shared weekends, Debbie came very close to learning the truth about the way Louis spent his time when he was back in Jersey.

It was about noon on a Sunday. Louis had arrived home on the Friday evening complaining how hot London in June could be and how he would have liked to stay in Jersey. Debbie had said nothing — she was very afraid of rocking the boat — and after a pleasant evening at a riverside club his humour had improved. He had some business to attend to on the Saturday but to her delight he had taken her along, and in the evening he had managed to wangle an invitation to the country house estate cottage where he had taken her in the winter.

The covers were off the pool now and with the others in the party they had shared a barbecue and drinks at the poolside and swam until it became too cool to be pleasurable any more. Louis and Debbie had been invited to stay overnight but to Debbie's relief Louis had declined the offer. He had a business appointment arranged for the following morning, he explained, and Debbie was glad. Much as she was enjoying the company, now that she saw Louis so rarely she preferred to have him all to herself. They drove back to London, Debbie driving the white convertible Louis had bought her.

Next morning Louis had got up early and gone off for his business meeting leaving Debbie in bed. After a lovely lazy lie-in when she marvelled at how little sleep Louis could exist on she got up, took a leisurely bath and went through her beauty routine. They were going out for lunch and Louis had said he would be back in good time to pick Debbie up.

She was in the bedroom deciding which dress to wear when the telephone rang. She ran to the living room, wearing only her frilly lace body, to answer it.

'Hello.'

'Oh!' The voice at the other end was startled, little-girlish. 'I think I must have the wrong number.'

An intuitive prickle ran up Debbie's spine.

'Who did you want to speak to?'

'Louis Langlois. But . . .'

'This is Louis Langlois's home but he's not here at the moment.' Debbie's tone was icy. 'Can I tell him who called?'

'Yes.' Beneath the childish tone was something that might have been aggression. 'Please tell him it was Molly. He can call me back if he likes.'

'Will he know where to reach you?'

'Oh yes, he'll know.'

Debbie was seething as she put the phone down. The cheek of it! A woman — calling him here! To her knowledge it had never happened before, not since she had moved in certainly. She went back into the bedroom but she was completely unable to concentrate on deciding what to wear, pulling out dress after dress and discarding them on the bed. By the time Louis came home she was in a fine state and still wearing only her lacy body.

'Not ready then?' he said, coming into the room and eyeing her impatiently. 'I have a table booked for one o'clock — didn't I tell you?'

'Never mind lunch! I've had other things to think about.'

'Such as what?'

'A woman phoned for you. She wants you to ring her back.'

'A woman? Who?'

'She said her name was Molly and you'd know where to reach her.'

'Molly! What did she want?'

'How should I know? You'd better ring her back and find out.'

He laughed. 'Come here, Kitten. I love it when your claws are showing.'

'No. It's not funny, Louis. Who is she?'

He reached for her anyway. 'Molly is my sister-in-law. She is married to my brother Robin. So you see you don't have a thing to worry about.'

'Oh.' The relief was so great she wanted to cry; so great that it did not occur to her to wonder just why she knew so little about Louis's family.

Neither did she realise, as he kissed her and ran his hands over her body, displayed to its best advantage in the pretty ivory lace, that in telling her Molly was his sister-in-law he had only given her half a story.

*

442

For almost as long as she could remember Molly had been hopelessly in love with Louis.

She had begun life as Molly Feraud and she had grown up with the Langlois boys. It was Molly's mother, Susan, who had rescued Sophia on the beach the day that Robin was born and as a result the two women had become firm friends. They visited one another regularly, and took the children on joint outings, picnics, holidays, and Christmas trips to the theatre. Molly loved nothing better than tagging along behind the two boys on her plump little legs though they thought her a dreadful nuisance and escaped from her whenever they could, bringing down the wrath of Sophia on their heads when Molly, sobbing and red-faced with temper at being left behind, went running home to tell what had happened.

'How would you like to be left out?' Sophia would demand furiously.

'But she's a girl. She can't do anything. She's stupid.'

'She is not stupid. She's just smaller than you. And you were supposed to be looking after her.'

'But she gets in the way. If we climb trees she stands under-neath and cries. If we go on the rocks she slips down into the pools and gets her socks wet and then we get into trouble. It's not fair.'

'Fair or not you will include Molly in whatever you are doing.'

'Oh sucks!'

Both boys thought Molly a nuisance but it was Louis who suffered most. As the oldest he was expected to be responsible for her and to make things worse he was Molly's favourite. She hero-worshipped him, dogging his footsteps, holding on to his jersey and even, horror of horrors, trying to kiss him sometimes. Louis made a great play out of how much he hated being the object of Molly's affection but secretly he was flattered. When she put her chubby arms around him and planted her sticky lips on his cheek he wanted to be sick, but there was something rather pleasant about being put on a pedestal. Louis couldn't explain the way it made him feel, he was far too young to understand it himself — if he had been older he would have recognised the heady pleasure associated with power. Whatever Louis told Molly to do, she would do it, short of taking off all her clothes and rolling in a bed of stinging nettles, perhaps! Louis enjoyed the sensation of omnipotence it gave him — and he didn't even have to be nice to Molly to retain her slavish adoration. Once when she was annoying him he pushed her backwards into one of those very rock pools he had complained she was prone to falling into, laughing as she sat there crying, her dress and knickers soaked, legs flailing helplessly, elbows grazed. He had been quite prepared to tell Sophia and Susan it was an accident, that he had slipped himself trying to help Molly over the rocks, but there had been no need. Molly never told a soul about the quick shove in the chest and a day or so later she was as hunky-dory for Louis as ever.

As the three of them grew up Molly began to assert her femininity. She no longer tried to keep up with the boys but she was still around a good deal and she made it very clear where her affections lay. As her childish plumpness turned to a prettily rounded figure she took to wearing clothes that showed it to its best advantage whilst remaining almost little girly — pretty little figure-skimming shift dresses, denim jeans with cheesecloth blouses, hot pants and fringed Red-Indian look skirts. She had a flick-up hair-do that made her face look round and very pretty, she outlined her big eyes with kohl pencil and wore pearly pale lipstick and nail varnish. Anyone with half a brain could see it was all done for Louis's benefit but Louis ignored her just as he always had.

Until Robin began to take an interest.

From their very earliest childhood the rivalry between Louis and Robin had been intense and both the boys to a certain extent had a chip on his shoulder about the other.

Louis had always been the more outgoing of the two. He had charm, charisma, good looks, a quick lively intelligence and the sort of easy-going self-confidence that was a hard act to follow. He was very good at hiding the darker side of his nature, the vanity, the selfishness, the ruthless streak, the tendency to cruelty and the hedonism that would mar his golden image in later years. But however much others might be drawn to him Louis nursed a secret certainty that whatever he did he could never please his father. The inner certainty that he meant less to Bernard than Robin was a cancer eating away at his guts and in later years even when he was openly opposing his father and, to all intents and purposes, hating him with a fierce and fiery hatred, yet still there was a part of him that craved Bernard's approval and love.

Robin, on the other hand, never really appreciated the fact that he was Bernard's favourite. Always in Louis's shadow, he saw how Sophia favoured her elder son and did not have the insight to realise she was in fact compensating for Bernard's coolness towards him.

Sophia had always felt protective of Louis and, in a way, protective of Bernard. She was never able to forget Bernard's generosity in accepting Louis as his own and she was determined he should not have cause to regret it, whilst at the same time she was highly sensitive about Bernard's feelings towards the boy. She covered up Louis's naughtiness and hated it when Bernard chastised him, taking it almost as a personal rebuff to her. In her heart Sophia loved her children equally, but Robin never realised this. He saw the preferential treatment meted out to Louis and the natural mothering of David, so much younger as to always need to be treated a little differently, and saw himself as being, not unloved exactly, but certainly inferior in his mother's eyes. At the same time he took his father's attention so much for granted that it offered him no real compensation.

It was this sibling rivalry — and the secret desire of each of the boys to outdo the other — that made Molly the bone in the undignified tug-of-war which followed. Would Robin ever have found her quite so attractive if she had not been so obviously 'sweet on' Louis? She was pretty, yes, but no more so than many other girls he met — it was the fact that she was so attracted to Louis which gave her that added glamour in his eyes. And later when she despaired of ever getting so much as a second glance from Louis and turned her attention to Robin, Louis was unable to resist throwing her the few crumbs he thought would be sufficient to keep what was rightly his.

Sophia, when she realised what was going on, was horrified. She had seen the awful effects of a similar tug-of-war between her own brothers and she was terrified at the prospect of history repeating itself. All very well for Bernard to say comfortingly that they would work it out between themselves in the end —

Sophia could not help thinking that Paul and Nicky never had done. Nicky might have been alive today if Paul had not married Viv and she was sure the tragedy had marred their relationship and spoiled any chance of real happiness. She shuddered at the thought that something similar might happen to Louis and Robin. As their mother she wanted nothing more for them than that they should both be happy. Added to this, she felt a sense of responsibility towards Molly, whom she had watched grow up and of whom she was very fond. It wouldn't do her any good in the end, caught in the middle and bandied between the two boys like a trophy of war. But Sophia was loath to interfere for she knew instinctively that nothing she said would do any good as long as they were intent on swimming in this tight little circle chasing one another's tails. All she could hope for was that Bernard was right and they would sort themselves out in the end, preferably by meeting and falling in love, all of them, with someone quite different, and so putting an end to this relationship which somehow had the unhealthy tang of the incestuous about it.

Unfortunately for all of them, however, things had not worked out that way. The merry-go-round went on turning, Robin with eyes only for Molly, Molly with eyes only for Louis, Louis arrogantly doing exactly as he pleased with both of them, until the year when Louis was to be twenty-one. Then crisis point was reached, though oddly neither Robin nor Molly figured in the showdown. That was between Louis and Bernard.

It had been brewing for a long while, that showdown, ever since Louis had left school and gone straight into the company. Bernard would have liked him to go to college first but Louis, though he had a brilliant brain, was a lazy scholar. He had no intention of studying a day longer — he was impatient to get on with the serious business of life — making money.

When he saw that Louis's mind was made up Bernard took him into the company though he explained he would have to work his way up and learn as he went.

This did not altogether suit Louis, who had his own ideas as to the way both he and Langlois Business Enterprises should operate. The clashes began almost immediately, made worse by the fact that the following year Robin, who had not the slightest intention of being left behind, also refused to go to college and joined the company wet behind the ears. There was a difference, however. Where Louis wanted to march in and impose his ideas on an organisation that had been rolling along on oiled wheels for years, Robin was willing to learn. Bernard could not resist making comparisons and soon sparks were flying. In the year Louis was twenty-one matters came to a head. After one last flaming row Louis walked out of the company, convinced his father was favouring Robin yet again, and took off to build a new life for himself in England.

The moment Louis had gone Robin moved as far as Molly was concerned. He caught her hurt and vulnerable — and determined to show Louis she could live without him and be worth something in someone else's eyes, if not his. Their courtship was short — Louis had scarcely gone, it seemed, before Molly was wearing Robin's ring and the date was set for the wedding.

'Wait a little — you are both so young!' Sophia begged them, but they were in no mood to wait.

The wedding was the event of the decade — Molly wore a fashionable ballerina length gown, as did her bridesmaids, one in pink, one in blue and one in lemon yellow, and as they entered the church Sophia held her breath. Louis had come home for the wedding, though Robin had chosen David to be his best man, and Sophia found herself watching Molly for the look in Louis's direction that she dreaded, the look that would tell her that Molly's affections still lay with Louis.

To her relief, however, Molly glanced neither to left nor right, sweeping past Louis as if he were not there and as she stood beside Robin at the altar exchanging vows Sophia was aware of an overwhelming wave of relief. Perhaps after all it was going to be all right. They looked so good together, as if it had always been meant to be.

At first it seemed she was right. Louis returned to his life in London, making money and plenty of it, in his own inimitable style, and Robin and Molly settled down to married life. Ten months after the wedding little Juliet was born.

'It's too soon,' Sophia had said again when they told her Molly was pregnant, but the moment she saw the baby she changed her mind. Juliet was beautiful, the most perfect grandchild she could have wished for and Sophia hoped she would cement her parents' marriage. Molly seemed blissfully happy though in many ways she was little more than a child herself and Sophia thought that at last she had put her yearning for Louis behind her.

She was wrong. For when Bernard died so suddenly and tragically leaving his shares in the company equally divided between the three boys and Louis came back to assert his influence it had all begun again.

Louis regarded the fact that Molly was now his brother's wife as a challenge and Molly, as hopelessly attracted to him as she had ever been, was powerless to resist his advances.

Why was it, she sometimes wondered? What was it about Louis that made him so devastatingly attractive? She did not want to be unfaithful to Robin, she did not want to betray her child. Yet Louis undermined her resolve just as he had always done. One glance from his cool blue eyes and her knees turned to jelly, one touch and she was on fire with longing. She met him secretly and the danger added zest to their lovemaking, though when they were apart she wanted to weep with shame. She knew he was playing with her but it made no difference. He was like a powerful drug and she was addicted. Hating herself for her weakness was no remedy, fear of bringing everything she cared for tumbling about her ears, real though it was, could not stop her.

And Louis, with a foot in both worlds, revelled in the sense of power, recognising it now for what it was and not caring. He did not need Molly any more than he needed Debbie, except to feed his physical hunger and satisfy his huge ego. The difference between the two women was that whilst Molly knew the truth, Debbie most certainly did not.

Chapter thirty-three

'I want you to come to Jersey with me, Kitten,' Louis said.

Debbie experienced a great leap of joy.

It was autumn now — winter really, except that the mild weather had meant the leaves had remained on the trees in a blaze of red and gold much longer than usual — and the shortening days had intensified Debbie's sense of having been abandoned.

Last winter, she remembered, Louis had been there almost all the time and she had felt wrapped around by love, happy with the present, daring to become confident about the future. It had been the first time in her life she could ever remember having felt like that and it had been wonderful. Now she was back to uncertainty and longing, waiting alone for the person she loved to come home. Even the modelling jobs seemed to be fewer — 'the image' was changing, she was told; it frequently did — a new sharper look was the 'in' thing. Debbie did not mind about the modelling too much. The only thing that really mattered to her was being with Louis. But he seemed to be away more than ever and Debbie had grown more and more wretched.

If he loved her why did he leave her in London? Why didn't he take her with him? But when she asked him this he always had a plausible excuse or, failing that, he would simply say he liked having her here to come home to. Business and pleasure didn't mix, and when the business was done he liked to be able to relax and forget it, close the door and leave the world outside.

It sounded quite reasonable when he said it; Louis could make anything sound the way he wanted it to. But when she was alone Debbie was haunted by doubt.

Her friends were no help either. Grace, although great fun, could be very self-centred and she hated talking about anything that did not directly concern her and was likely to murmur

449

comfortingly that she was quite sure Debbie was worrying unnecessarily and change the subject. So Debbie stumbled on, clinging to the hope that next time he came home things would be different, next time he would convince her he really did love her. And when he told her he wanted her to go to Jersey with him Debbie thought that at last her prayers had been answered.

'When?' she asked eagerly.

'I'm not sure at the moment. I'll let you know.'

'Oh, right.' Debbie was puzzled but she did not ask any questions. Louis could be very impatient about that sort of thing.

She contented herself with the lovely thought that if he was taking her to Jersey, it must mean that at last she had been granted entry to that other part of his life. In Jersey he was bound to introduce her to his family. Perhaps he would even ask her to marry him. Whatever, she thought, it must mean that their relationship was entering a new and more satisfactory phase.

She could scarcely have been more wrong.

A few days later something rather horrible happened. Debbie answered the door to find a strange man standing on the step — a big, balding man with a face that looked as though it had been in more than one fight. Although he was wearing an expensive-looking leather jacket he reminded Debbie of a bouncer from one of the less salubrious clubs and instinctively she recoiled a little.

'I'm looking for Louis Langlois,' he said. His voice was rough East End.

'He's not here. He's in Jersey.'

'Are you sure?' The man seemed on the point of forcing his way into the flat. Debbie stood her ground.

'Of course I'm sure.'

'Hmm.' The man considered. 'When are you expecting him back?'

'I don't know.' The man looked disbelieving. 'I don't!' she reiterated.

'You'd better give him a message then hadn't you? Tell him George wants his money. And if he doesn't get it there's going to be trouble.'

450

'Who's George? What money?'

'He knows. If he doesn't pay up soon I'll be back. And next time I shall have company. Just tell him — right?'

He ran a swarthy hand across his chin, blue-shadowed from a growth of beard that needed twice-daily shaving. Debbie was not sure if it was rings she saw glinting on his fingers or a knuckleduster.

'I'll tell him,' she said, slamming the door and leaning hard against it. She was very frightened indeed.

It was almost a week before Louis telephoned; Debbie stayed inside the house with the safety chain on the door. She trembled every time she saw a car pull up in the street outside and hid behind the curtains pretending to be out on the couple of occasions the bell rang. Where was Louis? Why didn't he call her? She wondered if she dared to try to get in touch with him but he had forbidden her to do that so she waited, scared out of her wits until the day when — oh bliss! — it was him.

'Louis, I'm so glad to hear from you!' she almost sobbed when she heard his voice, languid as ever, on the line. 'I've been so worried!'

'Why? What's wrong, Kitten?'

'There was a man here — a really horrible man. He said he had come from someone called George and you owed him money. He said if he didn't soon get it he would be back. I think he was threatening me, Louis. He really frightened me!'

'Kitten — calm down!'

'But Louis . . .'

'Stop worrying about it. Leave it to me. I'll sort it out. Just don't answer the door, all right?'

'I don't intend to, I promise you! But what did he mean? What money do you owe him?'

'It's business, Kitten. George and I did some business together and he's an impatient sod. Now listen, do you remember I said I wanted you to come to Jersey?'

'Oh yes.'

'Well, can you get on a plane tomorrow?'

Her heart leaped. 'Of course. What time?'

'You'll have to check that out for yourself. Use my usual

travel agency — the number is in the jotter on my desk. When you arrive in Jersey take a taxi to the Pomme d'Or Hotel in St Helier. I'll get in touch with you there.'

'Louis . . .'

'I can't stop, Kitten. I'll see you tomorrow.'

There was a click at the other end of the line and he was gone. Debbie stood holding the receiver, a puzzled look in her clear turquoise eyes.

She hadn't heard Louis mention the Pomme d'Or before and she'd thought she knew the names of all the Langlois hotels — when Louis had first gone back to Jersey she had recited them like a litany — the Belville, The Westerley, La Maison Blanche and Les Belles Fleures. But not the Pomme d'Or. No definitely not the Pomme d'Or. Very odd. But tomorrow she would be with Louis again. He would explain everything. Debbie was smiling with relief as she replaced the receiver.

'I'm really glad for you, Debbie,' Grace said. 'Louis has been treating you very badly indeed.'

The two girls were sharing a bottle of champagne, curled up in the deep leather chairs that were the only concession to real comfort in the London house. Since speaking to Louis and book-ing her flight to Jersey Debbie had telephoned Grace, telling her she might be away for quite some time, and now they were spending a quiet evening together.

'He doesn't really treat me badly,' Debbie protested — how-ever worried or upset she was she always stood up for Louis if someone else criticised him.

'He does too! I wouldn't stand for it! I was beginning to think something very odd was going on, especially when that heavy came round threatening you. To be honest it wouldn't have surprised me to hear he'd just cleared off and left you.'

'Oh Grace it's nothing like that! It's just that Louis is so busy and he doesn't think . . .'

'I'd make sure he *did* think!' Grace said darkly. 'Now if Valen-tine treated *me* like that . . .'

Valentine, the titled gentleman, was still the love of Grace's life. Her short concentration period on a subject that did not

452

directly concern her exhausted, Grace returned to a discussion about her own torrid lifestyle.

Debbie walked around her room at the Pomme d'Or, lifted the net curtain that covered the window and peered out at the street below.

She was beginning to be very anxious. She had been here for four hours now and not heard a word from Louis. She was hungry and longing for a drink — the alcoholic sort — but she was afraid to leave the room in case he telephoned while she was gone. Now, more than ever, she was longing for the sound of his voice to dispel the sense of puzzled apprehension that was making her more uneasy with every minute that ticked away.

Where the hell was he? Why hadn't he been in touch? And why was she here at the Pomme d'Or? The literature on the dressing table had confirmed what Debbie had already suspected; it was certainly not a Langlois Hotel — it belonged to another group entirely. So why had he told her to book in here? Surely it would have made more sense to use one of his own hotels, even if he hadn't felt able to invite her to his home? The sick feeling gnawing at Debbie's stomach told her all too clearly that it did not bode well. If Louis had intended to introduce her to his family and bring her to Jersey permanently then he was going about it in a pretty peculiar way. It was almost as if he had shoved her out of sight so that none of them should know she was here at all.

So why had he asked her to come over? Since he had first mentioned the visit over a week ago, it wasn't that he had been overtaken by a sudden irresistible longing to see her and anyway, if that was the case, why wasn't he here with her now? Where the hell *was* he?

Debbie boiled the kettle on the courtesy tray to make herself another cup of coffee. Damn — she'd used the last of the little sachets, either she would have to ask for some more or settle for tea — not her favourite drink. Debbie glanced at her watch, wondering if the bar was open yet and if it was if they would send her up a gin and tonic via room service. She picked up the telephone to enquire and almost jumped as it seemed to be answered by a knock on the door. She dumped the receiver and ran across the room, fumbling with the catch and opening the door.

'Louis!'

She had known intuitively it was him the minute he knocked, as if he had somehow been clearly visible through the solid wood. He was wearing dark slacks and a leather bomber jacket over a striped shirt, casually open at the neck and her heart lurched as it always did when she saw him after a separation. She threw herself at him. Even in her stockinged feet (she had kicked off her high-heeled shoes) she was almost as tall as him yet because she was so slender she still managed to appear almost waif-like against his sturdy bulk.

'Let me come in then!' There was a hint of impatience in his tone.

'Oh Louis, I thought you were never coming! I was getting really worried.'

'Why would I not come?'

'I don't know.' Suddenly all her fears seemed too foolish to mention. 'I've missed you so much . . . I was just longing to see you, I suppose.'

Her hand was in his, she was leading him, without even thinking about it, towards the bed, but there was no eagerness in Louis. He seemed almost preoccupied and Debbie sensed it suddenly.

'What's wrong, Louis?'

'What do you mean, Kitten?'

'I don't know. You seem . . .' She broke off as he pulled her abruptly into his arms, kissing her, unbuttoning her shirt and sliding down the zip on her denim jeans. His hand moved over her breasts, behind and flat stomach, coming to rest in the soft tuft of hair between her legs and she began to forget her misgivings. It wasn't possible to think of anything else when Louis was loving her; he was so expert that he was able to bring her to peak after peak of delight, until she wanted him so much she was at screaming point. Then and only then did he undress himself, discarding his clothes in an untidy pile on the floor and making love to her so hard that the screams did come, and he stifled them with his hand pressed over her mouth while his body ground into hers. Afterwards he made love to her again, more

454

slowly and sensuously, standing in the shower cabinet with the warm water cascading over them, their bodies slippery with shower gel. But when it was over he moved away from her in an almost businesslike manner and she realised her misgivings had not gone away, only lain dormant whilst her senses had taken over.

'That was good, wasn't it?' she said, following him back into the bedroom and trying to recapture the mood of a few moments ago.

'Yes.' But his back was towards her as he towelled himself dry and he picked up his slacks and pulled them on without so much as a glance in her direction. 'Why don't you put some clothes on, Kitten?'

Still totally nude she ran to him, throwing her arms around him. Her hair dripped a wet patch on to his shirt.

'For goodness' sake, Kitten, you're insatiable! Give a man a chance! You've had it twice — what more do you want?'

I want you to act as if you love me, she wanted to say, but she knew she could not.

'Besides, you're making my shirt wet.' He put her away from him with a firmness that was cold and oddly disconcerting. 'Look, Kitten, I want to talk to you. There's something I want you to do for me.'

That was more like it. Anything . . . anything . . .

'What?'

'Do you remember telling me a story about Frank de Val?'

Debbie frowned. 'Frank de Val?'

'Come on, you must remember. He's a senator in the States, the island parliament. You were telling me about his perversions and how you'd met him at one of Simon Chambers' orgies.'

'Oh him. Well I never met him exactly.'

'But you did see him there?'

'Well yes, but don't say "One of Simon Chambers' orgies" like that. It makes me sound a real little raver. I only ever went to one and that was by mistake. I got out as soon as I could without making an exhibition of myself — I told you that.'

'But not before you'd seen Frank de Val.'

'I suppose not. But why are we talking about him?'

455

'I think that orgy could turn out to be the most profitable party you ever went to.'

'What are you talking about?'

'Look.' Louis towelled his hair dry and ran a comb through it. 'I have plans for expanding the company to give Jersey a bit of real night life. The trouble is the laws are archaic — strictly for the birds. Imagine not allowing legalised gambling in an island awash with money! But they don't. And getting the law changed is an uphill struggle. To do it I need a friend inside the enemy camp. I didn't have one. But now I think I have. Frank de Val.'

'I'm sorry, I still don't understand.'

'Come on, Debbie, use your brains! I'm quite sure now I can talk Frank de Val into coming down on my side and using his powers of persuasion on his friends in the States.'

'How?'

'Frank is a highly respected man. He has a reputation to protect. I don't suppose he'd like it to get out that he spends his free time cavorting about stark naked except for — what was it? — a frilly white apron and black stockings? It really wouldn't do much for his image, would it?'

'You mean . . . blackmail?' Debbie was shocked.

'Not a very nice word, that. But I suppose there's no point dressing it up in euphemisms, not just between ourselves. Black-mail — persuasion — whatever you call it, it comes to the same in the end. I get some help getting the law changed and Frank gets to keep his image as a fine upstanding senator.'

While he was talking Debbie had wrapped herself in a towel, sarong style. She stood holding it around her, hair dripping in wet stringy strands down her back, a shocked expression on her face. Her own life might not have been exemplary but Debbie had very definite ideas of what was right and wrong, and this was most certainly wrong. She didn't know Frank de Val as a person, and owed him no allegiance, but the thought of Louis using what she had told him to try to get his own way in direct opposition to the due processes of democracy struck her as being not only immoral but also repellent.

'I think that is the most disgusting suggestion I ever heard in my life!' she said.

456

'Really?' Louis's eyes were chips of blue ice, cold and hard. 'And you don't think it's disgusting that a man entrusted with the duties of a senator should be behaving the way he does?'

'Not really, no. I've seen people behave a good deal worse. It's not my scene but he wasn't doing anyone any harm and if it makes him happy . . . what's wrong with that.'

'I wonder if the electorate of Jersey would see it like that. I'll bet they wouldn't! What electorate would? And they are the biggest load of hypocrites going over here.' He laughed suddenly. 'I wonder what they would say, for instance, if they knew that I had a German father? They hate the Germans, you know, because of the occupation during the war.'

Debbie blinked. 'Your father? But your father was Bernard Langlois!'

'No, he wasn't. My father was a German, one of the occupying forces. My mother doesn't even know which one. She admitted as much to me. Rich, isn't it? That would be a wonderful scandal if it ever broke. But frankly it doesn't bother me too much. I'm not liked here anyway. I'm far too radical. So I have nothing to lose. Unlike some . . .'

'Louis.'

He stood up, gripping her by the arms. 'Look here, Kitten, I need Frank de Val's help and by God I mean to get it. I could have told him myself what I knew — the very fact I could describe his antics in such detail might have been enough. But then again it might not. I want impact. And you are going to give it to me. I'm going home to change now and then I want you to come with me to see him.'

'Oh Louis, he wouldn't remember me! I was only there for a few minutes.'

'It doesn't matter whether he remembers you or not,' Louis said. 'He'll see a girl who looks just the type to have been there.'

'What do you mean "just the type"?' Debbie demanded angrily.

'Obviously a showgirl.'

'I am not a showgirl!'

'Model, then. I'm not going to split hairs. He'll see you and he'll know I'm not bluffing. I think we'll find Mr Frank de Val will co-operate.'

457

'Louis, I don't know that I am going to do this!' Debbie said. 'I don't like it one little bit.'

'You mean you don't want to help me?'

'It's not that. But it's . . .' She stopped, searching in vain for the word to describe the degradation she felt with Louis even suggesting she should behave in this fashion. 'It's not a very nice thing to do,' she said lamely.

'Business isn't always very nice.' His tone changed to one of cajoling. 'You don't have to actually do anything. Just be there. I'll do all the talking. Now listen . . .'

'No, Louis, I can't. I don't like it.'

His eyes blazed cold blue fire. For a moment she thought he was going to hit her. Then he turned away.

'Well, if you won't you won't. I thought you, at least, would want to help me. After all, it's to your advantage too.'

'I couldn't!'

'I thought you liked the London house. I thought you would want to continue living there.'

She froze. What was he saying? He walked to the window, leaning on the sill, shoulders hunched. He looked oddly vulnerable suddenly.

'I thought you might have realised, Kitten, that I have financial problems. I am owed quite a lot of money which I am not likely to get in a hurry and in turn I have considerable debts of my own. The man I owe it to is getting restless — and he is not a nice person to tangle with. I'd have thought you would have realised that.'

Debbie shivered. 'The man who came to the house . . . was he . . . ?'

'One of his henchmen, yes. Quite honestly you are not safe there if George sends in the heavies. They are not fussy who they hurt. But in any case unless I can get things moving over here and make some money fast the London house is going to have to go. I can't afford to keep it on. So really, Kitten, the ball is in your court.'

Debbie swallowed. 'Why not sell the house, Louis? You're hardly ever there any more. And I could move over here with you.'

'No. I don't want that at the moment.' He saw the hurt look

458

in her eyes and went quickly: 'I'm living with my mother at La Grange. You wouldn't like it there at all. She can be a tartar. It's not what I want for my kitten. Now when I have some money it will be a different matter. I'll be able to buy a place of my own, move you over here, perhaps get married even. If I could make the hotels a viable proposition . . .'

But Debbie was no longer listening. In her excitement she did not stop to query the financial status of Langlois Leisure, or how Louis expected to benefit from changed legislation (even if his plan worked) in time to avert some imminent crisis. Least of all did she query Louis's sincerity. The magic words had been spoken — nothing else mattered.

In that moment Debbie would have gone to the ends of the earth for Louis — and he knew it.

Chapter thirty-four

Compared with Benny's the Jersey Lily Nightclub was a staid sort of place, ever-so-slightly faded and lacking in entertainment now the summer was over and the holidaymakers gone. At the height of the season the tables were much in demand at least until the cabaret was over and there were always some who would stay drinking as long as Jersey law allowed, but tonight, with a keen November wind buffeting the flags and the string of fairy lights along the front of the building, the place was almost empty.

It was not only the weather keeping them away, Louis explained to Debbie, there was an important gala going on in St Helier and many prominent islanders who might otherwise be spending the evening here at the Jersey Lily would in all probability be there instead. What Louis did not add was that his own mother was at the gala. The less said about his family the better.

Louis steered Debbie towards the bar. A dark swarthy man in black tie and dinner jacket was sitting on one of the stools smoking a cigar.

'Evening, Raife,' Louis said. 'I've brought someone to meet you. The young lady I told you about.'

The man swung round, hooded eyes narrowed behind the screen of smoke. Debbie was disconcerted by the intensity of his gaze but brazened it out. She was used to men looking at her. She lifted her chin and smiled at him.

Raife ignored her. 'Is this who I think it is?' he asked Louis shortly.

'It is. This is Debbie, a friend of mine from London.'

In spite of herself Debbie was unable to avoid feeling a little slighted at the wording of the introduction. Surely Louis could have said something a little more personal.

The hooded eyes swept over her again, taking in her hair, restored to some semblance of style by her Carmen rollers, smooth shoulders above the virginal white lace cocktail dress, shapely figure, endless legs. As his eyes lingered on her Debbie found herself hoping her stomach wasn't looking fat — slender as she was it had a tendency to bloat after a meal. When she had worked at Benny's she had never dared eat until it was almost time to go home but tonight she had been too hungry to care. When Louis had left her to go home and change, she had had two rounds of prawn sandwich sent up via room service, and then Louis had bought her steak, mushrooms, salad and French fries before bringing her here.

The inspection over Raife turned to stub out his cigar and reach for his drink. 'Well, I never thought you'd go this far, Louis.'

His tone was cool but Louis merely smiled. If Debbie had not been in love with him she might have described it as a sneer.

'You know how I feel about our project. And I'm prepared to do whatever is necessary to see it works out.'

'Hmm.' There was a distinct lack of enthusiasm in the other's non-committal response. 'We'd better talk about this in my office, I think. Shall we get some drinks in first? What are you having?'

'Debbie drinks g and t. I'll have the usual.'

'Two double whiskies and a g and t,' Raife said to the bartender. 'Don't ring them in. I'll settle the bill later.'

With a drink in her hand Debbie felt a little more confident. She followed the men along a narrow corridor to what was obviously Raife's office. Raife closed the door, went around to sit in his big leather swivel chair, offered Louis a cigar and lit another for himself. Louis perched on the edge of the desk, Debbie crossed to look at the bank of photographs on one wall, teetering on her high heels. The photographs were mostly publicity portraits of the various acts that played the Jersey Lily; some showed Raife with what must obviously be guests at the club. Debbie did not recognise any of them but studying them was preferable to listening to the conversation Louis was having with Raife. Debbie was still not happy about Louis's plan —

and from the tone of his voice it did not sound as if Raife was too enamoured of it either.

'Why have we got to bring someone else into it?' Debbie had asked Louis when he told her he was taking her to the Jersey Lily to meet Raife, and Louis had explained that Raife was his partner and friend. Well, it didn't sound as if they were going to be partners or friends much longer, judging by the way voices were beginning to be raised.

Debbie winced, sipped her g and t and concentrated even harder on the photographs, but she could hardly avoid hearing the angry exchanges.

'How the hell do you expect to ever make a success of anything if you're not prepared to give it your best shot?' Louis was demanding.

'This is a small island, pal. You want to play with fire. If something goes wrong . . .'

'What is going to go wrong?'

'Anything could. De Val could decide to come clean rather than be blackmailed.'

'Not he. He's got too much to lose.'

'And so have I. If he did shop you, or even talk to his friends about what you intend to do, you'd be finished in Jersey and so would I. What you do, Louis, is up to you. But leave me out of it. I've got a good club here.'

'You call this a good club? You've hardly got half a dozen customers in the whole damned place!'

'I make a living. In the season . . .'

'Not what I call a living!'

'You've got big ideas, Louis. You always have had. For God's sake, man, forget this one before it ruins us both.'

'Raife — I've got a keg of gunpowder I can stick under de Val.'

'And blow us up with it, maybe. Haven't you got enough stinking mess-ups in your life already without adding this one?'

'What the hell do you mean by that?'

'Shagging your sister-in-law for a start. One of these days your brother is going to find out what you're up to — if he doesn't know already.'

There was a short loaded pause. Debbie had begun to shake,

the gin suddenly making her want to be sick. She hadn't heard right. She couldn't have heard right! But in those few moments she was remembering, all at once, the phone call and that woman's voice, childlike, sweet, asking for Louis. 'Who can I tell him called?' 'Say it's Molly.' 'Who is Molly, Louis?' 'Molly — oh, she's just my sister-in-law.'

And now this man, this Raife, was accusing Louis of 'shagging his sister-in-law'.

Oh God, Debbie thought, that's why he doesn't come home to London very often any more. That's why he doesn't want me over here. He is having an affair with his sister-in-law. Molly. Whoever she is.

Over the ringing in her ears she heard Louis's voice, low and dangerous.

'Is that some sort of threat, Raife?'

'It might be — yes.'

'You bastard.'

'Fair's fair. You resort to blackmail against my wishes, so will I. I don't want to be dragged into this, Louis, and by implication I will be. I value my business if you don't. I've worked damned hard to build it up. I don't want to come unstuck because you've got greedy. I won't let you do it.'

Louis laughed. It was the most chilling sound Debbie had ever heard.

'And how are you going to stop me? You think I'd fall for that one? If you think you can threaten me, Raife, you've got the wrong man. I don't give a monkey's cuss who knows about me and Molly. She might care. Robin might care. But I sure as hell don't. And if you don't want to be in on the biggest thing that's ever going to hit Jersey that's your loss. But I assure you — I intend going ahead. And you, pal, can go to hell!'

He slammed his glass down on the desk and grabbed Debbie's wrist, jerking her across the room, out of the door and into the dark corridor. Shocked and shaking she could do nothing but go with him, past a couple of staff who had overheard the raised voices and come to see what was going on, and out into the night. The wind had really got up now, it whipped at Debbie's stole, and dragged along in the darkness, her eyes not yet accustomed to the change, she stumbled.

463

'Louis! For God's sake!' she sobbed.

He stopped, waiting for her to wrench her stiletto heel out of the crack that had trapped it, but she could feel his fury still running down his arm and coming out of the tips of his fingers like electric current.

'What the hell is the matter with you?' he barked.

She couldn't answer, couldn't ask him if it was true that he was having an affair with the unknown Molly. In truth she did not need to. She already knew the answer. It was tearing her apart, a pain so bad she wanted to die. She couldn't confront him with it. She couldn't even cry yet.

'Come on, you silly bitch, get in the car!' he snarled.

Debbie could do nothing but obey.

Wherever he took her it was only a short journey. She sat in the front seat hugging herself with her arms, still too stunned to really take in what had happened.

'Come on — get out!' he snapped at her.

'Why? Where are we going?'

'To see Frank de Val. Isn't that why you're here?'

Tears were pricking her eyes, burning in her throat. She couldn't believe he was talking to her like this. In all the time they had been together she had never seen this side of him before.

'You might think that's why I'm here,' she returned sharply. 'It isn't my reason. I came to please you, to be with you. I won't be threatened like this, Louis.'

For a moment she thought he was going to strike her. A pulse throbbed in his temple, his lips curled into a snarl and she shrank back in her seat, closing her eyes and covering her face with her hands.

'Kitten!' She opened her eyes again, peeping between her fingers. He was running his fingers through his hair, looking more perplexed than angry now. 'Kitten, I'm sorry. I didn't mean to upset you. The truth is I'm worried — very worried. I need money urgently and I don't know how to get it. But I shouldn't take it out on you.'

'No, you shouldn't!'

'I said I'm sorry. Am I forgiven?' He reached for her. For a moment she resisted but she could feel herself weakening.

'I — I don't know.'

'I don't deserve to be, I know, but I'll make it up to you, I promise. Just do this for me.'

'Louis . . .'

'I need the money, Kitten. *We* need the money. Come on now, I've always been good to you, haven't I?'

'Yes.'

'And this is your chance to do something for me. Come on, sweetheart, you don't have to say a word, just let me do the talking.'

'Oh Louis!' One part of her knew she was being played for a sucker. One part of her knew but somehow could not care. She loved him too much; she had to believe there was at least hope for them or she simply could not bear it. He kissed her, leaned over and opened the door for her.

'It won't take long. And it won't be half as bad as you think.'

But it was as bad — worse. Standing beside Louis, listening to him put his propositions to the senator, and back them up with threats of exposure of his private life Debbie cringed inwardly, wishing she could be anywhere but here on the front porch of what she might have described as a 'stately cottage' if she had been in the mood for quips.

The senator was smaller than she had remembered him; dressed now in jacket and cords it was difficult to imagine this was the same man she had last seen wearing nothing but a frilly apron. There was something familiar about his face but she could not have put it more strongly than that. But Louis had told her there was no need for her to speak and it seemed he was right. The senator was obviously so shocked to be confronted by Louis and Debbie on his own doorstep that he did not query for one moment Louis's assertion that Debbie could — and would — identify him to the world if he did not go along with the suggestions Louis had made.

'All right . . . all right! I'll do what I can. I can't promise anything — you know that. I'm only one among many.' The voice that could fill the States was low and trembling and de Val kept glancing nervously over his shoulder.

'Ah but we both know how persuasive you can be. You'd better be persuasive, Frank, if you value your reputation. I hope I'll soon hear there is to be a debate on changing the law, otherwise Debbie might have to go to the newspapers.'

'I told you . . . I'll do what I can. Now for God's sake go, before my wife comes to see why I've been so long at the door!'

'Tell her it was one of the people you represent, with a problem, Frankie. That's no more than the truth.'

'All right. But go, go!'

By the light of the porch Debbie could see the sweat glistening on his scalp where his hair had receded and she felt a qualm of pity for him. Men like de Val weren't wicked or even bad, just rather pathetic. They couldn't help being what they were, but that didn't mean they were proud of it. Who knew the depths of shame and self-loathing someone like Frank experienced when he came down from the high of indulging his fantasies? Bad enough to have to live with the knowledge of an inconquerable — and very undignified — vice, how much worse to be threatened with exposure! Debbie began to feel sick again and it was as if de Val's humiliation was also somehow her own. What was more it was somehow inextricably bound up with the way she had felt in Raife Pearson's office. She couldn't forget the things Louis had said, especially about Molly. Even though she was not consciously thinking about them now yet the shadow remained, dull and heavy, adding to the terrible sense of degradation.

This whole trip, for which she had had such high hopes, had turned into a horrible sick nightmare. Nothing had turned out as she had expected or hoped, nothing at all. Even Louis's promises now held a hollow ring.

Debbie felt suddenly as if she might be going to faint. There was a ringing in her ears and her vision blurred. It was awful — awful. Just as she thought her legs would collapse beneath her if she had to stand there a moment longer looking at that pathetic sweating little man, she felt Louis's hand beneath her elbow.

'Come on, Debs. We'll leave Mr de Val to think about what we've said.'

'Why did we have to go to his house?' she asked when they were in the car again. 'Why couldn't you have written to him or talked to him somewhere else?'

'In the States building, you mean?' Louis slammed the car into reverse, turned in de Val's drive and shot off along the lane. 'He'd have been delighted to have been confronted with the evidence of his carryings-on there, I'm sure.'

'But surely there was no need for me to be there at all. It made such a business of it.'

'Frank wouldn't have believed I had a scrap of evidence unless I produced you. That's why it was so necessary for you to come over.'

A nerve jumped in her throat and the nausea worsened.

'We wouldn't really go to the papers would we? You wouldn't expect me to . . . ?'

'Well of course,' Louis said smoothly. 'If he won't play ball I shall have to make my money by some other means. I shall sell the story to the highest bidder.'

'*My* story!'

He ignored her, laughing as he swung the Porsche at high speed round the winding country lanes.

'It might almost be better! Perhaps the gambling laws wouldn't be changed and the clubs and hotels would have to stay staid but we'd be assured of money on the nail. What could I screw them for, I wonder? Thirty thousand? I should think so. And would I enjoy it! Seeing some of those stuffed shirts turn the colour of ripe aubergines over the story you could tell would be a prize in itself! I can see the headlines now — 'SEXY POLITICIAN IN ORGY SCANDAL' or 'FRANK AS FRANK!'

'What about me?' Debbie demanded. She was close to tears. 'I'd be telling the world I was at that orgy too!'

'That doesn't matter does it?'

'What do you mean — it doesn't matter? It matters to me! I didn't want to be there — it was horrible — embarrassing. Surely you wouldn't want to put me through that? Surely . . .'

She broke off as the truth hit her. He didn't care. Louis really did not care about her feelings at all. And that could mean only one thing. He did not have the slightest intention of marrying her or even bringing her to Jersey permanently. She had never been more than a diversion and now, when the de Val business was over, she would have outlived her usefulness.

He was swinging the car into a tree-lined drive.

'Where are we going?' she asked.

'Home. La Grange. I want to make a phone call.'

'Oh.' In spite of herself she felt one last desperate shard of hope. She was going to La Grange, the family home. Perhaps she was wrong and he did not intend to discard her after all.

The house was in darkness.

'You can come in if you want to,' Louis said. 'Mother is at a gala in St Helier and David is ill in bed with flu.'

Debbie's heart sank. So she wasn't going to be introduced. 'I'll wait in the car,' she started to say, then changed her mind, curiosity getting the better of her.

She followed Louis into the hall. Once, not so long ago, the grandeur of it would have overwhelmed her but the life she had led since going to London had changed all that. The fascination of La Grange lay in the fact that this was Louis's home, these walls had seen him as a child and a young man — days she could never share — and would see him, perhaps, through all the years ahead. Louis disappeared into what was obviously a study. She heard the ring of the phone as he lifted the receiver to dial and occupied herself looking at the paintings in the hall and running a finger over the carvings on the wooden chest that stood at the foot of the staircase. And what a staircase! Had Louis ever slid down these bannisters, she wondered. Most children surely would, given the chance and Louis had been a daredevil, she imagined.

An unexpected sound made her turn. The front door opened and a tall fair haired man came in.

'Who the hell are you?' he demanded.

Though a little taken by surprise Debbie returned his hostile gaze.

'I'm with Louis.'

The man snorted. He looked, Debbie thought, very angry.

'Where is he?'

She indicated the study. 'In there — on the telephone.'

The fair haired man made straight for the study. His familiarity with the house as much as any passing likeness to Louis told

468

Debbie who he was even before she heard Louis say in a surprised voice: 'Robin!'

And then all hell broke loose.

In the years to come, when she tried to remember exactly what was said that night, Debbie always found she had an almost total mental block. So terrible was what followed that it was as if her brain was trying its best to shut off, to eliminate the whole scene from her memory. But although the actual words of the accusations and counter-accusations were lost in the whirlpool of emotion Debbie was never, for a single moment, in any doubt about what was behind the terrible sound of two men tearing one another apart.

Raife Pearson had carried out his threat to tell Robin of Louis's affair with his wife, and Robin, like a mad bull, had come chasing over to La Grange to have it out with Louis. Like most gentle men who are slow to anger, his temper when finally aroused could be terrible. Frightened, Debbie shrank away as the two men followed one another round through the downstairs rooms of the house, shouting at one another. Yet in a strange way she was very calm, very aware of an ice-cold place deep inside her, a despair she could no longer deny and a sense of total humiliation and worthlessness.

Whilst she had been waiting for Louis in London, longing for him, loving him with all her being, he had been being unfaithful to her here in Jersey with his own sister-in-law. Worse, he had not the slightest intention of making their relationship permanent. She was here now only because he wanted to use her for his own ends and he did not care how much he cheapened her in the process. She was nothing but a pawn now in the game he was playing to get what he wanted here in Jersey. That was all she meant to him now — perhaps all she had ever meant to him.

Debbie cowered in the hall, frightened and hurt beyond belief. She no longer knew where she would go or what she would do now. She only knew that it felt as though her heart was breaking.

Chapter thirty-five
Jersey, 1991

Dan Deffains' office looked as if it had been struck by a bomb, more chaotic even than the usual organised clutter under which it disappeared when he was working on a story. The wastepaper basket had overturned, spilling half a dozen floppy discs on to the carpet and in the middle of the floor a huge pile of paper, newspaper cuttings and photographs resembled nothing so much as an unlit bonfire. Dan scooped the lot into a black plastic dustbin liner then reached for the last file remaining on his desk, a dog-eared manilla folder with pink legal tape hanging loosely from it and labelled both with a black marker pen and a typed stick-on label — ATTORNEY GENERAL v. SOPHIA LANG-LOIS — November 1972. For a long moment he looked at it, remembering the day, over a year ago now, when he had found it whilst clearing out his father's office, and the excitement it had aroused in him. Then, with a heavy sigh, he tossed the folder into the dustbin liner on top of all the rest of the paraphernalia associated with the Langlois case.

What a bloody fiasco it had turned out to be! He had had such high hopes that the case might provide the basis for a new scoop in investigative journalism, perhaps even a book. His instincts had been right. But it was a story he could not use without hurting Juliet. That was not something he was prepared to do.

How ironic it was, Dan thought, giving the sack containing the fruits of many hours of his labours a vicious kick. From the moment Catherine Carteret had telephoned and told him certain startling facts he had known he could not go on with it. It would have made a story and a half, of course, if he had used what she had told him, and she must have known it. She had taken one hell of a chance, spilling the beans to him. But she had called on his loyalty to his father: 'You know he really would

470

have been very distressed to know you were taking advantage of his privileged position as Sophia's advocate,' she had said in her sweetly reasonable tones. He had explained to her that he had never had any intention of violating the trust Sophia had placed in his father, that he had hoped, indeed, to prove her innocent. And it was then that Catherine had dropped her bombshell and he had known, with a great swoop of disappointment, that this was one story that must remain untold for a number of reasons — not the least of which was to protect Juliet.

Had his father known what lay behind Sophia's confession, he wondered. Or had he at least suspected? If he had, he had done the very best he could in the circumstances — though Dan, with his inherent respect for the truth could not help feeling it might have been better if the facts had been allowed to come out at the time. But not now. Now it was far too late. So, in accordance with Catherine's request, he had written off his hopes of a story and tried to steer Juliet away from investigating any further. And what had happened? Somehow she had found out about him and was convinced he had simply been using her.

Not that he could blame anyone but himself for that — and to be honest, in the beginning it had been true. But that had been before the totally unexpected had happened and he had fallen in love with her.

Fallen in love. It wasn't a phrase he was used to using, never mind applying it to himself. He had, of course, been deeply in love with Marianne, but after her death he had never expected to feel that way about a woman again. Then Juliet had come into his life and suddenly all the old preconceptions had been blown away. He had found himself wanting her, and not only on a physical level. She had made him feel alive again, reawakened emotions he had thought he would never again experience, and after that last evening they had spent together he had been ridiculously cheerful, certain that he could fight her Australian boyfriend for her — and win.

Now all his hopes were shot to pieces, totally scuppered by his failure to be honest with her.

Why the hell hadn't he been, he thought. He was usually honest to a fault. But without giving it any great deal of thought he knew the reason well enough and it didn't make him proud of himself — he had been too damned afraid of losing her. And, it seemed, his fears had been justified.

The dustbin bag looked in danger of toppling over. Dan twisted a tight-tie round the top, picked it up and carried it downstairs. He couldn't put it out with the rubbish, there was too much dynamite there to risk it blowing about on a refuse tip. He'd see to shredding it personally when he had the time.

The coffee pot was bubbling invitingly. On the point of pouring himself a cup he changed his mind. Early in the day it might be but the way he felt this morning he was going to have a stiff whisky instead!

Halfway through the whisky a thought occurred to Dan. He lowered his glass, eyes narrowing, trying not to be carried away by the sunburst of excitement that was beginning inside him.

Raife Pearson had warned Juliet that someone was 'not quite what they seemed' and with her reason blindfolded by emotion, she had translated that as a warning against him, Dan. But he couldn't have been the subject of Raife's warning. Raife wouldn't even have had any reason to know Juliet knew him, and even if he had known it was unlikely he would have made any connection between Dan and Harry Porter. No, he must have had someone else in mind — but who? Who, in Juliet's circle, was employing some kind of duplicity? Why? And how did Raife Pearson, of all people, come to know about it?

Dan's skin prickled and he knew it had nothing to do with the whisky. He picked up the telephone and dialled the Jersey Lily Nightclub. But when someone answered and Dan asked for Raife he was told that the owner was away for the next few days.

'I'll be in touch when he gets back,' Dan said, disappointed. He was impatient to find out what Raife had meant, but he had long since learned that impatience was an impotent emotion. He would simply have to wait until Raife got back — and hope Juliet was still in Jersey when he got his answer.

'I'm very worried about you, Sophia,' Deborah said, arranging the cushions at her mother-in-law's head. 'I think it's high time Dr Clavell had the consultant to see you again. Your "turns" are coming a lot more frequently, aren't they? I don't like it at all.'

Sophia smiled gently. 'Neither do I, but I don't think there's very much I can do about it.'

'That's nonsense and you know it. I'm sure if you went into hospital for a few days, so that you could be properly monitored or whatever it is they do to you, you'd be fine again.'

'Perhaps. But I have no intention of doing that whilst Juliet is here. My time with her is far too precious. Do you realise I haven't seen her since she was four years old? And once she goes back to Australia heaven knows when — if — I'll ever see her again. Unless, of course . . .' she added, brightening, 'something comes of this business with Dan Deffains' son. Now if they were to get together it could be quite a different story!'

Deborah said nothing. She felt quite bad enough already having to warn Juliet off Dan Deffains junior.

Why is it I manage to bring trouble wherever I go, Deborah wondered. Yet perhaps she was being too hard on herself. In the last twenty years she had been a calming influence if any-thing — at least she had tried very hard to make it so, doing everything in her power to be a good wife to David and a good daughter-in-law to Sophia. And she had been — she *had*! She loved David very much and he loved her. Perhaps in the begin-ning she had been attracted to him because he was Louis's brother; perhaps he had been attracted to her for much the same reason. There was, she knew, a certain amount of glamour surrounding her in David's eyes for he had hero-worshipped Louis. But that was all a long time ago. David knew all about her now. He had accepted her for what she had once been and forgotten about it. Their marriage had been good and Deborah was now quite certain of David in the comfortable way that comes from almost twenty years of loving and sharing.

As for Sophia, Deborah had made every effort to be whatever Sophia needed most. She had been a nurse and ladies' maid, confidante and friend, and she and Sophia had become closer than she would ever have believed possible. Perhaps, she some-times thought, they had fulfilled a need in one another — Sophia did not have a daughter; she, Deborah, had to all intents and purposes never had a proper mother. Between them they had forged a relationship closer than one of blood — and certainly a great deal more cordial than most relationships by marriage. But then of course her closeness to Sophia had predated Deborah's marriage to David; predated their meeting, even.

Abruptly Deborah switched her mind forward again to the present. Some things were too painful to remember. Some things were best left alone. And they had been now, for years and years. Only the fact that Juliet was here now had resurrected it all. She was the reason, perhaps, for Sophia's deteriorating state of health. Sad though Sophia would be to see her go, at least when she had things would be able to return to normal. Perhaps in a way it had been all for the best that she had disillusioned Juliet about Dan Deffains. Even if he had not been an investigative journalist, digging up their secrets to make a fat buck, he would have been an uncomfortable addition to the family. His father had known too much — far too much. Who could say how much of it he had passed on to Dan?

As for Juliet herself, whether she had been egged on by Dan or not she had been asking far too many questions. Better that she should go home to Australia and leave the rest of them to return to the normal peaceful lives they had carved out for themselves.

Debbie plumped the pillows behind Sophia's head a little more and Sophia touched her hand lightly.

'Never mind, if it doesn't happen I still have you, Deborah. I really don't know, my dear, where I would be without you.'

'And I don't know where I would be if it weren't for you,' Deborah answered truthfully.

Juliet phoned home during the early afternoon; it was evening in Australia and she felt quite homesick as she heard her mother's voice coming down the line as clear, almost, as if she had been in the next room.

'Juliet — darling — we'd almost given you up! I was only saying to Daddy this morning, we haven't heard a single word from Juliet!'

'I know. Time flies. But you could always have rung me.'

'Rung you? Where?'

'Well — *here*. La Grange.'

'Oh yes. I suppose we could. But I didn't want you to think we were chasing after you as if you were two years old again.'

'No, you've never fussed me, have you — thank goodness!' But she was thinking: That's only half the story. They didn't want to ring here. They never do.

'So — when are you coming home, darling?'

'Next week. I'll confirm times.'

'Yes, do. We'll meet you at the airport. Sean will be pleased. He's been here several times trying to find out if we had any news of you. You should have been in touch with him really, you know. He misses you dreadfully.'

'Yes — and tell him I miss him.'

'Juliet . . .' A strange loaded pause. Then Molly said awkwardly: 'Everything is all right, is it?'

'Yes of course. Why shouldn't it be?'

'Oh . . . nothing.' Molly laughed, a high, childish laugh. 'I suppose they've been telling you all kinds of stories about us.'

'What sort of stories?'

'Oh — when we were young . . . that sort of thing!'

'Not really. I must go, Mummy. I'll be in touch again.'

'Yes, all right darling.' Juliet heard the relief in her mother's voice and wondered about it. Relief she would soon be home again, relief that she hadn't been raped, kidnapped or murdered on the other side of the world? Or something else entirely?

An hour later Juliet parked her hired car outside Catherine's cottage. She had half expected to find her aunt in the garden but today she was indoors, listening to a radio play and ironing at the same time. As always Juliet was struck by the difference between the life styles of the two sisters — Sophia waited on hand and foot, living in the lap of luxury, Catherine living a perfectly ordinary, almost lonely life, doing everything for herself.

'Juliet, how lovely to see you!' She reached across to turn the radio down. 'What are you doing here?'

'I've come to see you, of course,' Juliet smiled, trying to appear more cheerful than she felt. 'I'm probably going home next week so I thought I'd come while I had the chance.'

'I see.' Catherine stood her iron on its heel, looking at Juliet slyly as she folded a pillowslip. 'You haven't decided to stay on then? Last time we were talking I thought there was a romantic attachment in the offing.'

'No, that's over now,' Juliet said quickly, ignoring Catherine's ill-disguised curiosity, and not even noticing the look of horrified guilt as her aunt wondered if perhaps her phone call to Dan was behind the sudden demise of what had seemed such a promising relationship. She did not want to talk about Dan and how he had used her, it was too painful. Besides which he had made a fool of her, she thought, and that was almost worse. 'I shall be back again, though, you can bank on it,' she added. 'Just as soon as I get some holiday and save up the air fare. I shouldn't like to leave it too long. You know Grandma had another turn the night before last?'

Catherine nodded, looking anxious. 'You found her downstairs, I understand.'

'Yes.'

'In the very spot Louis was murdered. That must have given you a dreadful fright.'

'It did.' Juliet hesitated, suddenly realising the way Catherine had worded that comment: 'the very spot Louis was murdered', not 'the spot where she killed him'. Juliet frowned. It almost sounded as though Catherine *knew* Sophia had not done it. But that wasn't possible, surely? She shook her head. Better not to go down that path. Catherine had warned her off. Perhaps she had been right to do so. But there was something Juliet wanted to know, something that had been puzzling her not just since she had been here but, in one form or another, for as long as she could remember but which she had not felt able to raise with her grandmother, especially in her present state of health.

'Can I ask you something, Aunt Catherine? Why did Mum and Dad go out on a limb so completely after . . . what happened? The rest of you seem to have closed up into a tight family unit but they cut themselves off instead. And Grandma never came out to visit, rarely wrote or telephoned, to them anyway. She hardly even talks about them. It seems really strange. I've wanted to ask her about it but I haven't liked to — I don't want to upset her. Do you know the reason? Did she think they had abandoned her?'

476

'Oh, I don't think it's that . . .' Catherine's face was in shadow. 'No, I don't think it's that. She wanted them to go. It was her suggestion, I seem to remember.'

'But why?'

'Well mainly I think because she wanted a good future for you. Poor Sophia, she never wanted anything but the best for any of her family, but things had a habit of turning sour for her. It's strange, when you come to think about it. She bore three sons. One of them is dead, another is on the other side of the world. But at least she has David and Deborah. They have been very good to her.'

Against her will Juliet found herself remembering what Sophia had said — 'I couldn't let him take the blame' — and the terrible suspicion it had aroused in her. No wonder David had been good to his mother if she had taken the blame for something he had done! Supporting her would be the very least he could do!

'Did David get on with Louis?' she asked before she could stop herself.

Catherine pulled another pillowslip out of the ironing basket.

'Oh I think so. David has always got on with just about everybody. And he never really had the chance to fall out with Louis. He was much younger, remember, and if anything he hero-worshipped Louis. It was a very different story where your father and Louis were concerned, though. They were always fighting from the time they were children. It was inevitable really, I suppose, the way things were. Your grandma did her best, just as she always did, but I'm afraid she just made things worse.'

'I don't understand,' Juliet said.

'Well now I am really going to tell you some family history.' Catherine put down her iron. 'Maybe I shouldn't, but I will. Bernard — your grandfather — was not Louis's father.'

'You mean Grandma . . . ?'

'She was already having him when she married your grandfather. Most people never knew the truth, of course. It was at the end of the war and everything was in chaos. Louis was passed off as Bernard's son and most people accepted it without question. I'm not even sure if your father knows what I'm telling you — that Louis was only his half-brother. I know Sophia did her best to forget, and I honestly think Bernard tried too, but

477

it wasn't so easy. He favoured Robin, naturally — or at least, your grandmother thought he did. Every time he corrected Louis she was there, rushing to his defence, taking up the cudgels on his behalf. The result was that the family split — Bernard and Robin, Sophia and Louis. From the time they were children that was how it was and when the boys grew up it just got worse. They squabbled over everything — toys, pocket money, who should do what, and then, later on over more adult things like the business. Louis had big ideas, Robin was like Bernard. Louis and Bernard fell out over it and Louis went off to London, though I never saw him there — we lived in two very different worlds. Then Bernard died and the trouble really started.'

She broke off, remembering the misgivings she had experienced when she had heard the terms of Bernard's will, dividing everything equally between the three boys. She had known it would cause trouble and she had wished heartily that Bernard had not done it, though she could understand his reasons perfectly. He had wanted, in the end, to show Louis that there had not been any preferential treatment for Robin, however it may have seemed. He wanted to prove he loved all his sons equally. And in so doing he had set up an explosive situation.

'Louis was a rather unsavoury character from what I can make out,' Juliet said. 'Did he take after his father?'

'I don't know. Sophia never knew for certain who his father was. The only thing she was sure about was that he was a German. The island was occupied at the time and Sophia had a German boyfriend, Dieter, someone she'd been in love with before the war when he was a waiter at the guest house. He could have been Louis's father, but I don't think so. However much we might have hoped that it was so, I don't think so.'

'Then who?'

'She was raped by another soldier who took advantage of the fact that she already had a German boyfriend. It was a matter for terrible shame, you see. "Jerry-bags", they used to call the girls who consorted with the Germans, and to this day they are looked down on as collaborators. That is why Sophia was so anxious to keep it quiet when she was pregnant — and why Bernard pretended for her sake that the baby was his.'

'Poor Grandma!'

'Yes. I often wonder what she must have suffered every time she looked at Louis. Before he was born she wouldn't get rid of the baby in case it was Dieter's, but afterwards she must have known, I'm sure, that he had been fathered by that pig. All his childhood years she tried to make something of him but it's hopeless, going against nature. Everything she and Bernard did for him was thrown back in their faces, even Bernard's last gesture in splitting the business equally between the boys in spite of all their differences. Louis was simply taking advantage of it, using his position as the eldest to try to do things to the company that would have had Bernard turning in his grave.'

'No wonder Dad hated him!' Juliet said. 'If he was trying to take over and do things Dad believed to be wrong who could blame him?'

'And it wasn't only that, I'm afraid. There was Molly too . . .' Catherine broke off, horrified as she realised what she had said.

'Molly? You mean my mother? What has she got to do with it?'

'Oh my dear . . .' Catherine was thoroughly distressed now, desperate to remedy the situation but not knowing how. 'I didn't mean . . . Well, not like that . . . my tongue runs away with me, it always has. Please don't think for a minute. . .'

'Aunt Catherine, stop blathering for goodness' sake! Are you saying my mother was involved with Louis?'

'Well no, not exactly . . . it wasn't like that . . .' But her face was telling a different story, flushed with embarrassment at her gaffe, anxious, concerned, indecisive.

'I see,' Juliet said grimly. 'Yes, believe it or not, I really do begin to see. Louis and my mother. That's what is behind it all. Not the business at all. I thought there was something that didn't ring true. I mean, it really is not easy to imagine Dad getting so steamed up about the business. But if Mum was involved then it's a whole different ball game. He would certainly get very worked up indeed. But I still don't really see why they went to Australia. A future for me — yes, I suppose so. But I would have had a future here. And Louis was dead by the time they went. There would have been no danger of anything starting up again.' She broke off suddenly as the first terrible hint of suspicion flashed into her mind. 'Oh my God! Oh no!'

479

'Juliet — stop it this instant! Stop it, please!' Catherine said insistently, but her distress only served to remind Juliet of how desperately Catherine had tried to warn her off investigating when she had first come. She hadn't been able to understand her aunt's impassioned plea then, hadn't known why she should have tried so hard to make her leave the past well alone. Now the first glimmerings of comprehension were coming and she did not want them to.

'Aunt Catherine — you're not trying to tell me . . .' She stopped again, unable to voice her fears. Her throat was dry and going into spasm; she thought she might be going to be sick.

'I am not telling you anything, Juliet, except that you must stop this here and now!'

Juliet's throat closed again. Catherine did not need to say a word. It was all there in her eyes.

'Thank you. I think I'd better go now.'

'Juliet!'

'No! Now now!'

She had to get out of here. If she didn't she would choke. Or faint. Or both.

'Juliet!'

She fled to her car. The engine fired first time. Juliet let out the clutch with a jerk and drove away from Catherine's cottage, tyres screaming.

Catherine could do nothing but stand helplessly by and watch her go.

Fortunately there was not too much traffic on the roads this afternoon. Juliet put her foot flat to the floor, driving as fast as she dared as if sheer speed would somehow take her away from the nightmare that had closed in around her in Catherine's cottage. But after a few minutes common sense took over and she slowed down. There was no way she was going to leave this behind. Wherever she went it would go with her.

There was a car park at the side of the road, a gravelled square surrounded by trees and obviously meant for tourists who wanted to leave their vehicles here and walk down to the beach below. Juliet pulled on to it, switched off the engine and sat gripping the steering wheel and staring unseeingly at the vista

480

of green and blue below her. She still felt sick, not as violently as she had done in the cottage, but a heavy dragging nausea, and she struggled with a sudden urge to scream hysterically.

No! No! Not Dad! He couldn't have killed Uncle Louis! I don't believe it!

But she did. That was the trouble. It all fitted together too well. It all made sense. The fact that they had left Jersey for the other side of the world, the reluctance to talk about the family they had left behind, the secrecy, even the concern about what she would discover. What was it her mother had said on the telephone? 'Have they been telling you stories about us . . . when we were young?' Presumably she had been referring to the possibility that Juliet would find out that she had been having an affair with Louis. And that because of it Robin had killed him.

Juliet covered her face with her hands, trying to shut out the images, trying even now to find some evidence that it was not true. But everything pointed towards his guilt. Everything. Even the fact that Sophia had willingly confessed to something almost everyone who knew her was convinced she could not have done. That most of all.

'I couldn't let him take the blame,' she had said. Juliet had thought she meant David. It had never for one moment occurred to her that all the arguments applying to David also applied to Robin, only more so. Robin had been older. Robin had had a perfectly good motive — two motives — whilst David was still too young to have cared much about the business. The fact that he now headed it had sidetracked her, Juliet supposed. It was possible, of course, that he had been an unusually ambitious nineteen-year-old, but she couldn't see it somehow, and Aunt Catherine had said he hero-worshipped Louis. No, the obvious candidate for jealousy on all counts was the brother who was so much closer to him in age, the brother who had competed and fought with him from schooldays on, the brother whose wife Louis had been trying to steal. That, most of all. Juliet knew how much her father adored her mother. She was the only thing in life that Robin cared passionately about. It must have torn him apart to know that she was having an affair with his own brother.

'And Cain slew his brother Abel . . .'

I should have known, Juliet thought. I should have realised what they were warning me about. How could I have been so blind? I was intent on proving Grandma's innocence and I never really stopped to take stock of the implications. She would never have taken the blame for anyone but one of her beloved sons. It could have been David, her baby. But it was not. It was Robin, the one she felt she had neglected in her efforts to over-compensate Louis for the fact that he was not Bernard's son. Robin. My father.

How could he have let his mother take the blame? Juliet could not even begin to understand. Except of course that Sophia was a very powerful personality. Perhaps she had persuaded him that she would be dealt with leniently and told him to leave while he could for the sake of his wife and child. To give her a good start in life, wasn't that what Catherine had said? Well, he'd done that. In Australia. On the other side of the world.

'And the Lord set a mark upon Cain. And Cain went out from the presence of the Lord and dwelt in the land of Nod, on the east of Eden.'

Juliet laid her face against her arms on the steering wheel and wept.

Chapter thirty-six

When Juliet had left Catherine went straight to the telephone and dialled the number of La Grange. Deborah answered, Catherine asked for Sophia and a few minutes later Sophia was on the line.

'Catherine! What a nice surprise!'

'No, Sophia, I'm afraid it isn't. Something really rather dreadful has happened. Look – I don't want to upset you but I think I must tell you. Juliet came to see me this afternoon. She asked me some very pertinent questions. Sophia, I think she knows.'

'Knows?'

'About her father.'

'What do you mean? What do you think she knows?'

'Oh Sophia, don't let's beat about the bush. I'm talking about Louis's death.'

There was a lengthy silence. Then Sophia said: 'How?'

'I don't know. I think she put two and two together.'

'Are you sure you didn't tell her?'

'Sophia – as if I would! I have to confess though that it might have been something I said that put her on to it. I was talking about Louis and I said Robin hated him because of Molly . . .'

'Catherine, you didn't! Won't you ever learn how to stop that tongue of yours running away with you?'

'Probably not,' Catherine said ruefully. 'I'm really very sorry, Sophia. It just slipped out – only one word, but she picked up on it. The next thing I knew she was practically asking me . . .' Her voice tailed away. 'I think she's upset,' she continued. 'And I thought you should know.'

'You didn't actually tell her anything?' Sophia asked.

'No.'

'All right. Thanks for letting me know, Catherine.'

'Try not to upset yourself, Sophia.'

'I think,' Sophia said, 'that I have known ever since Juliet came that something like this was going to happen.'

She replaced the receiver and sat staring into space. It was true – in a strange intuitive way she had known. And she was almost glad.

How strange it was, she thought, it had been talked about so little over the years, this momentous thing that had changed all their lives. Perhaps it was the curse of their generation that so many subjects were taboo. She had talked to Catherine about it at the time, of course, but only because it had become necessary when Catherine had come dashing home to Jersey, determined to prove Sophia's innocence. 'I'll never forgive you if you tell a soul,' she had said then and Catherine, though shocked and not in complete agreement, had gone along with her wishes. They had never mentioned it again.

But even Catherine did not know the whole truth. As for the others . . .

Sophia closed her eyes briefly, remembering that November night almost twenty years ago. How clear it still was in her memory! Clearer and sharper than many things that had happened since.

She had been to the gala, she remembered. She was wearing a gown of midnight blue lace and silver lamé with a corsage of freesias – the scent of them never failed to bring it back to her in all its shocking detail – the insistent little worry that had nagged at her all the way home, the growing sense of foreboding that had filled her when she saw that the lights were burning in the ground floor windows. Louis, she had thought. It must be Louis. Sophia had sighed. The last thing she had wanted that night was another scene. She hated the arguments, hated the rows. But Louis had become such a monster they were inevitable.

'Thank you, Le Grand, I'll see myself in,' she had said. She had walked up the steps and opened the door. All the lights in the hall were blazing but there was no sign of life. 'Louis?' she had called, crossing the polished floor.

And then she had seen him and gasped in shock and horror.

He was lying in the doorway of the drawing-room, a patch of scarlet spreading across his white evening shirt and soaking into the carpet. She tried to move towards him and her legs almost gave way beneath her. Then she was on her knees beside him.

'Louis! My God – Louis!'

He was dead – there was no doubt of that. Sophia looked wildly this way and that. Had he surprised a burglar? Was that it? She couldn't think straight. Her mind simply refused to work. And then she saw the gun, his gun, lying on the floor of the hall. She reached out and picked it up.

Louis's own gun. Oh God, she'd *told* him he shouldn't have it! For one thing it was illegal – he must have smuggled it into Jersey. And besides she hated guns – always had done since the war. It had worried her dreadfully knowing he carried it. He'd got it in America, he had told her, and he had it for self-protection because of the business he was in. 'What business?' she had asked. 'Your father never needed to carry a gun!' But Louis had only laughed. Now he was dead. His gun hadn't done him much good in the end.

A small sob caught like a hiccough in her throat. What the hell was she going to do? What did one do first in a situation like this? Call an ambulance? Too late for that. The police then? She levered herself up, started for the phone. Just as she was about to pick it up it began ringing. She reached for it, shaking as if in fever.

'Hello?'

'Mother? It's Molly. I must speak to Louis.'

'I'm sorry. That's not possible.'

'I have to! It's terribly important!' Molly sounded almost hysterical. 'Please – please!'

In some strange way her hysteria had an almost calming effect on Sophia.

'Why, Molly?' she asked. 'What's wrong? Why is it so important?'

'I have to speak to him . . . warn him. Robin knows about us.'

'About you?' But she knew only too well to what Molly was referring.

'Yes. Louis and I . . . we've been . . .'

'I know what you have been doing,' Sophia said coldly. 'I'm

not quite blind. I hoped you'd have the sense to keep it from Robin.'

'I did . . . we did . . . but Raife Pearson found out. He phoned Robin tonight and told him. God knows why. Robin is in a terrible state about it. He said he was going to kill Louis.'

Sophia had begun to tremble again.

'And where is Robin now?'

'I don't know – that's just it. He slammed out of the house and he hasn't come back yet. He's been gone for hours. I'm scared – really scared!'

As Molly spoke Sophia felt her whole body go weak just as her legs had done a few minutes ago and shock flooded her with a hot tide. Yet at the same time she was aware of a strange feeling of inevitability. Robin. Louis and Robin. She had always known something like this would happen one day. Only she had never expected it to be Robin . . .

Suddenly Sophia was very calm. There was not a single moment's doubt in her mind – she knew what she had to do.

'Have you told anybody but me about this?' she asked.

'No – no, I wanted to tell Louis – to warn him.'

'Then don't tell anyone. Do you hear me, Molly? Whatever happens – *don't tell anyone*.'

'But . . .'

'Just do as I say and everything will be all right. When Robin comes home tell him the same. Keep him there and tell him to say nothing.'

'I don't understand.'

'I haven't got time to argue with you, Molly. Just do it.'

She replaced the receiver, looked back for a moment at Louis lying there.

How she had loved him! Because of the circumstances of his birth it had sometimes seemed to her that he was hers alone. She had wanted so badly to make it up to him; at times it had seemed to her that the whole purpose of her existence was to try to bring him up properly and make him happy. But she had allowed herself to become obsessed – she could see that now. She had defended Louis too enthusiastically against what was probably no more than normal everyday disciplining on Bernard's part, and created divisions that might not otherwise have been there. She had refused to accept Louis's faults, failed to see what she was doing to her family. In so doing she had discriminated against the others, particularly Robin.

There had been times when she had hurt him, she knew, by what he saw as her favouritism of Louis. No wonder he had been unable to bear to see Louis winning the other woman in his life, Molly, his adored wife and the mother of his child. No wonder he had been driven to . . . God alone knew what. Well, if she had failed him before she was not going to fail him now. It was too late to do anything for Louis. Her first priority must be Robin – and her little granddaughter who could so easily be branded the daughter of a murderer.

A crime of passion, the French called it. Would it stand up here in Jersey? she wondered – and decided she dared not take the chance.

With a determined movement she lifted the receiver again and asked for the police.

'Could you come to La Grange, please? This is Sophia Langlois. I have just shot my son.'

Now, twenty years on, Sophia sighed, shaking her head as she remembered. It had all turned out so very differently to the way she had imagined it would and now, perhaps at last, the truth was about to come out.

If I could see my time over again would I do the same again? Sophia wondered.

And knew, without question, that she would.

Juliet was getting ready for dinner with the family when Deborah looked into her room.

'Telephone – for you.'

'For me? Oh!' Juliet's reactions seemed to have slowed down to half their normal rate. She could think of nothing but her terrible discovery so that everything else was overshadowed. Simply washing, changing and freshening up her lipstick and eyeshadow seemed to have become weighty chores. As for deciding who might be wanting her on the end of a telephone line, that was certainly quite beyond her mental powers at the present moment.

'Take it in the hall,' Deborah suggested. 'But I should step on it. It sounds as if it might be international.'

Juliet pulled on her towelling robe and ran down the stairs, trying to force her brain to do a mental time zone calculation. Early evening here – it must be the middle of the night in Australia!

'Hello?'

'Juliet – it's me, Sean.'

'Sean!' He might have belonged to another world. 'What time is it there?'

'Late – but I couldn't sleep. I wanted to talk to you. Your mother said you are coming home next week.'

She froze. Home. To her mother and father who had kept it hidden from her for the whole of her life that her father was a murderer. Only a few hours ago Australia had seemed like a haven where she could escape from the underhand way Dan had treated her, recharge her batteries with people who loved her. Now, suddenly, she was not at all sure she wanted to go.

'Juliet – are you there? I miss you like hell, you know. Your mother said they were going to meet you at the airport but I told her I'd do it. Do you know your flight times yet?'

'No.' Claustrophobia, closing in. Dan deceiving her here. Her parents deceiving her in Australia. Sean trying to tie her down. Her grandmother sick. Aunt Catherine pretending to be her friend and lying to her. 'Sean, I've changed my mind. I might not come home. At least, I might make a detour via the USA.'

'The USA?' He sounded shocked.

'Yes. I think I need some time on my own.'

'But what about your job?'

'Oh, I can't be bothered about that. It's the least of my worries. I'm sorry, Sean, but I'm all mixed up and I really don't know what to do.'

'Do your mother and father know about this change of plan?'

God, she thought, he sounds really staid and middle-aged. His long hair is really only a camouflage. Underneath it he is so conventional it's ridiculous. But the thought of speaking to her mother and father made her feel nauseous.

'They don't know. Could you tell them please? I don't want to speak to them at the moment. Please – look – I can't explain.

488

I just don't want to speak to them, right?' She knew her voice was rising and did not care.

'Is something wrong, Ju?'

She laughed, a brittle sound that was almost a sob. Was something wrong? Just ever so slightly. My world has turned upside down, that's all. Nothing much really.

'No,' she heard herself say. 'Nothing is wrong. I just want some time to myself, that's all. I have to sort myself out. At the moment I'm not very sure of anything. Look, I have to go. Thanks for ringing. And . . .' she hesitated, wondering how to word it, to make him realise that it was over. 'Don't feel you have to wait for me.'

'Juliet!'

But she had put the phone down.

You wouldn't want me anyway, Sean, if you knew the truth, she thought. You were a bit worried when I told you my grandmother was responsible for killing my Uncle Louis. Wait until you hear the truth!

She turned, saw, as if through a scarlet haze, Deborah at the foot of the stairs.

'Excuse me, will you?'

'I couldn't help overhearing,' Deborah said. 'You sound upset, Juliet.'

'You could say that.'

'Would you like to talk about it?'

'No. No, thank you very much.'

She pushed past Deborah and ran up the stairs.

It was a little after eight when Dan drove into the pub car park. He scanned the other vehicles that were parked there, looking for Phil Gould's Citroen. He could not see it but that did not necessarily mean Phil Gould was not there. He could have got a lift with someone else or he might be using one of the unmarked CID vehicles. They would all have been changed since he was in the force, Dan knew, and he would not recognise any of them.

He pushed open the door, made his way across the crowded bar and got himself a Scotch, looking around all the time. There were several faces he recognised and nodded to but not the one he wanted. Damn. This would have been a good deal easier than ringing Phil Gould again and asking for another meeting. His old inspector was bound to want to know why he was still digging around in the ashes of the Langlois case if he did, and Dan was not at all sure he knew how he would have answered him. His motives were so confused now. All he knew was that he was still hoping he might unearth something that would change the final scenario of the case and prove that Sophia – and Catherine – had been wrong to believe Robin guilty of Louis's murder.

Dan ran a hand through his hair once again running through all the arguments that had been going round and round in his head since Catherine's shocking revelation to him on the telephone and still failing to come up with any plausible alternative. Sophia would never have confessed and served time for the shooting unless she had been certain of her facts. She would never had put herself on the line if she had not been convinced her sacrifice was necessary. Her determination to protect Robin was the reason she had forbidden her attorney to put up any real defence, the reason she had blocked any investigation into the killing. There was no doubt about it, it all hung together very well – too damned well! And yet . . . and yet . . .

There was more to it than that. Dan was certain of it without knowing why. Was it just wishful thinking, because he wanted them to be wrong for Juliet's sake? Or was it that sixth sense that had made him a good policeman nagging away at him? He did not know.

The one lead he had was that parting remark of Raife to Juliet that 'someone was not quite what they seemed'. Dan had been hoping Phil Gould might be able to shed some light on what he could have meant by that. But Phil Gould was not here. Damnation, it really was not his day. Well he'd wait just a little longer, have one more drink.

Dan was just about to give it up as a bad job and leave when he saw Phil Gould come in. He gave him time to get his drink, then made his way across.

'Evening, Mr . . . Phil.'

Phil Gould was taking a long swig of his pint; as he lowered the glass he sighed deeply.

'Man, I needed that! Evening, Dan. Do you by any chance

490

remember how good a pint tastes after a four-hour question and answer session?'

'I do. And after pushing a pen in that smoke-filled den of iniquity otherwise known as the CID office, and plenty of other times as well.'

'You sound quite nostalgic.'

'Yes, I suppose I feel that way sometimes. Other times I remember how the bastards treated me.'

'They had no choice, Dan.'

'You didn't say that at the time.'

'At the time my blood was up on your behalf. Perhaps I'm older and wiser now. How is your leg these days, by the way?'

'OK. It doesn't really give me any trouble any more.'

'But you haven't thought about rejoining the force?'

'After being virtually told I was on the scrap-heap at age twenty-seven? Not likely.'

'Pity. I still think you're a copper through and through. You're never happier than when you're chasing up the leads in some case or other.'

Dan shifted uncomfortably. As a chance remark that really was a little too close to home for his own peace of mind. But at least it gave him a lead in to what he wanted to ask.

'Funny you should say that, Phil,' he said conversationally. 'You remember I was telling you about Juliet Langlois, Sophia's granddaughter?'

'The lovely girl who was going to make an honest man of you again. Yes. Has she done it yet, by the way?'

'No, and she's not likely to. I think I blew any chances I might have had in that direction.' His tone was determinedly light, hiding the sick ache inside, still surprised that the thought of not seeing her again could hurt him. He had never expected another woman to get to him in this way.

'You must be losing your touch, lad,' Phil Gould said heartily. 'A member of the fair sex turning down Dan Deffains . . . I find that hard to believe.' He chortled into his beer.

'Believe what you like. It's true,' Dan said shortly. 'But I don't want to talk about my personal life, Mr Gould . . . Phil.'

'Wise man.'

491

'But I do want to talk about Juliet. She went to see Raife Pearson.'

Phil Gould spluttered foam into his moustache. 'Christ, Dan, you didn't tell her I . . .'

'Of course not. She dug up the connection for herself and went to see him,' he lied. 'I don't think she got very far. But Raife said something pretty funny to her. He told her not to take everyone at face value, that there was someone who wasn't quite what they seemed to be. You don't know who or what he could have been talking about, do you?'

'Hell, no. Someone who wasn't what they seemed? That's pretty melodramatic stuff. No, I haven't a clue.'

'Oh well, never mind. I don't suppose it's important.'

They chatted for a while and Dan bought Phil another pint. He owed it to him, he thought. Conscience money.

'I think I'm for an early night tonight,' he said eventually. 'I'll leave you lot propping up the bar as usual.'

Phil laughed, wiping his moustache with the back of his hand.

'We earn it, laddie. Work hard and play hard, that's my motto. And if you ask me you should be doing the same.'

'What is that supposed to mean?'

'Re-apply for the job, Dan. Whatever it is you're doing now, you're wasted in it. You are a policeman through and through and you always will be. Come on now, it's a good life – admit it.'

'I thought you couldn't wait to retire, Phil!'

The older man laughed.

'Oh, I say that, yes, but as it comes nearer I don't mind admitting I'm dreading it. I wake up in the night in a cold sweat sometimes – and not only because I can imagine all the bloody embarrassing things the chief will say at my retirement do. No, take it from me, I shall miss the job. And if I could see my time over again I wouldn't look twice at any other career. With all the drawbacks, I still wouldn't do anything else – and I think you're a damned fool to be so stubborn. OK – you don't think they treated you as they should have and you may have a point. But you were so upset at losing Marianne I don't think you saw things straight. Can't say I blame you – if anything happened to Di I expect I'd be the same. But there's no point going on bearing grudges. You're just cutting off your nose to spite your face.'

Dan nodded, unexpectedly moved, and pressed his old inspector's arm.

'You might have something there, Phil. Perhaps I will think about it.'

'Do, Dan, do. Before it's too late.'

Dan walked out into the warm windy night. Could be Phil Gould was right, he thought. At least when he had been a policeman he hadn't felt a heel like he did now. He might have upset a few of the less law abiding members of the population, but at least he had been honest and up-front about what he did. And without a doubt he had missed it, missed the challenge and the companionship and the sense of anticipation that came from never knowing at the outset what a day would bring. He had been so angry – so damned angry – about what had happened to him and Marianne he had let it colour all his thinking, and perhaps he had been a little unreasonable in turning so bitterly against his former employers – yes, if he was honest, he almost certainly had been.

Now Dan felt drawn suddenly to the life he had left behind. When all this was over he would give some serious thought to seeing if the force would have him back, he decided. But for the moment he still wanted to follow his nose and see if there were still a few unsuspected twists and turns in the Langlois case.

Dan unlocked his car and got in, sitting for a moment deep in thought. There was nothing much he could do now until Raife got back but when he did Dan intended seeing him and asking him point blank what he had meant by his allusion to 'someone not being quite what they seemed'.

Would Raife tell him? He really did not see why not. This was one occasion when *not* being a policeman might prove useful. And if his intuition was not playing him false he believed the answer might prove very important, a clue that should never have been overlooked. Dan was determined to follow it up and find out exactly where it led.

Chapter thirty-seven

After dinner was over Juliet pleaded a headache and went up to her room early. She was almost ready for bed, still in a daze of shock and misery, when there was a tap at the door and Deborah looked in.

'Would you like me to get you some aspirin or something?'

'No, it's all right . . .' Juliet began, then changed her mind. 'Well, perhaps an aspirin might be a good idea. I do have a stinking headache.'

'I can see that.' She disappeared and was back in a few minutes with a bottle of tablets and a glass of water. 'Take these. I'd have three if I was you. I know you're only supposed to have two but you really do look dreadfully grotty.'

Juliet swallowed the tablets. One stuck in her throat, effervescing acidity in her mouth. She coughed at it and drank some more water. Heavens, the food at dinner had stuck in her throat, but she'd have thought she could get down a silly little aspirin!

'Sometimes you must feel as if you spend your whole life ministering to the sick,' she said apologetically to Deborah. 'First Grandma, then me!'

'Oh, I don't mind. I quite like being useful. But I'd never have made a nurse — not a real one. It upsets me to see people feeling ill or unhappy and I don't think I could bear it if my patients didn't get well.' She laughed lightly. 'That's the sort of person I am, I suppose. I only want to see the nice pleasant side of life. I close my eyes to the ugly and the sad or anything that makes me uncomfortable and pretend it doesn't exist.'

Juliet said nothing. The last thing she wanted just now was a conversation on psychology as it applied to Deborah. As for shutting things out and pretending they did not exist, she only wished she could!

'Juliet, what is wrong?' Deborah asked gently.

494

Juliet picked up a hairbrush, tortoiseshell-backed, from the set on the dressing table and twisted it round in her hands. She could feel Deborah looking at her and she somehow knew that the look was not merely curious but also anxious and sympathetic.

I have to tell someone! Juliet thought. If I don't tell someone I think I'll go crazy! And who better than Deborah? She was involved yet not involved, she had been part of the family for long enough to care what happened to it, but she didn't know Robin. They lived on opposite sides of the world and would probably never meet. Besides, it was possible she knew the truth already. She was, after all, very close to Sophia.

'I'm sorry, Deborah,' she said, wondering why she should be apologising about it. 'I know I'm being a pain but I've had a pretty ghastly day.'

'Because of Dan Deffains, you mean? Oh, Juliet, I really am sorry if you've been hurt, but I had to tell you. He's not worth upsetting yourself over.'

'No, it's not just Dan. It's something else. Something much worse.'

A small frown puckered Deborah's forehead.

'Worse? What do you mean? I don't understand.'

'No, I don't suppose you do,' Juliet said drily. 'It's something I found out, by accident almost — although God knows I've spent practically my entire time here trying to do just that. But I had no idea how dreadful the answer would be.'

'Juliet, you are not making much sense. What have you found out that is so terrible?'

The bristles of the hairbrush were digging into Juliet's hand, making vivid patterns on her palm. She didn't know even now if she could bring herself to actually put it into words. Then, quite suddenly, she heard herself say: 'You know I had this feeling it wasn't Grandma who killed Uncle Louis? You know I wanted to get to the bottom of the whole thing? Well, I think today I did.'

'Oh.' Deborah's voice was oddly toneless.

'Yes. And I wish I hadn't. Grandma confessed to protect someone. I think I've known that right from the beginning. What

495

I didn't know was that the person she was protecting was my father.'

'Your father?'

The reaction was so swift, so horrified, that in spite of herself Juliet looked up, seeing Deborah reflected in the dressing table mirror. She seemed to have frozen into a slim beautiful statue but her shocked expression reinforced the immediate impression Juliet had gained from her tone.

So Deborah hadn't known, she thought. Well, it was done now. She couldn't take her words back even if she wanted to.

'I know — it's awful, isn't it?' she said shakily. 'You can see why I'm not feeling so good. It takes a bit of coming to terms with — that one's father is a murderer.'

'Oh no!' Deborah said. Her voice was urgent and breathless. 'No, Juliet, you have it all wrong!'

'I don't think so. I wish I did. Frankly, Deborah, I don't know what I am going to do. I know I don't want to go home. All those lies . . . I don't think I can face him again, not yet, anyway. And it feels so bloody . . .'

'Juliet!' Deborah was beside her, touching her arm. 'You don't understand. You *have* got it wrong. I don't know who you have been talking to but they've misled you. I'm not speculating – I'm telling you. Your father did not kill Louis.'

Her tone was urgent but firm. It rang very true. Juliet turned, hope sparking — perhaps after all she had been right in the first place.

'You mean . . . it was David?' she whispered.

'No. No, Juliet, it wasn't either of them. Not Robin and not David.' She hesitated, her voice breaking. Then, in the same firm tones she had used earlier she went on, 'I know neither of them shot Louis. Because, you see, it was me!'

For a moment Juliet gazed at Deborah in sheer total disbelief. She felt as if someone had knocked all the wind out of her.

'You?' she whispered.

Deborah nodded. 'Yes, me. I shot Louis.' Her voice was low, her face deathly pale so that her carefully applied blusher stood out suddenly in russet streaks high on her cheekbones. 'Oh, don't look at me like that, Juliet, please! I loved him so and he . . . didn't want me any more. He was having an affair with your mother.'

'But you don't shoot somebody because they're ditching you!' Juliet interrupted incredulously.

'You don't know the way it was,' Debbie said fiercely. 'You don't know anything. You have always lived a good life, secure, loved . . . you don't know how important that is unless you have never been lucky enough to have it. Louis was the only good thing that ever happened to me. Or so I thought at the time. I couldn't see what he was, I blinded myself to it. And then I found out that he didn't really want me at all. He only wanted to use me. To blackmail someone.'

'Frank de Val.'

'Yes. He took me to his house that night. It was so humiliating — so degrading. And then he brought me here, to La Grange. I still thought that meant I was going to meet his family, be accepted. That shows you how naive I was.'

She broke off, remembering the way it had been. That whole day had been like a terrible nightmare, the waiting in her room at the Pomme d'Or, the visit to the Jersey Lily and to Frank de Val, the way the Louis she loved seemed to have turned into a monster, hard, cold and unfeeling. She had thought when he took her to La Grange that perhaps it was going to be all right after all, but that too had become part of the nightmare, with Louis's brother arriving and having a terrible fight with him because Louis was having an affair with his wife Molly. Right across the years Debbie could remember only too clearly the way she had felt — hurt, used and heartbroken because in spite of everything she still loved him; frightened by the violence that was flaring, terrified of what the consequences of the evening's work might be, numbly, coldly afraid for the future.

When Robin had eventually left, slamming the door and screaming away down the drive, Louis's mood had become even more peculiar.

'So you want to see La Grange?' he had said and he had taken her on a tour of the downstairs rooms, showing her each one not so much with pride as with gloating. This is my home, he seemed to be saying, one day this will all be mine. But take a good look, Debbie baby, because you won't be seeing it again.

She had gone with him, mute with misery, and in the drawing-room he had made love to her on the priceless Aubusson rug. Made love? No, those were not the words to describe that act. There was something cold and vengeful in the way he took her, something almost evil, and suddenly she had realised what it was. The gloating had not only been for showing her a life in which he had no intention of letting her share, rather it was as if he was showing her to the house, without love, without respect, without anything but a desire to defile. She had not fully understood it at the time, that had only come to her painfully over the years as she learned and accepted the truth about Louis, but she had known it instinctively then and it had hurt her so deeply it had made her physically sick. She had gone to the bathroom, that elegant Victorian-style bathroom, and retched helplessly into the blue-and-white 'Express' bowl.

When the spasm had passed she had washed her face and gone back downstairs. She could hear Louis's voice coming from the study and she guessed he was on the telephone again. She followed the sound of his voice. Her mind was made up. 'Please take me home,' she was going to say. 'I won't be your pawn any more.'

Louis was sprawling elegantly back against the desk, speaking into the heavy black receiver as he cradled it into his shoulder.

'Yes, darling, I'll see you soon. Tomorrow?' she heard him say. She froze. Already tonight she had learned that Louis was far from faithful to her but it was still a shock that he could actually telephone one of his lady friends while she was in the house. He looked up and saw her and smiled, not in the least perturbed at being caught red-handed. Then he turned his back, shutting her out. 'Love you too, Kitten.'

Kitten. If he had struck her she could not have been more shocked or hurt. It was his name for her, the special pet name that had made her feel so wanted, so loved. Now he was using it for some other woman. Quite suddenly the last slender thread that had been keeping Debbie's reactions under control snapped.

Earlier, showing her around, Louis had opened a drawer in the desk and shown her a little gun he kept there — showing off as usual, playing a role. Now she ran across the room, jerked open the drawer and snatched the gun out, pointing it at him.

'Put that phone down! Hang up, do you hear?'

Louis almost laughed, then turned pale. It must have been in that moment, she supposed, that he remembered the gun was loaded.

'I have to go now. I'll call you tomorrow,' he said into the mouthpiece.

She stood unwavering, the gun pointing at his chest.

'Who was that?'

'No one. Now don't be a silly girl. Give me that gun.'

'Who was it? Was it Molly?'

'No, it wasn't. Now look, Kitten, give it to me. It's not a toy.'

'Don't call me Kitten! Don't ever call me Kitten again! I hate you, Louis!'

'Don't be so bloody melodramatic.' He was pale, but in an effort to defuse the situation he walked out of the study, along the hall towards the drawing room. She followed him, still holding the gun.

'You've used me!' she sobbed. 'How could you do this to me, Louis? I loved you so much and all the time . . . how many others are there? How many?'

'Calm down, for Christsakes! Just calm down!'

'I am calm.' But she wasn't. She was shaking and sobbing.

'Kitten . . .'

'*Don't* call me . . . !'

And that was when the gun went off.

She hadn't meant to do it. She'd only meant to frighten him. She screamed at the crack, screamed again as the bullet hit him and the blood spurted scarlet on to his white shirt front. He went down slowly, sagging like a sack of potatoes, his expression more surprised than anything, the only sounds a choking, gurgling glug, and his breath rasping in the quiet house.

'Louis! My God — Louis!' She dropped the gun, running to him, falling to her knees beside him. 'I didn't mean it! I didn't mean to . . . Louis!' She lifted his head, cradling it in her lap. 'Louis – please — please, Louis!'

But within a matter of minutes, less maybe, the awful rasping breathing shuddered and stopped. Louis was dead. Debbie screamed again as she realised it, scrambling to her feet, relinquishing all contact with him as if he had suddenly become too searingly hot to touch. She backed away from him, hands covering her tear-streaked, mascara-stained face. She crossed the hall, bumped into the door, fumbled for the handle. The door swung open and she ran down the steps to where Louis had left his car. The November night was chilly but she did not notice it. She yanked open the car door, half-fell into the driver's seat. Louis had left the keys in the ignition; she turned it on, let out the clutch and the car surged forward,

How she managed not to be stopped by the police that night Debbie never knew. She was not much of a driver, she had never passed a test though she had her own car in London, and she seldom drove anywhere. Now desperation made her reckless, and surprisingly she yanked up from the depth skills she had not known she possessed. She drove like a wild thing, all accelerator and brakes, squealing tyres and crashing gears, but at first she did not know where she was going. Anywhere, as far as possible from La Grange! Then, as she hit the outskirts of St Helier, the plan occurred to her.

She was booked in at the Pomme d'Or Hotel. Almost opposite it, beside the harbour, was a public car park. If she left Louis's car there no one would connect it with her and certainly no one at the hotel would connect her with him.

Sometimes the car park was full, tonight luckily there were a few spaces. Debbie drove into one, summoning up all her concentration to make sure she did not collide with the neighbouring cars. The last thing she wanted to do was draw attention to herself. Then she locked it, threw the keys into a nearby rubbish bin and dodged the thin stream of late night traffic to run across the road to the hotel.

No one took the slightest notice of her as she scurried through the lobby and up the broad staircase. When she had gone out earlier she had forgotten to hand her key in to Reception. Now she thanked her lucky stars for that. She didn't think she could have faced speaking to anyone just now, not even an anonymous hotel clerk.

In her room she leaned against the door for a moment, feeling the remains of her self-control drain out of her, then she went into the en suite bathroom, ran a bath and climbed into it, scrubbing herself feverishly because she felt she would never be clean again.

After a while the hot water relaxed her body a little but her emotions still churned in an oddly heavy and numbed fashion. Tears filled her eyes. She got out of the bath, swallowed a handful of tablets, and paced the room, Then, when exhaustion and the effects of the tablets began to creep up on her she crawled into bed and eventually, curled protectively in the foetal position, she fell asleep.

Next morning as the news of Louis's death was breaking Debbie flew out of Jersey. At that time she had no idea of the family mayhem she was leaving behind.

'I can't believe I'm hearing this,' Juliet said. 'You're making it up.'

'No. I only wish I were, but I'm afraid it's quite true. I shot Louis. I didn't mean to do it. I only meant to frighten him — punish him — I don't know. I certainly did not intend to kill him. I didn't even wish him dead — not really. I was besotted with him. That's the ironic part of it, really. Practically everyone else hated him. His death was the answer to an awful lot of prayers. Apart from his mother and perhaps Molly, I think I was the only person who really grieved for Louis. Yet I was the one who killed him.'

'I see.' It was true, Juliet thought, she had been busy looking for someone who had hated Louis enough to kill him and she had forgotten that love — obsessive love — could be an even stronger motive. But of course there was a great deal more to this than simply solving the puzzle. 'You killed Louis,' she said slowly, 'but Grandma confessed. Why should she do that?'

'Because she believed Robin — your father — had done it.'

'She didn't only confess — she went to prison for it. How could you let that happen?'

Deborah crossed to the window so that she was no longer looking at Juliet and the whole of her stance seemed to change in some mysterious way so that she looked not self-possessed and totally sophisticated, but young and vulnerable as if her memories had somehow transformed her once more into the young girl she had once been.

501

'I've never been able to forgive myself for that,' she said softly, speaking more to herself than to Juliet. 'I've spent my life trying to make it up to her but I know I never can.'

'I should think not! My God, Deborah, she went to prison for you! Didn't you know what was happening? Why the hell didn't you have the decency to own up?'

'I didn't know she had confessed — truly I didn't. I flew back to London but I knew I couldn't stay there. I couldn't go on living in the house with Louis dead and anyway I was afraid the man who had been threatening Louis over his debts might come back. Besides, I wanted to cut all contact. A girl I had known at a club I used to work at was going to the USA, to Las Vegas, and I went with her. Big as the story of Louis's death was over here it wasn't big enough to reach the USA. By the time I got to hear what had happened Sophia's trial was over. I couldn't understand why she should have confessed, it made no sense to me. I followed it up, tried to find out and put things right. That was when I met David.'

'For heaven's sake!' Juliet shouted. 'This just gets worse and worse! You mean to tell me that you not only let my grandmother serve a sentence for you, you then wangled your way into the family by marrying David. You're disgusting! Well, I think it's time Grandma knew all about you. I think it's time she found out what sort of person she has had living under her roof all these years.'

'Oh Juliet!' Deborah turned. 'You still don't understand, do you? Your grandmother knows — she's known all along — well, almost all along.'

Juliet blinked. 'But you said she confessed because she thought Dad . . .'

'Yes, that's true. Robin had found out just that night that Molly, your mother, and Louis were having an affair. He had left the house in a terrible temper, intending to have it out with Louis, threatening to kill him. Eventually Molly telephoned here in a terrible state because he had not come home and she didn't know where he was, and your Grandmother, who had just found Louis's body, came to the wrong conclusion. She decided to take the blame rather than let the police arrest Robin.'

502

'But why didn't she change her story and tell the truth when she discovered that it was you?'

'I think you'd better ask her that.'

'No! I'm asking you! I don't understand how you could allow something like that. What sort of person are you, Deborah?'

'At the time I was very young, very alone and very frightened.'

'You're not any of those things now.'

'No, it's true, I'm not. But let me tell you what happened. I went to see your grandmother in prison. I tried to explain to her what had happened. I got so far and then she stopped me. She said she did not want to know. The one thing she did ask was that we should keep in touch. I visited her regularly and when she came home to Jersey I used to come over to see her. I met David and we fell in love.'

'And Grandma didn't mind?'

'She's a very special person, Juliet. No, she didn't mind. She was actually pleased. We had grown very close, she and I. She's been far more of a mother to me than my own ever was.'

'Does David know?'

'No. And I hope he never will.'

'That's deceitful too, isn't it?'

'What useful purpose would it serve? Oh yes, perhaps it is deceitful. But it's the way Sophia and I want it. And who are you, Juliet, to come here and judge us?'

It was a cry from the heart. Juliet, shaken to the core, did not know how to answer it.

'Oh my dear!' Sophia said. 'Oh my dear, I am so sorry you have been so upset by all this.'

She and Juliet were in her room; Deborah had gone up and quietly told her what had happened, and now grandmother and granddaughter were alone.

'I'm not upset for me, Grandma! I'm upset for you!' Juliet said vehemently. 'How could you go on letting the world believe you killed Uncle Louis when you knew very well . . .'

Sophia smiled, a faint faraway sort of smile.

'A lot of reasons, I suppose, really. Firstly because Deborah reminded me of myself. She really was very young then, you know, and very frightened. She had had a terrible childhood, a mother who didn't want her, no father, then a succession of men taking advantage of her.'

'But surely that wasn't in the least like you, Grandma. I understand you had a very happy family.'

'Yes, I did. But I do assure you, Juliet, I knew only too well what it was to be alone and terrified. Heaven knows I once came very close to shooting someone — by design, not by accident. Sometimes I wish I had.' She broke off and with a rush of discomfort Juliet realised she was remembering the German who, according to Catherine, had raped her during the war.

'Was that the only reason?' Juliet asked. 'Because you empathised with her?'

'No, there were two other very good reasons. One, I felt responsible in a way. Louis was my son and he had treated her very badly. I was ashamed of him. I couldn't blame Deborah for what she did — I am very much afraid Louis asked for what he got, though I don't think for one moment it was her intention to kill him. And lastly David was in love with her. I didn't want to blight things between them. Besides, it was a little late to start making waves. I'd served a very light sentence — much lighter than Deborah would have got, I'm sure. Say what you like, background does make a difference and the justices were biassed very much in my favour.'

'But Grandma, you've gone on letting everyone think that you . . .'

'What good would it have done to re-open it all again?'

'It would have cleared your name!'

Sophia laughed. 'That is the least of my worries. I realised a long while ago that caring what people think is a great handicap. Perhaps if I hadn't tried so hard to cover up the fact that Louis's father was German none of this would have happened. I wasn't going to make the same mistake again.'

Juliet shook her head in bewilderment. Her grandmother's reasoning was almost beyond her yet she admired her for it all the same.

'What about Dad? Why did he and Mama go to Australia?'

'To get away, of course, there's no doubt about that. They wanted to leave behind the bad memories and the shame and make a fresh start. And of course your father had a very serious

504

side to him. He was shocked, I think, by the whole thing. At the time I took it for guilt. But then I misjudged him, didn't I? Another mistake. I should have apologised to him years ago, I suppose. But I couldn't really, without implicating Deborah, and I didn't want to do that.'

'Well, Grandma, I have to say I think you are very wrong. I think the truth should be told and your name cleared.'

'Oh Juliet, Juliet, you are so young and fierce! Look a little further than your nose, my dear. What good would it do now? And besides, I think I have gained far more than I have lost. I have already said I don't much care about what people may think — there are plenty of things in life much more important than that. And see the good things that have come out of it all! I have a wonderful daughter-in-law who has been more to me than I could ever have hoped for, and because of what we share we are far closer than most blood relatives could ever be. No, without a doubt, my dear, I have been a winner in all this. So won't you please just let it all die before you upset the applecart completely!'

Juliet nodded. 'I suppose so.'

She did not agree. Not completely. But one thing was clear. With her generous spirit her grandmother was indeed a winner, loved by all who knew her. Perhaps in the end that was really all that mattered.

Chapter thirty-eight

'Do you know, I dreamed about Nicky the other night,' Viv said.

She and Paul were sitting in the garden enjoying a drink and the last of the evening sunshine but at her words a shadow crossed Paul's face.

'Really?' he said, taking a quick slurp of his whisky.

'Yes. It was as if we were all young again in the days before the war. I don't know what made me dream it — Juliet coming here, perhaps, and talking about the past. When I woke first it all seemed so real, almost as if I could reach out and touch it all. And then I suddenly realised — it's nearly fifty years since those days. Fifty years, Paul — a lifetime!'

'Yes.' The sadness was still there in his voice. 'But they cast a long shadow, don't they?'

Viv turned to look at him. Her green eyes were sharp with remembered joy and sorrow but also with something else, a tenderness for so much that they had shared; so much that perhaps they had failed to appreciate.

'Perhaps we've been wrong to let it, Paul,' she said gently.

'What do you mean?'

'The way things were . . . they marked us. To a certain extent I suppose that's inevitable. But Sophia suffered too and she's risen above it somehow. We've had the chance to do that and we've let it slip by. We've had good times, haven't we? Perhaps those are the ones we should remember, not the things we feel guilty about or regret. What happened is all a very long time ago now. We've had almost fifty years together and they haven't been all bad, have they?'

Her tone was almost pleading; he looked at her and saw for a moment an echo of the old Viv, the girl with flaming red hair who could wind any man around her little finger. Yes, it was true. There had been plenty of good times. They shouldn't let them be marred by the shadow of a man who had been at rest now for almost half a century.

'It wasn't only Nicky I dreamed of,' Viv went on softly. 'I dreamed about you too, that night you came to the show I was doing with the repertory company. You looked so handsome in your uniform! I think I fell in love with you that night, only perhaps at the time I didn't realise it.'

'Because of Nicky . . .'

'Nicky was part of my youth,' Viv said firmly. 'Nicky was a golden boy from the golden years. I don't know if he and I would ever have stood the test of time together — as we have, Paul.'

'Viv Carteret, the gin is making you maudlin,' Paul said.

But he was smiling, and in the softening evening light he reached out and took her hand.

'I am going home on Monday, Grandma,' Juliet said. 'I've booked my flight.'

'Oh dear, have you really?'

'Afraid so. I can't stay here forever, you know.'

'Why not?'

'Well . . .' She hesitated. The one very good reason why she could not stay was one she could not bring herself to tell Sophia about. She was ashamed, as well as hurt, that Dan had used her to try to gain information for his project and she knew that it would hurt Sophia too.

Sophia reached out and took her hand.

'It's all right, my dear, you don't have to explain! I know you have your own life on the other side of the world. Just promise me you won't leave it quite so long before you come back again.'

'Twenty years, you mean?' Juliet said, laughing. 'Oh, I think I can quite safely promise you that.'

'Good.'

'Telephone for you, Juliet,' Deborah said, putting her head around the door. She was still slightly stiff and awkward in Juliet's presence though she made a great pretence of there being nothing whatever out of the ordinary.

'Thank you, Deborah.' Juliet too found herself speaking in a

507

slightly unnatural manner. It wasn't possible, she thought, to discover something of such importance and simply put it all behind her, much as she knew that was exactly what her grandmother would have liked her to do.

She went to the telephone in the hall and lifted the receiver. 'Hello?'

'Juliet?'

She recognised his voice instantly, recognised it and began to tremble, partly from anger, partly because that was the response he was able to awaken in her.

'I'm sorry, Dan, I thought I'd made it clear I didn't want any more to do with you.'

'You did.' He sounded rueful. 'Abundantly clear. You never gave me a chance to put my side at all.'

'Do you blame me? I feel very used, Dan. I don't know why you are phoning me but you might as well know I haven't changed my mind. I still think what you did was pretty disgusting.'

'I know that's what you think and I won't try to argue with you now.'

'I'm glad to hear it!'

'But I really do want to see you. It's important. For more reasons than one.'

'Dan, there is no point. I am going home on Monday.'

Dan's heart lurched but he steeled himself to stick to the script he had decided upon.

'I can't explain over the telephone. At least, I have no intention of trying. Do you remember the pub I took you to for lunch? I'll be there tonight at eight. I'll look out for you.'

'Dan . . .'

'Eight tonight,' he repeated.

'I don't know . . .' But the phone had been put down. Dan was gone.

'Who was that?' Deborah asked behind her.

Juliet experienced a flash of annoyance, both for Dan, for daring to ring her, and Deborah, trying to re-establish friendship.

Perhaps in time she would be able to forgive Deborah, if not forget that she had killed a man and left someone else to take the consequences. Perhaps in time her subsequent kindness to

508

Sophia and the fact that she had owned up in the end to save further misunderstanding would allow Juliet to feel more kindly towards her. But not yet. Not yet.

'It was just a personal call,' she said coolly.

All day she kept thinking about the phone call, wondering why Dan wanted to see her and what he wanted to tell her.

Was he simply trying one last shot — hoping still that if he could regain her confidence he might still be able to put together the final pieces of the jigsaw for his story? Surely even he could not expect that? So perhaps there was a more personal reason. Hope flared in her. Perhaps she had been right to believe they had shared something special, perhaps it hadn't all been an act to further his own ends. That spark — that electric current of mutual attraction that had made her senses swim — couldn't have been all in her imagination — could it? But even if he did feel something for her, did she want to pursue it? What sort of future could there be with someone who could practise deception on her so readily?

She tossed the arguments back and forth, stacking them first this way, then that. And all the time she knew in her heart she had already decided. This was one time when her heart would rule her head. The thought of seeing him again, just once more, was irresistible, if only to find out what he was going to say to her. She was going to go.

At least it should mean I can get him out of my system one way or the other, she told herself. And knew that she was lying.

He was there waiting for her, standing near the bar with a clear view of the door. The moment she saw him she felt her stomach fall away and knew without a shadow of doubt that she had been fooling herself if she believed it would really be so easy to put him out of her mind.

'Juliet. You came.' He sounded almost surprised.

'Didn't you expect me to?'

'To be honest, no, I didn't. Not after what you said to me on the telephone, and not considering what you must think of me. But I am very glad you did. What can I get you to drink?'

'Orange juice, please.'

'Oh surely . . .'

'No, I want a very clear head. And I wouldn't like you to run away with the idea that you can soften me up with alcohol.'

'Very well, orange juice it is.' He ordered her drink and another whisky for himself.

'Well?' she said. 'What did you want to see me about? I'm not going to tell you anything, you know, so it's no good you thinking I am.'

'No, *I* am going to tell *you* something. But not here. Let's find a quiet corner.'

One of the window seats seemed reasonably secluded. They slid into it and Juliet was annoyed with herself for being so ridiculously aware of how close he was to her.

'Well?'

'First of all I want to say how sorry I am you had to find out about me the way you did.'

'Not as sorry as I am.'

'I should have told you the whole truth, I know, but somehow I left it too late and there wasn't a right moment. Stupid as it sounds, I was very afraid of losing you.' Her heart was hammering. She looked away from him.

'I wouldn't worry about it. Lots of people are deceitful and anyway it's all water under the bridge now.'

He leaned forward.

'Juliet, I know this will probably sound very hollow but I promise you I have no intention of writing a word about your family. In the beginning, yes, I admit I did think it would make a marvellous story and yes, I was going to use it for my latest project if I could turn up enough new and startling facts. But somewhere along the line my priorities changed. It was brought home to me, rather forcefully, that the truth might do a great deal of harm.'

'To the person really responsible.'

'Not just the person responsible. I really couldn't care less about castigating the guilty. They deserve to be found out, at least, that's my philosophy. But I realised the innocent might well be hurt too, and I couldn't justify that.'

She smiled but her lips felt tight.

510

'An attack of conscience at last! Is that why you asked me here? To publicly beat your breast?'

'Partly. It does matter to me very much what you think of me.'

'You surprise me! I thought investigative reporters had skins like rhinoceroses. But couldn't we get to the point? You said on the telephone you had something to tell me. What is it?' She did not know quite why she was being so sharp, unless it was as a defence against being hurt again.

A muscle tightened in Dan's cheek but he did not rise to her jibe.

'There is something I thought you ought to know,' he said quietly. 'Do you remember Raife Pearson telling you someone was not quite what they seemed?'

'I thought you were dropping your investigations!' she flared.

'I am. Most of my files are shredded already and I promise you that what I am going to tell you will go no further. This is totally and absolutely off the record.'

'So you say.'

'I don't know what else I can say to make you believe me. Except that time will prove it, I suppose. And the fact that I am passing this on to you because I think you should know.' He paused. 'The person Raife was referring to was David's wife, Deborah. She knew Louis, you see. She was at the Jersey Lily Nightclub with him the night he died.'

'I know,' Juliet said.

'You know?'

'Yes, and I really don't want to talk about it.' Juliet was surprised at how protective of Deborah she suddenly felt. 'Let's just leave it at that, shall we?'

He nodded but she could see she had non-plussed him. Quite a feat, she thought grimly, taking the wind out of Dan's sails! But the victory was a hollow one. She had hoped he had asked her here to tell her he really had felt something for her, that it hadn't been a charade, but it hadn't been that at all. He had just wanted to stir a little more.

'Well if there's nothing else I think I should be getting along,' she said coolly. 'I'm going home on Monday and I really should be spending the little time I have left with my family.'

'Oh, so you really are going?'

'Yes. I have a job waiting for me. And my fiancé.' Again, she didn't know why she had said that when the thought of Sean was like a gate closing behind her. A desire to keep the initiative perhaps. Or to show him she had a life that had not been touched by their encounter and hide just how much she was hurting inside.

'Oh, yes. Your fiancé,' he said. A note of bitterness had crept into his voice. She interpreted it as sarcasm. 'Well in that case I won't keep you from the people who are obviously important to you.'

She looked at him, at the hard line of his mouth, and suddenly she knew she was going to cry. Clearly it had meant nothing to him at all; that powerful attraction had been just a passing thing. It was one of the perks of the job to him, perhaps, seducing the girl in the case whoever she might be. She'd been a complete fool to think it might be otherwise.

She stood up, somehow managing a small bright smile in spite of the ache in her throat.

'Goodbye, Dan.'

She turned and fought her way to the door. Outside the night air whispered softly the scents of spring. A small crescent moon and just one star hung over the purple skyline. Juliet saw them through a haze of tears. She half-ran across the car park, fumbling in her bag for her keys. But her hands were shaking too much and with her eyes full of tears she could not find them. She leaned against her hire car, head bowed against the cold metal, and wept.

Dan watched her go through the door and tossed back his drink moodily.

Damn and blast, he'd buggered that up and no mistake! He hadn't said one of the things he'd intended to, she hadn't let him. She obviously despised him for what had happened and who could blame her? She had even thought he was still investigating because he'd been stupid enough to tell her about Deborah. He wasn't, of course. He'd just thought she ought to know – and telling her had been one way of putting off the moment when he had intended to bear his heart and tell her . . . what had he been going to tell her? That he was in love with her? Even now, even feeling as he did, the putting it into words was close to impossible. He was too rusty on that score. One thing to chat up the girls, another to say those three trite little words he had only ever spoken to Marianne.

And yet it was true. If wanting someone so much stirred up this torment of emotion then yes, he loved her. If being prepared to give up weeks of work to save her from being hurt, then yes, he loved her. If thinking of her with that bastard fiancé of hers made him want to go and kick his face in then yes. . .

For God's sake you can't let her go like this! he thought. If you sit here and let her walk out of your life you're a bloody idiot and you have no one but yourself to blame. He slammed down his drink on the table and made for the door.

The car park was dark and looked deserted. His heart thudded with sick despair. Too late. She'd gone.

And then he saw her. Standing beside her car, head bowed, hands covering her face. He raced across the car park.

'Juliet!'

She looked up, startled. To his surprise he saw that she was crying. He wanted to put his arms around her, hold her, wipe away the tears. Instead he said awkwardly: 'Juliet — don't go. Not yet. There's a lot more I want to say to you.'

She swallowed her tears, looking up at him with that same hard edge. But he felt he could see beyond it now.

'Really?' she said.

He nodded. 'Really. And I promise none of it has anything to do with your grandmother. It's more to do with you . . . and me. Look, I know we've got off to a pretty bad start, but don't go like this. Not before we've had a chance to . . .' He broke off. He still hadn't said it, damn it — still didn't know how he was going to even.

'Oh Dan!' she said softly and suddenly he knew he was halfway there already. Just by coming after her he had begun to break down the barriers, the rest would follow.

'I've been a bloody fool, Juliet,' he said. 'Give me the chance to start all over again.'

She fumbled in her bag again, this time, miraculously, the keys came to hand almost immediately.

513

'Let's sit in the car,' she said.

'There is just one other thing,' Dan said a good deal later. 'I know you hated the thought of me as an investigative reporter — do you think you could cope with me being a policeman?'

'A policeman!'

'That's what I was before my accident and to be honest it's all I ever wanted to do. I know I let myself get eaten up by bitterness over what happened but I suppose they didn't have a lot of choice really — a policeman has to be fit. I over reacted I expect — I was damned hurt and I wanted someone to blame. But I think I've got things in perspective now. My leg is healed. There's no reason why I shouldn't reapply for the job. And Phil Gould — my old inspector — thinks they'll have me back without any trouble.'

'Dan . . .'

'Don't say you hate the idea!'

'I don't. It just takes a little getting used to. This all takes a little getting used to.'

'I know. Pretty staggering, isn't it? An hour ago I didn't know how to tell you I loved you and now I've bloody well asked you to marry me!'

She grinned. 'Don't swear at me, Dan Deffains!'

'That's probably something else you'll have to get used to. My language is not always beyond reproach. But for you — I promise to try.'

She snuggled into him, loving him, feeling as if at last she had come home.

'No, Dan. I really don't want you to change a thing.'

'So,' Sophia said softly, 'I got my wish. You are staying, Juliet.'

'Yes. And Mum and Dad are coming over too, to meet Dan, so you'll see them again.'

'That might be very embarrassing at first, after so long, but it will be very nice to have all my family together again if only for a little while.' She smiled at Juliet. 'It seems to me that everything has worked out very well. Everyone is happy — you, me, Dan, your Aunt Catherine is over the moon to hear you are

514

going to marry the son of the one man I think she ever really cared for. Yes, everyone is happy.'

Everyone but Sean, Juliet thought. He had been dreadfully upset when she had telephoned to tell him the news. But he'd get over it. Now she was out of the way he'd soon find someone else — Australia was full of long limbed bronzed beauties and what they had shared had never been right.

'I know it sounds very trite, Sean, but I know you will find someone who will make you much happier than I ever could,' she had told him. 'My heart was never really in it; you deserve better than that.'

And he had said, sad but resigned: 'I knew, Juliet. I think I knew the moment you got on that plane that I had lost you.'

'Be happy, Sean,' she had whispered but she thought he had already put the phone down.

'Yes, everyone is pleased as punch,' Sophia said now. 'And I hope you are finding it in your heart, Juliet, to forgive Deborah. You really must not hold it against her, you know. I don't, and I don't want you to either.'

Juliet smiled, the smug happy smile of a woman in love. 'I suppose I can't, really, since if it weren't for Deborah, Dan and I would never have met.'

'Have you told him the truth about what happened?' Sophia asked.

'Not yet. I probably will one day. Do you mind that?'

Sophia shook her head. 'My dear, I trust Dan completely. As I did his father. He knew I hadn't killed Louis, I'm sure he did. But he went along with my wishes. I'm sure your Dan will do the same.'

Juliet nodded. In spite of a very unpromising start she was sure of it too.

'Did you ever sort out the Langlois mystery?' Phil Gould asked Dan Deffains.

Dan smiled. 'Oh, I sorted it out all right.'

'And what was the answer?'

Dan Deffains, newly married and back in the island police force, tapped the side of his nose and laughed.

515

'Now, Phil, I'm sure you know better than to expect me to share family secrets,' he said. 'Come on, man. I'll buy you a pint. But better make it a quick one. I have a home to go to!'